DATE DUE

Chihuahua

STOREHOUSE OF STORMS

Pancho Villa, symbol of revolt,
a legend which galloped out of the Chihuahua hills in 1911.

Chihuahua

STOREHOUSE OF STORMS

Florence C. Lister
&
Robert H. Lister

THE UNIVERSITY OF NEW MEXICO PRESS

The publication of this book is made possible
by a grant from the Ford Foundation

Manufactured in the United States of America
by the University of New Mexico Printing Plant

Library of Congress Catalog Card No. 66-21935
First Edition

CONTENTS

ILLUSTRATIONS

FOREWORD

THE WORD CHIHUAHUA has a stirring ring to it. Its syllables roll off the tongue with dramatic, bold rhythm. Although its origin is obscured by time, its stridence makes the seemingly meaningless word an appropriate name for a stark, unyielding land. That land is the largest of the northern tier of Mexican states. It is a segment of Mexico which has had a turbulent, bloodstained history in which many Americans have played serious parts for the past one hundred and fifty years.

Chihuahua's citizens—sometimes miners, sometimes ranchers, sometimes clerics—ever have been warriors. Seldom have they been warriors for an ideal, but always they have been warriors for survival. This is because theirs is an environment which has demanded the utmost, and one measure more, in tenacity of spirit, in courage, in strength of fiber of mortal man. There is no verdant, responsive paradise here. This is a somber, silent realm of tawny, denuded plains with little water and shade or high, rugged mountains cut by vast canyons. Sudden storms of sand or rain come and depart violently. Torrents fall either to meet resistant clayey soil and lie stagnant in desert basins awaiting eventual evaporation or to pour down rocky gorges swirling away a heavy tribute of silt and boulders. The sun blisters and cracks, the wind sears, and in time the land subtly instills fear and disloyalty. "Ay, Chihuahua!" is an expletive understandable to all Mexicans as an oath of anger, of melancholy, of resignation.

The demands of such a homeland are soul constricting. Distant horizons offer no hope, no reward. Altruism survives only with greatest difficulty. A man who must be on daily guard against extermination has little time for the luxury of imagination or song. Thus the gay *mariachi* serenades of Jalisco, the lively *huapangos* danced in Vera Cruz, or the colorful arts and crafts of Michoacán have no counterparts in Chihuahua. A race of strong men was needed to survive here, with enough love of the land to fight back.

This is the story of the men of Chihuahua who for four and a half centuries have chosen to make their area a testing ground of Spanish Empire and Mexican Republic, a drama played against a backdrop of an Indian background of even longer duration. Obviously, in an effort to compress such a span of time between the covers of a single book, no one period or one personality can be treated exhaustively. Reliance, therefore, has been placed upon the works of others who already have done the spadework in primary source materials dealing with limited segments of that chronicle. This, then, is an attempt to weave together these many threads of events into a fabric of history.

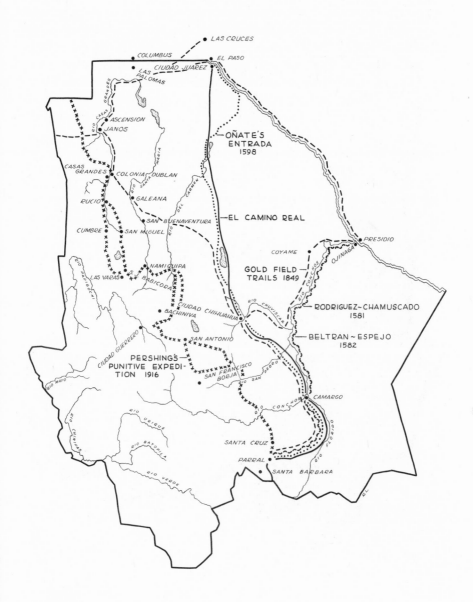

LAS CRUCES

COLUMBUS

EL PASO

CIUDAD JUAREZ

LAS PALOMAS

ASCENSION

JANOS

OÑATE'S ENTRADA 1598

CASAS GRANDES

COLONIA DUBLAN

RUCIO

GALEANA

EL CAMINO REAL

CUMBRE

SAN BUENAVENTURA

SAN MIGUEL

PRESIDIO

COYAME

OJINAGA

NAMIQUIPA

GOLD FIELD TRAILS 1849

LAS VARAS

BABICORA

CIUDAD CHIHUAHUA

RODRIGUEZ~CHAMUSCADO 1581

BACHINIVA

SAN ANTONIO

BELTRAN~ESPEJO 1582

CIUDAD GUERRERO

PERSHINGS PUNITIVE EXPEDI- TION 1916

SAN FRANCISCO BORJA

RIO MAYO

CAMARGO

RIO URIQUE

RIO BATOPILA

SANTA CRUZ

RIO VERDE

PARRAL

SANTA BARBARA

CHIHUAHUA

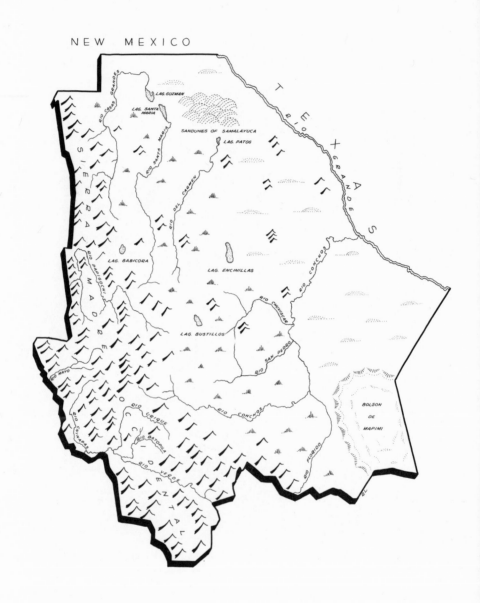

CHIHUAHUA, NATURAL LANDSCAPE

CHIHUAHUA, POINTS OF HISTORICAL INTEREST

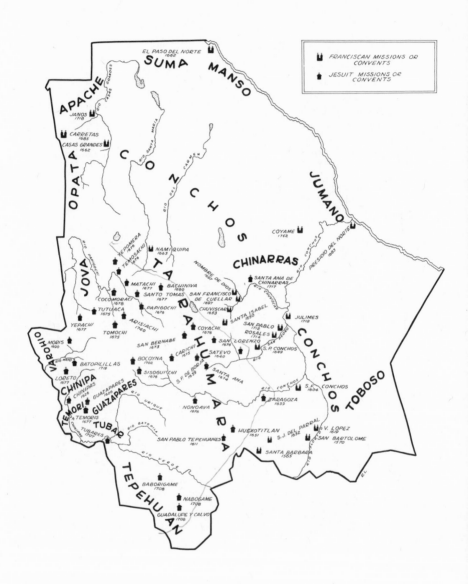

EL PASO DEL NORTE
1662

SUMA   MANSO

APACHE

JANOS
1718

CARRETAS
1685

CASAS GRANDES
1662

OPATA

CONCHOS

RIO CASAS GRANDES

RIO DE SANTA MARIA

RIO DEL CARMEN

JUMANO

JOVA

PEROMERA
1676

TEMOSACHI
1676

NAMIQUIPA
1663

TARAHUMARA

NOMBRE DE DIOS
1697

COYAME
1752

CHINARRAS

SANTA ANA DE
CHINARRAS
1717

PRESIDIO DEL NORTE
1683

MATACHI
1677

BACHINIVA
1680

SANTO TOMAS
1677

SAN FRANCISCO
DE CUELLAR
1697

COCOMORACI
1678

PAPIGOCHI
1678

CHUVISCAR
1653

SANTA
ISABEL
1650

SAN PABLO
1712

ROSALES
1714

JULIMES
1718

TUTUACA
1675

ARISIACHI
1740

YEPACHI
1677

TOMOCHI
1675

COYACHI
1676

SAN LORENZO

SAN
ROQUE

RIO CHUVISCAR

RIO CONCHOS

VAROHIO

MORIS
1690

SAN BERNABE
1673

CARICHI
1675

SATEVO
1640

S.P. CONCHOS
1649

CONCHOS

TOBOSO

RIO MAYO

BATOPILLAS
1719

LORETO
1677

BOCOYNA
1702

SISOGUICHI
1676

S. F. DE BORJA
1639

SANTA ANA
1674

CHINIPA

CHINIPAS
1626

GUAZAPARES
1686

NONOAVA
1676

S. F. CONCHOS
1604

S.F. CONCHOS

ZARAGOZA
1639

TEMORIS

TEMORIS
1677

GUAZAPARES

TUBAR

RIO BATOPILA

HUEXOTITLAN
1651

S.J. DEL PARRAL
1632

V. LOPEZ
1619

SAN BARTOLOME
1570

TUBARES
1709

SAN PABLO TEPEHUANES
1611

SANTA BARBARA
1565

RIO VERDE

TEPEHUAN

BABORIGAME
1708

NABOGAME
1708

GUADALUPE Y CALVO
1708

CHIHUAHUA, PRINCIPAL INDIAN GROUPS, MISSIONS, & CONVENTS

ONE

INDIOS

TO A.D. 1550

THE MANNER in which man secures his food determines his way of life. In the long ages before the advent of the Christian Era those men who, because of instinct for survival, infiltrated the great west of North America diverged into two distinct streams of development.

The bands who drifted out of Alaska into the vast sweep of plains which lay at the eastern skirt of the Rockies devoted their energies to pursuit of large herds of game animals which browsed through belly-deep grass. They became the big-game hunters of the continent, roamers and trackers who left behind them little else but stone implements of the chase.

The ones who penetrated down into the arid intermountain provinces west of the bony continental divide found themselves in a land uninhabited by large animals. They were forced to gain sustenance from other sources. They learned to gather wild seeds produced by ripening grasses, to grub out roots and bulbs, to harvest acorns from scrub oaks or beans from thorny mesquite, to snare small animals who shared the harsh environment. Their material culture centered upon milling stones to grind their plant harvest and basketry to contain it, possessions of necessity both portable and utilitarian.

Both the hunter of the plains and the gatherer of the desert were poor comparatively in the paraphernalia of living. Both ways of life were unchanging for millennia, and both were highly mobile. But each demonstrated man's remarkable adaptability, without which the marginal areas of the globe would never have been populated. In each case the balance between success and failure was delicate.

It is likely the first Chihuahuenses, people of Chihuahua, followed the two traditions. To the east on the *meseta central*, or central plateau, the hunters of the bison might have stalked their prey along the shores of lakes which lapped the slopes of parallel, bald

crests. To the west in the *sierra madre*, or backbone of the mountain divide, the seekers of wild plants and foragers for small game
probably moved along the escarpments, occupying the numerous
caves and overhangs to be found there while they continued in
their endless quest for food. It was with this latter group that the
prehistory of Chihuahua really began, because in their culture,
meager and low level as it was, lay the roots of what was to come.

For untold centuries the Chihuahua gatherers lingered in the
northern mountain valleys utilizing the resources of their chosen
homeland as completely as possible, the edible products of the
uplands supplementing those of deserts which encircled them.
Camps were made in arched shelters in buff-colored cliffs several
hundred feet above the fertile bottomlands. A number of families
dwelt together without benefit of protection from the elements
other than that afforded by the rock walls, ate together at the cook
fires, and together built up refuse deposits in the recesses of the
caves. Discarded plant materials, stone flakes left as a residue of the
manufacture of spear points and tools, and other debris of human
occupation, in time drifted over the outer fringes of the rock living surfaces and left for the archaeologists a scant record of sheer
survival. From analysis of the assemblage of stone tools recovered,
those students of the past could state that these first residents were
culturally akin to a group archaeologically known as the Cochise
of southern Arizona. They, in turn, were related to others of the
Desert Culture who occupied the broad expanse of eroded plateaus
and basins west of the Rockies from northern Mexico to Oregon.[1]

As traditional users of plant products, the Chihuahua Cochise
stood ready to meet one of the greatest revolutions known to man.
That was not the revolution which let the blood of men stain the
souls of their brothers, the revolution of white man's Chihuahua.
It was the revolution of a way of life itself, when a dramatic
achievement diverted the whole pulsating stream of action. It was
the revolution, the potent miracle, of agriculture. From some undetermined source, probably the heart of Mexico, they acquired
the knowledge of sowing of food plants to ensure a fuller and more
dependable larder. With that practice came implications of radical
significance to hasten man along his route from savage nomadism
toward sedentary civilization—the first glimpse of security, the opportunity for fixed abode, the attainment of leisure.

The Cochise men of Chihuahua most surely did not overnight metamorphose from foragers into farmers. For great periods of time they must have indulged in digging-stick planting in a most haphazard uncontrolled way and for even longer remained on the horticulturalist plane, concerned with the tending of individual plants rather than the seeding of large crops. But the fact that they recognized that the marvelous cycle of fertility and fruition could be worked to their own advantage had import not only to themselves but to modern archaeologists in their study of prehistory. A theory often stated by students of culture is that, in the past, agriculture and pottery-making always diffused together, as inseparable as Siamese twins. However, from deeply stratified deposits in one Chihuahua cave came shriveled cobs and kernels of corn, the most important domesticated food plant of aboriginal America, associated with lithic materials but not with ceramics. Thus it is apparent that at some remote day the inhabitants of the sierra madre raised a few hills of stunted corn while remaining ignorant of earthen vessels in which to cook or cache their harvest.[2]

Botanists concerned with the evolution of maize believe that it derived from a wild plant native to northern South America or southern Mexico and from there spread north. At some time prior to the Christian Era the increasing population of Chihuahua accepted the stabilizing influence of crops needing methodical seasonal care. In New Mexico, just north of the modern international boundary, in deposits free of pottery was found corn dated at 2000 B.C. by the carbon 14 process of measuring a deceased organism's remaining radioactivity.[3] Chihuahua corn, thousands of miles from the scene of initial domestication but on a direct route from south to north, proved to be of a similar primitive type.[4] Its tiny, age-darkened cobs were a link between the highly evolved, profuse cultures of highland Mexico, whose economy was based upon the raising of corn, and those of far lesser complexity which were gradually forming in the Southwest.

The route, or routes, of the diffusion of the revolutionary concept of maize agriculture is not positively known. The Sierra Madre Occidental of Chihuahua, with its deep intra-peak troughs allied in north-south direction, most certainly must have been important in that transmission. Rising sharply from the creosote-covered eastern plains, these mountains level off on a high plateau called "The Top of the Mountain," and descend abruptly to Pacific waters. The western escarpment is severely gashed and fretted with steep-walled *barrancas*, or canyons, which become deeper, more complex, and more numerous in the southern extension of the state. Because of the tremendous gorges created by the headward eroding action of elaborate river systems such as those of the Yaqui, Mayo, and Fuerte striving to reach the sea, this area for all human history has been the most impenetrable mountain massif on the continent. It straddles the boundary between Chihuahua and the coastal states of Sonora and Sinaloa, making east-west contacts nearly impossible, but allowing for north-south travel through declivities pointed like a compass needle from the Mexican state of Durango toward Arizona and New Mexico. Knowing that in modern times the Indians travel freely north and south through the cordillera, but avoid the hot waterless stretches to the east and the humid coast to the west, it seems not unlikely that in ancient days the same situation prevailed. The elevated sierra, with its temperateness, occasional water, and many caves, was a bridge rather than a barrier in the determined progress of man. The Cochise before the time of Christ were in a geographical position to feel the full impact of diffusion from the south. The first benefit of that northbound tide was one of the great molding forces of civilization —agriculture—which in this instance was dedicated to the cereal corn.

Beyond the facts that the Cochise trailblazers made use of natural caves in the Chihuahua highlands, fashioned various sorts of stone implements, and supplemented their menus with corn, little can be said of them. So rudimentary a culture as was theirs passed from the human scene with few reminders of its achievements. No remains of the men themselves have been found.

As the lakes out on the prairies spent themselves as tribute to a demanding sun, leaving playas and rocky terraces in their wake, and the denuded ranges began to lose their sharp identity in piedmonts of wind- and water-borne soils and gravels, the game animals must have withdrawn and with them the hunters. No such major ecological changes took place in the sierra. Yet because of lack of research, the next page in the story of Chihuahua is a blank. Surely the mountains were not untenanted for a block of time estimated to be several centuries, but at the present time there is a gap in the known sequence of occupation. It is anticipated that in the future the mountains and the foothills along their eastern feet will be shown to have known human life from Cochise foragers and then horticulturalists to the time of the next clear-cut invasion—that which occurred about A.D. 900.

The new arrivals moved into Chihuahua in much greater numbers than had the old Cochise, fanning out of southern New Mexico and Arizona along both flanks of the sierra madre into the verdant drainages of the Bavispe, Piedras Verdes, and Aros, where they inhabited caves, or along tongues of land at the edge of the mountains, where they constructed subterranean pit houses. Just as were all their contemporaries in the American Southwest, these new Chihuahuenses were farmers, more reliant than their predecessors upon the fundamental rhythms of seasons and the capacity of the untrampled valleys to produce crops, not only of corn but also of beans and squash. They were possessors of a well-developed sense of home and property, the latter with foundations seated in the Desert Culture of the past. In the discards of their living, they showed themselves to have been allied to peoples residing a few hundred miles to the north.[5] These folk, called Mogollones by students of aboriginal life in the Southwest, had acquired many of the basic skills of other regional cultures that had also evolved from a desert-dweller substratum. They knew how to fashion firm-walled baskets from strips of yucca and willow. They could weave from the fibers of the yucca simple cloth for garments, durable sandals for their feet, cordage for a thousand uses. From splinters of bone they were capable of producing smooth, sharp-pointed needles, punches, and awls. From stone they could shape grinding, pecking, or hacking tools. From wood and sinew they knew how to manufacture stout, taut bows and arrow shafts whose tips customarily were of hard wood. From clay their women made containers baked into imperviousness, the idea or actual practice of pottery-making having reached their ancestors from Mexico some seven centuries earlier.

With the flowering of their culture in the Chihuahua sierra, the Mogollones, as did their kinsmen to the north, came under the strong influence of the virile Anasazi-Pueblos of the Río Grande drainage of New Mexico and the San Juan drainage of New Mexico, Arizona, Colorado, and Utah. It was the process, familiar to students of culture dynamics, of an advanced group imparting some of its luster to neighbors of lesser development. As a result of this contact, or at least absorption of Anasazi ideas, the southern Indians began to assume a northern coloration. The outstanding change which took place in their lifeway was the adoption of a generalized style of Anasazi architecture. The mountain caves sheltered cubelike houses, some with as many as thirty rooms misshapen and molded to conform to the individual peculiarities of the cave in which they were located. These structures, like proper Anasazi dwellings, possessed doorways, window openings, and ceilings of spaced, peeled logs covered with earth. Their walls were of adobe mud daubed over a skeleton of lashed poles. Occasionally buildings were of two or three stories, with access to upper levels gained by exterior ladders. Granaries to keep safe the surplus corn were constructed of coils of grass cemented together with large amounts of mud.*

In steadily increasing measure the southern Mogollon folk were operating under a great stream of Anasazi-Puebloism which in time would completely submerge their own complex of material traits. Yet as long as the bulk of their numbers lived deep in the cordillera, they clung to their native simpler way of living. They continued to reside in their small cliff dwellings in the mountains or their pit houses in the foothills, to bury their dead in unlined pits sunk into the subsoil and—unlike the Anasazi—to leave few funeral furnishings with them, to exhibit little finesse or artistic excellence in their crafts. Architecture was of poor quality; basketry was of the simplest types; pottery remained characteristically thick and soft and dull brown in color, decorated only by various styles of manual texturing or by a lifeless red pigment.

About A.D. 1000, the Chihuahua Mogollones stood on the thresh-

---

* Olla Cave in Cave Valley, Chihuahua, located some forty miles west of Cases Grandes, has the most famous of such granaries. Formed of coils of grass coated with mud, this granary created in a bulbous shape resembling a huge *olla*, or jar, dominates the cave front in which a small aboriginal house is located. Rounded openings appear at irregular intervals up its sides to aid in the ready removal of the corn stored within. A comparison of a picture in Lumholtz, 1902, 64, and one in Lister, 1958, plate 5, reveals little change in the structure in the last half century despite the fact that it is disfigured with names of many visitors scratched into its soft plaster surface. Reports that vandals have demolished the structure have not been verified.

old of a new era. They forsook their elevated fastnesses and slowly spread like a human glacier down upon the eastern basins. What remained of their cultural purity was doomed.

Along the few river valleys which knifed out of the mountains toward the desert, or atop the broad, loamy floodplains which lay at the juncture of plateau and ridge, the farmers settled in small communal groups. They erected settlements and tilled fields which in most instances were dependent upon natural precipitation for life-producing moisture but in a few cases were irrigated by canals cutting off from perennial streams. Their basic pattern of life continued along the paths already well established. But now Anasazi influence hit them full force and sought to eradicate them. In open areas where they had established residence in earlier times, they abandoned their old circular subterranean houses and constructed above-ground, Anasazi-type adobe structures. However, they did not adopt the Anasazi kiva, or ceremonial chamber. From that it might be inferred that in spite of all the drift toward an Anasazi-Pueblo culture, they did not endorse Anasazi religion in its totality. Other factors also were at work upon the Chihuahua Mogollones. There were defensive features to the settlements as though attack across the seemingly empty basins were an imminent possibility. Wall apertures were minimal. Watchtowers topped scattered pinnacles.

Not only did their architecture reflect emulation of their northern contemporaries, but the lesser aspects of material culture took on a decided Anasazi enrichment. Pottery assumed new colors, new shapes, evidence of new technical competence. Great emphasis was placed upon personal adornment as bracelets, beads, pendants, and mosaics came into vogue. Burial customs modified, with inhumation within the house compound becoming customary. Bodies often were accompanied by numerous offerings. Trade in pottery with other regions grew, particularly with the Mimbres area of southern New Mexico and the Middle Gila of Arizona. The importation of shells from the Gulf of California increased. Turquoise was secured from the north. A rich hybrid culture—basically Mogollon overlaid by a thick veneer of Anasazi—flourished during the eleventh century in the Chihuahua bolsons, those flat-floored desert valleys, leaving for posterity several thousand mounded ruins. Cultural orientation was toward the north.

Along with small villages of several families, there was in Chihuahua, paralleling a similar development on the Colorado Plateau, a gradual concentration of the population into a few large centers. The most impressive was one today called Casas Grandes, covering some one hundred *hectares* near the present village of the same name. It was a city of many units which contained numerous large rectangular rooms and at least three stories of thick, puddled-adobe walls. This city was a thriving metropolis during the twelfth century, perhaps occupied by ancestors of the Ópata tribe encountered by Spanish explorers west of the Sierra Madre Occidental. It undoubtedly was a melting pot where, under the yeasty stimulus of prosperity and exchange, the Chihuahua civilization was reaching its zenith. Presumably its late occupants no longer felt need for protection against attack because the town structures of this period, built over a few subterranean houses of earlier days, had many door and window openings. Adobe or wooden stairways led to upper floors. A hand-dug aqueduct system of stone-lined canals and reservoirs with spillways allowed water to be taken from a source four miles distant and brought into the houses. A fifteen-meter well was dug within the village confines. An outpost on a nearby hill served as a link in a communication system with neighbors. In focus of daily life, Casas Grandes seemed an extension, a further elaboration and sophistication, of the period which had preceded it. But then there came about a shift of emphasis which gave the city a dual personality.

During the twelfth century the advanced societies of central Mexico were approaching the full glory of their development. With the lusty vigor of a people on the advance, they were bursting out of their highland domain, moving in all directions. Their influence, if not they themselves, came up the bleak corridor from central Mexico, moving along the inland passageway of the Sierra Madre Occidental, and eventually reached the camp of the Mogollon-Anasazi at Casas Grandes. There that influence led to erection of specialized architecture associated with an elaborate ritualism.

A ceremonial area which was out of the pattern of the usual Southwestern community separated several units of adobe houses. It consisted of cobblestone-faced pyramids, I-shaped ball courts, stone-veneered effigy mounds in bird and serpent form, and cobblestone-covered platforms thought to have been used for astronomical observations. All of these features would have been at home in Mexican Middle Culture towns.[6] A number of minor central Mexican items appeared to have been in use at the same time. Among these were copper bells and ornaments produced by the lost-wax process, cloisonné, grinding stones of legged varieties, ceremonial ax heads, plumb bobs and animal figures of serpentine, and spindle whorls of a sort reminiscent of some made in the Chalchihuites culture of the Mexican state of Durango. Turkeys and parrots were confined in an elaborate series of pens and were used in certain ceremonies. However, the major influence of the central Mexicans was largely confined to nondomiciliary architecture and, one must assume without definite proof, to the religious views of the Casas Grandes residents.

Pottery, usually a very sensitive indicator of change, remained Mogollon-Anasazi in nearly all its attributes except for the creation of an unusually large number of zoomorphic effigies. A harmoniously decorated polychrome ware and a polished black pottery—two types with genetic relationships to the previous periods of development in Chihuahua—were the most common pottery styles. Mexican legged pots were not in use.

The discovery of such a complex of buildings—to date the most extensive cluster of central Mexican architectural traits in the far north—leads to provocative questions about the events which promulgated their erection. Did a group of priests, powerful enough to force labor to participate in their building and persuasive enough to ensure their usage, arrive from central Mexico? Did some cult overtake the Mogollon-Anasazi of Chihuahua with the fervor of a revivalistic movement, causing them to embrace a new set of religious customs which entailed massed physical efforts? Aside from the ruins of Mexican-inspired buildings, there is little left to guide those attempting to understand the cultural processes involved. Apparently, human sacrifice, which was assuming great importance farther south, was not practiced as frequently and there are few signs of the new religious motivations having altered the fundamental courses of Mogollon-Anasazi life. Therefore, the culture of the Chihuahua foothills which for several hundreds of years had been a blend of Mogollon and Anasazi (a new result from old ingredients, as are most civilizations, in the final analysis), in its terminal days had a third infusion. This gave it Mexican gloss and theological direction but little else. A developing theocracy may have contributed to final disintegration of the culture.

The reasons which underlay abandonment of Chihuahua by the Mogollon-Anasazi after a three-hundred-fifty-year tenancy are not certain. Agriculturalists dependent upon favorable amounts of rainfall may have succumbed to one of the cycles of prolonged drought known to have gripped the area from the beginning of man's occupation. They may have fallen victim to disease, to pressure from nomads who were penetrating the intracontinental plains, to decadence which often follows florescence. Or with their tradition of self-government in jeopardy, they may have chosen to cast out the foreigners and their imposed beliefs and withdraw up the Río Grande or over the mountain divide to the security afforded by the towns of their relatives. There is some evidence of great physical strife and wholesale destruction of houses, a state of disorganization which probably developed sometime during the last half of the fourteenth century. In saddened, disconsolate bands, the Casas Grandes residents must have loaded their portable possessions upon their backs and drifted out across the sere plains and dunes toward the Río Grande or northern Sonora, where in absorption by other peoples they lost their individuality.

The silent houses were left to the mercy of the elements which conspired to return them to the womb of the earth from which they sprang. Gradually, ceiling beams rotted and split asunder. Walls of mud melted down and piled their residue about the base. Cobblestones loosened and tumbled down the slopes of the pyramids. Rows of cultivated fields smoothed over and became obscured under a new mantle. In a few score years there were left only rolling mounds of silt and clods where once a hardy breed of men had flourished. The era of the Mogollon-Anasazi passed into history.[7]

At the beginning of the historic era, Chihuahua was homeland for a profusion of tribes, subtribes, and bands of Indians, culturally and physically divergent, linguistically complex, and none obviously related to the archaeologically defined cultures which once had flourished there. Of the estimated eighty to ninety-five separate groups,[8] some were nomadic and some were sedentary.

Some ranged over the burning deserts, traveling from one stinking water hole to another. Others dwelt high in the cold mountain crags, living in natural caves and foraging for small game with the use of the bow and arrow. Still others preferred an easier life in the tropical recesses of deep barrancas, where nature provided lush growths of certain foodstuffs and where the climate was more moderate. A few were small-scale farmers, growing patches of corn and beans on clearings along stream courses cut across the high plains. After the horse became an integral part of the life of certain Indian groups on the Great Plains to the north, Chihuahua was swept from north to south and back to north again by flashing hordes of hard-riding savages. But whether the residents were farmers or hunters, there were no concentrations of Indian population into rich centers of culture such as had existed three hundred years previously in the Casas Grandes vicinity.

As the *blancos*, the whites, slowly pushed fingers of exploration, colonization, and missionization up the coastal plains of Sinaloa and Sonora, they inadvertently drove such peoples as the Chínipa, Varohío, Guasapar, Jova, Témori, and Tubar back farther into the knots of digitate canyons and towering mountains, through which flow the torrents of the Urique, Mayo, Fuerte, and Yaqui rivers and above which rise the highest peaks in the state. Because of the roughness of the terrain and its general poverty in the eyes of the Spaniards, the barranca aborigines were unmolested. Even now, some of the men dwelling there have preserved a primitive culture relatively free of Mexicanization.

At the time of the Conquest four main groups occupied the high mountains. The Pima Bajo and the Ópata held valleys and slopes on the Sonora side of the range, occasionally crossing into the area now Chihuahua. In the long extension of the mountains and spreading out into the fertile vales east of the masif, were the Tarahumara. Today this is Mexico's largest group of nearly pure-blooded Indians and one of its most backward and least acculturated. In the southern mountains and basins bordering Durango lived the superstitious warlike Tepehuán, who created one of the fiercest holocausts in Spanish colonial history. As conquest proceeded, they gradually retreated southward until at the present time Chihuahua is virtually out of their range.

Seminomadic Concho Indians claimed the southern and central Chihuahua plains as their habitat. They ranged from the headwaters of the Río Conchos to its junction with the Río Grande and northwest as far as Casas Grandes. A subdivision called the Chinarra wandered around the salt lakes and sand dunes of northern Chihuahua. Their southernmost extension was near the present town of Aldama, some twenty miles east of the Conchos River and into the Big Bend vicinity of the Río Grande. The culture of all these Concho was in a low stage of development. It was based upon occasional farming where conditions were suitable. It was the fate of the Concho, since they occupied territory near the early *reales de minas,* or mining districts, to be pressed into the service of mine and hacienda owners. As a result, theirs was the first Indian stock in Chihuahua to disappear completely.

Another desert band destined to give the Spaniards a great deal of trouble was the predatory group called Tobosos. These nomads came out of the frightfully barren Bolsón de Mapimí in southeastern Chihuahua and northeastern Durango to roam west to Parral and north to the Río Grande. The Concho were their traditional enemies prior to white conquest.

In the sand dunes along the northern border near El Paso and south to Casas Grandes, lived the Suma and Manso. Their first contact with the white man was with Cabeza de Vaca in his fabulous trip westward, across the area that is now the southern United States, to the settlements on the west coast of Mexico. They were farmers on occasion, especially along the Río Grande, but depended upon mesquite beans and mescal pods for their staple foods.

Where the Río Grande and the Río Conchos united, the first explorers met the naked and painted Jumanos and Patarabueye. There is much confusion concerning the identities of these two groups, although anthropologist J. Charles Kelley calls the latter peripheral Southwest in affiliation[9] and the Jumanos, Southern Plains in cultural association.[10] These seminomads forayed on the eastern plains after the buffalo, but they also farmed along the river lands. The Jumanos were great traders and were thus agents for the diffusion of culture between the southern plains and northern Mexico.

In the northwestern part of the state were various Apache bands coming south from what is now Arizona and New Mexico. They, too, were semiagricultural, establishing small *rancherías*, or settlements, where there was protection and water. With the introduction of the horse, and increasing pressures upon them by the western migration of white settlers in the United States, the wild Apache set Chihuahua on fire in the colonial period, maintained those fires over two hundred years, threatening the state with bankruptcy, abandonment, and disaster.[11]

The tribes mentioned are mere islands in a sea of names left by the early Spanish chroniclers. The names have little meaning since they cannot be pinpointed as to definite groups or localities. The conquistadors wrote of their poverty, their nakedness, their acceptance of the Faith, their attitudes toward the incoming whites. They mentioned the Cocoimes, Gavilanes, those of the small hat, the sons of the earth, the sons of the rocks, the sons of the mud, the little black ones, Satapayigliglas, Cuazapayogliglas. Osata, Cacuotaomes, Otauay, Batayogliglas, Guamuchicat, Boomes, Colorados, Ajames, Tuimamare, Sinibles, Mopututur, Bacopo, Pobas, Estoyto, Esauqui, Trimomomos, Cuurbipicas, those of the fish, sons of the mountains, white heads, peoples of the nuts, and so on. These names, some of which are descriptive and some attempts at phonetic translation, are mainly mere tags, without ethnic significance, but they do serve to point up the great diversity of tribes then in Chihuahua.

Colonization by the European conquerors meant great upheavals in the patterns of culture as they had existed in Chihuahua. Some groups were killed off through wars with the Spaniards or by heavy physical work of a type for which they were unsuited. Other groups became refugees, going farther out into the deserts to escape the yoke of the white man, or retreating into the almost impenetrable mountain reaches. The wealth of the Spaniards, especially in the matter of herds of cattle and horses, attracted preying nomads who came into an area where they had hitherto never ventured. Groups who formerly had wandered in small bands were forced into settled communities around missions. People from the mountains were brought into settlements down on the plains. With the possible exception of those isolated in the barranca country, no tribe remained untouched. Some submitted peacefully to white domination and, diminished through disease, were assimilated through intermarriage, mixed with other Indians and Negroes imported into the region by the Spaniards. Others vanished through suicidal warfare against the invader. However, never was there any such mass subjugation of the natives as occurred in the heart of Mexico.

TWO

BLANCOS
Men of Destiny
1550 – 1810

SPAIN was singularly suited to the conquering, converting, and colonizing task she chose for herself in the New World. Paradoxically, there were broad areas of basic similarity between the conqueror and the conquered allowing these alien cultures to mix, to mingle blood, to produce the Mexican mestizo. Formal in behavior, given to temperamental extremes, callous to pain and death, respectful of age and wisdom, class conscious, and quick to religious fanaticism, Spaniard and Indian met on mutually understandable terms. However, there was operative a force which compelled the Spaniard to make himself the master of the Indian. This was an unquestioning belief in the superiority of his Crown, his Church, and himself. It was this same motivation, plus a desire for quick wealth, that drove him to the frontiers to cast the image of *Hispanidad* upon the land. And it was the continual lure of the unknown territories to the north that were to initiate Chihuahua's recorded history.

By 1546 the northern frontier of Spanish-controlled Mexico had reached Zacatecas, a productive mining settlement which crawled up barren hillsides of the interior tablelands, and as life there began to assume a pattern of monotonous routine, the restless and the adventurous sought to push the boundary of empire still farther north. The second viceroy of Mexico, Luis de Velasco, was petitioned for authorization to explore into the northern unknown, crossed years earlier by the lost Cabeza de Vaca. Velasco, in turn, requested of the Crown concessions "to explore the lands Coronado had seen superficially, to locate suitable sites for towns, and above all, to look for mines." Finally in 1563 the standard bearer for the official movement northward up the central plateau was selected. He was Francisco de Ibarra.[1]

Ibarra was cast in the heroic mold of the conquistador. He had been weaned on a diet of proud family name and valorous fight against enemies and elements. An adolescent already a man, at sixteen he took up the role of explorer, a career which was to cost him his fortune and his life. In an auspicious eight years, Ibarra traveled through western and central Mexico, into the realms of the ancient people of Chicomostoc and Chalchihuites, leaving behind him those landmarks of Mexican mining—Fresnillo, Sombrerete, Nombre de Dios. Now at twenty-four he was named by the viceroyalty to carry on the task of taking lands north of Nueva España in the names of the King of Spain and the Holy Father.

Perhaps the influence of his uncle, one of the founders of Zacatecas, was partly responsible for Ibarra's selection. Maybe Velasco was reminded that young Francisco was a son-in-law of the former illustrious viceroy, Mendoza, a favorite of the Spanish court who had been promoted to the governing position in Peru. Unquestionably some consideration was given his ability to finance the undertaking, for he was wealthy. His previous success in acquiring new territories for His Majesty must have been recognized. Whatever the reasons for the choice, Francisco de Ibarra was a credit to his nation and his time. Through his efforts history marched into southern Chihuahua and, being unimpressed, marched out again.

In this first expedition into Chihuahuan territory, a volunteer military party, under the newly named Captain General of the northern provinces, wearily skirted the plains and rolling hills of the central corridor of present Chihuahua, restored itself on the wide banks of the Río Conchos, and hastened back southward to the mining town of Indé, Durango. The grazing and agricultural possibilities of the wide, flat basins might have been appraised by the youthful leader, but obviously since he established no mines, he did not suspect the presence of stupendous ore veins beneath the red-mantled flanks of the southern mountains. His subordinate, a Basque named Rodrigo del Río, did make note of that brilliant coloration.

Ibarra's second and more ambitious advent in May 1565 was through the back door. Departing from Zacatecas in central Mexico, he commanded a group of sixty soldiers armed with harquebuses, each with five mounts, and a number of Indian servants and an interpreter. He hoped to have a more mobile party by dividing his expedition into small groups, each independent in rations and beasts, each with its own servants.

The small party blazed a route to be frequently used later in travel to the northern settlements. They avoided the unhealthy tropic lands by marching up the interior basin, crossing the tremendous knife-edged crests of the sierra madre west of Topia in Durango before descending to the warm west coast. They made their way past Culiacán, the last outpost on this segment of the frontier, and into a rain of arrows from thousands of hostile Indians. Ibarra proposed "to explore the lands Coronado had seen superficially." This was the road to Cíbola. Unfortunately the Conqueror of New Mexico had suffered a serious defeat at the hands of various Indian tribes of Sonora, and the Indians had not forgotten their victory. They planned to drive out his successor; men of the barrancas united with their coastal neighbors to force the frightened Spanish army to change the direction of its march. Fighting for survival, the expedition sought sanctuary in the high, brush-covered mountains which served as a western bastion to Chihuahua.

The exact route taken by this army in flight from the Mexican west coast to the central mesa is in doubt. Most likely the demoralized little band worked its way northward through the Bavispe basin of Sonora, east through the narrow Púlpito Pass, and out on to the Carretas plains of northwestern Chihuahua.[2]

Their welcoming committee was a band of friendly Sumas who soon conveyed to Ibarra the same message of the Cíbola mirage that had been told Cabeza de Vaca and his three companions years before as they passed along the Río Grande. Off there to the north was said to be a golden dream. But hungry, tired, and frightened men—even empire builders—could not arouse themselves to high pitch over new horizons to conquer, especially horizons which seemed to produce only fatigue and disappointment. Cíbola and its promise must await the future. Their major concern at that moment was a safe return to some frontier settlement.

The ragged troops proceeded slowly southward toward an abandoned city of which the Sumas had spoken. Moving across bolsons and mesas swept by cold, raw winds of approaching winter, through snagging chaparral and mesquite, the men came down a

river to the ruins of Casas Grandes. They were the first white men
to explore its plazas and its rooms of puddled-adobe walls and,
perhaps, to ponder the reasons behind its abandonment. They
called it Paquimé.*

For five more days they marched to the south, and then Ibarra
turned his army west and back into the mountains. Had he continued southeastward on the plains, eventually he would have
reached the Río Conchos previously visited. To travel back to
Indé from there would have been an easy retracing of an old trail.
He might have avoided near-death from starvation and exposure
for himself and his followers. Unfortunately, he did not know
enough of the geography of his command to realize that he was
headed into certain trouble.

The men feared coming back into the territory of the Ópatas
and Jovas who had been bellicose earlier. Instead they ascended
the sierra, crawled down into cavernous gashes, and waded through
the waters rushing to break out of the mountains. From Casas
Grandes, or Paquimé, they went south to the area of Chuhichupa,
continued into the deep gorge of the Aros whose cliffs sheltered
Mogollon cliff houses, to the Sahuaripa district and the Río Yaqui
of Sonora. Energy needed to keep alive had to be used to search
for lost beasts or to build reed balsas for floating across rivers. Lost,
separated, cold, famished, inescapable hunger forced half-crazed
stragglers to eat their horses and whatever nature could provide.
Even ants were not overlooked. All were weak and ill. At last,
trapped in a slitlike canyon out of which there seemed to be no
exit, the horse-mounted men were faced with the difficult decision
of whether to turn back and seek a new route or to forsake their

---

* The ruin made quite an impression upon the first white visitors, as Bancroft quotes Beaumont, "a most beautiful city, adorned with very sumptuous
edifices extending over three leagues, with houses of three stories, very grand,
with various and extensive plazas, and the houses surrounded by walls that
appeared to be of masonry." Bancroft, 1886, 190. Bandelier, 1884, has a fine
description of the ruin as it appeared in 1884 (544-47). *Turismo*, January,
1961, has a recent description. It long has been customary for Mexican and
American historians (for example, Almada, 1945, 94-95; 1955, 9; Evans, 1945,
135; Terrazas, 1942b, 146) to regard Paquimé, now Casas Grandes, as a stopping place for the Aztecs who are thought to have arrived in the Valley of
Mexico from some undetermined northern hearth. There is no archaeological
evidence to support such a conclusion.

animals and scale the sheer cliffs on foot, gambling on not encoun-
tering war-bent Indians. But to be without a horse under those
circumstances would mean unquestionable, though perhaps desirable, death. The historian of the expedition, Baltasar de Obregón, volunteered to make the ascent to determine what lay ahead.
Not a man had a hope that the end of the terrible ordeal could be
near. But up on top, Obregón looked down upon rolling Sonora
plains, as a man gazing out of a darkened room into blinding
noonday light. The explorers were saved. Their reward was a ten-
year exemption from taxes.

As governor of Nueva Vizcaya, a post given Ibarra for his services to the Crown, he began at the capital of Guardiana* the com-
plicated job of establishing a workable government for the newest and largest Mexican province. Boundaries of Nueva Vizcaya,
named in honor of the section of Spain from which the Ibarra
family had come, were hazily defined to encompass "lands north
of Zacatecas." Thousands of square miles of vastly varied terrain
were included. Craggy mountains of the eternally cold *tierra fría*
and tropic barrancas and coastal shores of the steaming *tierra
caliente* were the extremes found in certain regions of Nueva Vizcaya. Mostly it was a province of elevated undulating plains and
arid deserts of the temperate zone called *tierra templada*. An involved diversification of native peoples, languages, and customs
matched the geographic complexity.

While the army continued to make exploratory reconnaissances,
Ibarra made a name for himself as an able, moderate, and just administrator.[3] He actively furthered exploitation of mining properties, encouraged establishment of cattle and farming haciendas,
provided help and protection for evangelical projects of all religious orders. Under his hand Nueva Vizcaya was born and began
to grow. Progress, however, was slow. Although the Spanish Crown
considered the north to offer great potentialities, the number of
European colonists remained pitifully small for the first hundred
years of occupation.

Before his death in 1575 at the age of thirty-six, Francisco de
Ibarra saw the founding of Chihuahua's first mine and first hacienda,[4] setting the pattern of the two industries, mining and graz-

---

* After 1620, the city of Durango. Almada, 1955a, 58.

ing, that were to enrich the state and the nation. He stretched his provincial frontier line from Saltillo and Parras on the east to San Felipe at the mouth of the Sinaloa River on the west and had invested over 400,000 pesos of his personal funds in the great venture of the north.

Upon Francisco's death from tuberculosis resulting from the ordeal in the sierra, his younger brother in Spain was named his successor as governor of the province of Nueva Vizcaya, but he died before reaching America. Diego, the rich uncle from Zacatecas who had been constant advisor to Francisco, became the new governor.

Thirty Spanish families had moved into Chihuahua's first town, Santa Bárbara, by the end of this initial period. Ten years earlier Captain Rodrigo del Río, himself later a governor of Nueva Vizcaya, had been ordered north from Indé to prospect for new mines. He had remembered the scarlet-stained hills on the old route to the Conchos, and there at the mouth of a canyon on the northern face of the Sierra de Santa Bárbara, he made the beginnings of what he hoped would be a mining strike. La Vazqueña, Santa Clara, San Francisco, Pallares, La Antigua, Embajadoes, and Cinco Pozos were silver mines opened up during this early period, but their romantic names obscured their general lack of promise. Isolation from the growing center of Spanish culture at Guardiana and the lack of laborers added to the difficulties of profitable exploitation of weak veins. Early appeals to Governor Ibarra for slave labor from central Mexico failed. In later years, when necessity overruled humanitarianism, the viceroys allowed Tlaxcalan and Tarascan slaves to be worked in the mines. But in 1575 thirty Europeans using primitive techniques of extraction failed to make an impressive showing.

Other Spaniards moved east to the Río Florido valley and there established San Bartolomé del Valle which was to become the center of an active development of stock raising and farming. Tepehuán Indians who worked scattered plots of land along the streams were dispossessed by this settlement.

The work of the Church was begun in Chihuahua in this same period. Franciscan friars came to both the mining and the hacienda settlements to serve the Spanish population and to make a start at conversion of the Indians.

By the last quarter of the sixteenth century, the foundation stones for the future state of Chihuahua were in place.

THOUGHTS of "the north" continued to prick the restive Spaniards' undiminished hopes of fortune without effort and their sincere desires to spread Christianity. The closing thirty years of the sixteenth century witnessed three historic groups departing from Santa Bárbara bound for that region which lay beyond the northernmost sphere of Spanish influence. The first expedition, the Rodríguez-Chamuscado, ended tragically. Neither of the two leaders returned. Here is what happened.[5]

Spanish objectives were two-fold—conquest of souls by the religious and conquest of bodies by the military. For conquest of souls, the religious team of three Franciscans—Fray Rodríguez, Fray Francisco López, and Fray Juan de Santa María—had asked permission of the viceroy to proceed to the north to bring more souls to God. Rodríguez had read the 1536 accounts of the nine-year wanderings of Cabeza de Vaca, but he apparently did not know of Coronado's military march. Nor did he know that other clerics before him had preached to the northern Indians. His own interest in that area was stimulated by reports from the Conchos, and other Indians with whom he worked, of people far up the big river who wore cotton clothing and lived in large cities. After the Fathers' request was granted, a squad of nine volunteer soldiers under the command of Francisco Sánchez Chamuscado was alerted to escort them to New Mexico. The soldiers were to be allowed the right of bartering with the Indians.

The party of approximately twenty men, including Indian servants needed to drive the six hundred head of cattle and ninety horses, rode over the red hills beyond Santa Bárbara to the valley of San Bartolomé, then up the Río Florido to its junction with the Conchos. They clung to the green thread of the Río Conchos valley as it cut northeast through desert hills to drop two thousand feet to spill itself into the big river of the north, Río Grande del Norte. The Fathers happily recorded large numbers of new converts as they baptized natives who came to greet the white men traveling through their tribal lands. At the junction of the two rivers, the naked Jumanos were eager to talk to the Spaniards, remembering the four others who had come among them years before, working healing miracles.[6] Rodríguez must have felt a sense of excitement in the realization that his path was now crossing that of de Vaca.

After almost a month of hot, dusty, summertime travel, Rodríguez and Chamuscado brought their men into the Río Grande valley of what is now central New Mexico and to Tigua and Keres villages once occupied by Coronado's army. Fathers Rodríguez and López stayed at Puaray, west of the Río Grande near modern Bernalillo. Fray Santa María was dispatched alone to return to Mexico to report on the arrival of the expedition in New Mexico and on the state of affairs there after the Spaniards' long absence.

Pueblo Indians remained sullen and unresponsive to the overtures made by these newest invaders. After forty years, memories of oppression, brutalities, and indignities at the hands of their predecessors were still burning.[7] Firm in their dedicated belief that these unlettered, unenlightened heathens needed their help and that of their God, the Franciscans demanded to be left behind as the soldiers prepared to return to Mexico. Chamuscado recognized the unspoken resistance of the natives but did not think the Fathers to be in physical danger. On the surface all was calm. Underneath, a storm was brewing. Two Europeans and three Mexican-Indian servants were left to attempt to carry out the monumental task of converting thousands of pagan Indians, without benefit of knowledge of the native tongues or customs and without comforting protection of a handful of His Majesty's soldiers. They were never seen again.

Within the sheltering adobe walls of the convent at San Bartolomé, anxiety was felt for the safety of the priests left to labor for God among the Pueblos in the north. Month after month passed without word or message of any kind from Rodríguez or López, but word came that Chamuscado had died on his return trip and had been buried on the banks of the Conchos. When his small army later rode into the Mexican outpost, the soldiers learned that Fray Santa María never had arrived back at San Bartolomé to make his report. The priest was presumed dead, either at the hands of hostile Indians or from thirst because of the hazardous desert shortcut he might have taken. When one of the Mexican servants left in Puaray succeeeded in making his way back to Santa Bárbara

to tell of the deaths of the friars, Fray Bernardino Beltrán, resident
at the convent, seriously began to talk to the men who had gone
with Chamuscado's troop. He gathered vital data as to available
water, possibilities of obtaining food, and probable temper of the
aborigines to be encountered on the arduous trip north. He meant
to determine the exact fate of his fellow Franciscans. And he meant
to see the north with his own eyes.

Antonio de Espejo, a rich fugitive from justice, was at the moment avoiding capture in escape to the northern colonies. Fray
Beltrán, knowing of his crime, persuaded him to finance another
northern expedition for the Franciscans. It was pointed out that
such an undertaking, if successful, might help clear the Espejo
name and re-establish him in the eyes of the government. It would,
at the same time, provide an enterprising man like himself the
firsthand opportunity of seeing that far-off fabled land. In November 1582, sixteen months after Rodríguez and Chamuscado had
ridden north, the Beltrán-Espejo expedition was under way.[8]

Traveling up the Conchos with the group was Juan López de
Ibarra, father of the first governor of Nueva Vizcaya, going north
out of curiosity to see the province his exploring son had never
seen. Several children and the wife of one soldier were the first
dependents to make the trek toward Quivira, that rumored area of
wealth in the north. In the following July the exploring party was
back at the Chihuahua frontier, showing several thousand examples of painted cotton textiles, pottery, and other curiosities
from New Mexico and telling news of disaster. All three friars
with the previous expedition definitely had been murdered by the
Indians—Santa María as he rode alone through the wilderness
somewhere near Pecos where he had wandered in an attempt to
set his course by the stars, and Rodríguez and López as they toiled
among the peoples of the Tiguex Province.

Beltrán returned to Mexico via the old Conchos route, but Espejo circled southeastward on a reconnaissance along the Pecos River
eventually to arrive back on the Río Grande and the Conchos.
Their combined reports to the government in the capital told of
finding three Mexican-Indians who had been a part of the
Coronado expedition still living in the western pueblo of Zuñi.
They described the entire Pueblo province from the Hopi villages

of northern Arizona to Pecos in northeastern New Mexico,* its large numbers of intelligent inhabitants anxious, they said, to receive Christianity. Almost incidentally they mentioned traces of potentially rich ore veins.

Souls and silver, the two stimuli of movement into Nueva Vizcaya, now became a lever for royal permission to push to a new northern frontier. Two expeditions out of Chihuahua, a mere handful of men meagerly supplied, had accomplished a great deal more toward bringing New Mexico into the realm of permanent Spanish influence than had Coronado's large expensive army. The time seemed propitious for a full-scale migration northward, thus assuring the development of strategically located Chihuahua.

THE ROAD to Cíbola had been up the coastal flatlands of Sinaloa and Sonora, but the road to Quivira—that newer pot of gold at the end of the rainbow—came through the corridor that was Chihuahua. Interest in New Mexico took great spurts after 1582. And Santa Bárbara found itself happily straddling the highway. Routine and officialdom hung like a grey blanket over central Mexico, driving adventurers of all sorts to the outposts to await license to move on. Mines, aided by Indian and Negro labor from farther south, began to pour forth a stream of wealth. Hills were stripped of their covering of scrub oak and juniper to supply fuel for mill furnaces. Haciendas developed along the river valleys, finding a ready market for their products in the mining settlements of the region. The population of Santa Bárbara reached seven thousand, making it the largest settlement of all of Nueva Vizcaya, including Guardiana, the capital. Everywhere was foretaste of a new adventure. It was the autumn of 1596 when the advance forces of Oñate's army of New Mexico made camp in the *rincon,* or narrow valley, below town.

Much could have been said of Juan de Oñate's admirable character and his proud family background, but patience surely must be considered one of his most outstanding virtues. It was a patience tried and tested during four anxious years of frustrating delays and countermanded orders. He had been granted the royal contract to conquer, colonize, and govern New Mexico. It had been

---

* Espejo actually visited seventy-four pueblos.

rescinded. He and his family had been conceded special privileges. They had been removed. He had been allowed to conscript funds and forces. He had been ordered to halt halfway on his journey to Santa Bárbara. He was told he was to be replaced by a man from the Spanish homeland, a higher bidder in the desired contract for New Mexico. He patiently waited. In February 1598, he submitted to the final government inspection at Santa Bárbara, was not found lacking, and was permitted to begin the actual migration northward.[9]

Blood of conquistador and emperor, of Cortez and Montezuma, were united in Oñate through birth and marriage. He was an outstanding example of the best hybridization produced through the Conquest. He was possessor of one of the largest fortunes in New Spain and was an intimate friend of all its prominent government and social leaders. He would bring to the new province a polish and a flourish with his velvet suits and white ruffed collars, his elaborate metal breastplates and carved leather trimmings, his morion helmet worn square on his head held high and erect. He would also bring broad wisdom and an unflagging sense of duty to Crown and Church. But like other conquerors before him, he would face many difficulties and much abuse. He would suffer imprisonment and disgrace.

There had been at least six others petitioning for the privilege of undertaking New Mexico exploration, including Espejo. They were denied for reasons of poor health, exorbitant demands, or personal characteristics deemed unsuitable. One petitioner had the misfortune to be arrested for the poison murder of his wife, her lover, and five servants! Three took it upon themselves to go north without royal permission and were judged to be traitors.

To risk one's fortune and person for the state in return for a lavish chain of titles—governor and captain general for two generations and *adelantado*—did not seem foolish or useless. This was not yet the age of cynicism. It was an era of government by contract.

According to Oñate's contract, he was to recruit at least two hundred men, fully equipped at his own expense, and to take cattle, sheep for wool and mutton, goats, colts, mares, wheat, jerked beef, iron for tools, medicines, gifts for the Indians, frieze and sackcloth, and numerous *quintals* of lead, powder, and quicksilver.

Governor Oñate agreed to supply horses, mules with harnesses, coaches, iron-tired carts, cavalry saddles, troopers' saddles, leather shields, helmets, harquebuses, swords and daggers, corselets, stands of arms, and horse armor. To secure all these items he pledged his own fortune. He also obtained the financial backing of many of the most influential men of the time.[10]

In the long wait at Santa Bárbara while King Philip and Viceroy Monterey vacillated between Oñate and the petitioner from Spain, Ponce de León, supplies such as the medicines, tools, and metals were stored in warehouses and corrals the settlers made available to the army. Much food was consumed. Cattle and sheep strayed off and were lost. It became necessary to make large purchases from local *hacendados*, or owners of the haciendas, in order to maintain the contract strength of the expedition.

An idle army quartered in a small town soon caused numerous disturbances with drinking, gambling, and brawling. The ardor of the men for the project had changed to discontent with constant delays. A notice was posted that all soldiers or colonists found guilty of stealing would have to make repayment at the rate of four times the value of the stolen goods and receive six lashes from the dreaded whip. Blame for the crimes committed by members of the expedition would fall directly on the shoulders of the commander. In 1609, when he was removed from the office of governor of New Mexico, Oñate was charged, among other things, with numerous robberies committed by his men on the march from Zacatecas to Santa Bárbara. He would be condemned with his captains, Gaspár de Villagrá and Gerónimo Márquez, for allowing the hanging of deserters from his army while bivouacked at Santa Bárbara.[11]

The last tedious inventory of the expedition was made on the desolate plains beyond the Río Parral. One hundred twenty-nine soldiers and colonists, eighty-three wagons, and seven thousand head of stock began to march. Riding beside the illustrious Governor and Captain General was his young son, burdened already with the rank of lieutenant, being apprenticed for duties he would have to assume in an early manhood. Behind them, soldiers moved into formal ranks as they pushed through the mesquite and cactus with partisan spears and lances catching the sunlight and reflecting skyward the sheen of brilliant metal. It was hot, even in February, for the plodding foot soldiers clad in heavy dress and carrying cumbersome arms and scabbards. Solid cart wheels of wood and metal gouged deep into the silty soil. A caravan of sweating men and beasts moved in a fog of strangling grey dust.

From the Río Parral the army marched up to the Río Conchos which was difficult to ford. Oñate planned to leave the river path to try to find a more direct route due north. A pontoon bridge was constructed using large wagon wheels as a base so that the sheep could cross; the first had become waterlogged and were pulled under the waters by the weight of their wet wool.[12] Once across the Conchos, the party progressed north to the Río San Pedro, where the agricultural center of Delicias is now located, to await the arrival of the Franciscans who were to accompany them.

By March 20, the expedition had arrived in the region of modern Gallegos. It was one of the most sacred days in the Catholic calendar, Maundy Thursday. A halt was called. No empire could be more important that that created in Heaven. A chapel of brush here instead of a chapel of mud, but the day was spent in adoration of the Blessed Sacrament just as in central Mexico. There were special prayers for the ultimate success of this venture. Flagellations were undergone by priests and followers until, according to Villagrá, the sands of the camping ground ran red.[13]

Two small parties went ahead to locate water holes and to blaze a trail through the wilderness of north central Chihuahua to be followed by the larger and slower moving body of colonists, soldiers, and stock. These scouts faced death from thirst and had some fierce encounters with Indians, but they sent word back to their leader that all was fine up ahead and to proceed. One month after Maundy Thursday, half crazed with thirst and endless hours of staggering through the bleached sand dunes of Samalayuca, the scouts thankfully fell on their faces in the softly oozing mud of the Río Grande bank just twenty-five miles below the crossing to be known as El Paso del Norte. Ten days later, April 30, 1598, amid as much pomp and ceremony as circumstances would allow, Oñate grandly took possession of the province of New Mexico for his King, his Lord, and himself. Hardships had not made him inarticulate. His proclamation filled a half dozen sheets of parchment closely written with sharpened goose quill. Now history could not pass him by.[14]

Oñate's expedition had, in general terms, traced a road to be used throughout the colonial period to tie its most far-flung colony to the central core of Mexico.* Chihuahua would be a most vital link in that chain of empire.

A minor result of the expedition was further confirmation of the martyrdom of Fathers Rodríguez and López. In a village on the central Río Grande, Villagrá wrote of seeing a mural which he thought depicted the details of the deaths of those two.**

WHILE SOME PRIESTS were concerning themselves with exploration hundreds of miles north of the settlements of the Valle de San Bartolomé, others were dedicating their lives to Christianizing the heathens closer at hand. One of these was Father Juan Fonte, Society of Jesus.[15]

Fonte had arrived in Mexico in 1600 after the long trip by land and sea from his native Barcelona. He had felt it challenging to be assigned to the fierce Tepehuanes already notorious for their dark superstitions. Zealously he strove to make a success of his work in the missions near the Durango mining camps of Indé, Guanaceví, and Zape. But always he recognized an urge to go even farther into country so rough and remote that no other Europeans had been there. In 1610 authority had been given for earnest missionary work along the gateway to the mountains. He had established a small mission headquarters in the green fertile valley of San Pablo (now Balleza), named it San Juan de Tepehuanes, administered to the Tepehuanes, and, at the same time, gradually attracted the Tarahumaras into the orbit of the mission's influence.

The padre had found the Tarahumaras, who inhabited the mountains north of San Juan, to be docile and friendly to him but bitter enemies of the Tepehuanes. Fonte was successful in getting the two tribes to forget, at least superficially, their ancient antipathies. They settled side by side at the mission forty miles west of Santa Bárbara. Once, Fonte had walked that distance to Santa Bárbara to plead with his countrymen dwelling there to be kind

---

* Bloom, 1937, 215. Eighty-three carts of this expedition were the first ones moved north on what was to become an important freight route.

** Archaeology at the site of Kuaua and subsequent analysis of twenty-seven successive layers of murals found in the ceremonial room believed to have been the one occupied by the Spaniards have disproved this notion. See Dutton, 1963.

to these Indians. The Tarahumara were so grateful for his interest that they had provided him with an honor guard of thirty of their finest warriors and had erected floral arches along the trail where the good Father could rest.

On November 16, 1616, Fonte and Moranta, his assistant, were to have a brief holiday. They were going southward to Zape where an elaborate ritual and feast were planned for the presentation of a new statue of the Blessed Virgin Mary. They would see old friends from missions, mines, and haciendas scattered throughout the northern Durango mountains. There would be a chance to forget temporarily the months of loneliness a missionary had to endure, cut off from his own people and the sound of his own language. It was an occasion the two men eagerly had awaited.

The pace of the missionaries instinctively quickened as they saw a familiar stratified and tilted, rocky cliff off several miles in the distance. It was a landmark for travelers coming to Zape. On its face were pictographs drawn by an unknown earlier people. At its feet were crumbling masonry-faced pyramids which archaeologists later would consider to represent an outwash of a tenth century Chalchihuites culture of central Durango. Zape and its promise of relaxation and fiesta were near.

These servants of God lived by divine omen and by the daily miracles He worked. All events were interpreted as manifesting His desires and His help. On this day He gave no warning or sign of what was to come, as His will came down with crushing force upon the two travelers.

A small band of Tepehuán men, angry and agitated, bareback on gaunt horses, rushed from behind concealing boulders aside the narrow trail. They spurred toward the priests who had turned to face them with an unearthly calm, savagely caught their robed bodies on spear tips, ripping cloth and flesh. Fonte and Moranta were left dead on the trail two miles from their destination. The first agents of Christ to the Tarahumaras had been killed.[16]

There was no fiesta at Zape. Instead there was a cyclone of terror funneling through central Durango, whirling in an orgy of mass hysteria, in a frenzied restatement of man's fundamental desire to pursue life in his own manner according to his own beliefs, dissipating itself in murder, arson, desecration, drunken oblivion. The Tepehuán nation was making its last mass effort at self-preservation. It was in full, misdirected rebellion. As a result, two hundred Spaniards were sacrificed, including ten friars. An estimated thousand Tepehuanes were killed. Mines, roads, and ranches were ruined.

The reasons for the disaster were intangible, undefinable. Spanish oppression here had not been physical. Rather, it was a tyranny of the soul. The Tepehuán people were highly superstitious and inclined to be guided by medicine men, *hechiceros*, practicing a simple black magic. At first they meekly had accepted Christianity as brought to them by the Jesuits. But some of their shamans, whether through jealousy of the power of the white priests or through the perception and honest fear of ultimate doom of their people, began to arouse the Tepehuanes against the intruders. Then a messiah arose.

Desperate people accepted desperate plans, clutching at straws of hope as Quautlatas, the hechicero, once baptized as a Christian, offered them promise. He foretold the complete destruction of the Spaniards and the emergence of Tepehuán domination of the land.

Ten priests met martyrdom, but only four bodies were found— those of the two Jesuits in Zape and those of Fonte and Moranta on the trail two miles north. By divine miracle, it was believed, the bodies were not decayed or odorous, although they had lain in the snow and rain for three months, still guarded by faithful dogs. They were removed to Guardiana by the army. At the outskirts of town a most solemn procession met the army cortege. Three hundred Christian Indians and the entire frightened European population of one hundred quietly watched as the Jesuit superior, Father Luis de Bonifaz, laid each body across a mule belonging to the governor of Nueva Vizcaya and draped it with a rich golden-colored mantle bearing the governor's coat of arms. The mules were led through narrow cobblestone streets to the Franciscan church where the bodies were laid out. Later they were taken to the Jesuit temple for the high mass of St. Thomas. The intense emotion of the occasion plus the overpowering odors of burning wax tapers and incense produced a macabre pageant dramatically Spanish. A large wooden chest containing four identical caskets was lowered into a flower-carpeted vault.

The Christianized Tepehuanes and the Spaniards repopulated the deserted settlements. Papasquiaro and Santa Catalina soon were rebuilt, but for seven years Zape stood empty, its chapel open to the sky and its homes decaying into heaps of brown mud. Then in 1623 new colonists once again came to the village on its quiet little stream by the big rocky cliff.

In an old well there, workmen found the statue of the Virgin Mary, the one whose erection was to have signaled the start of the celebrations that November day in 1616. A pious army captain had it sent to Mexico to be repaired and repainted by skillful craftsmen. Just as the scar of the war of which the image was a part never could be obliterated, so an ugly gash across its cheek would remain. The Lady of the Missionaries in the chapel at Zape became the center of a shrine of Santa María to which the devout came from all central Mexico. The waters of the well in which the image had lain those seven years were said to have produced miraculous cures.[17] Dark, somber oil paintings of the murdered priests, arrows plunged into their breasts, and brows capped with halos of clotted blood, were hung on the rudely reconstructed temple walls. A shrine was erected on the trail where Fonte and Moranta made their sacrifice. Stronger efforts than ever before were made to Christianize the wayward Tepehuanes and to keep them in the fold.

A second probing thrust of the Jesuits into lands to become a part of Chihuahua was to be parried by another outburst of native resentment and the martyrdom of two more priests. Julio Pascual, heir to a Venetian merchant empire, had been sent from the Jesuit dominion on the Sinaloa coastal plain, eastward into the tangled mass of the sierra madre. He had gone into the tropic areas of the headwaters of the great Mayo and Fuerte rivers, near the Barranca del Cobre. For six years Pascual had devoted his full time to introducing European religion and way of life to the Tarahumaras, Guazapares, Varohíos, and other tribes of this remote Chínipas region. Immediately after Padre Martinez, a native of Portugal who was sent to help him, arrived, rumors reached the priests of their impending doom. Calmly the Fathers prepared themselves and a few steadfast converts for death. Early one February morning a mob scaled the walls of the isolated church, which previously they had set afire, sent a rain of arrows down upon those trapped within, killing all but one. Padre Pascual, passionately aware of an exalted status soon to be achieved through death at the hands of his charges, cried as he fell, "We do not die as cowards but giving life for Jesus Christ and His holy law." Just two days after his arrival for duty, Padre Martinez lay dead. Pascual and Martinez had the dubious honor of being the third and fourth priests assigned to Chihuahuan territory to become martyrs.[18]

Faithful Chínipas Indians later came to the scene of the tragedy. They carried the bodies and belongings of their priests over a short range of mountains to a village called San Andrés de Conicari where the resident priest conducted requiem mass for his fallen associates. The year was 1632. Not for some two hundred seventy-five years would the world again be reminded of the heroic deaths of the Venetian and the Portuguese who had traveled thousands of difficult miles to attempt the dissemination of their culture and philosophy to a handful of unreceptive aborigines.

As soon as news of the massacre reached the outposts of Spanish settlement on the coast, an officer of His Majesty's army, Captain Perea, led retaliatory expeditions into the mountains to punish the wrongdoers. An uneasy peace was restored after the lives of eight hundred Chínipas and Varohíos rebels were taken. Many of the barranca people then were forcibly moved down onto the plains where they could be watched more easily and where they were assimilated by Sinaloan tribes. Others fled farther back into the deep twisted canyons to blend with the Tarahumara. These unheavals were to have lasting results. Spanish penetration into the area was virtually halted. This door to Chihuahua was closed.

But in the same year of 1632 another door was shown to both Franciscan and Jesuit religious orders. New floodgates of mineral wealth were about to be opened, bringing a revitalization of the colonization of the northlands and renewed vigor to the work of the Church. This gateway was called San José del Parral.

ONE HUNDRED YEARS had passed since the Spanish Crown and Church had laid claim to the strangely fascinating land and peoples of Mexico. The holdings in the center regions of the country—that belt of greatest native population and economic potentiality—were secured and were being exploited rapidly. Undreamed-of wealth had returned to the motherland. The realm of heathendom had been reduced, and thousands of new adherents to the Catholic faith could be counted. A new subrace—Caucasian, Mongoloid, and a bit Negroid—had been sired. In general, the provinces north and south of this new empire had been explored. The era of the proud conquistador was over. It was time for a second wind. By 1630 miners had opened the epoch of initial substantial development in the central section of Nueva Vizcaya. Here a Santa Bárbara resident by the staggering name of Alferez Real D. Juan Rangel de Biesma stuck his pick into a barren hill ten miles from home and pulled out ore samples sufficiently promising to cause a stampede of wealth-hungry men from the south.[19]

This first bonanza of large proportions in Chihuahua was at a hole called La Negrita punched high upon a rocky cliff. Below, a boomtown was spawned amid the thorny, fragrant-flowered *huisache.* At the end of Parral's first year it claimed a population of some three hundred miners, merchants, hacendados, clerics, slaves, adventurers, and drifters, all eager to be a part of the great strike. The *corregidor,* or magistrate, of Zacatecas was forced to establish heavy fines for anyone leaving Zacatecas for Parral without his permission.[20] Four hundred claims were filed in one year. Promise became reality when the diggings of the area came to produce more than 50,000 *marcos* of silver a year, valued at nearly 200,000 pesos.

Some of the genes of Parral's heredity were noble; some were ignominious. However, the settlement continued to thrive and to grow, in time to become known as the "City of the Bridges" as it stood over a treacherous river, which, on at least five occasions, has poured violent floodwaters through its streets, rushing houses and inhabitants headlong to frightful destruction.

First to Parral came the miners and crushing mill operators and, three years later, to San Diego, just to the north.* Then came the ranchers and the farmers spreading from the San Bartolomé valley up the Río Florido and Conchos, planting crops of corn and wheat and herding cattle, goats, and horses. Thus began enterprises destined to be most important throughout Chihuahua's history, supplementing and supporting each other. Mining would come to be dominated by foreign interests. Cattle raising, however, would remain a Mexican business.

In the vanguard of Spanish settlers were Franciscan priests sent

---

* Renamed Villa Escobedo, abandoned in 1929.

to carry out the Crown's desire of conversion of the native peoples. By 1604 Friar Alonso Oliva had constructed a simple whitewashed adobe chapel on a bluff overlooking the new *presidio* (garrison) of San Francisco de Conchos twenty-two leagues northwest of San Bartolomé. This mission was the twenty-first convent established under the authority of the Zacatecas Franciscan headquarters. Oliva lived at San Francisco de Conchos for forty years and set himself up as teacher and protector of the four thousand Concho Indians in the vicinity.

The entire Spanish colonial system was founded upon Indian labor, sometimes free but more often forced. Two words frequently used in connection with colonial policy were *encomienda* and *repartimiento* which added up to human slavery and debt peonage. In theory, the Crown supported a paternalistic policy. In practice, the abuses were many and regrettable as heavenly ideals were not allowed to interfere with worldly gains. As elsewhere, in Chihuahua these malpractices meant bloodshed and bitter war.

By the time of Parral's birth, the encomienda had been abolished by royal *cédula*, or decree, and because of the necessity of defending the frontier, tribes in these outlands often were excused from participating in the repartimiento. Nevertheless, through the mere fact of geographical location, the desert seminomads belonging to the Concho tribe were forced to be the laborers in the fields and in the mines. It was the first tribal stock of Chihuahua to be completely obliterated. The need for manpower became so acute that Negroes (who were arriving by the thousands from Africa) and Tlaxcaltecas and Tarascans, from the central highlands, were imported into Nueva Vizcaya where they, too, soon died off from an environment to which they were unacclimated and hard labor for which they were unfit. The local Indians—Tarahumaras, Tobosos, Sumas, and others, male and female—were captured and put up for auction in a growing slave market in Parral. Slaving raids were conducted as far away as La Junta on the Río Grande to supply the manpower needs of the mining district.[21] Service was demanded for ten years, except in the case of Negroes who were faced with a lifetime of bondage.[22] Free Indians and *mestizos* from other regions beyond the mountains came to work in the magic triangle of Santa Bárbara, Parral, and San Diego. Opportunity for the blending of the blood of the three great racial stocks of mankind was present.

A new strain, the Mexican, was in process of formation in Parral on the periphery of Spanish empire and the character and personality of the Chihuahuense were being created.

Using Parral as a toehold in the southern mountains, or Tarahumara Baja, by 1640 the black-robed Jesuits began an earnest campaign of "reduction" of the Tarahumaras; that is, reducing them from scattered paganism into settled Christian communities.[23] The Christian cross was carried from canyon to canyon, from crag to crag, where it met a Tarahumara cross used by these heathen long before contact with white men.[24]

A completed cycle of Catholic indoctrination was symbolized by the first leading Jesuit to re-enter the Tarahumara field. Padre Gerónimo Figueroa was himself an Indian from the state of Mexico, an ordained priest of a religion which had supplanted that of his ancestors. He and Padre José Pascual, originally from Valencia, established a chain of small missions, each with a constellation of circuit-rider outposts or branches through the Tarahumara Baja.

Pascual made his headquarters at San Miguel de las Bocas (now Villa Ocampo, Durango), a settlement of four hundred transplanted natives on a broad fertile plain through which flowed the Río Florido. Here he settled down to learn the Tarahumara language and subsequently wrote a trilingual book in Spanish, Tarahumara, and Tepehuán, with Latin footnotes. In time he was named rector of all the Jesuit missions to the Tarahumara and wrote a history of their development. It was a proud day when his Indians had saved enough money from the sale of their surplus crops to purchase two silver lamps to be sent to Rome to adorn the sepulcher of San Ignacio, founder of the Jesuit Order.

Figueroa walked north to found Huexotitlán, often considered the richest of the Tarahumara missions and noted for its skilled carpenters and smiths, and San Francisco de Borja and Satevó, two of the poorest. In 1641 he was commissioned by the government to explore the mountain chain to the north and west of Parral to suggest a route for a royal highway through the Tarahumara Baja to the Yaqui River on the western slope. As he trudged through the sierra, measuring the distances with an *agujon,* or sighting device, noting topographic features and feasible passes, he also observed the Indians, to whom his Order would send missionaries, and saw their huts of mud and stone scattered, as he said, like an "outbreak of smallpox" across mountain clearings. The road project never materialized beyond establishing a rough trail from Cusihuiráchi to Tomochi and Tutuaca and then over the divide to Sahuaripa. Another of Figueroa's feats was writing a book on the art of vocabulary of the Tarahumaras. After serving in the missionary field for forty years, he was called to Mexico City to become rector of the Colegio Máximo.

The Jesuits were dedicated missionaries of sublime faith and unfaltering crusading zeal. They were responsible for breaking through the barriers of ignorance and fear, for bringing Western civilization to these new outposts, and for holding the mountain frontier. These were men of unparalleled endurance, having to travel hundreds of miles on foot and on muleback, to face privations, torments of inclement weather, and possible death at the hands of fearful natives. They demonstrated the greatest intelligence and resourcefulness. A missionary had to know the rudiments of agriculture, construction, blacksmithing, cattle raising, leather tanning. He was expected to be a linguist, a cartographer, an author and historian. Often he was called upon to give advice to the government on developments along certain portions of the frontier line. In the words of the historian Bolton, the Jesuits were in effect the Indian agents of the day.[25]

The mission settlement itself was a stronghold of Christian living and a garrison. In its beginnings it usually was a shelter of indifferent sort built by the Indians for the priest and another hut where he could conduct his services. As the mission became established, permanent buildings were constructed. The main structure was, of course, a chapel, built on the plan of the Latin cross with arms of unequal size. Sometimes smaller chapels branched off the small arm of the cross. The walls were of thick stone or adobe-brick masonry and supported hand-adzed beams. Arches, domes, and fillagreed pilasters relieved the severity of design. The retablos behind simple altars had figures of the Bishop with his miter and cross, cherubs, doves, the Virgin, patron saints, or leaves and flowers worked with skill and delicacy in stone by a people who prior to this time had no tradition of sculpture.

Near the church were the homes of the resident priest and the Indians of the village. A compound was formed by shops and workrooms. Around this were the fields and corrals. Often the entire unit was walled and had defensive watchtowers. In the gardens, these priests transplanted to northern Mexico almost every fruit and vegetable known in Europe which could survive—oranges, figs, pomegranates, peaches, apricots, pears, berries, onions, garlic, mint, mustard, cabbage. One fruit denied the Indian was the grape, as the Spanish government sought to spare them the temptation of further inebriation (a prevalent weakness of the Tarahumara) and to eliminate competition for the wine merchants of the homeland. Domestic animals such as sheep, goats, horses, and cattle were brought to the sierra madre. The mission had to be self-sustaining, and, often, there was a surplus with which to supply Spaniards in the vicinity. It was not uncommon for missions to own twenty-five thousand or more head of cattle. These were used as meat for the priests and their neophytes and as undisguised lures to attract the timid, hungry Indians still lurking in the hills.

Most materials used in the construction and daily operation of the mission had to be gathered or created on the spot. Not everything could be so obtained, and it was necessary periodically for supply caravans to be dispatched northward from Mexico City. The Franciscan Order, for many years, operated its own supply service which brought necessary items to the missions on the central mesa and to those of New Mexico. These armed caravans, although controlled by the religious, came to be the main secular commercial links to the capital as well, as their ponderous wagons carried ores, crude salt, official papers, foodstuffs, garments, and even settlers, northward.[26]

The Jesuits of the Tarahumara Mission relied on such caravans to bring them new supplies each year. These were unloaded at a depot in Parral. There it was the responsibility of each priest to arrange with muleteers for pickup and final transportation to his headquarters. Alms lists still extant in colonial archives (archives of Hidalgo del Parral) give an insight into the needs of the missionaries for tools, seasonings, clothes, medicines, and writing supplies. They ordered *arrobas* of rich, spicy chocolate and sugar—two products of Mexico—bags of pepper, yellow saffron so necessary to Spanish rice dishes, cloves from the East Indies, and cinnamon from Ceylon. They asked for gunpowder, buhir wax, petards and firecrackers for festivities, flageolets for music making, widths of sackcloth for shirts, linens, cassocks of the thick cloth of the country, clerical bonnets, shoes for members of religious orders of a stated number of "points," spurs to fit those shoes, blankets, serge pants because, as one Father wrote, "they last so well." They needed pins, needles, thread, knives, dyes, and scissors. Orders were made for door locks and keys, golden tacks for the sacristy, plumbs, compasses, adzes, planes, joiners, hoes, chisels, stirrups and bridles, bells, bars of iron. To care for illnesses of various sorts requests were made to the Provincial (regional superior) to send borax, camphor in linseed, vitriol spirits in glass, powders of Malinalco, scammony cathartic, assorted antidotes. For their church services they wanted myrrh, rose aloes, candles, and books of the Canonical Right.

The tremendous importance of the mission was recognized by a Crown eager to convert the aborigines and anxious to expand and protect its economic investments. An initial grant of 1,000 pesos for each Tarahumara mission was made to the Jesuit Order. Military protection was to be furnished by the nearest presidio. What further funds were forthcoming usually were dependent more upon economic and political factors than upon religious ones. After ten years the missions were to be turned over to parish clergy for operation. The missionary's place was among the unconverted, not among the Christianized. However, because of unsettled conditions and lack of parish clergy, the Jesuits retained control of their missions longer than the stipulated ten-year period.

The work of the resident priest at a mission was aided by native Christians who formed a teaching corps to drill the new converts in the fundamentals of Church dogmas and service. Selected native officers enforced attendance at mass, special prayers, confession, and celebrations of certain feast days. Other Indians were put to work tending mission fields and livestock. Frequent complaints of the priest's exploitation of native labor compelled the viceroy to appeal to the Church to end such practices.

Meanwhile, colonists and government officials themselves were adding to Indian discontent which began to flicker up in gusts of hot wind from the desert. The warlike Tobosos took to raiding isolated haciendas and attacking caravans moving north and south on the Guardiana-to-Parral road. Neophytes fled from Franciscan missions at San Francisco de Conchos and San Bartolomé. Murders and robberies became the order of the day; with each successful skirmish, the audacity of the Indians grew. They were astute and had learned much from their overlords about the use of horses and the techniques of mounted warfare. It was they who may have been responsible for introducing the horse to the southern Athapascans to their north.[27] Troops marched from Parral to drive the Tobosos north across the Río Grande, but actual contact with the elusive rebels never was made.[28]

The Concho picked up the brightly burning torch of rebellion. They swept across southern Chihuahua plains, angry and destructive. Two Franciscans were murdered in the San Francisco church. Other villages were sacked, and the inhabitants were driven southward. First Atotonilco, then San Bartolomé, and, one by one, other settlements stood empty, with the crops drying in the hot sunshine and the houses open to the sky. At the end of the year 1644, the embattled Spaniards held only four towns—Indé in northern Durango, the Jesuit mission of San Miguel de las Bocas, the Franciscan mission at Mapimí (now in Coahuila), and the garrison and mines at Parral. The Tobosos returned, augmented by the Salineros, Julimes, and Colorados from the east. Raids and fighting continued through most of 1645.[29]

It was over as suddenly as it had begun. The Indians were tired and wanted peace. They surrendered to the officers offering them the best terms. The fire of revolt was about to go out. But then the Tarahumara, previously unorganized and without leadership began to stir.[30]

The basic cause was Spanish oppression. The gentle Tarahumara, once proud of a wild freedom amid peaks and canyons, were impressed as slaves in the Parral mines and were being pushed into ever deeper misery. Pre-Hispanic life for them had been difficult, but amelioration had not come with their white masters. They were driven, with a lash, to almost superhuman efforts in backbreaking drilling and shoveling, and then were forced to carry on their shoulders rawhide bags of ore up as many as four or more tiers of notched-pole ladders to be dumped for shipment to a crushing mill. Overheating of the human body, extreme fatigue, choking dust to clog the lungs, and insufficient food soon broke the hardiest. Disease and despair were their wages.

No longer were they free to ramble through the labyrinthian

sierra, moving as they chose from one cave home to another. The padres herded many of their number into mission settlements and strictly demanded their presence at lessons and ceremonies which they did not comprehend. They were told they must forsake their *petates** and sleep on beds, put crosses in front of their doors, raise dogs and cats and chickens. The padre's god, whom the good Fathers said was kind and just, did not seem to heed their prayers. He even withheld the rain. For five years crops had shriveled and died for lack of moisture. No longer was there sweet oblivion from drinking large quantities of the intoxicating *tesgüino*—lashes from a stinging whip, were their punishment. Drinking, games of chance, and even teasing sport with other men's wives were frowned upon by the Spanish clergy. The Indians were led to believe that everything pleasant in life was clothed in sin.

An inarticulate hatred and resentment suddenly found vent. One night in May 1646, San Francisco de Borja, where a stockpile of grain was stored, was set afire. Forty neophytes and Spaniards were slain. It was war again. A pursuit force of a hundred volunteers rode from Parral. Another of two hundred loyal natives was dispatched from Huexotitlán. Hastily, Governor Valdés, who had been ineffective in stopping the bloody disorders, was removed from office and was replaced by Diego Guajardo y Fajardo, who personally led a punitive force through the mountains, burning and destroying all Indian property encountered. Hunger was an even more invincible enemy than the Spanish governor. The Tarahumaras gave up, tossing the heads of their two former leaders at the feet of the conquerors.

On his military campaigns, the governor had selected a fertile valley on the Río Papigochi in the northern mountains, or Tarahumara Alta, to be the site of a new colony. Such an outpost not only would push the boundaries of Nueva Vizcaya still farther north toward the province of New Mexico, but it could well serve as a listening post against the agitated Tarahumaras. He did not know that his countrymen would ignore the rumble of new terror.

---

* Rush or palm mats universally used in Mexico for a myriad of purposes. A newborn baby may be laid upon one. He may sleep upon one as he grows to maturity. And when he dies, he may be rolled up in one as he goes into his grave.

Bloodletting was still too fresh a memory, and Fajardo encountered much reluctance among the inhabitants of Parral to move on to a new distant settlement later called Villa Aguilar (now Guerrero). There were only four volunteers. They traveled up to the Papigochi where they joined a military party of thirty. With them went Padre Godinez (also known as Beudin), a Belgian priest who had worked recently among the Concho. He immediately built a mission a mile from the town.

At first Padre Godinez made friends with many of the Indians of the area. His pleasant personality and sincere desire to help his charges overcame the language handicap. They trusted him as a child trusts his father. But just as a child becomes unreasoning at misunderstood actions of his well-meaning parent, so the Indians of Papigochi began to doubt, to question, to detest. The padre was held responsible, in their eyes, for the deeds of his countrymen.

Apparently the Spaniards had learned nothing from their recent disasters at the hands of the Indians, for they continued to enslave and mistreat them. The *alcalde,* or mayor, himself was guilty of crimes against the Indians. Father Godinez had told him so as he reminded the alcalde that the actions of the Spaniards were not only unchristian but unhealthy. Angry at the ugly truth, the settlers of Villa Aguilar condemned the padre for his objurgations and his warnings, calling him meddlesome. They said a priest should tend only to his flock and not interfere in political matters. The schism between the Spaniards of the town and the Belgian of the mission steadily widened.

Certain that trouble was inevitable, Godinez prepared himself for a crown of martyrdom. His decapitated body and that of his guard were nailed later to a humble cross in the atrium of the lonely chapel. He had been right. It was a new round of war without quarter.

Once more the royal troops marched in righteous indignation. General Barrasa and Captain Morales found the enemy dug in on an impregnable mesa, El Peñol—six hundred Tarahumara men bound together through hatred and fear into an unaccustomed tribal unity. The Spaniards waited at the mesa's skirts throughout the night for reinforcements. With the dawn, they quickly saw that it was the Indians and not they who had received aid. El Peñol was a mass of red humanity, likened to a giant ant hill. Over one thousand strong, they bitterly fought off the Spaniards, inflicting many wounds with their well-aimed arrows.

On the seventh day the battle came to an end. Godinez had been made the fifth Jesuit martyr in Chihuahua, and the Tarahumara had met their second defeat.[31] One more final gasp for freedom from oppression would be made before the spirit and the hope of these valiant people would be crushed.

To LOOK at Tepóraca one would not think him to be a leader of men.[32] He was small and lithe and possessed the beautifully muscled legs of his people, bred through centuries of half walking, half trotting through mountainous environment. His features were sharply defined, almost gaunt, with skin deeply burnished and shiny as if it had been well oiled. Long, straight, black hair, held at the forehead by a white headband, fell to his shoulders. His basic clothing was a breechclout and a pair of rawhide sandals; in cold weather he added a large, warm blanket worn crosswise across his body.

To hear him was to feel the sear of a flame of passion, for Tepóraca was an orator. His words, uttered with skill and intense feeling, aroused a war-weary tribe to yet another futile attempt to stop the incursions of the Spaniards. Other leaders of the 1650 rebellion had given up the battle and had returned to conditions as they had been before. But for Tepóraca there could be no surrender. The hatred and contempt he felt for his conquerors ate at his very soul, leaving him no peace of mind, no escape. So he traveled through the gorges of the Tarahumara Alta pleading or demanding that the Tarahumara unite once more to rid themselves of the scourge of the Spaniards. By March 1652, they were ready to strike.

The small mission a mile from Villa Aguilar again was the first target. Padre Antonio Basilio, who had made his way from sunny Naples, was crucified in front of a mud chapel in the sierra madre of northern Mexico. Some witnesses said they had seen his soul in the form of a child leave his mouth and ascend to heaven as he expired. He was the sixth Jesuit martyr in Chihuahua.

This time there were no white survivors. The entire population of Villa Aguilar was massacred. Later, Satevó and San Lorenzo were razed, and, ultimately, seven Franciscan missions lay in ruins.

All booty possible was carried away as the rebels scattered throughout the mountain chain. Tepóraca had his revenge.

Then the Tobosos struck from the east.

The hapless Spaniards were being pulled in many directions at once, like a victim of Inquisition justice stretched upon a rack. Tenacious and determined to hold on to their empire with its tremendous promise for the future, they were capable of much bravery in the face of overwhelming odds. Their defense was a mere handful, never more than fifty, ill-equipped, poorly trained soldiers aided by a few loyal Indians. They countered violence with violence, fire and pillage with fire and pillage. No quarter was given, none asked.

Governor Fajardo had sent troops into the desert in pursuit of Tobosos who threatened to disrupt completely the supply caravans coming from the capital. At this unfortunate time, the Tarahumara hordes of Tepóraca made their furious assaults. Loyal Indian runners brought frantic appeals for protection from scattered missionaries. The distracted governor was forced to immediately recall the troops from the desert and order them into the mountains where headquarters were set up at Tomochi, a town which throughout its long history was doomed to know deadly violence. Again outnumbered, the resolute Spaniards took the offensive. In fighting lasting a year, they pushed the enemy back farther and farther into the mountains, burning homes and crops, and at last defeated them by starvation. For months Tepóraca craftily managed to elude the Spaniards, only to be taken finally through the treason of one of his own men.

Bitter, disillusioned, and thoroughly beaten, the Indian leader was brought into Tomochi for execution. He was sentenced to death by the Spanish officers against whom he had fought. The chaplain urged Tepóraca to confess his great sins, to ask the Lord's forgiveness, to enter death as a Christian. A blasphemous snarl was the Indian's only answer. He had been made to surrender his body but never would they get his soul.

Tepóraca was hanged from a pine bough on March 4, 1653. With him died all Tarahumara resistance. From then on they would be a dejected, defeated people living in squalor and extreme poverty on the edge of civilization, coming to beg on the city streets. Their plight would, from time to time, prick at Spanish conscience, but, until recently, no concrete actions were taken for their betterment. Their misery and lack of acculturation would slow economic development of the modern state.

European culture continued to spread over Chihuahua. The remaining half of the seventeenth century saw the white population steadily increase in spite of frequent outbursts of resistance from the Indians. East on the plains were Franciscan missions, a small chain of military presidios, and a growing number of haciendas. This was still a war zone where trouble could develop at any moment. West in the mountains were an increasing number of mining operations and Jesuit missions. This, too, was a war zone.

Mining continued as an important activity. As new mines were discovered, there was a parade from the south of men seeking fortune and excitement even though the governor, for fear of arousing the Tarahumara, had issued strict orders that no one— whether he be Spaniard, mestizo, Indian, *mulatto,* or Negro—was to enter the mountains except by his personal sanction. Nevertheless, prospecting continued. Movement in the Chihuahua corridor was still to the north. In 1658 gold was found in a rincon three miles from Santa Bárbara, and San Francisco del Oro was founded. Urique, far to the northwest of Parral in a fantastically rough canyon country, and Cusihuiriáchi, south of Lago de Bustillos, were important centers of mining by the wane of the century.

The miners themselves were not getting rich. The government held a monopoly on quicksilver needed in the amalgamation process. It was sold to the miners at an excessive cost, and its nearest source was in Guardiana many hundreds of miles away. This made for delay and added expense. After repeated appeals by the governors of Nueva Vizcaya, the King agreed to allow the miners to obtain the quicksilver on a four-month loan and to set up a closer royal depository. Since the Crown had a one-fifth stake in all mining output, it was important to see that work was not halted.

The diseases and disasters to which miners around the world have fallen victim became common in the reales de minas. Tuberculosis, cave-ins, fires, and petering out of veins were a part of a hard life. The first hospital in Chihuahua was founded in 1680 in Parral.[33] It was located where the temple of the Virgin of Soledad now stands on Plaza Guillermo Baca. Building was initiated by funds donated by a group of free mulattoes. Its beds soon were filled with miners suffering from monoxide or mercury poisoning, accidents, and tuberculosis.

The love of the gamble goes deep with all miners, and these men would not give up. A trench here, a pothole over the next ridge, a pit in the canyon beyond, and maybe one day, *gracias a Dios,* a strike. Bonanza had replaced Quivira, but the urge was just the same.

Slavery continued in the mines, and again its victims were the Indians. A ban against slavery had been issued after the Tepóraca uprising with a fine of two hundred pesos and two hundred lashes for convicted slavers. Again in 1686 Governor José Neyra y Quiroga ordered that there be no enslavement of the Indians of this province. Nevertheless slaves were needed, and slaves were taken.

The Tarahumara Alta still was heathen. After the second destruction of the little chapel in the Papigochi valley and the death of the second priest there, efforts to bring Christianity to the Indians were abandoned for a time. It was as if the acrimony of Tepóraca had cast an evil spell upon the land. It was a period of epidemics and prolonged drought. There were many who held the Jesuits accountable, and so for twenty years the padres stayed in their southern missions and waited.

On an autumn day in 1673, the time for return was ripe.[34] Military braid and plumes mingled with flowing black robes and white Tarahumara breechclouts at a ceremony held in the village of Huexotitlán. It was a rededication service, a mass prayer for a successful reduction campaign to be launched in the high sierra. Fathers Francisco Barrionuevo and Juan Manuel Gamboa, with some Spaniards and friendly San Pablo Indians, walked again into the mountains as representatives of a culture and a religion violently expelled two decades previously. In the party was an influential chieftain, Don Pablo, who earlier had accepted Christianity and who did much to smooth the way for the priests. The following year Padre José Tardá replaced Barrionuevo, and another year later Tomás de Guadalajara took over the work of Gamboa.

Despite torrential cloudbursts and snow yards deep in places, rough trails, unreliable guides, and hostile attitudes of the natives, Tardá and Guadalajara planted the cross, sang the *Vexilla Regis,* fell on their knees and cried "Viva Jesús" in the mountain fastness from Huexotitlán to beyond San Pablo de Yepómera in the north and Tutuaca in the west. Two simple men, armed only with their Faith and their belief in the wisdom of spreading Christianity, covered one of the most difficult stretches of terrain in the whole of Mexico and turned sullen, embittered natives into willing neophytes. San Bernabe, Coyachi, San Lorenzo, Cárichi, Papigochi, Sisoguichi, Tomochi, Pichachi, Santo Tomás, Tejolocachi, Mátachi, Temósachi, Tutuaca, Yepachi, Cocomorachi, and Yepómera were missions or visitas they established. The limits of the Tarahumara range were sketched in.

At Yepómera the Jesuits and Franciscans had some bitter misunderstandings, since this represented an overlapping area of the Tarahumara and the Concho, and each Order considered it its rightful domain. The archival papers of Parral reveal a hot contest between the two Orders involving not only the Spaniards of the area but the bewildered Indians. Ultimately, the Río Papigochi was accepted as a boundary between the mission territories worked by the Franciscan Alonso and the Jesuit Guadalajara.

Reports made by Guadalajara and Tardá to their Provincial were filled with accounts of minor miracles worked each day by the Lord to aid them in their task of battling the Devil who had confined these Indians in such a hard environment to keep them from the Light. They began the work of baptism, trained native teachers to carry on, and even supervised the building of thirty churches. By 1678 there were seven missionaries serving five thousand Indians and one hundred Spaniards living in thirty-two pueblos in the Tarahumara Alta. By contrast, the Tarahumara Baja had three thousand natives and three hundred Spaniards in thirteen pueblos. At this same period, with the re-establishment of the Chínipas missions, penetration into the state via the southwestern barrancas began in earnest.

The outlook for the Jesuits seemed bright. Because of their industry and skill as missionaries and teachers, they had been given handsome gifts of money by rich admirers. An initial gift of 22,000 pesos from the governor of Nueva Vizcaya had enabled them to establish headquarters in Guardiana. Later, in 1686, a gift of 16,000 pesos was presented to them by Luis Simois, one of the two wealthiest landholders in the Parral area. The funds were to be used to maintain a Jesuit college in Parral. The Jesuits were fortunate, too, in the outstandingly high caliber of the priests coming from all parts of Europe. Forondo, Picolo, Prado, and Pecora— Italians; Neumann, Ratkay, Glandorf—Germans; Sánchez and Salvatierra—Spaniards.

Father Salvatierra spent ten years in the southern mountains, where in 1684 he was the first white man to descend into the awesome Barranca del Cobre. He returned to Guadalajara as president of the Jesuit college there, and went on to his greatest fame in founding a series of missions up the peninsula of Baja California. He returned on a visit to the Tarahumara Baja in the 1690's just in time to use his tremendous influence to keep the southern Tarahumara from joining a new revolt in the north.

Joseph Neumann was stationed for twelve years in the moon-shaped valley at Sisoguichi and forty years at Cárichi. His efforts at the latter mission made that church the most beautiful in the mountains. He encouraged his people to plant wheat and to operate the only flour mill in that portion of the sierra madre. Four times he served as rector and three times as *visitador* (inspector-general). Much of the history of the Tarahumara missions for a half century comes from his letters written in flawless Latin to friends in Bohemia. Neumann died among his converts at the age of eighty-five.

One of the most colorful priests of this period was Padre Franz Hermann Glandorf from Osnabrück, Germany.[35] After spending months at the settlement of Cárichi on the northern fringe, where he studied the Tarahumara language under the tutelage of Father Neumann, he was assigned the mission of Tomochi. This was a trouble spot, and Glandorf was an obvious troubleshooter. The people of Tomochi, then and now, had a reputation for easy violence. Neumann had written him, "Many heathen of a perverse race live there, and it has always been a nest of rebels." But fortunately the austerity and great penitence of Glandorf's life impressed the Indians. Furthermore, these fleet-footed folk were awed by the priest's ability as a walker. On arrival in Mexico he had walked from the port of Vera Cruz to Mexico City and then north to Chihuahua. There, the distances he had to travel from settlement to settlement, from one plank home to another, to work with his followers were great and arduous. He made his rounds frequently and apparently without fatigue, and in so doing, won friends. He inspired a myth of having wings on his feet, while in truth he was terrified of a horse and, because of a hernia suffered years previously, could not ride. So successful was Glandorf in dealing with his "bad boys" of Tomochi that he remained, alive and working, for forty years.

Out on the limitless buff-colored plains the Franciscans followed what had become a set pattern: advance, baptize, build convents; face death and destruction at the hands of angry savages and if not killed, retreat; return when conditions simmered down and start over again. It was a dreary cycle but one which gradually inched the frontier line northward. In this century they saw their Nueva Vizcaya chain of missions united with those of Spain's most remote colony, New Mexico. They were back at San Bartolomé by 1649 and at San Francisco de Conchos in 1667—in both, working with the Concho. About 1665 they had gone as far north as Casas Grandes, the Paquimé visited by Ibarra almost exactly one hundred years earlier, to bring the Sumas under their influence. A total of sixteen new missions were scattered over the state, including one in Parral.

The land that was Chihuahua was being divided according to Spanish law. Each mining settlement was granted community lands, an *ejido*, for the use of all the miners collectively. Other lands were considered to belong to the Crown, these being the *baldíos*.

A piece of land could be claimed by settlers if proof was established that the desired parcel was not populated or being used by either other Spaniards or Indians. A street crier stationed near the entrance of the principal church of the town read the pronouncement as mass ended, in loud, rhythmic Spanish. If no protests were filed with the authorities, a new owner could then show possession by standing on the property and throwing stones to the four winds, scratching the earth, and ordering his laborers to begin the initial tasks of settlement.

The legal size of a hacienda for grazing bulls, cows, horses, and mules was fixed at 1,755 hectares on a side; that for goats and sheep at 875 hectares on a side. Land for grazing could be bought and sold freely.

One of the largest fortunes accumulated during the last of the seventeenth century was that of Don Valerio Cortés del Rey.[36] Although he had come to Parral as a miner, through shrewd maneuvers he broadened his activities to acquire hacienda lands along the Río Conchos where by the 1660's he raised forty-two thousand head of cows, steers, and lambs for sale at the busy slaughterhouse in Parral. With the growth of his personal fortune, Don Valerio came to be a man both respected and feared in the area. In 1667 the Indians of Satevó, with the backing of the resident Jesuit, made official protest against him for continuing abuse of them. The statement, taken by a royal scribe at Parral, claimed that men working on Cortés del Rey's hacienda at Satevó stole seeds, lambs, and chickens from the Indians and allowed cattle to trample down their seedbeds. Presumably such practices were stopped, as a royal decree signed in Madrid by Queen María of Austria, mother of Carlos II, dated October 2, 1674, gave him the right to establish a family estate to be passed to his heirs, a *mayorazgo*.*

Cortés del Rey was a man of some consequence in Parral and the prototype of the hacendados of the fabulous pre-Revolution era. He cut a fine figure as he rode his big bay mare into the little plaza by the bridge, nodding his head and tipping his high-crowned Cordovan hat to those who smiled a "buenos días, Don Valerio." He swaggered—for who could help swaggering?—in his skintight pants buttoned from waist to ankle, his skirted coat of softest serge with its gold and silver trim, and his lush velvet waistcoat. He had the self-assurance that came from a fortune estimated at 287,842 pesos and twenty *ranchos* and haciendas in what is now the Jiménez district on the Río Florido. He enjoyed sitting across the plaza and watching work continue on the new cathedral to which he had donated 10,000 pesos. Don Valerio owned a home on the corner of Calle del Puente and Calle Pablo Ochoa facing the Plazuela Morelos (modern names). He also had an office, for the viceroy had named him assayer and weighmaster of the mines under Parral's jurisdiction. Cortés del Rey died with the century, but his estate passed to three male generations, then to a nephew and his successors until, in 1823, the newly created Mexican government out-

---

* The second *mayorazgo* was that of Conde de San Pedro del Alamo which was later acquired by Martínez del Río. The latter man became involved in confiscation proceedings after Maximilian's rout but the family still retains some Chihuahua property. Almada, 1945, 258; 1955a, 78-79.

lawed this bit of Spain's bequest. His fortune, his fame, and his inheritance long since have vanished, but the house with his oval stone coat of arms still stands on Plazuela Morelos.

In 1680 Nueva Vizcaya was on the sidelines of one of the most terrible defeats ever suffered by the Spanish colonial system. The Pueblo Indians to the north, in full rebellion, had killed or driven the Spaniards from New Mexico. Details of the causes of the trouble, the intrigue, the fierce fighting, and the withdrawal do not belong in this account. But the affair did have serious repercussions in the neighboring province to the south.

Some two thousand bedraggled Spanish and Christian-Indian refugees moved down the Río Grande to the area of El Paso del Norte about the new Franciscan missions of Guadalupe,[37] San Lorenzo del Real, San Antonio Senecu, San Antonio de la Isleta, and San Francisco del Socorro where they were out of the Pueblo Indian territory. There they were ordered to stay while strength—moral and military—could be gathered to recapture all that had been lost at Santa Fe and in the Río Grande valley.[38] Many colonists, however, had no stomach for return to the scenes of recent disaster and death. They wanted only to go back to central Mexico, to their own people, to the security offered there. Strict orders were issued that no one was to leave the encampment.

Spain would never accept retrenchment and withdrawal. The investment in New Mexico, in terms of both money and souls, was too great to be abandoned. However, it was to be twelve years before the white man again stood before the mud village of Santa Fe at the foot of the Sangre de Cristos and challenged the red man's supremacy. In those chaotic twelve years at El Paso del Norte, it was impossible to stop desertion. Quietly in the night, singly and in groups, disheartened colonists slipped away from the river valley to attempt to wade the sand dunes of Samalayuca and cross waterless deserts to reach white settlements in Chihuahua. Some made good the escape. Many did not.

The shock waves of revolt and revenge spread from the Pueblos to every other tribe in both northern provinces. For the first time in their history, many bands united for war. Janos, Sumas, Mansos, Jocomes, Concho, and others confederated.[39] Ethnic amalgamation was hastened. The Spaniards were in for trouble. When trouble did not actually exist, they suspected it. Plots and counterplots, espionage and plunder, quick raids and rapid escape, retribution and retaliation, white compassion misunderstood for white weakness—it was enough to drive away almost anyone. These, however, were men of empire. Spanish empire demanded peaceful and harmonious coexistence of whites and Indians. Naturally, the Spanish would dictate the terms. The Indians would make all concessions in the matters of creed and thought. Naturally.

So the Spaniards stayed in El Paso del Norte, where the trail to the north crossed the great river, and waited. They were capable of furious, sustained action when necessary, but they were masters at the game of waiting and watching. Some, like de Vargas, were anxious, even eager, to go back to Santa Fe at any cost. Others found that life along the warm river had its compensations. Seeds brought north from Parral and Casas Grandes sprouted quickly in the rich river silt. Wheat and corn did well on the terraces. Grapes grew large and sweet and fermented into a delicate wine. The two hundred head of cattle sent from Casas Grandes thrived and multiplied four times. The heat of day was tempered by the nearness of the river waters. The nights were pricked with myriads of blue-white stars. It was easy to forget the raging sandstorms sweeping off the mesas in the spring to bend double the tamarisks and pile drifts of dirt around the crude *jacales,* or shacks. But one was not allowed to forget the hostile Indians who had been there first.

News came of constant unrest among them. One group had sacked and burned the church at Janos. The Sumas had attacked Santa Gertrudis. Mines were ruined, haciendas set on fire, cattle and horses driven off. Only Casas Grandes, Torreón (near San Buenaventura), Namiquipa, and Bachiniva remained between the Río Grande and the settlements in southern Chihuahua.

Reverberations from New Mexico then reached into the Sierra Madre Occidental. Calamities seemed to pile up for the Indians. Epidemics of smallpox, measles, and dysentery—particularly virulent in areas where the Jesuits were creating mission communities —killed off almost one-third of their number. Spanish miners and ranchers were encroaching upon Tarahumara lands causing hardships and suffering. Violent cloudbursts beat upon the mountain crests, their hungry waters devouring the thin mantle of productive soil and spewing lifeless silt, rocks, and uprooted crops out upon the ruffle of tablelands. Drought in lower elevations sucked the sweet milk from kernels of maize, leaving plants stunted and cobs shriveled. Medicine men, in desperate hope of reversing the cycle of misfortunes besetting their people, chanted to unhearing gods who responded only with blazing comets speeding across the darkened dome of night. Around smoldering cook fires, rebellion was conceived.

The worried, isolated padres grew increasingly aware of the undertow of discontent pulling converts toward the pagan bands who openly were seeking coalitions with other nations and bluntly threatening those loyal to the Spaniards. They heard of a long knotted rope which was being passed from clearing to clearing, each knot to pledge willingness to push for freedom, and weekly learned of the growth of the number of knots and the shrinkage of the cord's total length. To government officials they sent pleas for military help at the missions. They advised placing extra guards with the mule packtrains moving supplies and ores through the sierra. Through the long, dry summer of 1699, they cautioned that attack might come with the completion of fall harvest.

As a result of the information sent by the priests, troops were marshaled along all mountain frontiers, marching from the west and east. Generals made official visits to mountain communities, taking a census to determine movements of natives, admonishing them to lead good Christian lives, investigating insurrection, and filing wordy testimony from Indians interviewed.[40] A few Tarahumara judged guilty of treason against the Spaniards were hanged. Others were exiled from the mountains. Ruthless reprisals were made for the murder of the missionaries at Yepómera and Tutuaca. A revolt at Casas Grandes which threatened to engulf the entire Tarahumara Alta was crushed.[41] By the end of the century it seemed as if peace had been restored. The harassed Spaniards took a deep breath.

But there could be no peace.

The current of influence in the corridor that was Chihuahua began, for the first time in the historic period, to move from north to south instead of in the opposite direction that it had taken for the past one hundred twenty-five years. Out of New Mexico thundered the wild Apache, increased in number by absorption of mission malcontents, to begin a two-hundred-year war. Out of Texas came a threat of French invasion.

SABEATA, a chieftain of the Jumano and Cíbola Indians living at the confluence of the Conchos and Río Grande and loyal to the Spaniards, had followed the river courses south to the capital of Parral to inform the authorities of the arrival in his territory of white men who were not Spaniards.* With him he carried some wrinkled papers written in French and tied in a dirty neckcloth of fine lace. He repeated stories told him by Indians living three days' travel down river from La Junta that a white man had set up a kind of court among them.

For some time, fear of French encroachment had been felt by the government of New Spain. La Salle's fort of St. Louis on the Texas coast brought them close. The vast potential wealth of Nueva Vizcaya was thought to be in jeopardy.[42]

Immediately, Captain Retana, commander of the presidial troops at San Francisco de Conchos, was ordered to proceed up to La Junta to subdue hostile Sumas and to go on to reconnoiter Espíritu Santo Bay where French forces were believed to be. His report would determine the future course of action. The governor, Juan Isidro de Pardinas Villar de Francos (in office from 1687 to 1693), knew too well that his army was inadequate and too dispersed because of the Indian trouble on the northern border to withstand any full scale invasion. Immediate appeals for reinforcements went to the viceroy in Mexico City.

But this was not to be the time of a showdown with the French empire builders. Before Retana's departure from San Francisco de Conchos, reliable information arrived that Fort St. Louis had been abandoned. The French would not invade Chihuahua at this time or from this direction. A century and a half later their troops would move up from the south.

The Apache, however, were no such shadowy phantoms. They were real enough to cause more trouble in the southwestern United States and northern Mexico for a longer period of time than any other group of Indians. For two centuries white settlers

---

* Kelley, 1955, 981. Sabeata had made the journey to Parral at least three other times.

lived in terror of sudden raids by these warlike people. Who were
they, and where did they come from?

Actually, people known as Apache were from a number of different tribes but all belonging to one of the great linguistic stocks
of North America, the Athapascan. These seminomads perhaps
represented one of the last large waves of migration from Siberia,
having filtered down through the great interior basins to arrive at
about A.D. 1400 in the American Southwest. They and their fellow
Athapascans, the Navajo, forayed around the frontiers of the
Pueblo Indian territory so successfully that one and then another
center of Pueblo civilization was abandoned and its inhabitants
moved to a more central location. By the seventeenth century,
Apaches were entrenched in the mountains of southern New
Mexico and Arizona fighting other Indians and all whites.[43]

Always bellicose and in need of loot which might be obtained
through making war,[44] the Apaches were quick to take advantage
of the Spaniards' weakened condition after the disaster at Santa Fe
in 1680. It must be stated in all fairness that the Apaches were
frequently the victims of forked-tongue white treachery not only
of Spaniards but later of U.S. Americans, and, at best, their hunting grounds were encroached upon by the white man's range, but
they took a terrible vengeance—indulged in savage torture, ferocity, and treachery that frequently paled the white brand. Both
north and south of the Río Grande, when they were rampaging,
the only good Apache was a dead Apache, from the frontiersman's
point of view.

Previously they had been the prey of some Spanish slavers who
sold them into bondage in Nueva España, an act which naturally
increased their hatred of the white men.[45] They fearlessly raided
ranchos in the El Paso and Mesilla valleys to secure horses and
food, and with each success became more brazen. Once the Apache
became mounted, his quivers of arrows meant death to anyone in
his way. Where once they had walked, they now rode and with
great skill. The Jicarillas of eastern New Mexico became outstanding horsemen; the Chiricahuas of western New Mexico and Mexico more often used the burro.

It was said that these Indian warriors could shoot their bone-,
stone-, or iron-tipped arrows with such tremendous power that at a

distance of three hundred paces an arrow could completely pierce a man's body. The arrows were made in such a fashion that the tip would be dislodged when the removal of the arrow was attempted. More frightful were the lancers who held fifteen-foot lances high above their heads with both hands and, guiding their mounts through knee pressure, charged down on the enemy. Their aim was sure. Escape was infrequent. It was war carried on by small bands, striking unexpectedly, fleeing and scattering in rough terrain. Reprisal was most difficult. It was seldom war of one army pitted against another.

The Apaches, especially the Chiricahuas, were almost completely predatory. Raiding was an occupation. They ate wild plants and berries, even mesquite roots, found across the sandy deserts. Sometimes they did small-scale farming. They were hunters, too, of deer and small game and were experts at stalking. But mostly they lived off the efforts of farmers and cattlemen such as the Pueblos and the Spaniards. Clothed in buckskin shirts, leggings, moccasins, and breechclouts, long hair flying, they swooped across northern Mexico to stir up such fear that many of the settlements were abandoned, and like the Pueblos earlier, the inhabitants withdrew to the centers of greatest population. "Apache" became synonymous with "barbarian." The cruelty and inhumanity of their merciless treatment of victims shocked a civilization which was itself barely out of agonizing Dark Ages.

The type of hit-and-run warfare waged by the Apaches was difficult to halt because of distance and dispersion. While the borderland colonists were becoming more dismayed, demoralized, and debilitated, the Indians were riding a high tide. Their audacious successes attracted recruits from other desert dwellers, and their numbers grew. They became an amalgam of heterogeneous peoples clad in a fantastic mixture of native and captured clothing styles, all equestrian by horse stealing and warriors by desire. They were cunning, proud kingpins of the desert. There seemed to be no stopping them.[46]

Measures taken to halt the Apache incursions in the north and those of the Tobosos in the south were ineffective, halfhearted, and reflected the state of decline of a motherland being pulled down by a weak and vacillating monarchy. Gone was the indefatigable conquistador. The hegemony of the men of the Iberian peninsula was at an end. Decadence, corruption, and ineptitude for government spread like a disease from the heart of the empire to all its limbs. Mexico became a victim of royal inertia and bankruptcy. Official positions were filled by funds and not faculty.

At a time when Nueva Vizcaya was a land of war and its leaders bore a martial title, the governor was seldom a military man. He obtained his office through purchase. In return, he received a yearly salary of 2,000 pesos and the right of appointing the civil subhierarchy. He was subject only to the King except in judicial affairs handled through the *audiencia*, or high court, of Guadalajara and in money matters controlled by the viceroy.

Those matters of money gave the men governing Nueva Vizcaya at the beginning of the eighteenth century many headaches, because, although the viceroy agreed in principle to the strengthening of military forces in the north, he did not provide the funds to do so. One appeal after another piled up on his desk. Add 6,000 pesos to the annual fund. Put more men in the field. Strengthen Parral, Conchos, and Janos. Offer rewards for the capture of Indian ringleaders. Mount expeditions to take to the deserts to hold the water holes. Pursue, punish, or perish.

The highway connecting Parral to Guardiana, its nearest neighbor to the south, was seventy leagues long guarded by one presidio, Santa Catalina de Tepehuanes, with an attachment of *eight* soldiers. What could eight men hope to do to discourage the bands of Tobosos who constantly preyed upon caravans moving along the road, robbing, killing, and plundering? An alternate route thirty leagues longer, by way Cuencamé, was under the feeble protection of troops at El Pasaje, El Gallo, and Cerro Gordo. The captain general made his headquarters at Parral and was assigned a detachment of fifty men. It was customary to reassign fifteen of these to Guardiana. Some twenty leagues north of Parral was San Francisco de Conchos whose presidio housed fifty soldiers, under command of Juan Fernández de Retana. From Conchos to the next link in the chain of forts it was one hundred leagues. Janos, in the far north, was founded to protect the only practical route to the Sonora coast via the Púlpito Pass. Top strength of Nueva Vizcaya fortifications was never more than one hundred fifty men.[47]

At last the emergency was recognized by the distant government, and extra monies were voted. The viceroy decided to authorize an investigation into the state of affairs in the north with Don José Francisco Marín the official inspector. Being a highly conscientious man, Marín made a thorough study of the deplorable conditions and recommended the following: 1) the presidios should be strengthened in manpower and material and relentless war should be waged against the enemy; 2) the subjugated Indians should be required to live near the presidios where they would be under constant surveillance and should be made to plant their crops and build their homes according to Spanish ideas of "the proper manner"; 3) the governorship should not be venal but should be granted on basis of intelligence and diplomacy (unfortunately, these two desired attributes had not always gone hand in hand with wealth); 4) the Indians should be incited against each other and allowed to kill each other off; 5) Nueva Vizcaya should be opened to colonization by the nonmilitary, but with the understanding that each civilian would also be a militiaman armed with harquebus and ammunition; 6) soldiers in the presidios should be allowed to marry and obtain lands; 7) settlers should be brought to the Río Grande valley from the Canary Islands and Galicia.

Marín's succinct report deftly pointed up the problems besetting Nueva Vizcaya. The lack of able leadership, skilled in making war or maintaining peace, was fundamental. Also, there was the matter of the poor caliber of underlings. The soldiers often were thugs and cutthroats exiled from central Mexico. Being assigned to a northern presidio was banishment from society. Naturally, such men were not overly eager to advance and meet the enemy. They had no real desire to protect, defend, or even keep Chihuahua. Many were engaged in contraband activities as corruption in government spread to corruption in the presidios. Captains too frequently were resentful of governors who were ignorant of actual conditions or possible means of helping them. Marín suggested changing the hired mercenaries into landowners and thus providing them with the purpose of defending their homes.

Despite Marín's advice, conditions on the border remained the same. Indian encounters were frequent and indecisive during the first twenty-five years of the eighteenth century, but it began to seem that peace could be maintained in the south of Chihuahua without further need of the presidios. Government economy outweighed public insurance, and the soldiers were withdrawn.

By a vote in 1709, the village of San Francisco de Cuellar was established, later to become the village of San Felipe de Real de Chihuahua, and finally the city of Chihuahua.* It was born of an argument democratically settled by sons of Iberia and of Mexico. The town created would not wholly reflect the Galicia or Valencia or Estremadura of some of its founders. Neither would it be completely "Mexican." It would come to be a blend of the Old World and the New and, in the twentieth century, a composite of elements found both to the north and to the south of the Río Grande. It would, however, remain democratic and place in its pleasant plaza a plaque dedicated to the founding fathers, listing not only those who were in favor of its establishment but those who were not.[48]

Seven years before, in 1702, miners restlessly drifting northeastward from the camp at Cusihuiriáchi had come to the barren hills in the heart of Nueva Vizcaya and had found outcroppings of silver-bearing lodes at two test pits. Twice before, claims were staked here, but Indian troubles had driven the miners away. Now again they had taken hasty title to the area and called it Santa Eulalia. Like a prairie fire, word had spread that another strike was on. Very soon the northward tide began to swell into a wave of sizable proportions. Claims were staked. Shafts were sunk. Jacales were constructed. And five crushing mills began operations, one of the most important being the property of Sergeant Major Trasviña y Retes. But silver alone was not enough to sustain life at the spot of the bonanza. There was no water for the men or their beasts.**

Some of the miners wanted to locate down on the river at a spot equidistant from both diggings. Others wished to remain in the nothingness of that silver-plated basin. The man appointed to serve as the first alcalde mayor of the new real de minas, General Juan Fernández de Retana of San Francisco de Conchos, favored

---

* There have been many suggestions of a meaning for the word Chihuahua, but none have been universally accepted by scholars.

** Until very recent times, all water used at modern Santa Eulalia had to be hauled in on railroad tank cars.

establishment of headquarters at the junction of the two rivers, just north of the two peaks above Tabalaopa. He died before seeing this project carried out. It was then that Governor Deza y Ulloa ordered the question of the new town put to a vote, and it was he who broke a tie vote and brought about its official establishment on the spot where it now stands.

From its inception, the city of Chihuahua occupied a strategic position on the royal road to New Mexico. The location was almost the exact center of what would become the state, and midway between Parral and Janos, the two poles of occupation. The government considered it a valuable vantage point from which to launch a counteroffensive against the barbarians. At the same time, a town even two hundred fifty miles farther north than Santa Bárbara would help bolster the nervous settlement at Santa Fe, so recently reoccupied. The locale, near the mountains and yet not on the desert, provided a generally temperate environment suitable for agriculture and grazing. These factors, it must be admitted, were secondary. Santa Eulalia sat on top of a silver treasure chest, and in spite of the absence of water and timber, the presence of hot, drying winds and screeching Apaches, men doubtless would have hazarded their futures to participate in her riches. The city of Chihuahua in its chosen location only made the gamble easier.

Life in the new community took on the feverish tone of a boomtown. Wealth grew at each shovelful. La Descubridora and other pits at Santa Eulalia would be known as the richest mines in the world, in two hundred years producing ores worth over 300,-000,000 pesos. Merchants and traders quickly arrived to set up business. Haciendas at Sacramento, El Sauz, Encinillas, Labor de Dolores, and San Gerónimo were developed to provide footstuffs for the town. The population increased so rapidly that soon it was the largest, though latest, town in the province.

In its isolation from the seat of power in Mexico City, the new town of Chihuahua teetered on the brink of bloody annihilation at the hands of savages. The settlement strove to live life to its fullest—gaily and sinfully. Drinking, card playing, concubinage, and other vices were enjoyed by men whose daily work was strenuous and whose fears of tomorrow often were boundless. A tempering agent in the yeasty mixture created by ambition coming up from the south and fear of death coming down from the north was the fact that the Brothers of St. Francis had been there first and had a nearby village called The Name of God—Nombre de Dios.[49] The Church, with all the power of Spanish conscience behind it, acted as a brake on the flight to debauchery.

This was Franciscan territory. In the course of the thrusts northward the friars had brought the Word to Concho Indians at Nombre de Dios and to Tarahumara at their ranchería at Chuvíscar in the late 1600's. The new stampede of Spaniards, this time to Santa Eulalia, was unwelcome, but the Fathers stood ready to serve both Indians and whites. Having risen from the ashes of many disasters brought on by avarice and ambition, they tried to shield and protect their Indians from the evils of the servitude system which sucked up labors of one-quarter of the aboriginal population instead of four per cent as prescribed by royal decree. Loudly, and frequently, they condemned the war of attrition waged through vice and disease against their charges. Considering the nervous tenor of the entire northern front, it would be foolhardy, would it not, to stir up further trouble? They demanded in the name of the Church that the conduct of the Spanish settlers be exemplary. All must attend Sunday church services. It was the Christian duty of every master to see that his slaves go to mass and other doctrinal sessions held throughout the week.

The friars goaded civil authorities into bringing order to this moral chaos. Fines were established for swearing and for drawing figures of holy images. Heavy penalties were imposed for carrying knives or pistols. Fighting in the streets, cattle rustling, and a long list of other misdemeanors were punishable by public lashings. All persons found drunk on the streets were dressed in a tunic and red beret, lashed twenty-five times, forced to drink water until made ill, and exhibited in the plaza for three hours. The bells in the tower of the *parroquia,* the parish church, rang out an evening curfew to send all inhabitants indoors and supposedly out of temptation from wrongdoing on streets dimly lit by lamps of burning fats.[50]

A Franciscan dream of creating in Chihuahua a temple to God as beautiful and inspiring as any in all of Mexico began to take form early in the town's history.[51] Just the presence of such a huge breathtaking structure would be a constant reminder of the higher purposes of the Conquest and exploitation of this heathen land. It would require great outlays of money. But was this not potentially one of Spain's richest provinces? Was not a mountain of silver at the city's outskirts? The authorities were persuaded by the eager friars to allow a tax of one *real* (equal to 12½ cents) on each mark of silver produced at Santa Eulalia and two hundred other nearby mines (a tax of about 1½ per cent) to be set aside for the cathedral's construction. In 1725 the cornerstone was laid, on the south side of the plaza. Work would continue for a hundred years, and it would cost nearly a million pesos before completion. This represented an even more impressive sum considering the impoverished condition of the military and civil branches of the government at this time of struggle with the Apaches and other aboriginal peoples. The cathedral proved to be a building of immense beauty, awe-inspiring to worshippers, and a source of pride for all Chihuahuenses.

A corps of architectural workers headed by *maestro** Nicolás Morín and his son Ignacio designed a twin-towered church of plain, buff blocks of rock, massive yet not overpowering. The center facade of intricately carved stone done in baroque style was divided into six sections by vertical columns. Stone figures of the twelve apostles stood in shell-shaped niches between these columns. In early morning light the native stone walls shone a deep golden, subtly changing color through the day to a light buff at twilight. Large, carved, wooden doors opened into a spacious vaulted interior. Elaborate encrustation detail was skillfully executed in materials from across the world and brought into Chihuahua by mule train. Maestro José María López was in charge of the gold and silver work. Maestro Santos Domínguez was the head cabinetmaker.

A green iron fence surrounded the church atrium outside, enclosing the graves which were placed there. In modern times these graves have been removed, and the entire area has been paved. Large and sonorous bells hung in the towers to announce mass to the populace and to drive away the numerous pigeons that roosted there.

Although the plains were out of the Jesuits' assigned realm, they petitioned for the right to establish a college in the city of Chi-

---

* In Mexico it is customary to call any top craftsman a *maestro*, or teacher.

huahua where priests might study Tarahumara linguistics and where neophyte assistants could be trained to carry on the work begun by missionaries. In 1717 they further asked for the privilege of working with the Chinarra Indians located in the desert east of town. To carry on this work, a charming domed chapel, Santa Ana de Chinarras, was built on a rise above the Río Chuvíscar near the hacienda granted to Captain Pedro Cano de los Ríos in 1671, now modern Aldama. These "intrusions" heightened jealous feelings among their ecclesiastic rivals, the Franciscans, which were worsened when Doña María Apresa Ibarra gave the valuable hacienda of Tabalaopa to the Jesuit Order. Such gifts did a great deal to bring about later expulsion of the Jesuits.

Much of the city of Chihuahua grew helter-skelter, with narrow streets conforming to the peculiarities of the topography. On the other hand, the main part of the *villa*, or town, had to be done in the "proper manner," laid out in the Roman grid pattern so characteristic of all towns founded by the Spaniards, with a central square upon which faced the *casa de ayuntamiento* (town hall) and the main church.

The plaza was, and still is, the core of the town. To know the plaza is to know the history of Chihuahua; for it was here that two foreign conquerors encamped; rebels gave *gritos*, the cries of rebellion; heroes were cheered. Through this plaza marched the father of Mexican independence in chains. A president of Mexico came in flight from a puppet emperor sent from Austria. A still later dictator was feted here enroute to visit the President of the United States. It was in this plaza where crowds gathered for community events such as Sunday mass, weddings, christenings, and funerals. Travelers arrived or departed, friends gossiped, sweethearts met, business was transacted, bands played, fiestas were enjoyed—all this the Plaza de Armas has witnessed interminably.

At first the plaza was a hard-packed dirt square with the wide *portales* of the ayuntamiento on the north side and the church opposite to the south. By the middle of the century, under Jesuit supervision, an aqueduct consisting of an open flume supported by a series of graceful masonry arches came from the Río Chuvíscar through the southeast part of town to empty its waters into a fountain here. Fountains have been an enduring passion with Spaniards, inherited by Mexicans, who even built them where there was no water. In this parched land, here was a fountain with tinkling jets of water to create a spot of beauty in what had been an ugly patch of dust in dry weather and mud in wet. With the arrival of a ready water supply, the plaza was landscaped with trees and flowers. Roses and canna lilies came into radiant bloom. A sense of civic pride surged through the inhabitants.

The eighteenth century was nowhere noteworthy for its sanitation. Neither medieval Spaniards nor Neolithic Indians kept clean settlements. The residue of human living was in the streets. Beasts of burden and transportation added their filth to that of their masters. In time, however, efforts were made to beautify the town. Streets were cleaned and straightened, some even paved with river cobblestones set in neat patterns. Where unpaved streets remained, servants used large quantities of precious water in sprinkling the dirt to lay clouds of dust raised by each passing wagon or carriage. Indians employed by the city swept public places with brooms made of fibers and brush bound together.

Most houses were one-story blocks of adobe bricks; rooms were added as the family grew. They had been unadorned mud in the beginning, walls crudely made and thick. Later their fronts, flush with the street, were plastered and painted in white and delicate pastels. Finer homes sometimes were two-storied and had tan-colored cut-stone facing on the corners and around door and window frames. Iron grillwork and carved wooden shutters covered the windows. Heavy beams and corbels were hewn from timbers brought down from the sierra. Wide passageways and rooms of generous proportions and great height gave one a sense of space inside to match that found outside. Just as life in the town revolved around the plaza, so life in the home revolved around the inner patio onto which most of the rooms opened. Here was seclusion made pleasant with plants growing in tubs and birds kept in reed cages. If the home possessed its own private well, it was usually in the patio, close to the out-of-doors kitchen. The patio was a place for the family to gather for relaxation, for the youngsters to play, and for the chickens to scratch. Most homes had their own small gardens of fruits and vegetables grown from cuttings and seeds carried up from the valley of San Bartolomé and watered by irrigation ditches branching off from the river. Religion being a very personal affair with Spaniards, each home—rich or poor— had its own shrine in the corner of one room.

Men who held shares in the shafts at Santa Eulalia and those who acquired hacienda and rancho titles realized substantial financial returns for their efforts. A class of wealth was in process of rising to the top in this melting pot. A man of this class was Andrés Carbonnel, one of the original settlers, whose estate was estimated at 176,000 pesos. Another was Ildefonso de Irigoyen who had title to the hacienda at Labor de Dolores and who had generously donated lands upon which to build the town's first houses. The homes of these and other "new rich" came to reflect the best tastes and traditions of the day, islands of luxurious living in a sea of mass hardship and discomfort. Heavy tapestries, rugs, and silks from the Far East brought to Mexico's west coast by the fleet of Manila galleons found their way north on mule caravans. Solid-silver table service was set with Talavera china and handblown glassware from central Mexico. Dark oil paintings in gilt frames hung over ornately worked wood and leather furniture imported from Spain. Cloth from the finest looms in Europe was made into furnishings and clothing.

IN NUEVA VIZCAYA isolation equaled insulation. The racial hatreds and antimonarchic tensions conceived in the central highlands had not penetrated to the far north. The populace had been too preoccupied with self-preservation to consider the doctrines of liberty, equality, and fraternity for the masses.

In central Mexico, uppermost in the stratified social system were the *gachupines*, those of Spanish blood born in Spain. In the regions of greatest Spanish occupation they considered themselves superior to those who had been born in Mexico. They acquired the higher posts in government and the more prominent social position. The *criollos*, persons of Spanish blood born in the New World, socially and politically subordinate to the gachupines, resented such discrimination and came to abhor all things Spanish.[52] As a result, they were the group responsible for igniting the fuse of the independence movements at the beginning of the nineteenth century, and they represented the future of the nation. At the bottom of the scale were Negroes, mulattoes, and Indians, the first two comprising a class of illiterate slaves.

On the northern frontiers, place of birth scarcely seemed important. Emphasis necessarily had been placed upon survival, and a criollo was as capable of shooting an Apache as a Spaniard direct from the peninsula. Pioneers, because of their very mode of life, had to be democratic and had to accept the tenets of human brotherhood. There had been insufficient leisure in Nueva Vizcaya to maintain an elaborate social hierarchy among the Europeans or for race prejudice among the native born, either in time of war or in the rare periods of peace.

It was the pleasure of the King to have his vassals, whether criollo or gachupín, enjoying peace, progress, and aggrandizement. To this end he periodically sent visitadores, or inspectors, into the outlying realms to make a check for him on all legal and social matters. The duties, far beyond the abilities of one man, were listed as follows: to cleanse the people of lewd living; to correct, castigate and enumerate the capital sins and offenses to God our Lord; to inspect the ministers, to see how they were using their offices; to investigate the archives and courts; to check titles of *denuncias** of mines; to punish cattle thieves; to ascertain whether employers were taking good care of the Indians; to examine brands on stock; to determine whether landowners were carrying out royal orders and whether labor laws were being obeyed; to audit hacienda accounts, salaries paid, and measures and weights used; to find out whether all fines were properly forwarded to the royal cashier; to see whether the poor and destitute were mistreated; to hear complaints of water rights or fraud; to inquire as to the teaching of the Catholic doctrine. The visitador was empowered to name mayors, justices, and constables. Everyone was ordered to cooperate with him on threat of a fine of 2,000 pesos. In a word, he was acting as the King's agent in all affairs which concerned subjects living within that distant domain.[53]

His Majesty, though removed, was aware of the inroads Indian depredations were making in the royal fifths, the Crown's share

---

* *Denuncia* in Mexican mining law is the instrument of "denouncing" or recording a claim.

of proceeds. He sought by mandate to further establish equality among his vassals. Royal cédulas were cried through the streets of Chihuahua by heralds, read from the pulpits by the clergy, nailed to church and town hall doors. The rights of the Indians were to be respected and their enslavement was outlawed once more. They were to be assured of good lands with ample water and exit rights-of-way through Spanish property. Spaniards and Negroes were to stay out of their towns. Spanish employers were not to victimize them, although account books at Parral show Yaqui and Tarahumara Indians working for twenty days for approximately six pesos. To save them from the damnation of alcoholism, sale of intoxicants to Indians was forbidden, and they were not permitted to own or cultivate vineyards to produce grapes for their own use. In return for this fatherly surveillance, the Indians were forced to recognize the authority of the Spaniards. They were forbidden to travel from the town of their residence or employment for a distance of more than four leagues without a written permit issued by the father minister or the alcalde. Anyone without such permit could be shot on sight. This measure was an attempt to curb the increasing numbers of robberies, assaults, and cases of woman-stealing which were being committed by itinerant bands of renegade Indians.

At the beginning of the second half of the eighteenth century, Nueva Vizcaya was guarded by only two garrisons five hundred miles apart.[54] This was scant protection for twenty-three thousand Spaniards and mestizos living in sixteen communities and adjoining ranchos and haciendas. The following year, after urgent appeals from residents of Parral and the Río Florido valley, a new garrison was established at Guajuquilla (modern Jiménez) with a double complement of men to supersede troops formerly stationed at Conchos, San Bartolomé, and Cerro Gordo. By 1760 another fortification was set up at La Junta, later moved to Julimes, to protect six Franciscan missions operating there. Ultimately the presidial system was reorganized under a government inspector, Hugo Oconor.[55] Fifteen presidios, forty leagues apart, stretched from Sonora to Texas, each with forty-three soldiers, a chaplain, and ten native scouts. Six of these forts were in Chihuahua: Janos; San Buenaventura moved to Valle de Ruíz near the Laguna de Guzman; El Paso del Norte transferred south across the sand dunes of Samalayuca to Carrizal; Guajuquilla relocated at San Elizario downstream from El Paso del Norte;* Julimes back to La Junta; Cerro Gordo established on the Río Grande forty leagues below the junction at La Junta.[56] In addition, five "flying companies" were activated to go to areas of trouble when needed. The cost of all this protection was great—19,000 pesos annually. In actuality it was but a small price to pay to keep an empire from ruin, as it was estimated that in a twenty year period over 16,000,000 pesos' worth of property had been destroyed or stolen by Indians, and in a five year span, one thousand six hundred seventy-four civilians had met scalping and agonizing death, one hundred sixteen haciendas and ranchos had been plundered, and almost sixty-seven thousand head of cattle had been driven off.

The year 1776, when American colonies were fighting for independence, was the year when Nueva Vizcaya also was gaining a certain degree of freedom from Mexico City. That province became part of a new viceroyalty called Provincias Internas under a *comandante general*. Headquarters at first were in Guardiana. Later, the seat of government moved to Arizpe, Sonora, from where campaigns against the barbarians might more easily be initiated. By 1785 the comandante general came to reside in Chihuahua, then a flourishing city with a population of over seven thousand.[57]

The first comandante general was Teodore de Croix, born in Lille, France, called Caballero de Croix and a brother of the viceroy of the same name, whose suave French manners and elegant uniforms caused a sensation in provincial Chihuahua.[58] There was an immediate urge to create a bit of France on this empty Mexican plateau. Rich matrons sent to Paris for the sweeping, many-petticoated, brocaded gowns of the day and powdered wigs to match. Beauty marks and painted cheeks were high fashion. Baths taken in enormous stone or pottery bowls were scented with leaves of sweet basil, thyme, and crushed rose petals. Creams and oils for facial treatments to rival those given in European courts were imported in great quantities. Lavish parties and elaborate *bailes*, or dances, increased, spiced by the presence of the officers of the newly organized provincial dragoons known as *blanquillos* from the

---

* San Elizario claims to have been the first military post in what is now the United States.

white facings of their jacket lapels. Too soon the dispassionate authorities in Mexico City, unconcerned with the social amenities, ended this French era, as Caballero de Croix was promoted to the post of viceroy of Peru. Before he left, however, he was responsible for granting ejidos, four by twenty leagues, to most of the settlements along the Carmen, Santa María, and Casas Grandes drainages in an attempt to encourage Spaniards to remain in the north.

Chronic warfare forced the colonial administration under Viceroy Galvez into a policy of extermination by trying to incite the Indians against each other, driving them into alcoholism, perhaps arming them with guns with which they were less skilled than with the self-bow, and by giving them gifts, or bribes, to remain at peace. It was to be peace at almost any price. The price grew to 1,000,000 pesos a year to maintain the military establishments, to buy gifts to lure the barbarians into camps where they were supported in idleness. There they lived on government-bought rations under a 1790 treaty gained by Captain General Ugarte y Loyola. It was a dire situation.

Nor could officials feel too happy with the negative results obtained with the mission Indians whose concept of Christianity seemed to be raising a patch of corn, living in a mud house, and celebrating Catholic feast days with liquor and licentiousness. The amount of absorption of true Christian ideals and Spanish mores was dubious by even the most charitable estimates. Neophyte apostasy was a primary problem facing the Church.

Missionary activity, which had been a deterrent to Indian wars along the frontier, was either on the decline or had not increased during most of the early part of the century. Removal of the Indian missions from the control of the missionaries was a continual threat, but because of lack of parish clergy and royal control, the missionaries were allowed to retain their missions until mid-century. In 1705 the Jesuits had seventy-one missions in Nueva Vizcaya; by 1748 they had added only four more, with fifty-one priests actively working with the Tarahumara. In 1753 all those Jesuit missions in Durango and the Tarahumara Baja were placed under authority of parish clergy whose duty it was to work with the converted rather than the unconverted. However, because of constant lack of funds and interest, under the new regime the structures and gardens so painfully built and tediously maintained by the missionaries were allowed to fall into decay and to grow rank with weeds. One Jesuit wrote his Provincial of visiting a mission church which had been abandoned by his predecessor where he held mass for a gathering of eager natives who brought the heads of three hundred of their dead to join in the services! Soon after, there were no Jesuits left in Nueva España to worry or to care.

KING CARLOS III was dominated by anticlerical ministers who aroused in him the fear that a state within a state, a Jesuit empire within Nueva España, was being created. These ministers urged immediate Jesuit suppression. Thus influenced, on June 24, 1767, Carlos issued a sudden mandate for expulsion from the New World of two thousand two hundred members of the Jesuit Order.

Orders for the expulsion, sealed with extravagant royal rubrics, were received in Mexico by the viceroy, the Marques de Croix, with instructions that they were not to be opened until the night of June 24. Secrecy was ordered under pain of death. Officers were instructed to go immediately to all Jesuit houses, to allow the padres to pack nothing except clothing needed for the trip, and to send them aboard vessels lying at anchor off Vera Cruz awaiting return to Europe. All priests were to be treated with dignity and respect, but with firmness. They were banished from the Spanish Western Hemisphere forever.

Two days after the Marques de Croix opened the sealed orders in Mexico City, a weary courier handed instructions to the captain of the infantry regiment of the Crown stationed in Parral. It fell to the lot of Captain Lope de Cuellar and Lieutenant Becerril to execute the painful orders in Chihuahua, where almost a dozen Jesuits had met death to bring some twelve thousand eight hundred Tarahumara and Tepehuanes into the kingdom of Christianity. Cuellar's first step was to arrest three padres at the Jesuit seminary in Parral. On June 30, accompanied by a royal scribe and sixteen soldiers, he courteously visited the Jesuit college on Calle Libertad in the city of Chihuahua where he took into custody three resident priests and another he took from the mission to the Chinarras. Vicente Antonio Mota, priest at the *parroquia*, was called in to make a complete inventory of the books in the well-stocked library and of the numerous sacred objects. The Fathers then were escorted south out of Nueva Vizcaya to Zacatecas, where they joined stunned Jesuits being brought in from other northern sections.

Earlier, the Tarahumara Baja missions had been turned over to parish clergy. The remaining Jesuit missionaries were all in the Tarahumara Alta or in the Chínipas barrancas. Captain Lope de Cuellar rode to their headquarters at Yecora and then to every distant mission where each time the same heartbreaking scene was re-enacted—surprise and disbelief, quiet obedience, a tearful farewell, silent resignation. Eighteen missionaries from the Tarahumara Alta and from the Chínipas area left behind them devoted natives and a complex task unfinished. Braun from Temósachi, Ruanaba from Mátachi, Palacios from Santo Tomás, Nortier from Tutuaca, Vivanco and Honorato de la Vega from Papigochi, Dias from Narárachi, Cuevo from Nonoava, Corro from Sisoguichi, Steffel from San Francisco de Borja, Badillo from Coyachi, Sterkianowski from Norogachi, Iranzo from Guaguachi, Kiylt from Temeychi, Mateu from Tonachi, Gonzalez from Tomochi, Kauga and Yanez from Cárichi—names which cut across European national boundaries to unite in selfless devotion. However, indoctrination of the Tarahumara was superficial, and was easily sloughed off in the succeeding generations.

At the deserted college in Chihuahua the priests were visited by throngs of Spaniards who came to pay their respects to the saddened clerics. The governor of the Tarahumara and a determined group of his Indians called for permission to go to Mexico to plead with the viceroy for Jesuit reinstatement. Cuellar knew the expulsion orders came not from Mexico but from Spain and so denied permission for the Tarahumara petition.

One month after the sealed order had arrived in Parral, the party of priests, escorted by a dozen young men, began their journey to the south. At Satevó, an old Jesuit mission, they halted to celebrate a special mass. At the banks of the Río Florido they were stalled for ten days because of raging floodwaters. Before they rode out of the province, they were met by a vanguard of Franciscans coming to replace them and stopped to answer worried questions about their abandoned mountain missions.

Each town through which the party passed turned out en masse to say its farewells to the priests. At Fresnillo, Zacatecas, and

Querétaro there were such demonstrations. At Zacatecas, Father Manuel Vivanco, a veteran missionary for half a century and then seventy-four years old and nearly blind, was left behind because of his inability to travel.

Fearing a serious incident, the viceroy had sent orders that the groups moving toward Vera Cruz were to bypass the capital. But he could not refuse a request from the padres to visit for the last time the most sacred shrine of Mexico, that of the Virgin of Guadalupe. There, throngs from the city crowded in around the band of priests, striving for an opportunity to kiss their hands or their robes, shouting blessings and cheers and tear-drenched good-byes. In comforting but sad triumph, the party moved off the highlands to the tropical town of Jalapa and down to the steaming port of Vera Cruz.

In October of 1767 and in January of 1768, seven ships carried six hundred fifty-eight Jesuits from the shores of Nueva España. The cost to the Crown of removing the Jesuits from that province alone was over 4,000 pesos. Many priests succumbed from hardships and illnesses suffered during the crowded voyages. Father Corro of the Sisoguichi mission died in Vera Cruz before sailing. A second Chihuahua Jesuit, Father Braun of Temósachi, died in Havana and was put to rest in the waves of the gulf. In prison in Spain, they compiled histories of their former lands. Clavigero wrote of California, Pfefferkorn of Sonora, Ducrue of Baja California. There were no histories of Nueva Vizcaya, only remembrances of toil, death, and few rewards. Sterkianowski completed a journal of the trip back to Spain, but no account of his activities in Chihuahua.

So far as possible, all property pertaining to the missions was removed to the city of Chihuahua where it remained for thirty years. Inventories taken at the time placed an evaluation of 61,500 pesos on the confiscated materials. The Colegio de Loreto in the city, not yet completed, passed to the Administration of the Temporalities and was used for government offices. The Colegio figured prominently in the coming fight for Mexican independence from Spain as it housed the admitted instigator of that movement. In addition to the Colegio, the Jesuits owned several business houses, a crushing mill, and parts of seven haciendas.[59]

Cuellar was made governor of the Tarahumara and captain general. He later was removed from office for maladministration and misappropriation of funds. He was accused of pocketing more than 10,000 pesos earmarked for the cathedral's construction and for the building of the city's aqueduct, and monies belonging to the *cabildo,* or municipal council, and to the Jesuits.

Fifteen Franciscan friars were ordered to the mountains from the Colegio of Guadalupe in Zacatecas and twenty-six from Mexico City, to continue the proselyting campaign. The King demanded a complete description of each mission including location, water supply, flora and fauna, visitas attached, Indians of the mission, their economy and dress, mines of the area, and antiquities. Such manuals were filed for Tomochi, Novagame, Santa Eulalia, Tutuaca, Cerocahui, Guazápares, Chínipas, San Buenaventura, Batopilillas, Cusihuiriáchi, Morís, San Miguel de las Bocas, Guaguachi, and Baqueachi. At the last-named mission the distressed Franciscan charged with its operation wrote, "This is the short answer which the minister of this mission has been able to make among the many hardships, inconveniences, and annoyances of these mountains."[60] Land too poor, people too disinterested, and weather too foul, made life unpleasant for this servant of St. Francis.

At the abandoned Jesuit missions, the new Order took over the stockpiles of grain and sugar cane. They assumed, also, the annual stipend to the synod of 300 pesos per mission. However, the number of missionaries declined steadily, and when the Crown stopped paying the synod, the economic condition of the missions was serious.

The Society of Jesus had been founded by St. Ignatius Loyola in 1540, the year of Coronado's entrance into New Mexico. The Mexican Province of the Order, organized by Padre Pedro Sánchez and fourteen members, was functioning just thirty years later. By the end of the sixteenth century, Jesuits had become active in religious affairs of Nueva Vizcaya. The mendicant Society was developed along military lines, each priest considering himself a soldier of Jesus Christ, dedicated to missionary educational work. Secular business and political activities were prohibited to all members of the Order.

The vigor and skill with which the Jesuits turned themselves into successful farmers, traders, bankers, and industrialists in order to support their missions and their schools made them both feared and lauded. But it attracted gifts from the wealthy. This gave them great power within the Church hierarchy and in Catholic courts. Jesuit asceticism was suspected by some. The vow of poverty was questioned. Certain of their reforms were condemned. Jesuits in Nueva Vizcaya, as elsewhere, incurred the wrath of civil authorities and landholders because of their role as protectors of the Indians.

Thirty-nine years after Carlos's edict another King, Fernado VII, rescinded the expulsion order and allowed the Jesuits to come again to Mexico. In 1819 a few were back in Nueva Vizcaya. The college in Parral reopened. No Jesuit returned to the sierra madre. Throughout the next century, as the battle between Church and State grew fiercer, the Jesuits were driven from Mexico and from Spain itself. In 1820, 1845, and 1856 they were expelled, only to be allowed to re-enter under a new administration. The mountain missions, however, remained unused, their walls crumbling and deteriorating, the future forsaken. By 1849 all had ceased any attempts at operating.

Many rumors lingered behind the *padres prietos,* or "black fathers" as the Tarahumara had called them, to be told and retold around the Indian cook fires. Some said that missionaries of Sisoguichi had fled to Bocoyna, deeper in the mountains, to take refuge in a natural cave where they ultimately starved for fear of being apprehended if they ventured out to seek food. Most of the stories concerned treasures which the natives liked to believe were left in caves or buried within the mission compound. Treasure seekers have gutted many of the mission floors but no cache of valuables yet has come to light.

WITH THE ARRIVAL of the 1800's the Apaches were at questionable peace.[61] In the north everything was comfortably prosperous. Once again tides were rolling up from the south carrying a new influx of colonists, small businessmen, and idle floaters on the current. The city of Chihuahua and the old mining camp of Cusihuiriáchi were the most populated centers. Crops had recovered from a severe drought in the nineties, and the number of irrigated farms along the leafy river valleys doubled. Men returned to the vast tablelands they had fled during the Indian wars. Herds of longhorn cattle and Spanish cow ponies tramped down the spongy earth around water holes dotted across northern bolsons. Hacienda settlements were reclaiming the land for the white men.

Each hacienda was a compound of owner's house, workers' quarters, workrooms, chapel, gardens, and fortifications. Many had watchtowers where guards could be stationed to sound the alert if raiders came pounding that way. Men were placed on the flat roofs where they slept, ate, and watched for Apaches. Thick exterior walls had no openings but presented a blank face to intruders. Heavy gates could be swung shut to block entrance. The source of water supply was enclosed within the walls, for they remembered bloody times on these plains. Also they remembered the luxuries known to the south and across the sea. The owner's ranch home was as pleasant as his home in town with imported furnishings of leather, carved wood, silver, brocades, and heavy handspun materials. The quarters for the families of the peons who did the actual work of the hacienda were crowded and crude. They provided the minimum essentials of four walls and a roof. It was a feudal pattern of living long known in the motherland.

Diversions on isolated ranches were based upon skills needed in daily work with animals. Aptitudes for riding and roping were fundamental, and Mexican men developed into superb, graceful horsemen. *Vaqueros* (cowboys) of this northern ranch tradition would, through the years, become more allied to the cowboys of the southwestern United States (who originally adapted their costume from the vaqueros as they did their techniques), than they were to the *charros* of Jalisco. Their typical costume would become the Levis, heeled boots, and Stetsons of American cattlemen,* not the embroidered sombreros and skintight suits seen at *charradas,* country dances.

Tailing the bull tested the ability of daring riders. A rancher using a long lance separated the wildest bulls in the corral and turned them loose to run on the plains. Horsemen galloped hard behind to reach out at just the proper moment, grab the tail of the bull, secure it under his right leg, and violently twist hundreds of pounds of fierce animal to the ground.

Another favorite sport was racing on horseback to a rooster tied

---

* Mexican methods of working cattle, types of saddles, and dress today are basic to the cowboy tradition of the Southwest.

to a tree or post, seizing the bird by its greased neck, breaking the thongs which bound the legs, and riding off with it.

Mining was the occupation in which the Spanish Crown had the biggest stake. It was the fundamental reason for Nueva Vizcaya. Mexico at this period produced more than half the world total of silver, and the northlands were the biggest assets in this output.[62] The saving of souls and the raising of cattle and the garnering of more land were all secondary to the compelling drive to tap the underground wealth of the mountains and plains. Had there been no hope of possible ore deposits, it is doubtful if the incredible maze of canyons and peaks west of the undulating prairie would have been penetrated. But they were, early, and ore was hauled out by pack mules up and down perilous trails blazed through rough passes and over precipitous cliffs.

The first mines of Santa Bárbara and Parral had been at the edge of the sierra. By the 1690's, Urique, the site of primitive Indian diggings located in craggy country, became the first seat of Spanish authority in the southern sierra. Then came San Francisco del Oro, Cusihuiriáchi, Chínipas, and Santa Eulalia. Alamos, on the Pacific slope, was developed. San Pedro, on the Arizona border, was worked after 1680, under the constant threat of the Apaches coming down from the New Mexico mountains. San Pedro ore was packed twenty miles to a Corralitos smelter whose furnace burned mesquite roots grubbed from the desert.

Batopilas, the deepest mountain infiltration yet, began to boom by 1740. By the eighties, seven thousand people had made their way into this remote camp, where the streets once were paved with silver bars to welcome a bishop, and where a common miner had been made a grand duke for his fabulous gifts to the King. In the *municipios* (municipalities) of Madera, Ocampo, Mina, Morelos, and Chínipas, scattered veins of silver and gold were claimed and worked, mostly by Indians and Spaniards engaged either in prospecting or in packing. In the early portion of the 1800's, a new center of mining activity was established at a town named for the unlikely combination of a saint and a governor—Guadalupe y Calvo. European-style palaces climbed rugged hillsides, and opera performed by traveling road companies made life gay. It was in the mad tradition of wild prosperity luckily gained and easily lost.

The government-controlled assay offices determined the prices paid, and collected the taxes on metals exported to Spain—two per cent on precious metals other than gold and silver upon which the duty was five per cent. The first assay office was in Parral. Another was opened in the city of Chihuahua after Santa Eulalia began its output. In the 1780's Alamos, Sonora, was given another assay office to serve the portions of southern Nueva Vizcaya nearer to the Pacific slope than the central corridor.

Mines gave fantastic wealth to some. To others they meant an unglamorous life of hard, dirty, physical labor, frequent frustrations and defeat, often danger, and victimization by mine owners who preferred to pay in inferior merchandise rather than in hard reales. Rarely, rewards were great, and that was enough for the gambler with the pick. A prayer and a candle lighted to the patron saint of miners, San José, on his day of March 19, on the parroquia altar, surely would bring luck. Men and beasts worked together to take the riches from the ground. Mules turned crude windlasses to draw ore up in basket loads from shafts many of which were a thousand feet deep. Other ores were carried up ladders of logs lashed with rawhide thongs, tier upon tier, to be dumped outside. In some regions, for example the Sierra Grande, those eastern desert mountains near Cuchillo Parado, torches lit the way into mammoth caverns (some said they were large enough to hold the cathedral), and the floors were worked for lead and silver.

Crushing mills operated by mules were of the types used in early mines of the southwestern United States.[63] Typically, the mill consisted of a circular pit in the ground, some thirty feet in diameter, lined with smooth, flat stone. In the center was an upright post through which a shaft of wood was suspended at right angles. At the ends of this crosspiece were large, flat grinding stones which were dragged around the pit by mules. The ores, first partially crushed, were thrown into the pit, watered, and ground into a mortar. The "amalgamation process" was one in which quicksilver, muriates, sulphates, and various chemicals were added to the mortar. Then the entire mass was dumped into stone tubs through which a continuous stream of water flowed, carrying off the lighter matter. The amalgamated metals sank to the bottom, the quicksilver was pressed out, the mercury was burned away, and the silver was ready to be molded into barras, or ingots. Each ingot weighed approximately fifty pounds, and during the colonial period, was valued at from 1,000 to 2,000 pesos. Ingots were weighed at the assay office, stamped with the weight, and were easily identifiable in case of theft. Rich men in Chihuahua were said to have had ingots stacked like cordwood in their cellars. Miners, hard pressed for ready funds, on occasion sold their ingots for cash at a lower price than the ingots would have brought in the city.

Another form in which the silver was carried was as coins, or specie, poured into sacks of raw beefhide. When the sacks dried, the skin contracted compressing the coins. A pair of sacks was worth the value of an ingot and represented one mule load. American traders in Mexico in the middle of the nineteenth century widely used this method of transporting money.

Twice a year, on June 30 and December 31, an armed caravan of hundreds of mules, each carrying two ingots, slowly moved south down the long road to the Casa de Moneda in faraway Mexico City. The big shipment filled the coffers of empire. Between 1738 and 1752, the northlands, even though torn by Indian warfare and internal corrosive corruption, managed to ship to the capital almost 16,000,000 ounces of silver molded into bars.

Muleteering was a proud profession and one of which resourceful frontiersmen seemed to have a natural flare. Back-packing had been a centuries-old cultural pattern in Mexico which, through generations, conditioned well-muscled legs to travel without exhaustion long distances over changing terrain. The *arriero,* or muleteer, walking or trotting behind the caravan of beasts, with a fistful of rocks or a stick to enforce his wishes and a loud "Anda!", knew he held a responsible position. He was the contact with the outside world.

They were a lusty lot, those arrieros, generally unkempt from their journeys over dusty trails, armed to the teeth for protection, living off the land and their skill at hunting and pilfering. Nineteenth-century arrieros were harbingers of a twentieth-century group of devil-may-care bus and truck drivers who have taken the wheel to practically every arroyo and rincon in Mexico. An earned reputation for rowdiness, as well as for the ability to cope with difficult situations, followed them like a shadow.

Custom and experience dictated ways in which pack mules had to be made ready for the trip. First, blinders were put over the mule's eyes. Then a saddlecloth covering a raw sheepskin was thrown over his back. A pad of stuffed leather was added next and was cinched under the belly with a broad fiber band. The cargo was placed either on top of the beast's back or divided and hung on each side, lashed securely and covered with matting. Speed in packing was an art and sometimes a necessity. Three minutes per mule was a fair average. The caravans embraced as many as two hundred mules, each carrying two to four hundred pounds, and could travel approximately fifteen miles a day.

Goods which did not lend themselves to being transported on the pack mules were moved in *carretas,* solid-wheeled, cratelike wagons drawn by a team of mules. Furniture, dishes, portraits, silver pieces, church vestments, jewels, silks and metallic cloth, foodstuffs, firearms, and a great variety of luxuries from Europe and Asia were taken north to the frontiers in this manner. One route led up the central mesa to Chihuahua. Another from Guaymas, Sonora, crossed the mountain barrier in the north and cut down southeastward to the city.

Once a year the caravans traveled up to Santa Fe on the Camino Real, two ruts worn deep over malpais and adobe, around sand dunes, through arroyos, up mesas, connecting the sleeping civilization of New Mexico to the vigor of the capital, a distance of eighteen hundred miles and as far removed in advancement. Although semimonthly mail service from Durango north was established by the middle of the eighteenth century, the first- and second-hand news brought in by the trade caravans was eagerly awaited. The arrival of the traders was newspaper, telegraph, radio, and barroom gossip all in one.

On the return trip to Chihuahua, wagons and mules carried booty of New Mexico in the form of hides and beaver pelts, Chimayo and Navajo blankets and rugs, piñon nuts, and turquoise. Sheep were driven south for sale in Chihuahua. At El Paso del Norte, more arrieros joined the party with strings of mules packed with fresh and dried fruits grown along the warm bottomlands of the Río Grande. Grape products, particularly raisins, *aguardiente,* and wine, were highly prized in the southern markets. They timed their arrival in Chihuahua to coincide with the annual fair held about mid-December in the southerly valley of San Bartolomé and the later one in the city in January.

Chihuahua's fair meant a chance to see and to buy, tax free, a wide array of merchandise from both north and south, as well as local products. It brought together hundreds of traders and customers. Booths were set up around the Plaza de Armas and the smaller plaza by the old Jesuit college. Here were displayed such diversified items as bolts of cotton and woolen materials, ribbon streamers, feather dusters, whimsical painted clay and wooden toys, and *metates* on which to grind cornmeal. Old crones huddled over small piles of medicinal plants brought in from the sierra—*yerba del oso* to break a fever, *tecomaca* for sciatica, *tianguis* for fever, or *yerba de San Nicolás* for snakebite. Hawkers loudly advertised their wares. Crowds pushed along the walks and spilled over into the streets where fancy carriages were hitched. Down the side streets of Las Golondrinas or Los Dormidos or Calle de la Ascensión was where one could buy a horse to ride or a chicken to be simmered in a *cazuela* (earthen pan or crock). Everywhere was the odor of cooking food as women fanned charcoal fires to prepare the chocolate and chile *moles* of fiesta to pour over tender pieces of turkey, or meatpies of goat meat ground with spices, enclosed in pastry, and fried in deep fat. Other stands offered tortillas folded over mashed beans and cheese topped with hot sauce. There were custards, sweet dainties, and candies made of guava or peach, gruel of flavored milk and rice cooked together for a long time, or spiced chocolate made frothy by a whirling hand mill.

Bullfights were held in a temporary arena to the west of town, near the sandy banks of the Chuvíscar. The darkness of the evenings was lighted by dazzling fireworks displays of paper castles, saints, flowers, and birds. There were monte games, and leisurely walks around the fountain in the plaza and up the drive toward the Santa Rita church. Rancheros proudly seated in silver-inlaid saddles astride the finest horseflesh exchanged views on the condition of the country. Dances in the parlors of fine homes were attended by men garbed in tight-fitting embroidered suits and women in snug-bodiced, voluminous-skirted gowns of rustly silk. Other dances were held in the streets where *huaraches* and bare feet kept time to polkas and *varsovianas*. Strolling musicians, with plaintive melodies brought from sad Spain, sang, for a coin, on the street corners. Even Tarahumara servants in their quarters joined in the music making with crude violins carved with penknives from models given them by the Jesuit missionaries.

Fair meant fiesta. It was a happy time for everyone. Who thought then of Indian wars, or who cared about intangibles of liberty and equality? What if black paper streamers had recently hung from a thousand doors because of epidemic deaths from measles and small-pox? Who remembered that the arrieros had brought news of insurrection at Dolores and Guanajuato? No one.

THREE

INDEPENDENCIA

1810 – 1910

WINDS OF UNREST had ruffled the calm waters of sequestered Nueva Vizcaya as early as 1806. Newspapers brought north by trade caravans had told of disasters Spain had suffered at the hands of England and France. In 1808 more news arrived that Napoleon had further worsened the Spanish situation by deposing King Fernando VII and putting his own brother on the Spanish throne. In the heart of Mexico, the criollos seized upon the distressing state of affairs in the motherland to begin violent agitation for freedom. The reaction in the north was loyalty to the Crown.[1] It was a loyalty of principle—a provincial conservatism. Just as they had been born into Roman Catholicism, so had they been born into a society ruled by a monarchy in Spain. It never occurred to the Chihuahuenses to question either.

Despite an apathetic detachment from the calamities crushing the Spanish bureaucracy, people in the north could not remain completely indifferent to the seriousness of the situation. They responded, as they always had, with money, not barras of silver this time, but pesos. Captain del Valle called a public meeting in the *casa consistorial* (town hall) to launch a subscription drive for funds for their brothers in Spain, to aid in restoring the beautiful cities, which, by this late date most New World sons of Chihuahua had never seen, and to push the Bonapartists back across the Pyrenees. Captain del Valle read a royal order from Seville recounting details of the French invasion and of Spanish glories and final defeat. He himself opened the fund with ten pesos. Persons prominent and not-so-prominent pushed forward to give their pesos and to have their names placed upon the role of donors. Names frequently met in a history of Chihuahua at this period were on the list—Trespalacios, Ponce de León, Irigoyen, Salcedo, Terrazas, Zuloaga—ironically Royalists then, but what of tomorrow?

Other subscriptions followed. One was initiated by the social leader of the town, Doña Margarita de Irigoyen y Valois, to aid the war widows and orphans. Threat of invasion from across the sea accomplished something that actual invasion by primitive hordes never had done. A large fund, voluntarily subscribed, provided armament for defense. It was two months before Hidalgo's grito, the initial cry for freedom. In the north, sentiment was for the Spanish Crown in its fight against Napoleonic France, not for autocracy of her colonies.

Brigadier Nemesio Salcedo y Salcedo had taken over the *comandancia* in 1802.[2] Shortly after being duly installed in office, he endeared himself to the society matrons of the quiet provincial capital by staging an elaborate wedding for himself and his bride from Spain. The bride's trousseau was discussed and analyzed in every fashionable drawing room in town, and adaptations of her gowns were made quickly by deft seamstresses. Her perfume, her hair style, her manner of speech already differing from theirs, eagerly were copied. Her coming broke the monotony of dull routine far from social centers. The cathedral, now nearing completion with the addition of a clock in one tower[3] and decorative embellishments in the vast interior, was aglow with hundreds of perfumed, white wax tapers turned out of molds in local candlemaking shops and was fragrant with roses, lilies, geraniums, and flowers in profusion gathered from patio gardens. Rich miners, landowners, businessmen, military and government officials arrived from all parts of the state to see and be seen. In that tranquility, small events such as this wedding loomed large.

Salcedo had faced a trying period of administration with firmness. No suggestion of proindependence feelings had been permitted. Inflammatory propaganda had been suppressed so completely that the men in the streets were unaware of the turbulent state of affairs farther south. Chihuahuenses remained passive and undisturbed.

Adhesion to the monarchy had meant arming to drive out foreign invaders, but even a cursory examination of available trained manpower and munitions would have shown a tremendous lack of both. A new generation had come of age since the end of the long period of Indian wars, and these young men did not know the tricks of water-hole warfare of the desert. An arms factory had been established on the northern approach to the city to produce firearms and gunpowder. The call for volunteer troops had gone out to the mountains and the plains, and *compañías patrióticas* were organized rapidly at Cusihuiriáchi, Parral, San Francisco de Conchos, Aldama, Carrizal, and other towns to drill with sticks for guns and bravado for a crutch in the dust of the plazas.[4] These *"fernandinos,"* or followers of Fernando VII, had prepared themselves for European-type battles of army against army and furious charges upon redoubts. This would not be the guerilla skirmishes their fathers had withstood from the Apaches. They itched for a chance to prove themselves in battle, to hold their homeland for Spain just as their ancestors had fought to obtain it. Yet the disappointing years passed with no invasion by the *bonapartistas* and no concrete indication that such a catastrophe ever would occur. Because of their distance from Mexico City, it had become unlikely that any force would move in upon them. Feet stopped marching. Lancers quit practicing. The dust settled back on the plaza walks across Chihuahua as the small flurry of excitement ended.

THEN CAME the shrill cries of "Long live our Señora of Guadalupe! Death to bad government! Death to the gachupines!"

With those words Mexico's battle for independence from Spain was begun. The place where it all started was an insignificant country village, Dolores, over the mountains from the mining center of Guanajuato, one hundred miles north of Mexico City. The man who gave the call to arms was a humble parish priest, an unknown. The time was two o'clock in the morning, September 16, 1810. The place was a village church. In the shadow of the altar, a revolution based on racial hatred was initiated by a member of the clergy under the banner of the dark virgin who first appeared before an Indian. The revolt was doomed to failure in its first attempt.

A rabble of criollos, Indians, and mestizos had joined ranks behind Father Miguel Hidalgo y Costilla and his commanding officer, Ignacio Allende, to pour victoriously over Guanajuato, Querétaro, Guadalajara, and the central highlands, killing all gachupines, and looting the countryside. Then with the first reverses came desertions. Peons, with a gun on one shoulder and a few tortillas tied up in a handkerchief, stole off to their homes. After a period of indecision and squabbling among the leaders of the revolt, it had been resolved to go north to secure aid from the young nation which not too long before had fought her own battle for freedom. Heaven, and not haven, awaited in the north.[5]

Some said Ignacio Elizondo had been a traitor because he was angry at not getting a promotion in the independence army. Others said he had revealed the whereabouts of Hidalgo and his men through a misunderstanding of orders.[6] But because of him the rebels were captured at Acatita de Bajan, Coahuila, and the revolt was doomed to die before a firing squad. Subordinates were summarily shot at Monclova. The higher officers, including Hidalgo, with legs chained, were marched in a unison they had been unable to achieve in freedom across the bitter, waterless Bolsón de Mapimí to the seat of the comandante general in Chihuahua. They were in the care of Lieutenant Colonel Manuel Salcedo, nephew of the governor of Nueva Vizcaya and himself later governor of Texas. Six priests were taken to Durango where they met degradation and death a year later.

At Chihuahua a proclamation issued by Salcedo had been posted on walls of buildings along the main streets of the city. In it Salcedo said he would allow the people of the city to witness the coming of the prisoners, but he took precautions to forestall trouble. No crowds were to be formed. No one was to go to the roof tops for a less obstructed view. The grito, as given by Hidalgo, was not to be raised. No foreigners were to be admitted to private homes. Actions contrary to the public interest—that of royal partisans—would be dealt with severely.

The procession of mounted soldiers and pedestrian captives came around the hill from Tabalaopa and down the rutted road into the streets of the town. There was only the clomping of the horses' hoofs and a distant bray of a burro to break the enforced silence. Solemn men, women, and children, with impassiveness bred through two centuries of looking death squarely in the eye, curiously craned their necks to see this monster whom the comandante general had said wanted to destroy them all. As he passed, they saw a fifty-eight-year-old man with head held high, with clear eyes full of a serenity born of inner peace, though he marched to his death. The crowd standing by the road could only feel that here was a man who believed in a cause enough to die for it, who had tried his utmost and knew he could do no more.

The prisoners were kept in the military hospital, formerly the building of the Jesuit college, while awaiting their trial by a high tribunal appointed by the comandante general. Twenty-three rebels were sentenced to be shot by a firing squad. Seven others were to do hard labor at the presidio of Janos and the textile factory on the Encinillas hacienda. One, Mariano Abasolo, owed his life to publicly denouncing the cause and to the passionate pleas of his beautiful young wife. He received a life sentence to a prison in Cádiz, Spain.

An ecclesiastical tribunal ordered by Bishop Olivares also sat in judgment of the priest Hidalgo. His liberal views had been questioned by the Inquisition in the period before the Grito de Dolores. He was suspect. Now, he was to suffer the pain of degradation for engaging in forbidden political activities.[7]

Public opinion began to favor the condemned leader. A priest at Parral backed an abortive attempt by Salvador Porras and another clergyman, Pateo Sánchez Alvarez, to help Hidalgo escape. Both these men had sat on the tribunals sentencing the rebels. Others involved in judgment were to join the movement for independence in later years and to hold important offices in the new government.

On May 6, 1811, the shooting of the condemned began. By July 30 only Miguel Hidalgo y Costilla remained to be executed. At daylight he was led from his dark tower cell, on the walls of which he had written a verse of thanks to his kind jailer (a gachupín!), down to the courtyard. Gathered there were the prominent government and religious leaders of Nueva Vizcaya. The bishop, who personally had sent a plea to the King to spare Hidalgo's life, tearfully stripped him of his sacerdotal garb and gave him the Holy Sacrament. A paper containing a retraction of his political conduct and reaffirming the authority of the Spanish monarchy was signed and was circulated among the witnesses as a vindication of the execution about to take place.* The priest was placed blindfolded before a squad of twelve of His Majesty's soldiers. In the nearly forgotten outlands, the empire was about to be protected. Captain Pedro Armendáriz raised his arm to signal for attention, then

---

* This retraction of his revolutionary policy has led to criticism of Hidalgo among Mexicans. Priestley, 1938, 221-22.

gave the order to fire. The Liberator of Mexico fell dead. The seeds of revolt scattered like a dry dandelion on the wind.

The heads of Hidalgo, Allende, Aldama, and Jiménez were cut from the cadavers by an Indian, were packed in preservative salt, and were sent south to the royal Brigadier Don Félix María Callejo, at Guanajuato. The Spaniards of the north had spoken in a manner that the Spaniards of the south would understand.

The heads of the four insurgents were hung on spikes at each of the four corners of the *alhóndiga* (granary) where, in the first engagement of the war, hordes had massacred all the Spaniards who had sought refuge there. A sign was posted which read, "The heads of Miguel Hidalgo, Ignacio Allende, Juan Aldama, and Mariano Jiménez, notorious deceivers and first heads of the Revolution, that sacked and robbed the property of God and the Crown, let run with major atrocity the innocent blood of loyal *sacerdotes* and just magistrates, and were the cause of all the disasters, disgraces, and calamities that were afflicted upon and experienced by the inhabitants of all parts of the Spanish nation. Nailed here by the order of Sr. Brigadier D. Félix María Callejo, Illustrious Vindicator of Aculco, Guanajuato, and Calderón, and restorer of peace in America."

In Chihuahua, the bodies of Allende, Aldama, and Jiménez were exhibited in the plaza and then were buried in the old San Felipe cemetery where now is located the park of Abraham González at the corners of Avenida Independencia and Paseo Bolívar. Father Hidalgo came to rest in the chapel of San Antonio off the Franciscan temple of San Francisco de Asís. It would be twelve years before heads and bodies would be united in burial.

A nervous home government recalled Governor Salcedo with instructions to bring with him all the transcripts of the trials of the insurgents over which he had presided. Enroute to his embarkation at Vera Cruz, his caravan was robbed, and all the documents were stolen. No written proof of Hidalgo's guilt reached the King.

The light of freedom was snuffed out. New Spain was saved for the Crown. Or was it?

IN 1812 IN CÁDIZ, Spain, a constitutional monarchy was proclaimed conceding the rights of citizenship to all inhabitants of Spain and her colonies, regardless of race. Upon arrival of this news in Chihuahua, a three-day fiesta was held. Two years later the Cádiz constitution was dissolved. Again there was another fiesta in the north by those favoring the absolute monarchy. At the same time a seditious plot against the government was uncovered in the city. The ringleader seemed to have been José Felix Trespalacios, a member of the tribunal which had condemned Hidalgo. He was first sentenced to death but later was sent to Spain for a ten-year prison term and perpetual exile from Nueva España.[8]

Official uneasiness increased in Nueva Vizcaya after the Trespalacios incident. A public security guard, headed by Pedro Ignacio Irigoyen, was charged with detecting and punishing plots against Spanish authority. Forty cases were considered, and if punishment was deemed necessary, the lash cracked across backs bared in the Plaza de Armas, and prison sentences were ordered.

After the term of an annoying comandante general, Bonavia, who insisted in establishing residence in Durango rather than Chihuahua, Alejo García Conde, quartermaster of the province of Sonora and later of Nueva Vizcaya, became the leader. He fathered three sons who were to serve the new Mexican government with distinction.

The ever weakening Crown desperately sought financial support from the colonies. Two more contributions were ordered. Nueva Vizcaya was given a staggering quota of 100,000 pesos to be raised by any method feasible. García Conde proposed a patriotic lottery wherein persons either could purchase a whole ticket or fractions of tickets. Since there was no printing press in the province, each ticket tediously had to be handwritten and sealed with rubrics. In this manner, 12,000 pesos were obtained.

IN THE BEAUTIFUL HIGHLANDS of Michoacán where the rows of corn grow green and tall, the seedlings of revolt ripened to burst upon the countryside under the sword of another fighting priest. José María Morelos y Pavón, like his idol Hidalgo, met death before a firing squad. But shooting a leader in Chihuahua or in Michoacán could not hush the ever increasing agitation for freedom from Spain. The child now grown stronger and more virile than the parent demanded the right of self-determination. Unfortunately, an unprincipled weakling set a pattern of government by *coup*

d'état and barracks revolt which was to plague Mexico for a
hundred years. Augustín de Iturbide was a royalist general who
transferred his allegiance upon sensing the swing toward independence. He joined a revolutionary leader, Vicente Guerrero, in
the south, captured a rich caravan bound for Mexico City from
Acapulco, and marched on the capital under a proclamation called
the *Plan de Iguala* after the town where it had been formulated.
On September 27, 1821, Mexico declared itself a free nation
under God and Iturbide. Three hundred years of Spanish rule
had left its indelible mark forever upon the peoples, the language,
the religion, and the cultural patterns of Mexico.

At this very time, when sentiment at the capital was overwhelmingly favorable to the independence movement, stout royalists
in the north collected 4,000 pesos and sent four hundred soldiers
from the presidial forces and the militia to aid the garrison in
Mexico City. At the southern borders of what was soon to be the
state of Chihuahua, the small army declared itself for the Plan de
Iguala and about-faced to march on Chihuahua. Being a practical
man and without troops, García Conde then joined the movement.
Nueva Vizcaya became a part of the new nation of Mexico.[9]

Independence was accepted with characteristic reserve. A *Te
Deum* mass was celebrated in the cathedral, and a minor fiesta was
enjoyed in the plaza. But there was no rejoicing in the streets, no
dramatic fireworks or eloquent speeches. Those came later.

The state of Chihuahua became a reality in 1823 with a population numbering 112,694. A cartographic project was authorized
the following year to ascertain obscure boundaries easily traced on
paper but which in actuality ran crazily over crags and down
barrancas in the sierra, cut across treeless plains, and uncertainly
stayed close to the Río Grande in the north. Because of its inhospitable and rugged 95,000 square miles, after two-and-a-half centuries parts of the state still remained unknown and uncharted.

In the new state government a legislative chamber of not less
than eleven members elected Simón Eliás González, who had sat
in judgment of Hidalgo sixteen years earlier, as the first governor.
He was in Sonora, however, and did not re-enter Chihuahua political life until 1829 when he became comandante general. Rafael
Bracho was named first governor of the state of Durango; he also
had condemned Padre Hidalgo. Trespalacios, once considered a

dangerous traitor, was allowed to return from Spain. By an ironic twist of fate many of those who were eyewitnesses to the death of a rebellion, later were to witness the birth of a nation. Amends had to be made.

September 16, the date of the Grito de Dolores, was established as a nationwide holiday.[10] At first, ceremonies were religious but gradually they took on a civic tone. Buildings around the plaza were draped with the new red, white, and green Mexican flag. Salvos were fired from cannons. Expressive poetry and eulogies dear to the hearts of Mexicans were read. Booms of band music counterbalanced booms of fireworks. A noisy parade marched to the Santa Rita temple where mass was held. At the hour of the first grito from the central balcony of the *casa de gobierno*, the first magistrate uttered again the words of fire.

Although the new national and state governments were in the hands of conservative criollos, recognition was taken of Mexico's unique Indian heritage. The flag itself carried the Aztec symbol of the fierce eagle perched upon a cactus. Its red band of color stood for blood, Spanish and Indian together. The Virgin of Guadalupe, who had appeared miraculously before an Indian convert shortly after the Conquest, became the patroness of the new nation. In Chihuahua, it seemed appropriate to raise a statue to the insurgent heroes in the form of a pyramid, an architectural form used by many pre-Hispanic, highland, Mexican peoples as a temple base. This pyramid for fifty years dominated the Plazuela Hidalgo between the Palacio de Gobierno and the Instituto Científico y Literario and then was replaced by a large figure of the padre himself.

IN THE SECOND YEAR of independence, Chihuahua was ordered to give up the bodies of the men considered to be the fathers of the new country.[11] Early that August morning, in 1823, a quiet crowd gathered in the atrium of the white convent of San Francisco. Present were the leading civil and military officials, each with a black band around one coat sleeve. Their ladies were dressed in stiff, black silk and enormous hats called *empanadas*, or "meat pies." Crowded about the enclosing fence were the ragged poor, some cooking over charcoal fires, some nursing babies, others merely squatting on heels waiting. About nine o'clock, the small bells in the tower began to toll in the slow, deliberate rhythm of funeral music. The officiating priests of San Francisco swung back the carved wooden doors of the chapel as the army bugler announced the start of the cortege. Solemn-faced priests, followed by bareheaded government dignitaries, walked from the church. The people outside stepped aside to let them pass. The alderman emerged from the darkened interior carrying a funerary urn covered with a deep-blue mantle. A police squad marched close behind to provide fitting escort. Up the cobblestone street they moved without sound or outward emotion, past the tower of the Jesuit college of Loreto where Padre Hidalgo had been confined, executed, and decapitated, across the plaza to the cathedral.

Another party of men went to the cemetery up the rise from the plaza and dug up the remains of Allende, Aldama, and Jiménez. The caskets, draped in black, were carried to the cathedral to rejoin the remains of the fallen leader. A solemn mass was conducted and witnessed by most of the citizenry. On August 21, Captain Mauricio Ugarte headed the military escort to Mexico for the heroes who conquered in death the capital they never had conquered in life.

South in Guanajuato, similar services were held for the skulls of the insurgents, those which had so long hung on the alhóndiga to be cleaned by buzzards and flies.

On September 16, the anniversary of the Grito de Dolores, the remains of bodies and heads, in urns richly adorned with crystals and overlays of gold and silver and with each name intricately inscribed, were paraded through downtown Mexico City. Streets were lined with throngs of curious spectators, under balconies hung with black banners, for this was a day of mourning. Homage was paid to those who had given their lives before a firing squad in the north. As the procession came into the zócalo, or public square, cannonading was deafening. A company of grenadiers and the Third, Fifth, and Seventh Infantry Regiments marched smartly past the officials on the balcony of the National Palace. The remains ultimately were deposited in the sanctuary of San José.

In 1925, after the terrible revolution overthrowing the Díaz dictatorship had ended, the heroes' urns were removed to the monument of Independence, built in the center of a traffic circle, a widening of the treelined Paseo de la Reforma. There they rest at the base of a shaft, on top of which stands a large golden angel, with a perpetual flame burning in a shrine and gigantic floral wreaths to honor them.

THROUGH LATER YEARS in Chihuahua, towns were renamed to keep alive the memory of the condemned men. Guajoquilla became Jiménez; San Bartolomé, Allende; San Gerónimo, Aldama; Santa Rosalia, Camargo; Santa Cruz Tlapalcones, Rosales; San Buenaventura, Galeana; San Pablo Tepehuanes, Balleza; and San José del Parral, Hidalgo del Parral. The Plaza de Armas became the Plaza de la Constitución. Plaques to Hidalgo were hung on the convent of San Francisco and later on the Palacio Federal. A society to preserve the objects used by the patriots of 1811 and to establish a cult centered around veneration of the Father of Mexico, called The Patriotic Society of Friends of Hidalgo, had a membership of many prominent persons in the capital including Captain Pedro Armendáriz who had commanded the firing squad and Padre José María Sánchez who had been involved in an unsuccessful plot to free Hidalgo from prison.[12]

Although racial hatred was late in reaching the frontier, it did, in time, ruffle the imperturbability of Chihuahuenses and seemed to grow in intensity in the formative years of the new state. The young legislature had voted down a measure to expel Spaniards. However, the people remained unsatisfied. Black rumors were widely circulated that the Spaniards were planning to recapture Mexico, that forces had landed in Cuba for final preparations. Anger and suspicions increased. It was during a civic fiesta in the town of Jesús María in 1829 that one overt act promulgated a chain reaction of violence against all Spaniards in the locality.[13]

Just who yelled "Death to the dirty gachupines!" no one knew. But like an uncontrollable contagion, other voices joined in to swell into a loud roar of bigotry based on fear. Someone threw a rock through a window of a Spanish-owned store. Other rocks began to shatter glass in homes and public buildings. Wooden sheds were tipped over or set on fire. Park benches were smashed. A full-scale riot lasted for several days.

After that outburst, thirty of the eighty Spanish residents of the state were expelled. This move proved to be an unfortunate one for the economic condition of the state because much of the wealth was in the hands of the Spaniards. When they were driven out, they took their money with them although their property was confiscated. Mining particularly suffered from removal of such financial support and acknowledged Spanish resourcefulness. Gradually, because of lack of capital and Mexican inability to strengthen mining interests, the mines passed to management of other foreigners, usually British, Canadians, or Americans.

To the credit of the people of the north, not all Spaniards were expelled. Some, because of their personal popularity, were allowed to remain. Melchor Guaspé was one of these. He had served as jailor of Hidalgo and had been honored by a verse written by Father Hidalgo with a piece of charcoal on his cell wall. After a number of years in the Spanish navy, Guaspé, a native of Majorca, had come to mid-continental, arid Chihuahua where the closest thing to sailing was a colloquial joke about navigating the wavy plains. He had found employment as bell ringer of the parroquia and caretaker of the public buildings and in such positions became acquainted with the officialdom which walked his halls. After the crisis over the Spaniards, he served as alderman of the ayuntamiento. One of the schools of the capital bore his name.[14]

Other Spaniards were excused from the expulsion decree through recognition of their services—military, scientific, or political—to their adopted land. On these grounds, Andrés Manuel del Río, a naturalist schoolmate of the famous Baron von Humboldt (who had visited Mexico himself early in the century) was permitted to remain. He had come to Mexico from Madrid as a young man and had served as a professor of chemistry in a seminary at Minas, publishing many scientific works on Mexico. In 1820, after manifesting his loyalty to Spain, he was appointed a deputy of Mexico by the Crown. In spite of his known royalist sympathies, Manuel del Río was an exception to the expulsion order.

REFORM, reorganize, refurbish—such was the keynote of the new era of self-government. Desire to improve standards of health, living, and education was genuine. Hopes were held for peaceful, orderly government and widespread prosperity. Legislation to those ends was profuse. Results, however, were negligible. Poverty and continual political discord hung like a shroud on the shoulders of the young state struggling to maintain the promising gains of the first quarter of the century and to improve the status of all citizens.

The capital city, now having a population of ten thousand, embarked on sanitation reform.[15] Thirty outlying smelter furnaces which burned charcoal poured smoke over the top of the basin in which the city lay and coated buildings with black soot. Owners of homes were required to repaint sooty structures and to repair or rebuild homes or sheds which had fallen into ruin. Heads of families were responsible for keeping streets clean in front of their houses, were ordered to sweep the sidewalks every Saturday and to carry the trash to lands set aside outside the city. Laws were passed controlling the disposal of household refuse and the offal from soap factories and slaughterhouses. Street lights consisting of lard candlesticks set on posts were installed,* and residents along those streets were asked to keep them in serviceable condition. Stray dogs were killed. Unhitched burros were not permitted to wander through the town.

Mexico's government functioned, as had Spain's, on enormous duties of fifteen to fifty per cent imposed on all trade and many monopolies. The duty on smelting metals was only two per cent, but the quantity of work done in Chihuahua made this tax important. All monies taken from one state to another were taxed two per cent; if taken out of the country, three-and-a-quarter per cent. A sales tax of two and three per cent existed. All farm products were subject to duty, as was all imported and exported merchandise.

Considerable revenue was derived from the manufacture of cigars. Since no tobacco was allowed to be grown in Chihuahua, it had to be imported. The Mexicans, then as now, were addicted smokers. Men and women enjoyed the vice and were willing to pay duties in order to get tobacco in any form. An American visiting Chihuahua in 1826 reported the arrival of two caravans loaded with cigars valued at 120,000 pesos which represented one year's supply! To avoid paying the tariff, substitutes for tobacco were used. Every man carried one pouch of *punche*, a plant resembling

---

* Pattie, 1905, 151-56. "It is the largest and handsomest town I had ever seen, though the buildings are not so neat and well arranged as in our country. The roofs are flat, the walls well painted, and the streets kept very clean." 153.

tobacco, and another pouch of corn husks.[16] He then had the makings of roll-your-own's which he lighted with flint and steel.

The Church also operated on large tithes, costly fees for baptisms, weddings, and funerals, and special contributions requested for the more than a hundred feast days. Many found themselves unable to pay for priests' services at funerals conducted for the eight hundred who died of cholera in 1833. The cost of living, and dying, was high.

In most quarters, money was scarce; in some, nonexistent. Other than work connected with mining and smelting operations, there was no industry in the capital. Groups of the poorer inhabitants of the town lived by hammering and reworking the scoria of the furnaces to collect bits of silver to sell. Many artisans and craftsmen carried on small-scale projects in their patios, making shoes, furniture, or saddles. Others found employment as arrieros with trade trains or as soldiers in the presidios. A few operated inns for travelers or stables for the animals used on the trail. Some upper-class men with a smattering of education served as scribes and clerks in federal offices or the branch mint. Money was in the hands of the merchants, mineowners, landholders, and those who occupied lucrative government posts.

Legislation to establish a primary school system was passed, but because of lack of money and trained teachers, few schools actually were opened. The secondary-level Instituto Científico y Literario was founded in 1827 under the leadership of Father Antonio Cipriano de Irigoyen, a native of Santa Fe.[17] For over a century its graduates have been Chihuahua's leading men. A beginning budget of six hundred pesos allowed instruction only in two subjects, Spanish grammar and Latin. Later a variety of courses in metaphysics, the humanities, ancient history, cosmography, philosophy, French, Italian, mathematics, and jurisprudence were added to the curriculum.

The first printing press began operation under government subsidies and strict supervision which permitted no printing without official sanction.[18] Government documents and legal papers were the main output of the press. In 1827 the head of the printing office was fined twenty-five pesos and relieved of his job for printing a harmless but unauthorized booklet, "Escuela Festiva." The first newspapers were circulated in 1829 with flowery names like *La*

Antoracha Federal (The Federal Torch), *El Patriotismo Manifesto* (The Patriotic Manifest), and *El Hombre Libre* (The Free Man). Men may have been free of Spain, but they were not free to write as they pleased. Governor Arce suppressed these papers because of their federalist tendencies. Copies of *Fanal* (Lighthouse) published in the capital in 1835 are the oldest newspapers of which examples still remain.

Laws regulating public conduct were numerous and severe.[19] Shops and stalls were closed promptly on the ringing of the cathedral bell. Circles of light revealed maids and houseboys scurrying across the plaza, lanterns in hand, to close and bolt enormous doors of their masters' homes. All persons on the streets not known to the authorities were under suspicion and were jailed overnight. Quiet after curfew time was maintained—no noise, no serenades for love-making or fun. Nighttime diversions such as dances could be held only by authority of the chief of the municipio. Sale of liquor was prohibited. No day laborers, artisans, domestic servants, or minor boys were allowed at ball games or pool halls on working days. No horse races were tolerated on the city streets. Although anyone carrying firearms without a permit was subject to fines, travelers reported frequent murders in the city, with the victims' bodies being carried through the streets to induce someone to pay for burial. Profligate women were said to have been the reason for many brawls.[20]

General lawlessness was so widespread that the cells of the ancient, towered public jail on Calle Libertad constantly were crowded. Police justice was despotic as administered by the Forces of Public Security. Lawyers were few and worked for a fixed fee of two thousand pesos a year. Appeal of a verdict was unheard of. This lawlessness, unrest, and injustice was symptomatic, for revolution still smouldered.

The central government changed hands so repeatedly that few citizens had faith left that Mexico could make itself into a strong respected nation. Continual strife among leaders and those desiring to become leaders led to indifference and defeatism. Maladministration through open dishonesty and through lack of preparation for governing was accepted with characteristic shrugs of the shoulders and openhanded gestures. "Es la vida, señor," they would say to each other. "Qué lástima!" That is life; what a pity. Many

remembered with nostalgia the halcyon days of life under the
Spanish monarchy. Heated debates in the capital for and against
centralized government or for more independence of the states
were not echoed in the north. Chihuahua then as always was too
far away to be vitally concerned.

Iturbide, who had set himself up as Emperor in Mexico City,
was ousted. He was replaced in time by the wily Santa Ana who
through the *cuartelada,* or military coup d'état, put himself and
his henchmen in power for forty years. During one of his poisonous
attempts to create a conflict sufficient to unseat the legal president,
Anastasio Bustamente, Chihuahua became aroused enough to
declare war on its southern neighbor. Durango had sided with
Santa Ana; Chihuahua had not. The area between the Río Florido
in Chihuahua and Cerro Gordo, the colonial presidio now within
the state of Durango, was disputed. After a farcical show of pitifully
weak force by each side, the treaty of San Pedro de la Noria was
signed. Chihuahua's army, under command of Governor Arce,
marched northward up the corridor to the capital. In this year
of 1832 these soldiers would ride again in pursuit of warring red
men.

FOR FORTY YEARS Apaches had lived around the squalid lonely
presidios in bribed peace. It was not the permanent calm of un-
conditional surrender but rather one of advantage to the Indian.
He had a keen awareness of his ability to rise up and strike again
when the times demanded. He saw the weakness of Mexican fortifications and the lack of aggressive spirit among the troops. He
sensed the ineffective leadership and deficit of funds which was
leading to daily desertions and increasing grumblings. He studied
the poor caliber of fighters stationed to guard the bleak frontier,
inexperienced in the strike-and-scatter brand of warfare in which
he himself was fearfully expert. Bored by idleness, he and his
brothers saw their opportunity and seized upon it. Chihuahua
once more was faced with the terror of Indian screeches in the
night and the sight of families slain, cattle driven off, homes
destroyed, and chapels desecrated.

Apaches first engulfed the area of Carrizal and El Carmen in the
north-central bolsons. Where once there were a hundred thousand
cattle grazing, in a few years there was only a tenth that number

left. Haciendas were deserted; buildings were surrendered to the furies of the Apaches and the elements; wells were filled in with drifting debris. Mines were only gaping holes along the border mountains, machinery rusting in the blazing sun, the owners and their work beasts either driven away or killed. The bloody pageant of the late 1700's was being repeated. Retrenchment and retreat were necessary.

Seeing the impunity of the Apaches, another plains group, heretofore peaceful, came to Mexico to raid for horses and slaves. Every September, the month they called that of the Mexico moon, the Comanche rode out of Oklahoma, Texas, and Colorado to ford the Río Grande and move down into the mountains surrounding the Bolsón de Mapimí. Each year they came in greater strength to go ever farther southward, until by 1835 they were a band six to seven hundred strong and traveled as far as the interior of Zacatecas.

The Comanches were a nomadic hunting group belonging to the huge Shoshonean linguistic stock of North America. They had been small in number and relatively unimportant prior to the advent of the horse, but with the adoption of that animal, they evolved rapidly into an aggressive, warlike people generally acknowledged to be the most skilled horsemen of all American Indians. They took on a fierce, untamed beauty as they sat atop their unsaddled steeds ready to spring from one side to the other at a full gallop or to hang under a horse's belly to draw an arrow from a beaded quiver.[21]

In 1835, Comandante General José J. Calvo declared war on the barbarians.[22] His predecessor, José María Arce, had been murdered during an inspection trip along the northern line between Rosales and Chihuahua. Calvo was caught between a disinterested, distracted federal government unable to subsidize increase in troops and weapons and worried landowners whose properties and lives were in constant jeopardy. Angry demands for protection and aid were placed before frustrated officials. The residents of El Carmen, in the heart of the zone of Apache invasions, stated their intentions, their *plan,* for a mutual assistance pact wherein everyone, not only soldiers and militiamen, would be armed to fight off the invaders. Calvo was able to get a treaty of doubtful value signed in El Paso between Mexican army officers and Comanche chiefs Isacaraco and Dueño de los Dos Palominos and subchiefs Coyote Gritón, Tecolote Cabezón, Zorra Alta, and Aguila del Aire. Comanche raids ceased for a time.

Officials in Chihuahua, paralyzed by fear, tried to buy off the Apaches with rations and by granting them the right to sell animals taken through plunder. Reaction from the neighboring state of Sonora, within the sphere of Apache sorties from Arizona, was immediate and inflamed. This plan could only be an irresistible incentive for wholesale raiding activity. Horses and cattle would be driven from Sonoran ranches to be sold in Chihuahua. It was buying time for one Mexican state at the expense of another. There could be no peace on those terms. Sonorans resolved to strike first.

The presidio of Janos sat upon the wide northern plains to guard entrance to the passes through the sierra that separated the Pacific coast from the central plateau. A colony of Apaches had been persuaded to work in settlements in the vicinity and to content themselves with occasional government rations. It was to Janos that armed invaders from Sonora rode. At the order of the comandante general of Sonora, soldiers charged into the town under the cover of a starless night, mercilessly killed fifteen Indian men, women, and children as they slept, and carried others away as hostages. The party departed as rapidly as it had come but paused long enough to send word back to stunned commanders at the fort in Janos that this attack had been a reprisal for other Apaches killing two dozen Sonoran soldiers and for raiding the corrals at the village of Fronteras.

Protests were made at once to the governor of Sonora. If peaceful Indians were to be ruthlessly struck down, how could there be any confidence in Mexican bids for peace? Treaties would have less value than ever before.

A struggle without evident solution dissolved into a policy of desperation. Hopes were pinned to a foreign mercenary as much feared by the Mexicans as by the Apaches. James Kirker, called Santiago Querque by the Mexicans, an Irishman trapping in the wild and broken country around northwestern Corralitos, was to be paid for Indian scalps.[23] He employed a band of Delaware Indians from the eastern woodlands of the United States to help carry out his one-man war. Without scruples or country, Kirker was a product of the dangerous life of a foreboding frontier, keeping alive by skill and wits. He was a daring horseman, an unexcelled shot, and having lived among the Apache for a time, knew all the trails and water holes across northern Mexico used by them. He could match treachery with treachery, torture with greater torture. He spoke their language and understood their mode of existence. With this knowledge and his confident command of his environment, Kirker was the most formidable enemy the Apache yet had encountered. So successful was he in Indian hunting that the poverty-stricken Mexican government was unable to make payment for the scalps. They would have cause to regret this breach of contract when war developed between the Americans and the Mexicans and Kirker allied himself with the *gringos*.

WE HAVE NOT HEARD the last of the Apaches, but what of United States relations in the early part of the century? Forerunners of American tourists were then making their debut in northern Mexico. Some had come as travelers and sightseers, genuinely interested in the customs and country so different from their own. Others were traders looking for new markets for the goods of the young United States. A nervous Spanish government regarded all with suspicion and jealously guarded her lengthy borders. For the last twenty years of Spanish colonialism, scattered numbers of Americans found themselves embroiled with Spanish officials because of illegal entry into the country, were frequently jailed for long periods, and sometimes executed.

About 1800, Philip Nolan, an American freebooter, sent a shiver of fear through the northlands.[24] Anxious rumors swept the capital in Chihuahua that he was heading an expeditionary force ordered to invade Nueva España. In this thinly populated desert country where four hundred souls represented a thriving community, that many soldiers stayed nearly half a year on the mesquite- and yucca-covered banks of the Río Grande waiting for an invasion which never materialized. Nolan, with a group of some thirty men, to outward intents on a horse-buying trip, was met in east Texas by Spanish authorities and was killed in the encounter. A half-dozen survivors were marched in chains south to San Luis Potosí, then to Saltillo, and finally were confined behind the huge wooden doors of the public jail in the city of Chihuahua. Their crime had been trespassing on Spanish soil without permission.

The capture and imprisonment of the Americans had been ordered by a monarchy distant and detached. The people of Chihuahua, however, were touched with compassionate curiosity about their northern neighbors. Similarity of environment and frontier problems offered a common meeting ground. With characteristic candid frankness, they liked the proud spirit of the Americans held in their jails. They chose to treat them more as friends than as enemies and allowed them to move freely about the city on their word that no attempt at fleeing the country would be made. Robert Ashley and Jack House were two who made good an escape. Another, Stephen Richards, was forced into service in the Spanish army.

One of Nolan's gang, captured and marched to Chihuahua, was Peter Elias Bean, a young boy of seventeen who had run away from his Tennessee home to go west to hunt buffalo along the Río Grande. In Mexico, his gentle, soft-spoken manner quickly won him sympathy from his captors and friendship from some of the town's leading inhabitants. Pedro de Valois was a rich merchant who saw in Peter Bean an unusual opportunity. Spanish Pedro and American Peter joined in a partnership to sell hats imported from the States. The enterprise became so successful that branch stores were opened in Parral and San Bartolomé. Young Bean became a popular, prosperous businessman, often consulted in matters regarding the Americans or as a translator of occasional English documents. Then came the word from Madrid.

All the Americans captured from Nolan's gang were to be hanged at once. Dismayed and sorrowful, Salcedo could not but question such a sentence upon men who were now friends, whom he felt never could have been any threat to Spanish security. He gave them a sporting chance by allowing them, through the roll of a pair of dice, to select one of their number to serve as the victim. The unfortunate one, E. Blackburn, was hanged publicly in the patio of the jail.

To prevent angered townsmen from helping the five remaining Americans to escape, they were taken under guard down the central highlands to the national capital where they met a caravan headed for the port of Acapulco. The prisoners were moved to the dank dungeons of the Castillo of San Diego. Before they left Chihuahua, Waters and Bean were baptized into the Catholic faith, with the alderman Pedro Ignacio de Irigoyen and the merchant Pedro de Valois acting as their godfathers.*

In 1800, the valuable domain known as Louisiana had been returned to France by a weakening Spanish monarchy. Three years later the United States, desirous of gaining control of the port of New Orleans and the length of the Mississippi River, bought all the French province for $15,000,000. In December 1803, Yankees moved next door to the Spanish territory of Texas. No Spaniard in position of authority felt that the Americans would be satisfied with Louisiana. The tide of Americans constantly moving toward the Pacific would soon engulf Texas, New Mexico, California, and even northern Mexico itself. Talk of American plots to invade those regions was common in the province of Nueva Vizcaya as it was farther to the east in Coahuila and Texas. Burr and Wilkinson, whose treachery scandalized official circles in Washington, were thought to be the prototypes of all land-hungry, power-drunk gringos. When an officer of the United States Army brazenly built a fort on Spanish land in the San Luis valley of northern New Mexico, it seemed certain the time of invasion was fast approaching.

That intruder was a twenty-four year old captain born and bred in the western army, Zebulon Montgomery Pike, who, three years later, was to become the celebrated discoverer of Pike's Peak.[25] He was captured, taken to Santa Fe, then on to higher authority in Chihuahua. His party was escorted south by a polite young Spanish officer, Lieutenant Facundo Melgares. A year earlier, the lieutenant had commanded one hundred regulars and five hundred militia with an animal train of two thousand beasts on a mission to the borders of Louisiana to intercept Captain Pike, mistakenly thought to be invading Nueva Vizcaya from that direction. False rumors of his *secret* coming arrived months before Pike did! Pike and his men joined a caravan of traders and the combined party made frequent

---

* Arellano Schetelig, 139a, 260-64. Good luck continued for Bean. Because of his youth, he was pardoned. He became an agitator in the independence movement and a valuable aid to Father Morelos who sent him north to the States on purchasing trips in behalf of the insurgents. As a reward for his loyalty to the cause, he was made a colonel in the Mexican army. He married a native woman with whom he spent his remaining years in the village of Jalapa, Vera Cruz.

stops along the Río Grande valley to enjoy hospitality proffered by scattered hacienda settlements eager to break the monotony of quiet routine with a gay round of dances, feasting, and cockfights. When captured, they were allowed to keep their firearms and to ride their own mounts, but they were not permitted to record notes of the country through which they traveled. The party reached the Río Grande in March 1807.

Once the traders had ferried their cargoes across in dugouts and had driven the empty wagons over a rock-lined ford, the party moved past fields beginning to green with young wheat sprouts and rows of grapevines spreading along rope arbors. Ditches full of water were bringing resurgence of life to fruit trees in delicate pink and white blossom. Stark branches of willows and cotton-woods were losing themselves in a pale-green veil of newborn spring. Neat adobe houses, some with fronts whitewashed, some with blue borders around windows and doors, stretched irregularly along the warm bottomlands for a number of miles. El Paso del Norte on the south bank of the Río Grande, six miles down from the ford, made a favorable impression on the men from the north. The welcome for the Americans was so pleasant that they were in no haste to continue to Chihuahua where, they were told, official displeasure awaited them.

The road went downstream for a few miles and then struck due south across basins and rocky terraces left by ancient seas. Thirty miles from the river, the extensive mounds of shifting sand dunes of Samalayuca crowded in on the trail, whirling in islands around the roots of sotol, mesquite clumps, and Spanish dagger, gradually moving eastward with the prevailing winds. Wagons heavily loaded with kegs of aguardiente and brandy, bags of raisins, dried fruits, and onions, and bales of fibrous *lechuguilla* could not churn through the deep sands without a double team of mules to pull them and many hands to push. It was often easier to traverse a wide arc around the eastern edge of the dunes, leaving the river valley south of San Elizario. Sometimes cargoes were taken from the cumbersome, floundering wagons and were repacked for shipment across the dunes on the backs of extra burros. In the first sixty miles south of El Paso there were only two fetid water holes, where men and animals drank together. Pike's men observed bones and abandoned equipment thrown along the trail, silent testimony of hazardous crossings not completed.

Beyond the sand lay the Laguna de Patos, a desert sinkhole where the waters of the Río Carmen came to die. In the rainy season the lake always spread out thinly over the basin to create a gigantic mud puddle to impede all travel. Solid-wheeled carts and the feet of many beasts gouged the oozing muck and turned it into a quagmire. The road improved as it turned slightly west to the walled fort-town of Carrizal where three hundred soldiers and their families drearily guarded the caravan road and the northern desert. Pike came through Carrizal at a time when it lay sleeping in the warm springtime sun, a time when there was no suspicion that its Apache neighbors would not remain at peace.

As the party continued to move southward across expansive plains increasingly carpeted with tall, native grasses not yet greened from summer rains, they noted an abundance of game and other animal life. Antelope and rabbits provided them with welcome fresh meat, but they had to be on the alert for the numerous snakes, tarantulas, and scorpions. They passed many springs, or *ojos*, some hot and large enough to offer the pleasures of bathing, exercise, and refreshment. Ojo Caliente, twelve miles south of Carrizal, was an oasis where all caravans were accustomed to make camp in order to enjoy temperate waters in natural basins worn into the rock.

The village of El Carmen on a bluff east above the river sprawled indifferently beneath inviting trees, its dirt plaza swept barren by spring winds. Dogs came to bark at the animals of the caravan and tousled children to gape in curiosity at the uniformed foreigners bringing up the rear of the train.

On they progressed to the cliffs of Gallegos where another spring seeped from the rock and supported a few cottonwoods to provide shade for hot travelers. Pike was not aware of the fact that this was the place where at another Easter season, two hundred thirty years previously, Oñate's men, on the way to conquer New Mexico, had undergone bloody penitence. For it was there that Maundy Thursday in 1598 was observed with flagellations.

The Pike party rode on down to the lake of Encinillas in the midst of a vast depression where antelope and herds of longhorn

cattle browsed in deep grass and cracked through the greyish, al-
kali crust of the shore. The trail kept to the east of the high, mud
walls of a hacienda establishment in the valley, but the men could
see occasional riders passing through its enormous gates.

El Sauz, another hacienda, was located some miles still farther
south in a broad, flat bolson edged by mountains high enough to
be topped with a few pines. Caravan scouts sometimes brought
deer down from these mountains to furnish food for the men of the
train. The road skirted the dry valley and wound through some
gently broken hills near a ranching community, Sacramento. From
there, the travelers jogged across more tablelands to come to the
original pueblo of the Chihuahua valley, Nombre de Dios. The
graceful spires of the cathedral of Chihuahua could be seen silhouetted against dark hills beyond. One could even hear their
sonorous bells as Melchor Guaspé called the population to mass
or sent it hurrying home at curfew. A few miles more would reveal
whether death or freedom would be in store for the little band of
prisoners now at least a month's journey and six hundred fifty
miles from the United States border.

Governor Salcedo was bewildered by the problem of dealing
with Captain Pike. He had been Spain's last governor of Louisiana,
had left that post after Napoleon had forced return of those lands
to French control. He was aware of American rapaciousness in
coveting the bayous and swamplands so strategically located. It
came as no surprise to this servant of the royal house of Spain that
French stupidity plus American cupidity placed Louisiana under
the Stars and Stripes. Was he, then, to consider Pike the forerun-
ner of a new expansion desired by the government in Washington?
Was the fiasco of Louisiana about to be repeated? Governor Alancaster of New Mexico had found papers in Pike's trunk definitely
incriminating in nature, perhaps linking him with the notorious
Aaron Burr. Why had Pike been allowed to continue on through
Spanish lands to observe the lack of fortifications and military
preparedness? Alancaster had committed a careless blunder, one
which might have dire consequences, and he, Salcedo, would urge
that New Mexico have a new governor.

Whatever his political feelings, Salcedo was the ingratiating host,
formally polite in the stiff code of the Spanish gentleman. He offered his city to the men whom he considered official representa-

tives of a foreign nation. They were not permitted to discuss with the natives either of the twin facts of Spanish control, government and religion, but those were the only restrictions placed upon them. The deserts to the north and east and the mountains to the west were considered sufficiently frightening to discourage flight.

Pike's courteous behavior and sincere interest in what he observed made him friends quickly. He and his party were entertained in fine homes in the city and joined in the lighthearted fun made of their language difficulties. They visited two Americans in jail who had been with Nolan in southern Texas. One had served in the United States Army under Pike's father.* They roamed the winding streets lined with oblong mud houses, peered into inner blooming patios with all the inquisitiveness of later American tourists, admired the massive cathedral with its statues of the twelve apostles and the beautiful arches of the Jesuit aqueduct. As they sat on sun-drenched benches in the plaza, they sampled foods and drinks new to them, offered for a few copper coins. They sipped *tepache*, a slightly fermented pineapple drink made from fruit brought up from tropical barrancas, and nibbled at *ates* of guava paste, and *pepitas*, fried squash seeds. It was difficult to remember that they were prisoners of a foreign power.

At length Salcedo determined to return his "guests" to their homeland and to send a strongly worded note to Washington protesting such violation of Spanish borders. He also advised his superiors in Madrid of the action taken. A gentleman to the end, Salcedo loaned the impoverished Americans a thousand pesos for the trip through Spanish territory and assigned to their companion of the journey from Santa Fe, Lieutenant Melgares, the task of escorting the group back to the north. They traveled east on the road to Coahuila and again crossed the Río Grande. By the end of June 1807, Pike had reached the new United States property of Louisiana.

No invasion of Mexico followed Pike's trip. The United States government preferred to ignore charges of spying, to insist Pike had been lost in the little-known western wilderness. Perhaps, though, Pike accomplished his mission. For he supplied Washing-

---

* David Ferro, Third Sub-Legion, in 1794 served under Captain Zebulon Pike.

ton with the most thorough and accurate account of the political and religious manners, the flora and fauna, and the general potentialities of northern Mexico (including New Mexico) of any American observer to that date. He had kept the papers secreted from the eyes of the escorting troops by stuffing them into the barrels of the rifles his men had across their saddles. Had he really been a spy? *Quién sabe?*

IN STEADILY increasing numbers, American hunters and adventurers began edging in on the Spanish territory of Texas. When captured, they were shackled and taken across dead and waterless deserts to Chihuahua. A royal inspector of the jails in Nueva España wrote of interviewing eight Americans languishing in the jail in Chihuahua charged with entering without passport. Two of them, Josiah McLanahan and Rubin Smith, were accused of trying to incite revolution. In 1813 six others were thrown into jail to sit for years. One of them, Robert McKnight of Missouri, imprisoned for nine years, later was famed as one of the operators of the Santa Rita copper mines in southern New Mexico. These mines had been worked by a Spaniard, Francisco Pablo de Lagera, who suffered expulsion after Mexican independence was consummated. McKnight, too, was forced to leave the area as a result of repeated raids by the Apaches who in one night drove off eighty pack mules.

Spain was feeling pressure not only from her own Mexican subjects but from outsiders as well. Her back was up. Futilely she tried to slam shut the sluice gates of the Chihuahua corridor to cut off the flow of influence and immigrants from the north.

After Mexico became a free nation, Americans traveling into that territory found themselves entangled in an even greater web of restrictions and prohibitions enforced by contrary agents. Had not the unexplainable lure of the hostile land been so great and the opportunity for financial gain so frequent, northern Mexico might have been spared the onslaught of foreigners coming during the first twenty years of the nation's existence.

Serious trading activity between Mexican merchants and American and French freighters came with the birth of Mexico.[26] William Becknell generally is credited with bringing the first caravan of wagons laden with an assortment of goods for sale across the mid-continental plains to the Río Grande. This venture proved to be so successful that a boom in traffic bound for Old Mexico began to cut row on row of ruts into the western prairie. In June 1824, ninety Americans and Frenchmen had made their way safely to the plaza in front of the Palace of the Governors in Santa Fe with loads of calico, cooking utensils, hair ribbons, lithographs, and medicines. Their enterprise was almost stopped because of a stubborn refusal to pay the high taxes assessed on each wagon. In the end, the new traders had to accept the Mexican government's ultimatum of no taxes, no trade. The amount of the duty was added to the sale price, and compromise was clouded.

Early spring brought out the Pittsburgh wagons like March snow brings up the crocuses. With the first open weather, spans of oxen or horses pulled them from outposts in Kansas or Missouri. It was the type of existence that appealed to the robust, virile men living on the frontier who thrived on a gamble with life or fortune. The journey from beginning to end was fraught with countless hazards. Indians and highwaymen, both in the United States and in Mexico, made it necessary to go in caravan formation, sometimes to travel at night. Maintenance of wagons, providing for the needs of men and animals and protecting merchandise from the vicissitudes of weather, were constant challenges to the ingenuity and skill of the drivers of the trains.

Once Mexican borders were reached, patience to last out frustration was a further challenge to the men turned traders, frustration as defeating as the robbers who lurked in ambush or the spring torrents that turned eroded plains to mud. Patience was an unexpected quality in these virile types. Although the Mexican government realized greatly increased revenues from the American trade, it seemed set on a petulant pattern of frustration, contradiction, piddling argument, and endless red tape.

Customs agents had to have bills of lading in Spanish. Any error or omission in translation of the papers led to confiscations of all the goods. If everything seemed in order and properly endorsed, a *guía*, or permit, was issued. The trader was allowed to deliver his goods only at points named in the guía and within a certain prescribed time limit. To be found off the route allowable in the guía, to be late in delivery, or at a market other than those named meant confiscation. Regulations stipulating what articles could be imported into Mexico constantly changed. At one time Santa Ana sent to the ports of entry a list of two hundred items which could not be brought south. A trader leaving Missouri with wagon loads of commodities which had been acceptable for Mexican trade the year previously might arrive on the border to find his entire shipment blacklisted.

The bulk of the traders coming into Santa Fe were bound for Chihuahua where higher prices could be attained that would more than justify the lengthier trip down the Chihuahua Trail.[27] Ports were opened in El Paso and Presidio del Norte (at La Junta) about 1830. After the defection of Texas in 1836, they were frequently ordered closed by an unpredictable despot acting in arbitrary fashion. Strong opposition was voiced in both Mexico and the United States to a decree prohibiting all foreigners to engage in the trade unless they were naturalized, married to Mexican women, or lived with families in Mexico. A year later the customshouses received instructions to modify these harsh restrictions. There remained an element of trying uncertainty attached to the international trade. Overnight a man might find himself faced with financial ruin because of change of position of the Mexican agents or delays caused by weather or official formalities.

At each Mexican village, the caravans were subject to scrutiny. Papers were re-examined, more taxes levied. If the destination was still farther south than Chihuahua, additional duties were paid in each state. The internal duties often were at least twenty per cent of the United States evaluation of the goods. With so many persons in the position of collecting duties, the opportunities for fraudulent practices were numerous and, according to the Americans, seldom overlooked.

Some traders passed through Chihuahua to penetrate into the central highlands at the time of one of the great fairs such as that held annually in December in San Juan de los Lagos in Jalisco. On the way north, they brought loads of textiles from the mills of Aguascalientes and León. A few preferred to be itinerant peddlers from settlement to settlement, village to village, surviving one hairbreadth escape from robbers and Indians after another, broadening constricted horizons of the widely dispersed inhabitants.

Most of the traders in the city of Chihuahua camped together at the bullring near the Chuvíscar, lining up the Pittsburgh wagons to await the long trip home before the plains were snowed in. Frequently they sold the wagons in Chihuahua and acquired a string of mules for the rapid return trip. They rented store space on one of the central streets of the city in which to arrange merchandise for display. They usually tried to dispose of their shipment in wholesale lots to be paid in bullion and specie. Retail trade meant copper money which was not negotiable in all sections of the country, but occasionally it was necessary to peddle. In the twilight and early evening hours, the streets came to life with throngs of shoppers and onlookers. It was a social period of meeting one's friends, of promenading through the markets and shops, and of sipping coffee or spiced chocolate in the crowded parlors under the portals by the plaza. This was the time when the American traders made most of their sales. Due to the large numbers of people pushing into the stores dimly lighted by spindly candles, merchants discovered it was also the time when they had to be most alert to prevent large-scale shoplifting.

To men unused to the bickering, agitated type of bargaining enjoyed by Mexicans, disputes over prices might seem monumental and ludicrous. Articles were sold by measured size rather than by intrinsic value. There were questions as to whether reading glasses should be measured lengthwise or crosswise, pocketknives open or shut, writing paper by the length or the width. All cotton piece goods, regardless of type or quality, had a set price of two to three reales per *vara* (one vara equals 33 inches), twenty-five to thirty-seven cents. Profits were tremendous. Sale price frequently was six times the wholesale figures paid back in Independence.

In the first years of the trade, the amount of business transacted brought a $15,000 return. The number of traders and the amount of merchandise increased until, by the time of the war of 1846, $1,000,000 was taken north in a season; a single enterprise brought in $150,000.

The main route of travel for the trade caravans was via one of the two branches of the Santa Fe Trail, which united in the valley of the Sapello and Mora rivers in northeastern New Mexico to come to Santa Fe from the east. From there the road continued in the Río Grande valley to El Paso, with the exception of an eighty-mile, waterless cutoff, thence south over the trail first traveled by Oñate's expedition in 1598.

Texas was eager to encourage traders to go to Mexico by way of

San Antonio rather than Santa Fe. Merchants of that Texas city subscribed eight hundred dollars to aid a group of men under John C. Hays of the Texas Rangers to find a suitable route across west Texas to the port of El Paso.[28] They went through many hardships and eventually were defeated by the inhospitable terrain, but fortunately they reached the Chihuahua border town of San Carlos, downriver from Presidio del Norte, before perishing from starvation. In 1840 James Magoffin, a trader owning land at El Paso, and Dr. Henry Connelly, a long-time merchant, led a hundred men and wagons west from San Antonio, crossing the Río Grande at Presidio del Norte and following the Río Conchos route to central Chihuahua. A Texas trail was not in great use until after the Mexican war when fevered prospectors going to the California goldfields would not be turned back by anything man or nature could put in the way. San Antonio never benefited substantially from the Mexican trade bound for Chihuahua.

The hard cash brought into the country by trade with the Americans understandably was welcomed by the destitute Mexican government. Two less-tangible influences which came with the traders were not appreciated. For the first time, Protestantism and Freemasonry were discussed in northern Mexico—discussed, argued, and rejected. Always conservative, sometimes reactionary, Chihuahua would not accept dogmas other than those advocated by the Roman Catholic Church. In central Mexico, in the years leading up to American invasion, there was increasing resentment of its power and wealth. Not so in northern fringes. Loyalty to the Church was as unquestioned and undoubted as loyalty to the Crown had been twenty years earlier. Clerics, with public approval, openly crusaded against these two undercurrents, Protestantism and Freemasonry, sweeping south with the American tides. One trader operating in a plaza shop fruitlessly complained to the alcalde that priests had entered his establishment, seized several dozen handkerchiefs marked with the Masonic stamp, and had carried them into the street for public burning. Such incidents were followed by neither indemnification nor apology.[29]

THE BOOMING trade relations between the two nations were briefly but seriously imperiled by the disastrous Texas-Santa Fe Expedition.[30]

In 1841, Texas dreams of empire evaporated before an aborted invasion of Mexico's northern colony of New Mexico could be consummated. Texans, proud of their costly new freedom from Mexico, were driven in irons from northeastern New Mexico, beaten, nearly starved, ruthlessly shot down as helpless prisoners. Captain Demasio Salazar, charged with bringing the American prisoners south to El Paso, was brutal. His violent actions later were repudiated by the commanding officer of the garrison at El Paso who sought to make amends through apologies and kinder treatment. General Francisco García Conde, son of the last agent of Spain in Nueva Vizcaya, himself once governor of the Federal District, chief of the fifth division of the Mexican army, and in 1840 governor of Chihuahua, expressed his regrets over the unfortunate incident. El Pasoans brought food and "pass wine" to the suffering survivors and gave them remnants of clothing to protect them from sharp winter winds. Father Ramón Ortiz of the convent of Guadalupe offered his services and sympathy and his carriage for men unable to walk.

On November 9, 1841, ragged and forlorn, the Texans commenced the severe test of a thirteen-hundred-mile shackled march to confinement in prisons in Perote and Puebla and the Tlalteloco convent in Mexico City. Over the dunes of Samalayuca to the wilderness towns of Carrizal, Ojo Caliente, Gallegos, and Encinillas they plodded, one weary mile after another, under the silent sun. On to Sauz, Sacramento, and the capital, they pushed in a fog of fatigue and numb despair.

After a respite in quarters once occupied by Hidalgo and his insurgents, they were led on southward out of Chihuahua. They left no scars, few remembrances. Their passing was the tragic prologue to the bitter drama about to come.

THE SHOWDOWN between the United States and Mexico, which long had been brewing, came in the year of 1846.[31] In New Mexico it proceeded quietly with the help of purchased treason. Manuel Armijo, governor of New Mexico, had been bought through the undercover efforts of an American trader, James Magoffin. Feeble pretense at defense of Santa Fe had been made in Apache Canyon on the town's eastern flanks while fat Armijo had fled southward like a winter duck on the wing, protesting he was routed because of lack of adequate support. General Stephen Watts Kearny and his Army of the West had moved rapidly into the shady plaza where the Santa Fe Trail met the Camino Real. The flag of the eagle and the serpent had flown atop the squat Palace of the Governors for less than a quarter century.

Caravan trade was at its highest peak in the mid-1840's. The grasslands and arroyos of the approaches to the Mexican colonies were deeply grooved by creaking wagon wheels rolling new wares to exchange for rawhide bags of specie. A million-dollar business was at stake in the conflict between the two nations. Anxious traders had hoped Kearny would be able to free them of the strangling net of increasing duties demanded by Mexican customs agents. They had urged that all the compromises be favorable to them. For protection, some of the westward-bound wagons in that year of 1846 had attached themselves to Kearny's military column and had followed him in a lengthy chain to the foot of the Sangre de Cristos. There they had waited with growing impatience for permission to travel on south to Chihuahua to dispose of their goods and return home before winter snows stopped all plains traffic. Permission had been withheld pending military decisions.

Trader merchants in advance of the column had been confronted with a difficult decision. To proceed to Santa Fe under a cloud of wild rumor of the approaching army of their nation meant possible, almost certain, confiscation of their wagons or further exorbitant duties levied by dishonest officials determined to get as many American dollars as possible while the opportunity presented itself. It meant exposing oneself to open insult and reckless violence from a populace aroused against the American invaders. To wait along the trail for the advancing army meant facing uncertainty and delay, perhaps prohibition of trade all together.

James Josiah Webb,[32] a veteran of two years in the trade, had reached Santa Fe early in the 1846 season to find himself in the ticklish position of selling at a loss and leaving Mexico before the impending crisis actually broke, or gambling on being able to reach southern Mexican markets ahead of war and competition from traders who might benefit from being allowed duty-free importation under cover of Kearny's guns. He chose to leave his sick partner, George Doan, in Santa Fe and to join a caravan heading down the Río Grande. Before he had finished packing and making arrangements for drivers for the wagons, New Mexico fell to the Americans.

Albert Speyer, whom Webb had joined, was a Prussian Jew traveling under both English and Prussian passports. Earlier he had been reported to Kearny by a government trail rider as a possible ally of the fleeing Armijo. It was considered not unlikely that he was attempting to get contraband munitions into Chihuahua to aid the Mexicans. As soon as the departure of the Speyer-Webb caravan was discovered, suspicion turned to certainty. A pursuit squad under Captain Benjamin Moore rode south, covering forty-five miles a day, to intercept the men and wagons. The soldiers never sighted the racing caravan and after some days swung back to headquarters to report Speyer's escape.

In the group, driving hard to evade American soldiers, was a German doctor making a scientific trip to northern Mexico. Intent on gathering collections of botanical and geological specimens and making astronomical observations, Dr. Adolph Wislisenius did not wish involvement in any international war, and so, once Chihuahua was near, he and a manservant departed from the caravan to travel the empty deserts alone. They risked ambush from frontier forces being hurried north to plug the gaping holes in the defense line and death by maurading Apaches operating near the lonely springs. They crossed the vastness of the northern belt of sagebrush and low cacti without incident, to ride unmolested into the capital of hysterical Chihuahua. News that the city of Monterrey, Coahuila, had been taken by the American army had just been received.

All the Americans in town, some thirty in all, had barricaded themselves in a small hotel run by Bennett Riddells, American consul to Chihuahua, where they hoped to remain safe from angry Mexicans. Wislisenius joined them. Several days later the governor of the state sent soldiers to escort them all southwest ninety miles to Cusihuiriáchi to wait until his forces had driven the enemy from the soil of Mexico. The doctor was released from custody a week later and returned to the city. The other men were kept at Cusihuiriáchi until after the Battle of Sacramento.

The caravan of wagons belonging to Speyer and Webb steadily moved toward Chihuahua, keeping to the established route to avoid confiscation. No delays were tolerated because each day lost might mean Kearny's traders were gaining on them. Competition was unthinkable because of the high duties they had already paid. Just when the end of the tiring trek was near, disaster struck.

As the train moved on in the dark of a moonless night to the hacienda of Penol, forty miles north of the city of Chihuahua, the riders thought they observed some figures on the roofs of the outbuildings. Expecting each day to catch up with Armijo's men escaping southward, they felt certain that at last they had overtaken them. The wagons passed the corral as the gates were flung open and out marched Mexican soldiers. A quick-thinking lead driver, seeing the soldiers armed and intent on capturing the caravan, jumped to the ground and loudly yelled orders for the wagons to charge into corral formation. The Mexicans had hoped to take them in a strung-out position. Speyer and Webb went immediately to the commanding officer in the house to protest this summary treatment. They learned that Governor Trías knew of their flight to Chihuahua and had been waiting for their arrival. They were ordered now to release the two wagons loaded with ammunition and guns to the officer before them so that the needed supplies could be rushed ahead immediately. The other wagons would be driven to the city in the morning by Mexican soldiers.

Webb was enraged at not knowing of Speyer's smuggling operation. But he was even more concerned for the fate of his cargo should the drivers learn they were to become prisoners, as well as pedestrians, with sunup. He and his new partner quietly ran the mules away from camp so no suspicious driver would decide to flee back toward the Río Grande during the night. Somehow the next morning the two traders persuaded their hesitant helpers to allow themselves to be disarmed and to find a spot on the load in which to ride while the soldiers took the reins to the city. For three days the Americans and the Mexicans traveled together in a spirit of comradeship, singing the *corridos* of the trail and recounting adventures. Speyer and his Spanish clerk were allowed to enter the city, but all the Americans were detained at the river bank for two weeks. Then they were permitted to move to the traditional traders' camp at the bullring.

Anti-American sentiment was increasing daily, not the least being voiced from the pulpit as it had in the war of criollo against gachupín. Territorial needs essentially economic were expressed

and repulsed in terms of race prejudice and religious bigotry—
Texan against Mexican, Catholic against heretic. Catholicism was
considered endangered. Chihuahuenses were fanatically aroused
against the antichrists coming to desecrate shrines and to preach
the doctrine of godlessness. Priests exhorted their people to organize for the most important battle in Chihuahua's history.

Webb and Speyer sent anxious appeals to administrators in the
Palacio de Gobierno to be allowed to go to more southerly markets
with their goods. They had already been detained six weeks. Speyer
arranged through a German merchant in Durango for permission
for the caravan to enter that state. Securing a pass to leave the
arena, Webb called on John Potts, an Englishman serving as director of the mint and a man of considerable influence with the
governor, to plead for help in securing papers enabling him to
travel to the interior. Some time previously Potts had drawn up
such papers for a traveler from Baltimore, had them signed and
sealed. For some reason, they never had been picked up. Luckily,
the name of the individual had not been written in the blank space
left for that purpose. Quickly that of James Webb was inserted,
and he had a paper of safe conduct to be used once he got out of
Chihuahua.

Embarrassed by the restless Americans, Governor Trías sent the
caravan south to a hacienda on the Río Florido. They were joined
by several Mexican families traveling away from what they believed would become a zone of war. The owner of the Moorish-
style hacienda was a former governor of the state and the father of
two lovely daughters. On seeing the crass, unruly behavior and
untidy appearance of the Americans, whom he regarded as burros,
he feared for the safety of the girls and was easily persuaded to allow the caravan to proceed out of the state. The drivers were to
"escape" to go eastward to join the military column at Monterrey.
In anticipation of this event, Speyer had hired Mexican drivers before the train left the city of Chihuahua. In La Zarca, a solitary
ranch on the edge of the *travesía,* or "crossing," a desolate eastern
area abandoned because of repeated Indian incursions, twenty-one
American mule skinners bought mounts and started for home.

One month later half of the twenty-one were dead. With faces
almost cadaverous, hair long and matted, lips cracked, and delirious from heat prostration, the survivors were found by sheepherd-

ers, sprawled in the scant shade of a ravine. They were brought to Jiménez where they were cared for by sympathetic townspeople. After they began to recover, the Americans recounted their misadventures. They had ridden east from La Zarca not into freedom but into a deadly bolson country without water or grass, into the heart of as vast and uncompromising a desert as any on the continent. The horses died rapidly, and soon, too, the men expired. Some separated to forage singly and to die alone.

An English army officer, George Ruxton, was northward bound on the Camino Real at this time.[33] After his arrival in Jiménez, he heard there might be survivors of the ill-fated party of American mule skinners alive in the desert and in desperate need of help. He organized a volunteer rescue party to go in search of the distressed men. Moving from rincon to ridge and scanning each segment of horizon as carefully as possible, they rode back to civilization with no further knowledge of the victims of Chihuahuan hell.

Speyer and Webb sold their cargo at the fair in San Juan de los Lagos and joined forces with George Doan, who had been captured at El Paso but was later allowed to enter Mexico on his English passport. Doan had rejoined his partner in San Juan. The double caravan turned north again with wagons loaded with ten tons of refined sugar, cones of crude brown sugar, *rebozos* (shawls), shoes, and chocolate. All along the way to Chihuahua they observed Mexican troops being organized to meet General Taylor's army of invasion to the east of them. Before passing through the customs station at Cerro Gordo in northern Durango, notorious for difficult agents, the guía had expired and the traders were forced to pay a high bribe to prevent abrupt confiscation of their cargoes. Webb kept his American passport concealed as he thought it a ticket to abuse, getting past officials with the English papers of his partners.

In Chihuahua, Webb rented a plaza store from Padre Terrazas, brother of the town's prefect. Doan engaged in further freighting to the interior. And Speyer entertained Mexican officials with lavish parties.

The autumn months of 1846 had seen laborers drafted to fortify the approaches to the city of Chihuahua and more southerly Santa Rosalía (modern Camargo). Prisoners from the crowded jails were

pressed into service. North at the hacienda of Sacramento, first denounced* by Captain Pedro Nuñez Falcón in the seventeenth century, Mexican strategists designed a series of entrenchments along
hillsides, hoping the American army would pass in a ravine below
and be annihilated. Governor Angel Trías, heading a junta to prepare for defense, solicited funds and arms and organized a national
guard of young men of the city ready to fight the hated Americans.
Five hundred Chihuahua volunteers and an equal number of dragoons from Vera Cruz and Zacatecas marched across the wastes to
El Paso to join forces with the men dispatched northward at the
time of the ill-fated defense of Santa Fe against Kearny. They were
confident of victory. Anything less was unthinkable. Had not the
padres told them the Americans, if victorious, had promised their
soldiers one hour in which to loot and ravish? Cords were already
being prepared in the capital with which to bind the feet of the
American prisoners to be paraded southward, as their Texan cous-
ins had been before them. Governor Trías would deal with these
heretical burros who came not to trade but to covet and then to
seize.

To Americans, Angel Trías was no angel.[34] He was an exceedingly wealthy hacendado who loved his scorched homeland but
passionately hated Americans, which involved him in much un-
pleasantness during the mid-century. His was a blind, unreasoning emotion which Mexicans intepreted as superpatriotism and
Americans as unprincipled tyranny. Trías had not been a true son
of the raging frontier but had spent much of his youth in Europe.
He had learned six languages, including a fluent, flawless English,
and was at ease in sophisticated, European, urban society. Baron
von Humboldt was among his large circle of intellectual friends.
When he returned to his native Chihuahua, he married into one
of the first families, the Horcasitas, and peremptorily set about to
control the enormous tracts of land belonging to his family. The
Camino Real to the Río Grande crossed his extensive haciendas of
Sauz, Penol, and Encinillas in grass-blanketed, central basins, and
traders coming south had to traverse the empire of Don Angel.
Trouble inevitably developed.

---

* The process often used in acquiring land was to utter a "denuncia" or
an oral proclamation or claim accompanied by appropriate ceremony.

In the late thirties and forties, Trías' domain was favorite raiding territory of the warlike Apache, not only because of its situation not too distant from sheltering mountains but because of the irresistible lure of herds of fat stock grazing belly-deep in wild grasses. The animals stolen in these attacks were driven to the El Paso vicinity and often were sold to men on the trail. By law each beast had to have a brand (fierro); if it was sold, it also had to have a sale brand. Some animals had changed hands so many times that the markings had become confused, making definite determination of ownership impossible. Apache horses and mules reaching American wagon trains seldom had acceptable brands. Confiscation by border agents followed. Since many of the readable brands showed the animals to have been Trías property, the traders, although sympathetic to the hacendado's losses, felt resentment at the long arm of Don Angel's authority which could take away that which had been bought in good faith with United States silver dollars. One of their number, Josiah Gregg, doctor and author of Commerce of the Prairies, had been jailed without a hearing because members of his starving caravan once had butchered a Trías calf to remedy their immediate unfortunate situation, fully intending to make payment later.[35]

They questioned the flawlessness of a government system wherein one man could own, or claim to own, so much of a state, yet where unrelieved poverty was the miserable inheritance of thousands of peons. They saw Trías as an unyielding dictator, completely subjecting the workers to his will, luxuriating in wealth sustained by their efforts. Missouri-bred freethinkers, reared on a rugged diet of independence of spirit and thought, could not stomach such conditions, and they spoke out. What started as anger at having their property confiscated turned into hatred for an individual and the type of society he represented.

Don Angel, for his part, saw the unshaven, dirty trail riders as bourgeois and uncultured forerunners of an undesirable influence from an aggressive nation. He found them distasteful and uncouth. He could not help but fear their adaptability, their competence, and their uninhibited speech. Fear found vent in hate, and war provided an escape valve for both.

Angel Trías—anti-American, antimasonic, and, some said, antidemocratic—served eight different terms of varying length as governor of Chihuahua. His son later followed him into office. Angel Trías *padre* and Angel Trías *hijo* made names for themselves in Chihuahua politics. Father was in office when "Yankee Doodle" was sung in the Plaza de la Constitución!

COLONEL ALEXANDER W. DONIPHAN, in civilian life an eminent criminal lawyer from the southern border state of Missouri, on February 28, 1847, led his bedraggled troops into the plaza of the capital city of Chihuahua. He saw them move its ornately scrolled iron benches to make room for supplies, saw them water their horses, even bathe themselves in its public central fountain, and saw them cut its priceless plaza trees for firewood. He ordered them to place their cannons in commanding positions at the entrance of the short streets leading into the plaza and to move into surrounding buildings vacated by the panic-stricken Mexicans, as he felt it urgent to prepare for an indefinite occupation. He had received no communication from General Wool who was to have converged on the city from the eastern sector via the San Antonio trade route. Indeed, Wool was supposed to have taken the city before Doniphan's arrival. If Doniphan had been abandoned in this lonely Mexican capital by his higher officers, he had no certain knowledge of it, only countless discomforting rumors. His men had routed its defenders, had chased them to the mountains and barrancas, and had sent its governors packing posthaste to ancient Hidalgo del Parral.[36]

The men out of Missouri who made up this invading force scarcely looked like conquering soldiers. Few had complete uniform or insignia. Fringed buckskin jackets associated with homespun pants or expropriated Mexican sombreros. Many had long, flowing hair and straggling beards. All were dirty and ragged after the trying march from El Paso and the three-hour fight up the slopes at Sacramento. They camped in the plaza, as they had fought at Brazitos and Sacramento, without plan or military correctness but with tremendous spirit. They joked and guffawed loudly in the fellowship of shared adventures, hardships mutually endured. They leered at girls brave enough, or brazen enough, to watch them from behind shuttered windows. They had enlisted to whip these Mexicans, and by George, they'd done it! Doniphan proudly said, "My men are ragged, rough, and ready."[37]

Ragged, rough, and ready—that had characterized the First Missouri Volunteers since their formation in Fort Leavenworth. Only half-outfitted through mismanagement and lack of funds, rawboned, adventuresome farm boys eager to see a bit of the world beyond Missouri, always scrappers, without military deportment, they would earn accolades from shocked military academicians. Part of the reason was a lifelong training at marksmanship, essential on the frontier. Important to their victories was the character of their leader.

Abraham Lincoln once said of Doniphan, "You are the only man I ever met who, in appearance, came up to my previous expectation." He was an Irishman of imposing stature and handsome appearance with a crop of sandy hair, hazel eyes, and a clear complexion. His civilian occupation as a lawyer had brought him considerable fame as a fearless, eloquent orator, shrewd and forceful in court, but kindly in his nonprofessional dealings with people, although he once had been a party to court action against the Mormons. Even though he had no firsthand knowledge of the country into which he was going, he had listened to so many accounts of traders outfitting along the Missouri border that he had acquired a great deal of strategic information which proved valuable. Most importantly, he was a natural leader of men and one who thoroughly understood the rustic background and abilities of his men and their unquenchable feeling of independence. He was confident of channeling this spirit sufficiently to produce group victory without regard to professional military procedures. The stalwart First Missouri Volunteers became so esteemed after the Chihuahua campaign that General Wool asked them to stay with his army for another hitch, tempting them with plentiful rations and cakes of soap. While the rations might have trapped them into one more chance at the Mexicans, it may have been the soap that sent them streaming back across the Río Grande to heroes' acclaim to Missouri.

A colorful addition to Doniphan's motley crew was James Kirker, hired exterminator of Apaches. Kirker galloped into the American encampment in mid-Río Grande valley, long, black hair trailing from under his sombrero, supple leather pants and jerkin emphasizing his rugged massiveness, silver spurs with huge rowels jangling, and a saddle bearing a small armory of pistols, rifles, and knives, all obviously well used. He wished to volunteer his services. This was no patriotism or high-flying impulse to aid fellow Anglo-Saxons. He wished to revenge himself upon defrauding Mexican magistrates who had refused to pay the stipulated bounty (in the amount of 30,000 pesos!) for Apache scalps, claiming—and was it not plausible?—that not only were Kirker's successes greater than their budget would allow, but that they were unable to distinguish Apache scalps from Tarahumara scalps or, *madre de dios,* even scalps of the Mexican *campesinos!* True to an era when murdering an Indian was no crime against society, Doniphan had felt no qualms about allowing Kirker to associate himself with the army as a scout, and indeed found valuable the accurate detailed knowledge which Kirker and his Indian deputies possessed of the topography and its fickle climate.

The "army," one regiment of Missouri volunteers, had been encumbered by three hundred fifteen wagons belonging to the traders under its protection and eighty-five of its own, carrying hospital, ammunition, commissary, and sutlers' stores. It was not an expeditionary force designed for speed. Nor was it one to overwhelm the enemy through sheer force of numbers, considering that many hands would be required for the noncombatant duty of holding reins of horses and mules to prevent them from bolting at the sound of battle.

Trías had been anxious for the trade caravans to reach Chihuahua before the army so that he could collect taxes not paid at Santa Fe and use that money for armament. But he truculently sent word upriver that all wagons, regardless of the nationality of the owners, must have Mexican drivers. The Americans balked at this restriction and chose to stay with the army. Five traders—Connelly, Doan, McManus, Valdez, and James Magoffin—proceeded to El Paso in advance of the army to determine whether commerce across the border would be allowed. The English army officer, George Ruxton, on his journey north after his unsuccessful attempt to rescue those American mule skinners from the desert, brought back news of the traders' capture and their removal to the city of Chihuahua on charges of spying. Connelly, being a naturalized Mexican citizen, was under suspicion, but the Mexicans were particularly angry at Magoffin for his part in the unsavory Armijo affair at Santa Fe. His brother and new sister-in-law, William and Susan, in the caravan camped at Valverde waiting while Doniphan and his men rode west to subdue some rebellious Navajos, were alarmed for their brother's safety but were unable to go in pursuit.

Baptismal fire for the First Missouri Volunteers had come at Brazitos, thirty miles north of El Paso, where, on Christmas Day, Mexican dragoons and artillery surprised the Missourians in a bivouac where they were waiting for word from Wool to the south and artillery support from Price still at Santa Fe. Traders rushed to guard their precious wagons while the soldiers, caught unprepared and low on gunpowder, calculatingly had held their fire until the Mexicans were nearly upon them and then had aimed calmly with deadly, telling results. The defenders of the "honor and the glory of the Republic," as Trías had called his troops, were routed, leaving behind their cannon and all hopes for an easy victory.

Jubilant on the successful outcome of their first taste of battle, the Americans had moved to El Paso del Norte at the bend of the Río Grande where a population of four thousand now dwelt on prosperous farms in the vicinity. They had pre-empted needed food from the natives, paid by valid drafts on the quartermaster. Doniphan remembered a joke of which he had been the butt when, in procuring supplies, he had confused the English word *mice* with the Spanish word *maíz*, meaning English maize or Indian corn. The soldiers had liked the easygoing El Pasoans and had soaked up not only the warmth of the midwinter sunshine but the fire of great quantities of "pass whiskey." Doniphan had met his most difficult task in controlling their idleness. Games of monte and chuck-a-luck had blocked the streets. Drinking to excess and subsequent fighting nightly disturbed the peace. Some men had taken to amusing themselves at shooting coyotes raiding the corrals. Others made promiscuous love to full-breasted, brown-skinned girls. For forty-two days the army blissfully lounged on the south bank of the Río Grande, the soldiers content to linger in this happy town which always had welcomed Americans, while their colonel worried about lack of communication from either General Taylor or General Wool in Mexico and the upsetting news of rebellion at Taos with threat to Price's men at Santa Fe, and the traders on guard by their wagons in the plaza chafing to get on to business.

Having made the decision to press on to Chihuahua without waiting longer for orders from General Wool, Doniphan organized the traders, whom he now regarded as a worrisome responsibility, into two military companies under Skillman and Glasgow and headed by Samuel Owens. Julian K. Glasgow had been the United States consul at Guaymas, Sonora, and had come to Chihuahua to join in a business partnership with Dr. Henry Connelly, an old-timer in the trade. Owens was one of the wealthiest members of the trading party. He owned a store in Independence and was favorably regarded for having grubstaked numerous Santa Fe traders, including Webb. He was also the half brother of a girl once courted by Lincoln.

Troubles soon descended upon the party after leaving El Paso. The soft dunes of Samalayuca were a real obstacle to the large number of heavily loaded wagons. Weak, struggling teams sank to their bellies and had to be pulled out. Some of the men did not own canteens and had to carry water in their saber sheaths. Young Father Ramón Ortiz, who was being escorted south in his carriage under suspicion of spying, gave his water to the thirsty and ill-prepared and dispatched runners back to El Paso for more water. Lagging rearguard troops were forced to camp on the dunes without water and wood, but a nighttime rain had packed the sand and had provided drinking water. Several men perished in the ordeal, one from bloating after finally reaching a spring. Robards died and was buried at the foot of the stony bluff at Gallegos.

On the approach to Encinillas, a grass fire, started through a soldier's carelessness, was whipped by gusty winds. The flames crackled through the tall, dry grass spurting closer and closer to the trapped caravan. They shoved artillery pieces and ammunition to the boggy shores of the lake where they might be readily immersed. Frantic men chopped a wide swath through the grass and trampled mules back and forth to pack a firebreak. Then the capricious wind changed, and the scorched army was saved.

American soldiers stealthily approached the hacienda buildings at Encinillas, then with drawn sabers charged into the walled courtyard expecting to take Mexican soldiers stationed there off guard. They found that seven hundred Mexicans recently had been withdrawn, and all the herds of cattle and sheep had been driven off in anticipation of their arrival. From the frightened peons left to operate the hacienda, they learned that fortifications and the Mexican army awaited them at the hacienda of Sacramento.

This news had come as no surprise because Ruxton, Kirker, and other travelers passing though Chihuahua had brought detailed information about fevered Mexican preparations for defense of the capital. Doniphan knew that he could have outflanked the twenty-eight hillside trenches, but he knew, too, that a battle sooner or later was inevitable, and so he deliberately chose to meet the Mexicans at a site of their own selection. His victory thus would seem all the greater. He placed the merchant wagons at intervals in the column to avoid being cut off without support and drove his army caravan four abreast so that at any time they could fall into corral formation. They did not come to Sacramento down the valley but swung in from the side, causing confusion among Mexican troops set to fire straightaway. After a bitter, exhausting, three-hour struggle, the rough-and-ready men from Missouri stormed the heights and scattered Mexican defenders. Twelve hundred cavalrymen from Durango, Chihuahua, and Vera Cruz, twelve hundred infantrymen from Chihuahua, three hundred of the artillery and fourteen hundred civilians, armed only with lances, machetes, and lassos, had been cowed by twelve hundred excited American farm boys and traveling salesmen. Mexican losses were estimated at three hundred dead, forty prisoners, ten pieces of artillery, and the black flag with its piratical skulls used at Brazitos.[38] Americans counted two casualties, one of them a possible suicide.*

Samuel Owens, prominent in the Mexican trade, had been killed in an assault on one of the dugouts. Captain Reid and a small detachment of men had dashed along the fortification to attract the fire of the Mexicans, forcing them to reload their guns. During the momentary pause caused by reloading, American troops rushed the trench and overwhelmed it. Owens, however, had not obeyed orders and had run his horse straight into the redoubt, to pass into romantic legend. Stories immediately circu-

---

* Connelly in Hughes's reprint (1907) gives the American loss as one killed, seven wounded. 436. Hughes earlier stated that one American was killed and eleven were wounded, three of whom later died. Fn. 115.

lated, to expand and become adorned by later campfires, of how that day he had deliberately worn a distinguishing white suit and had ridden a white pony to make himself an easy target. Spicy speculations of marital difficulties, financial entanglements, and hopeless illness were lugubriously relished.

Doniphan was thrilled by the performance of his raw army of individualists and realized that his unwavering faith in them had been justified. He leaned on the side of the dusty carriage of the priest-prisoner from El Paso as he boasted, "Well, Ortiz, what do you have to say about the Mexicans whipping my boys now?"

"Ah, señor Doniphan," Father Ortiz quickly had answered, "they would have beaten you if you had fought like men, but you fought like devils!"[39]

Devils was just what the Chihuahua populace expected them to be. Large numbers of townspeople had trooped to the battleground in carriages, on horseback, and on foot to sit in vantage points on the ridges to watch sadistically the almost certain defeat of the untrained gringos and to be on hand to claim the spoils of battle, particularly the fleet of canvas-topped merchant wagons. When they came to the painful realization that it was not the invaders who were being crushed, they had rushed headlong in bitter, blinding disappointment back to their homes in the city to either barricade their doors or to pack for immediate withdrawal. Their leaders had warned of the doom and disorder to come in the event of American victory.

The few Americans still in the city sought refuge with the Englishman Potts and his brother on the flat roof of the mint. Since prisoners had been freed, there was some apprehension concerning the money in the mint. Some of the liberated prisoners joined the defenders, but others took this opportunity of official distraction to rob, loot, and rape. The men on the roof were armed with guns and several leaden tubs of acid. They could see the battlefield off to the north, but because of the haze of distance and smoke of the skirmish, they could not make out just what was happening. They soon learned to distinguish the sharp report of American guns from the deep, prolonged sound of Mexican artillery. At times it seemed the Americans were winning, and then the Mexicans. They held no hope for the outnumbered invaders because they, too, had been influenced by the local press. There were fleeting misgivings about their own fate in the heat of a Mexican victory. After several hours they began to see a few sightseers coming back from Sacramento. Then more and more horses and carriages raced crazily toward town in terrorized confusion. Tearful shouts of "Ya vienen!" ricocheted through the winding streets, and the refugees on the mint roof realized the impossible had happened. They would be able to see Old Glory fly over the green plaza.

In the days following the triumphal entry into the city, Doniphan, in the pattern of conquerors, issued a florid proclamation. He wanted to reassure the populace. Mexicans were urged to continue life as before. Word was sent to Parral asking Trías, Heredia, and García Conde, the whipped, classical strategists of Sacramento, to return to the capital, but they refused. Doniphan's chief concern was merely to keep Chihuahua out of the war raging to the east. Zachary Taylor's great victory over Santa Ana at Buena Vista was then only rumored. He wanted internal free trade in Mexico for Americans but did not object to national import duties. He demanded security for American citizens residing in the state. The band of Americans confined at Cusihuiriáchi for six months traveled north to the city to join those from Missouri in a rebirth of commerce. Bustling shops appeared around the plaza. It was business as usual. Albert Speyer was taken into custody immediately, charged with smuggling arms to aid the enemy. Some thought hanging was too good for him. However, he was tried and acquitted. Perhaps his extravagant entertaining and the elegant gifts of silver bridles and silver fans he presented to the American officers had some influence. Who can say?

The cathedral was the scene of a pompous funeral for Major Samuel Owens. All of the local priests participated. This service gave rise to a popular feeling that a holy shrine had been profaned just as the clergy had predicted.*

Day followed routine day with no word from the American forces to the east. To the south in Vera Cruz, Winfield Scott was reported to have taken the Caribbean gateway to Mexico, but where was General Wool? Doniphan felt deserted, not knowing

---

* Owens was not a Catholic although many writers since have called him one. See Gibson, 1935, 354.

what his course of action was to be. Should he march his disorderly regiment still farther south hoping to meet General Zachary Taylor, or should he move east to find General Wool? Or should he return to Missouri? What of the merchants who had fought side by side with his volunteers? Should they be abandoned to the mercy of irate Mexicans only too anxious for revenge and for profit from American merchandise, or should they be ordered north? It was becoming increasingly difficult to control his men. Many of the one-year enlistments were up. Most men had not been paid. And none seemed capable of tedious garrison duty. Unhappy grumblings were drowned out in abandoned carousing and all the excesses of leisure without need. Trouble was apt to erupt at any time.

In desperation, Doniphan gambled on sending an express to find Wool and request instructions. Twelve riders, led by the trader James Collins, were dispatched to race across five hundred miles of majestic, but barren, enemy territory, avoiding encounters with Indians or Mexicans by traveling at night. Orders were sewed into saddle pads. Guns were cleaned and made ready. They moved swiftly south to Saucillo where they attempted to angle eastward, but lack of water forced their return to the main corridor. At Jiménez they succeeded in swinging into the Bolsón de Mapimí, keeping near the customary route to Saltillo. Luckier than Speyer's mule skinners, fifteen days later the express arrived in a lather at Wool's headquarters.

Doniphan's camp held out faint hope for the success of the express. When unfounded rumors spread, and were believed, that all the gallant men of the mission had been killed, it seemed time to call a general meeting to discuss the entire problem. Already thirty-eight men had been discharged at the end of their enlistments and had left Chihuahua following the Conchos route to Presidio del Norte on the Río Grande, cutting across Texas plains to Fort Towson on the Red River. Colonel Doniphan proposed to take his restless army out of Mexico that way if contrary orders were not received soon. He stood before the troubled gathering as he formerly had stood before juries, forcefully pleading his cause, artfully persuasive and deeply angry. He banged on the table by which he stood, shouting, "I'm for going home to Sarah and the children!" Not everyone agreed with him. Some of his lieutenants were for going on to Mexico City itself, if need be. But preparations were begun to evacuate Chihuahua on April 25 and for the march northeast to Presidio and San Antonio. Suddenly the entire army was homesick and wanted to go home to all the Sarahs and children left on the Missouri farms. They were tired of what seemed a war without purpose or direction.

Two days before evacuation day, forty-two men returned from Saltillo bringing orders for the First Missouri Volunteers to join Wool's column there as soon as possible. The Collins group and some Arkansas Volunteers under direction of Captain Albert Pike had retraced the trail from the east. They had traveled openly, proclaiming themselves scouts of Wool. Fear of reprisals from the oncoming American army kept Mexicans outwardly friendly and eager to furnish supplies.

In the party from Saltillo was Josiah Gregg. He wished to claim his effects which had come south from Santa Fe in the thirty-wagon caravan of Samuel Owens. He reported having met the feeble survivors of the band of teamsters "escaped" from Speyer's caravan in southern Chihuahua and also the train of the wily Señor Armijo.[40]

On April 28, 1847, the fifty-nine-day American occupation of the Chihuahua capital ended. Silently, the citizens, impassive and unemotional in the wake of defeat, stood on street corners to watch wagons pull out of the bullring and soldiers dismantle their cantonment in the plaza. The predicted disaster had been a dud. Occupation had been raucous but not ruinous. Complaints had been made of sacking the historical archives in the Palacio de Gobierno,* of seizure and distribution of the grains stored in the public granary, and of general disrespect for the beauties of the city. But 800,000 pesos were left untouched in the mint, and personal lives and property were unchallenged. Damage had been relatively slight. Some natives nursed a sense of acridity years would blur but not obliterate, but this was owing principally to ruffled pride—to insult rather than to real injury. Unabashed, others had enjoyed the boisterous fun and unrestrained debauchery of living as if there were no *mañanas*, and who cared?

---

* At a later date the remainder of the archives of the colonial Comandancia General de Provincias Internas was sold by the French forces to merchants to be used as packing for merchandise. Almada, 1938c, 73.

Traders universally were disgruntled over what they felt was a sudden decision to leave. They protested that some of them had no wagons nor could they obtain any on such short notice. They questioned the wisdom of routing the army via Saltillo and Matamoros, pointing out that if they returned via Santa Fe, it would not be necessary to depart so soon. They refused to recognize the hard fact that Washington, then, did not care a tinker's damn what happened to them. The regiment had been ordered east, and east it went. A number of the traders traveled with it, but experienced great difficulties in maintaining the fast pace set by Doniphan.

They moved down through Bachimba, San Pablo, and Saucillo to Santa Rosalía at the junction of the Conchos and Florido. There they saw the meager fortifications which had been prepared to meet their original advance should they have bypassed the city of Chihuahua. At Jiménez they saw signs of recent Indian raids. On they rode to San José de Pelayo, a decayed colonial presidio, to the broad saline lakes on the eastern desert which for centuries had supplied salt for the smoking smelters of Parral.* On May 6, the American army of invasion left Chihuahua soil and entered an unenchanted region claimed by the Comanche. It was still five months before the hill of the grasshopper, Chapultepec, would be taken by Scott's army to bring an end to the war.

The unmitigated heat and suffocating dust of the late dry season made travel exceedingly unpleasant. Nostrils clogged and tongues swelled. Trader Gregg was the butt of much sarcasm as he jogged along holding a large, red umbrella overhead and fretfully worried over botanical specimens. Fatigued soldiers slumped and almost fell from their saddles. Obstinate mules became more unmanageable. When the army bedded down at night, the desert produced scorpions and lizards. Grumbles were heard as men tried to make themselves comfortable on the hard ground. With increasing frequency as the wet cycle moved in, the skies glowed with brilliant lightning, thunder burst from horizon to far horizon, and rain beat down suddenly and relentlessly, whipping at rags of clothing and soaking equipment. Dr. Wislisenius, now a practicing doctor with the troops, had much to do to keep the army moving.

---

* After the middle of the seventeenth century, salt also came from northern Chihuahua and New Mexico, with Mansos and Pueblos being the main suppliers. West, 1949, 37.

Indians added to their difficulties. Sixty-five Comanche were defeated in one engagement, and a thousand head of stolen horses and cattle were recaptured and returned to their rightful owners. The irony of risking their necks to fight the enemies of men who had so recently been their own did not escape the volunteers. Straggling trader wagons, such as those of young Magoffin, had to be hurried to the main body of troops to prevent Indian ambush.

In Parras, a famous wine center, the hardships of the trail were forgotten in a brisk round of drinking and revelry which came to an abrupt end when one celebrating soldier was brained with a rock by a zealous Mexican pickpocket.

At Saltillo, the brave but almost ignored battalion was honored in review by General Wool. The swaggering general, resplendent in military finery, stood at stiff attention as the men of the First Missouri Volunteers paraded in irregular, unmilitary formation, but still full of heart, in rags caked with desert mud. They sailed from the Halls of Montezuma in overcrowded, stinking transports "to Sarah and the children" and thundering, cheering ovations upon arrival in New Orleans and St. Louis. With them went the infamous James Kirker.[41] There they deposited the black flag captured at Sacramento with the Missouri Historical Society and went back to rural hamlets to assume roles of community heroes until they were superseded by participants in the upcoming Civil War. They had walked, joked, brawled, and cursed their way over thirty-five hundred miles of the middle girth of America. The historian De Voto called the adventure "The Anabasis in Homespun."[42]

Ten merchants elected to remain in Chihuahua. One of these, James Aull, a business partner of the dead Owens, was murdered two weeks later. Another, Alfonso C. Anderson, so popular before the war that he had been permitted to stay when all the other Americans had been expelled to Cusihuiriáchi, became a United States vice-consul to Chihuahua. Forty other traders went north by way of a circuit to Corralitos and Santa Rita and then up to Socorro to avoid any possible trouble at the El Paso customs station. In their haste, they carried only heavy bags of specie. James Webb, still a lone wolf, followed the Camino Real and re-entered New Mexico without incident. He later became a legislator from the territory of New Mexico and still later a senator from his home state of Connecticut.

The American forces in Santa Fe had been divided into four groups. Three of them ultimately penetrated into modern Mexico. General Kearny had led one party west along the Gila River to the Pacific and, after the treaty of Guadalupe Hidalgo, became governor of the new American territory of California. Another group, and the first one actually to enter and to leave Chihuahua, was the Mormon Battalion.[43] Five infantry companies of converts to the Church of Jesus Christ of Latter-day Saints were organized in Missouri to trace a satisfactory wagon route from Santa Fe to San Diego. This preceded by a year the other Morman movement into the depression of the Great Salt Lake. The men of the battalion were to be in the service of their country for one year, to be mustered out in California where they had wished to colonize, and to be allowed to keep their firearms. Under command of Philip St. George Cooke, the only battalion in United States Army history composed of members of one religious sect traveled down the Río Grande, departing from the road in the lower valley and moving out southwestward into the Apache homeland of southern New Mexico.

From there, on advice of their scouts, the valiant Mormon boys trekked south of the Santa Rita mines toward the high sierra hoping to find a pass through which to take their ponderous wagons. For a time they followed the old trail toward Fronteras, Sonora, and then rode more northwesterly to the Guadalupe Pass. They were endangered by continual lack of potable water and a dim trail leading them through hazardous country nearly impossible for wagon traffic. Stouthearted and not easily swayed from the dogged determination to reach new homesites in California, all refused to turn back. They pushed and shoved, raised and lowered, took wagons apart, carried them up perpendicular cliffs in pieces, and reassembled them. After stupendous physical efforts, the crossing was negotiated in a wild region north of the actual pass. Had they gone due west from the point where they had left the Río Grande, they would have had fairly flat, easy going. François Aubry, Santa Fe trader with a reputation as a fantastic rider, first covered this route to California, and later it was the way surveyed by the Southern Pacific Railroad in its push to the west coast.

West of the Guadalupe Pass, the Mormon Battalion looked down into a beautiful, green valley once occupied by the flourishing San

Bernardino rancho. Continual Indian depredations had forced abandonment of a promising cattle range well supplied with good, clear water and lush vegas, or meadows. In curiosity, the men probed the rambling adobe establishment, musty rooms with mud roofs sifting through the beams, carved doors unhinged, mighty bastions disintegrating from force of elements and vandalism. The cattle, those which had escaped capture by the Apache, had been turned loose to run wild and forage for themselves. Huge and ferocious, they attacked when challenged, thoroughly frightening the Mormon soldiers.

BY THE TREATY of Guadalupe Hidalgo, the international boundary was set a little north of the 32nd parallel; the Mexican government was paid $15,000,000; and all claims of American citizens against the Mexican government were assumed. Upper California, Arizona, and most of New Mexico became United States property.

One month after the treaty was signed, Sterling Price, commandant at Santa Fe, ordered fifteen hundred American soldiers into Chihuahua once again. This time Governor Trías met the army at Sacramento with a white truce flag and the information that the treaty had been signed. Price, distrustful of the Mexican governor known to be violently anti-American, marched on to Chihuahua and Santa Rosalía. At the fortifications prepared to halt Doniphan, the Americans and the Mexicans staged a postwar battle. A heroic but hopeless defense of the little plaza gave the Mexicans a third defeat. Price's men moved on out of the state. Nothing was accomplished by this comic opera episode except to enhance the position of Angel Trías, the father, with his own people.[44]

The drama of the war in Chihuahua was ended. Fame and misfortune awaited some of its leading characters. Colonel Doniphan and Brigadier General Price were awarded ceremonial swords in recognition of their efforts in the campaign. Doniphan came face to face with stark tragedy in the accidental deaths of two sons, one by drowning and one through mistaken administration of poison during an illness. Price, active in Missouri politics, became governor of the state. He later returned to Mexico to fight for Maximilian and to attempt a colonization project which failed. John T. Hughes, self-proclaimed historian of Doniphan's regiment, wrote a book of its madcap adventures and, in so doing, became one of Missouri's best known men. General Kearny, ordered to Mexico after the war's termination as a governor of Vera Cruz, contracted a tropical fever, and died.

None of the traders received indemnities from the government, which ruled that Doniphan had no official sanction to press them into military service. Many of them continued to return each year to the inviting Chihuahua markets. Webb became a wealthy merchant and politician and remained active in the trade until the Civil War. Albert Speyer, the man suspected of being an agent for the Mexicans, went to Europe in 1848 to buy goods for the Mexican market which he freighted overland via the south Texas route. After retiring from this work, he moved to Kansas City and then to New York. There he was involved in a stock market crash and committed suicide. Henry Connelly, once a Mexican citizen, served as governor of New Mexico under the Lincoln administration. James Collins, the trader who had acted as translator for Doniphan and who had headed the daring express to General Wool, published the *Santa Fe Gazette*. One morning he was found murdered in his office. The trader whose name has appeared most frequently in accounts of forty-niners going west through El Paso was James Magoffin, he who had persuaded Armijo that American control of New Mexico was inevitable. He, like Speyer, had bought his freedom with champagne and conviviality. He became one of the three American owners of property on the north bank of the Río Grande opposite El Paso del Norte, where he operated large repair shops and well-stocked warehouses to outfit travelers, and gained fame secondarily as a lavish host.

The battle reverses, which critics of the Mexican president called the Santa Anan betrayal of the Mexican people, resulted in the loss of half their national territory. It was the eve of one of the most fabulous gold rushes in history. Within a year, gold in quantity was recovered from a Mexican colony just lost. Within that same year, a new procession of American adventurers passed through the Mexican northlands.

EL DORADO, Cíbola, or Quivira—the golden mirage which beguiled a nation into monumental exploration—for three hundred years haunted the misty frontiers of Spanish America only to become a reality too late. On January 24, 1848, just nine days before the signing of the treaty at the national shrine of Guadalupe, gold was seen in the millrace on the American River in the high mountains of California. After three hundred years of hardship, travail, hope, and discouragement, fortune beyond count had slipped through the numbed fingers of Hispanic empire. The Johnny-come-lately Americans, who seemed to have luck riding on their shoulders, had claim to the treasure, not the Mexicans. It was then all the more grievous to have many of the highways to the riches cut across Mexico.[45] As they had been made to do many times in the past, Chihuahuenses resigned themselves to an unfortunate situation.

Roads westward were many and difficult, but none were more trying than those charted through northern Mexico. Veterans of the Mexican campaigns with some knowledge of the terrain to be crossed were in demand as wagon-train masters. James Kirker returned to serve as guide and interpreter for the westbound gold seekers.[46] Men who only a year before had gone home to dull, peacetime occupations were once again on an exciting march through Mexico.

San Antonio long had been attempting to break in on the traffic to Chihuahua. The Texas city now became the jumping-off center, a thriving market where argonauts bound for the Pacific could be made ready for the crossing of the thousand-mile vacuum which lay between. Suppliers stocked shotguns, six-shooters, knives, ammunition, mirrors, compasses, riding and pack saddles, bridles, nails, rope, blankets, clothing, and horses and mules. Packs had to be well planned and compact. No essentials could be overlooked because lives might depend upon having some particular item, but nothing extra could be hauled to hinder rapid progress.

Organization of the caravans usually was along military lines with elected officers in full command. They stopped on holidays and Sundays, which were celebrated with religious services, community sings, or group games. Mules were used to carry provisions and water for a hundred-mile stretch. Each man started with at least a gallon of water in gourds and canteens hung on his mules. As the provisions were used each day, more water was added. Additional supplies were hauled in wagons.

One well-used road followed a trail blazed by Lieutenants Whiting and Smith from San Antonio through the sage and mesquite of southwest Texas to El Paso, now a booming town athwart the muddy Río Grande. In the first year of Mexican independence, a tract of land on the north bank had been granted to Juan Ponce de León, known as Ponce's Hacienda. After the upper side of the river became American territory in 1848, Ponce had sold out to trader Benjamin Franklin Coons, who created a caravan center called Franklin. This property lay near Magoffinsville, home of James Magoffin. By 1857, the American settlement also took the name of El Paso, and in 1859 it was made official with the establishment of a municipal government. In 1849, however, the area was a vital crossroads for north-south, east-west travel. By midyear four hundred wagons had pulled through the cluster of adobe buildings toward the land of golden opportunity after having bartered with local Mexicans for provisions from the productive valley farms. El Paso always had impressed American travelers as a delightful oasis in an otherwise desolate region, and it never had looked more welcome than it did to forty-niners.

From El Paso the trail went upriver about thirty miles, the established Camino Real, to the site of modern Las Cruces (where the roads crossed or intersected). At this point was a junction. Caravans could either turn due west to Tucson or swing southwest to Janos and then over Cooke's route to Guadalupe Pass and northern Sonora.

From San Antonio another road ran south to the Río Grande, now the international boundary, and kept to the river up to Presidio del Norte where an American named Seaton operated a combined fort and trading post in an abandoned Franciscan mission to deal with the Indians of the river and Mexicans on scattered rancherías. During the period of the mass migration to California, this settlement, because of its location on a junction, also thrived. A northern road continued near the twisting river to El Paso. Another branch led down the Río Conchos, the route of the first conquistadors, looped west to the isolated town of Coyame where needed food and pure water always were obtainable, then southwest again along the Conchos to Santa Rosalía and the main Chihuahua corridor. Wagon trains turned south toward Durango and ultimately to the port of Mazatlán, after traversing an almost unbelievably confused knot of mountains, to wait for occasional ships which sailed for San Francisco. Or, the wagons went west to the city of Chihuahua. From there the Camino Real was followed to the north end of Lago de Encinillas where a branch road cut west through a rocky pass and north to the yellow plains of Galeana, Casas Grandes, Corralitos, and Janos.

A further trail came into Chihuahua at the eastern border village of San Carlos, hazardously traversed the arid deserts and mountains of Serranias del Burro to Presidio. A route most used by men landing on the Texas coast came overland to Saltillo, Parras, and then into southern Chihuahua at Jiménez, retreading the line of march of Doniphan's regiment.

All across the States men hung up their plows and boarded up their shops to join the mad rush. Many were physically unfit and materially unprepared for the strenuous trip involved. A goodly number were buried on grey Mexican deserts with the hushed reading of the Twenty-third Psalm, victims of starvation, thirst, scurvy, or Indian torture. A year of deadly cholera epidemics in the southern states and in Mexico was 1849, and many on their way to gold camps went instead to Paradise. One of the six thousand Mexican cholera victims of that year was the former governor of Chihuahua, Francisco García Conde.

The routes through Mexico were considered expensive; one hundred pounds of provisions, enough for one man, cost seventeen dollars! Mexicans and American residents in Chihuahua profited by the growing wave of tourists which provided a ready market for food products and for beasts. Salt, flour, *pinole*, sugar, coffee, hard bread, and fruit-jelly pastes were sold at high prices. Flour, for example, was eleven dollars for three hundred pounds. Beef cured by drying and pounding with lard and chile sold for thirty-three dollars a hundred pounds. A pinch of the preparation added to a pot of boiling water and thickened with cornmeal made a filling meal. Rooms in Riddells' hotel off the plaza rented for a dollar and a half a day, with animal board at the stables being thirty-seven cents a day. Some Mexicans found lucrative employment in manufacturing leather canteens and packsaddles used by the wagon trains.[47]

THE RETURN to Chihuahua of the Americans was overshadowed by stepped-up Indian activity. For a number of years Mexicans were inclined to believe that the Americans were really the guilty ones in the perplexing situation with the Indians, particularly the Apache. They felt that Washington encouraged raiding into Mexico by permitting the Indians to keep their guns and by not sending pursuit forces into the Indian homelands. Mexico demanded large indemnification. Actually, the United States had no authority in that region of southwestern New Mexico and was hamstrung in chastisement. The Animas, Peloncillo, and Chiricahua mountains technically were Mexican, although Mexican patrols had not been mounted there for years. Americans were suffering at the hands of the same Indians.

Sensing the weakness of Mexican defenses and the low morale following the American invasion, Apache hostilities increased southward in strength and audacity. Northern Chihuahua withered and decayed like a melon snapped from the vine. Adobe walls of abandoned ranch houses melted back to earth. Garden plots strangled in weeds. Herds of stock were dissipated. It was estimated that ten thousand head of horses annually were driven north out of Mexico by Indians to be sold to Texans and other Southwesterners. A country normally lonely now became empty. Despair led to revival of the despicable bounty system, although it was vetoed by Governor Trías on grounds of its inhumanity. A dead Apache warrior's scalp was worth 200 pesos. Each male captured alive brought 250 pesos, each woman or child under fourteen years of age, 150 pesos. Americans, as well as Mexicans, joined in the hunt.[48] Boldly, flauntingly, the Indians struck at the outskirts of the capital itself, killing peons as they worked in the fields.

The federal government proposed to establish a chain of military colonies along its new borders for protection against both the Americans and the Indians. Four companies were designated for Indian duty in Chihuahua. A general conscription of all men between the ages of eighteen and fifty-five for short tours of military duty failed because those who should have led flagrantly disregarded and abused the law. Brave intentions were negated by surprising public indifference and chronic impoverishment. A government atrophied by prevailing low morality in public office and a citizenry influenced by a dismal, fatalistic outlook on the one-hundred-fifty-year-old Indian war were incapable of resolution.

Despite screams of "subterfuge" and "underhanded dealings," in 1853 the United States further dismembered Mexico by the pur-

chase of land in southern New Mexico and Arizona for $10,000,-
ooo. Angel Trías, the elder, was notified that New Mexican troops
had taken possession of La Mesilla and the territory to the west.
Once again Trías was put in the role of defender of the fatherland.
War had swept around with a stinging backlash, and Trías would
not be caught unprepared. He sent two trusted men, Antonio Ja-
quez and Tomás Zuloaga, to confer with the New Mexico governor, while Luis Zuloaga mobilized forces and marched up and
down the border. Santa Ana, in secret, without ratification from
any Mexican congress, had sold another large part of Mexico,
45,535 square miles, to the American minister to Mexico, James
Gadsden. A grandson of one of the delegates to the Continental
Congress which had sought American sovereignty, Gadsden now
aided his nation to become landlord of a piece of Mexico inhabited
principally by rattlesnakes, coyotes, and warlike aborigines. The
crafty Mexican president who liked to be called "Supreme High-
ness," for whom the Chihuahua state flag had flown at half mast
during an imprisonment in Texas, ordered obedient Trías to accept the new boundary. Trías, duty bound but discontented with
his old leader, delayed six months in publishing the treaty in Chihuahua.[49] Meanwhile, Zuloaga and his men did sweating squads-
right and -left in the wilderness.

Superficially, the United States bought the region involved south
of the 32nd parallel so that controls on the Indians might be enforced. That was what the Mexicans had said they wanted. Another, but undiscussed, reason was to gain a level, all-weather
railroad route to the Pacific.

Some Mexicans preferred to remain under the red, white, and
green banner with its Aztec symbol. New border towns grew from
clusters of migrants from Texas and the Mesilla valley. Ascensión,
near Janos, and Zaragoza, downriver from El Paso, were two such
centers.[50]

President Polk had appointed a commission under John B.
Weller to survey for the new international boundary. John Russell
Bartlett succeeded Weller and did much toward a detailed scientific study of the little-known country on both sides of the border,
even to a description of the ruins of Casas Grandes a hundred
miles in the interior. Lieutenant Colonel W. H. Emory took over
after the Gadsden Purchase and completed the long and difficult

task. A Mexican team, headed by engineer José Salazar Ilarregui, worked with the Americans. Both commissions had financial and physical setbacks. The Mexicans were forced to sell their technical library by "cubic weight," so a government report said, in order to meet field expenses.[51]

One of the members of the border commission was Pedro García Conde, younger brother of the former Chihuahua governor. He had had an illustrious career as director of the military college in Mexico City and had begun a reconstruction program at the National Palace. During the American intervention, he had led the cavalry forces at Sacramento and later wrote an account of the fateful battle. From the hardships and privations suffered during the cartographic survey, García Conde developed severe rheumatism and went to Arizpe, Sonora, to rest and recover. He died there in the arms of his boyhood nurse.

ON BOTH SIDES of the Río Grande, oppression, treachery, poverty, and slavery bred civil war. It erupted first in tormented Mexico, hopelessly shackled by the two pervading forces left from Spanish domination: military miasma and medieval clericalism. Dynamic leadership passed from the hands of conservative criollos and Santa Ana partisans to liberal mestizos and pure-blooded Indians. Basic protests were agrarian. A landless peasantry in an agricultural economy suffered mass misery. Relief was demanded from a parasitic Church which monopolized half the money and land in a nation of potential wealth and actual bankruptcy. Again, Chihuahua was out of step. The fundamental problem was geographical and ethnic. Whether the Church or the hacendados had legal claim to her plains and her valleys did not matter. The Indians were the true masters. Landowners, large or small, could not challenge them. A central government, secure for three hundred years from overthrow by Indians, frequently failed to appreciate the northern dilemma. Confederation of the northern states was the topic of discussion in cafes and *cantinas*.

The modern game of Mexican politics began in the north. The Laws of Reform and the Constitution of 1857 of Benito Juárez and his intellectuals divided the state and the nation into two camps. Political parades and posses, pro and con Juárez, armed with *manifestos, pronunciamientos*, and pistols, marched or rode over stony ridges and gritty, alluvial fans to remote, dusty plazas to proclaim local victories, leaving adversaries crumpled in the streets. Power shifted from side to side, from caudillo to caudillo. Sometimes the conservative *santanista* Zuloaga brothers (one of whom had named himself president of the nation after endorsing a Plan of Tacubaya) were in control, with the wealth and crushing power of the clergy openly used to further their reactionary cause. Luis Zuloaga had served for a time as governor, but his enormous gambling debts and general inefficiency led to his removal from office. At other times, the warrior-lawyer Coronado swept through the state and beyond to bring fleeting victory to the liberals and renewed hopes for a northern coalition. Trías, the old war-horse who for over a decade had been Santa Ana's hatchet man, deserted the ranks to fight for the liberal movement gaining momentum everywhere. For his defense of the capital, the legislature authorized a golden medal, but it was never presented.

When conservative invaders rode from the *monte** of northern Durango to rout liberal defenders hurriedly rushed to southern Allende, then conquered the city of bridges, Parral, and the capital itself, factions under a *juarista* banner united to drive them out. Domingo Cajen, a fanatically religious Spaniard who saw himself as a reincarnation of the conquistadors of the 1500's dedicated to conquer New Spain for the glory of the Roman Catholic Church, placed a puppet governor, Juan Barcenas, in the government building on Plaza Hidalgo.[52] Seeking to force him out were Juan José Méndez, Joaquín Terrazas, and Luis Terrazas, representatives of a new provincial intellectualism which opposed the stifling power of the hierarchies of Church and army. Fighting through the cobblestone streets of the city, in the dry arroyos under the arches of the aqueduct, across the farmlands by the Chuvíscar, liberal guerrillas, sustained by a corps of sharpshooting riflemen from the sierra, succeeded in slaughtering the Cajen soldiers from Durango. Cajen was executed, presumably as he tried to escape. The Laws of Reform triumphed in Chihuahua.

In 1860, within a month after the Cajen incident, Luis Terrazas, with the rank of colonel bestowed for a single raid on the treasury when Barcenas was looking for Méndez in the mountains, was

---

* Literally mountain, used colloquially as dense, scrub plant growth.

designated governor of the state. He was thirty-one years old, still not the legal minimum age for the high office.[53] But he was the man of the hour, so an exception was made. In a country noted for contradictions, Terrazas became the greatest contradiction of all. He was beloved, his honor and name defended with voluminous, biased prose and oratory. He was scorned, condemned, suspected, and held up as a tarnished symbol of a decadent era. He was to become "Señor Chihuahua."

Strong monarchial sympathies, though quiescent, were still alive in Mexico. The reactionary faction played on these sympathies. In 1810 and again in 1823, royalist Chihuahua had been reluctant to climb on the bandwagon of independence. Now widespread poverty, lack of constructive development in education, economics, and political life, uncurbed depredations of the Indians, and the ridiculous and devastating events of the American war of 1848 easily were blamed on ineffective, often illiterate, Mexican leadership. In the confusion of the period of the administration of Juárez, the arrival of foreign troops did not seem earthshaking. The United States was itself in the throes of a death struggle and unable to back up the widely touted Monroe Doctrine. Spain, France, and England, at the invitation of conservative envoys, eyed the rich Mexican plum. In this grab bag of international politics, France drew the prize. A mere fifteen years after young cadets had given their lives in defense of the hill of Chapultepec, French forces with an Austrian king came to build a castle there. Juárez sought refuge in the relatively stable north.

To men of the northern frontier, where all efforts were devoted to survival, where work often brought no fruition and religion little gratification, no enemy other than the Indians on horseback could be comprehended. Alone they had faced the Indian menace. Had anyone in Mexico done more than offer solace and advice? Had the central government sent relief from the American occupation? Had Juárez channeled financial aid to the brave ones who toppled *tacubayistas*? No! Now when a quota of two thousand soldiers was ordered to help repel an imperialist invasion in the central highlands at the expense of safety at home, Terrazas felt justified in refusal. It seems plausible that he meant no treason or insurrection.[54] A lifetime on the borderlands had taught him that the Apache would attack at the slightest sign of weakness.

To unsmiling Juárez, called a champion of law without soul, there was no excuse for disobedience. Danger was relative. To him, the strength of a ruthless, greedy Napoleon, encouraged by conservative elements in Mexico willing to forfeit sovereignty in return for hollow pomp and circumstance and ecclesiastical status quo, was a far more serious threat to his country than a handful of bloodletting Indians who rode like shadows through the night. Added to Juárez's calloused disregard of desperate pleas for help against the Indians were thorny problems of administration which Terrazas as a green governor had not been able to solve to the president's satisfaction. Touchy matters of amortization of Church properties and their resale, of adjudication of public forest and grazing lands, and of proper deposition of customs funds collected at Chihuahua's northern ports of entry—these were complex problems, the solution of which cried for men of vision and fortitude. For a butcher and small landholder turned governor, pitfalls were everywhere. Some were the work of cunning political enemies who had Juárez's ear. Terrazas had the misfortune of coming to power at the wrong time.[55]

From his temporary headquarters in Monterrey, Juárez declared Chihuahua in a state of siege, replaced Terrazas with knee-bending Jesús José Casavantes and General Patoni to enforce his dictates.[56] Many felt this move to be a high-handed rebuke for an honest difference of opinion. Other liberals were encouraged by what they considered a strengthening of their position in the north. At this time Trías, as military commander, had to confiscate the property of his young friend, Terrazas, now dethroned and sulking at El Paso del Norte but soon to be back in the charmed circle.

Juárez was president of a government on the run, and he ran for the border. The dour-appearing, dusky Indian who had come to be the white hope of many Mexicans rode into Chihuahua's Plaza de la Constitución on October 12, 1864.[57] In later years, October 12 was a day to be celebrated north of the Río Grande as Columbus Day, south as Día de la Raza, Day of the Race, when sentimental stanzas glorify the great Indian substratum of which Benito Juárez was an outstanding example. However, in the middle of the last century it was not fashionable to have had Indian ancestors. In Juárez's case, as in that of many of the leaders of the Reformación and their fighters in the hills, the racial fact was accepted but not lauded. Perennial Governor Don Angel, who doubled as military commander, had awaited the president at Rancho de Avalos south of the capital. His gilded carriage drawn by matched high-stepping Spanish horses discreetly followed the dust-blanketed one in which Juárez rode as a procession formed at the outskirts.

Tattered remnants of a nationalist army escorted their indomitable leader for two months across a hostile wilderness to safety. Yet safety is an illusion. There can be no refuge without hope. Juárez did not know the true enemy of the north. He had eyes and hatred only for the French interventionists who sullied the central mesas. His traveling party foolishly went through land of easy ambush, thinking not of the danger of sharp wheels miring accidentally or of untimely carriage breakdown. Yet monarchial sympathizers known to be lurking in the northlands, lost behind distant clumps of cottonwoods, patrolling boulder-strewn passes between desert hills, did not disturb the president. His enemies, he fanatically and falsely believed, were those of all Mexicans, the miserable French grenadiers and their blond Maximilian, Archduke of Austria, now Emperor of Mexico. It would seem, though, he had not an enemy in the world as he rolled into the Chihuahuan capital.

Never in the history of the young republic had the highest officer of the land visited this outpost. Many of the shadowy figures to float through the presidential palace had not held office long enough to tour the states. Many had known no need or desire to show themselves to the ignorant multitude. All had been too preoccupied with ending one revolt and starting another. Now Chihuahua, rebuffed by the administration, its domain sold off and its affiliations forced northward, was to be host to the president. It mattered not that he was a president without a government or a man without glittering uniform or flowery title. Nor did it matter now that he had angered the padres and scorned the generals. He *was* the president to the Chihuahuenses, and he had come to the shelter of their city.

Arches made of evergreen boughs and fall flowers spanned the street, soon to be renamed Juárez. Banners reaffirmed adhesion to the liberal regime with large letters reading *Chihuahua con Juárez.* In a display of emotion, children vigorously waved small tricolored flags and grown-ups shouted "Viva!" as the stoic Indian sat erect and nodding in his carriage. No glimmer of pleasure or satisfaction crossed his stern features. The fiesta-minded citizens did not care. They ignited rockets to boom a rousing welcome as an honor guard led by Joaquín Terrazas smartly paraded around the plaza, new guns from the States on their shoulders. Back up Calle Libertad the procession moved toward the hallowed shrine of Papá Hidalgo. Here Juárez, in a rumpled black frock coat, spoke a few solemn words in memory of the man who willingly gave his life for the sacred cause of independence just as they, the citizens of a new and better Mexico of the future, now must be prepared to do. It was said hardly a dry eye could be seen in the emotional throng, thrilled with a sense of high destiny, packed into the patio of the building.

Outside, other spectators sat hunched on heels or leaned against the building, content just to be in an atmosphere of excitement. One president or another, one strutting general or an alien king, made no difference to them. Republic or monarchy, there still were never enough *frijoles*, the Mexican staff of life.

An occasional Tarahumara in from the high mountains edged his way through the congestion, curious to look upon the face of a man some said was Indian, too, who aspired to be a leader of white men. Not being able to get inside the palacio, he quietly continued on his way, eyes down on sandals and dirty feet, aware that this was not his problem.

Notably absent was Luis Terrazas. Through fear or discretion he had remained in El Paso, uncertain of his reception should he return to Chihuahua. Never one to enjoy being on the outside, he resolved to cross the dunes and take his chances. Back in the city, Juárez, with the aplomb of politicians everywhere and needing friends wherever they were obtainable, gave him *abrazos*. Luis was in.

Through the winter, decrees and proclamations poured from the pen of the fugitive president to be printed in volume by local presses. Trías, in his familiar role as an executive officer carrying out unpleasant tasks, forced a "loan" of 10,000 pesos from the residents of the city and 100,000 pesos from those living outside the capital to underwrite the cost of the liberal campaign. In March, Trías staged a mammoth banquet at the home of American trader McManus in honor of the president's birthday. There were laudatory speeches and many a toast held high. Someone recited suitable passages from the poetry of Guillermo Prieto, himself a reformation leader and cabinet member. There was stirring band music, and there were throbbing songs of unrequited love and "Las Mañanitas," the birthday serenade. It was a gay, costly celebration, and it should come as no surprise, masterminded, engineered, and financed by that arch politician, Luis Terrazas.[58]

Terrazas, with behind-the-scenes backing of Juárez, was reelected to the governorship in early spring. Before his inauguration, other foreign soldiers had set up camp and cannon in the plaza, Juárez had fled and Terrazas was replaced as governor by one of the conservative Zuloagas backed by a vanguard of two hundred French soldiers, recently from African duty, who took over the city.[59] There was no open resistance, although a group of merchants led by a Spanish shopkeeper, Domingo Leguinazabal, armed to prevent looting of their stores. Juárez and his advisers, including Terrazas, had moved north past the cliffs of Gallegos and the Indian-infested Sierra de Candelaria and La Magdalena to asylum afforded by the international boundary.[60] Eleven hours later, tramping through the inky blackness of midnight, General Brincourt arrived with fatigued companies of the Eighteenth Infantry and four pieces of artillery. With great noise and confusion they erected tents, moved materiel, and pointedly disturbed the sleep of the men who had come earlier. Some of their number had been left to occupy Parral.

Brincourt was welcomed by the local priests, and Father José María Terrazas sang the *Te Deum* mass. Regional conservatives offered their aid to the French forces, glad for the chance to strike back at the exiled president and his court of anticlerical officials. Tomás Zuloaga was made chief prefect of the city. It was his job to advise the foreign commander of the best ways in which to win over the populace, known to be strongly loyal to Juárez. A good beginning was made in allowing Chihuahuenses to purchase needed corn at attractive prices. Brincourt proposed to allow municipal elections and a restoration of government on the local level. His was to be a paternalistic policy. Despite his best efforts, resentment of the occupation began to spread. Then Zuloaga played into the hands of the liberals when he failed to inform Brincourt of the usual ceremonies attendant upon September 16, Mexican independence day.

In the past, several days before the holiday, the plaza walks always were scrubbed with strong-smelling soap made from a species of cactus and swept with brooms of straggly, stiff ixtle fibers. Red, white, and green bunting was draped in full swags across the facades of public buildings. Under them were hung giant pictures of a balding Hidalgo and the words "Liberty, Equality, and Fraternity." The oil lamps were filled, wicks replaced. Brass candlesticks and chalices of the church were polished, and the altars were decked with flowers. But in this year of 1865 no permission had come from the commander of the occupation and, although there was much defiant mumbling, the town's residents were fearful of proceeding with the preparations. When Brincourt at last found out that he was on the verge of insulting the town by ignoring its national holiday, hasty civil and religious festivities were organized. There would be a fiesta, but the zest for it was gone with the lack of joy of anticipation.

During Juárez's tenure in office, there had been no public processions. This was part of the controls put on the Church, because such public parades sometimes led to violent demonstrations. Brincourt, however, ordered a parade from the plaza to the chapel of San Francisco. There were a few carefully worded speeches and properly polite references to their French "guests." And then the people mobbed into the chapel where the remains of Father Hidalgo had been kept.

As if a torch had been dropped in gunpowder, suddenly, without warning, the whole congregation exploded in a stupendous, crashing brawl. Fists were swinging. Feet were kicking. Catcalls and obscenities echoed through the vaulted domes of the church. Soldiers, clergy, and civilians punched wildly, shoved, screamed. The pent feelings of the past weeks burst into the open. Ringleaders of the anti-French demonstration seemed to have been the youthful students from Chihuahua's Instituto Científico y Literario, the preparatory school which most of the upper-class boys of the town attended. The director of the school, Padre José de la Luz Corral, had been an open critic of Brincourt. He had given a political sermon in the temple of San Francisco and had blessed the national flag. Eighteen of his school's boys were hauled off to the municipal jail to quiet down.

Brincourt had an uneasy choice of letting the youngsters go scot-free and chance being regarded as spineless and lenient or keeping them under guard and stirring up the further animosity of their elders. He ordered all but one released. Young Jesús Escobar was to be an object lesson. Punishment would be by ridicule. Jesús was ordered to sweep the manure from the streets each day, for all Chihuahua to see him and to mock him. The women of the city came to the quick defense of their son. They openly expressed their contempt for an interloper who would intimidate a child. Each morning, as Jesús came down the streets with his ixtle broom and his shovel, large-eyed girls and their solemn mothers, without a word, tossed freshly picked flowers in his path. It was a simple gesture but profoundly significant. Brincourt knew he was defeated. He could not fight the women nor could he set Jesús free. He shipped him off to Durango, where he was detained until the end of the occupation.

Mexico was not fated for a bauble of Napoleon. For once, the Mexicans behind Juárez seemed to be united in purpose and determination. The French found they could control those areas in which they actually undertook occupation. As soon as royalist forces pulled out, republican forces moved in. This nationwide pattern was repeated in Chihuahua.

Brincourt left on October 29, reminding the inhabitants through the local paper, *La Nueva Era,* that Juárez had deserted them— had, in fact, fled to the disliked Americans. Juárez returned from El Paso in early November. French troops under General Billot came back up north in December. Juárez retreated to the Río Grande, where he was safe because Maximilian had forbidden his men to go farther north than one day from the city of Chihuahua, to avoid any possible trouble with the Americans. In February, French troops withdrew, leaving Chihuahua in the care of imperialist Mexicans. It was time for "General" Terrazas to attack.[61]

The Terrazas duo, Luis and Joaquín, concentrated their forces at Aldama, twenty miles from the capital. Five hundred fifty men —volunteers from Carrizal, cavalry from Durango, lancers from Julimes and Camargo, and the presidential battalion—made up the force. High above town rose a denuded rocky hill called Cerro

Grande. Joaquín made for its crest. Colonel Félix Díaz gained an eminence on the aqueduct. Between them—the aqueduct and Cerro Grande—the town was swept with cannon fire and gunshot. Imperialist troops began to scatter and disappear in the night. Those remaining in town were driven into the cathedral towers to surrender. One of the tower's resonant bells was cracked during this bombardment. Chihuahua belonged to Luis. Earlier, Maximilian had offered him a government post, but he had declined.

Republicans had reverses. Manuel Ojinaga, temporary governor, was killed by French sympathizers in Arisiáchi. The political *jefe* of the town of Guerrero, a republican, was creating a fortune for himself by imposing heavy "contributions" on the residents of that area. French agitators used discontent among the people there as a lever to swing them to their side. Ojinaga was shot, and a load of munitions being sent from El Paso was stolen. Colonel Méndez, comrade-in-arms of Terrazas when Cajen conservatives were annihilated, met his death at Cusihuiriáchi. The imperialists permitted friends to bury Méndez, only to exhume the body for public display and to impose a thousand pesos' fine on the grieving family. In April, a third French invasion of the state was attempted. Atotonilco, a village in the extreme south, was sacked, looted, and laid waste.[62]

Chihuahua again became the temporary seat of the federal government when Juárez crossed the desert from El Paso for the fifth time. In December 1866, he left the state to return to the heart of the nation. By June, his opponent, Maximilian, and two Mexican generals who had led the fruitless campaign stood before a firing squad by a hill near Querétaro. Señora Terrazas had been among those who had sent pleas for mercy to President Juárez.

Luis had been in the escort of dignitaries riding south with the president to the Chihuahua-Durango border. The man who had come north as a foe departed as a staunch friend and was responsible for giving Terrazas at least a good beginning toward his big empire and long political career.

With the war's end, several new names appeared on the maps of the state to commemorate fallen heroes—Ojinaga (Presidio del Norte), Meoqui (San Pablo), and Villa López (Atotonilco). The latter town was omitted from tax rolls for five years because of the disastrous French raid, and Terrazas launched a public conscription for aid. Juárez himself was not honored in Chihuahua until 1888 when his name was given the Mexican settlement on the south bank of the Río Grande, opposite El Paso.[63] Padre José María Terrazas was fined and expelled from the state for his open advocacy of the French occupation. And Governor Luis Terrazas acquired his first large estate, part of the historic hacienda at Encinillas.

Reconstruction in Chihuahua, as elsewhere in Mexico, was difficult and disheartening. Terrazas was checked at every turn by financial deficits and unending squabbles between political rivals. In 1872, at the time Juárez was running for re-election, revolt stirred in the Tarahumara Alta. It favored election of one of Juárez's ablest generals, Porfirio Díaz. Terrazas remained loyal to his benefactor, Juárez, but he was defeated by a Díaz leader, Donata Guerra, in a fierce encounter at the Hacienda de Tabalaopa on the road to Aldama.[64] The death of Juárez, however, quickly ended the northern revolt, putting Lerda de Tejada into the presidency. Terrazas met with Díaz at the Hacienda el Charco near the capital. He demanded that all the arms Guerra had captured at his victory at the Hacienda de Tabalaopa be turned over to state forces and that Díaz himself never again set foot in the state. He was *persona non grata*. Strong words to be remembered with mixed feelings in the years ahead!

Four years later, Díaz openly coveted and won the high office of president with the issuing of the Plan de Tuxtepec. In Chihuahua it was now time for Angel Trías, the son, to enter the arena of vicious political life. He pronounced himself in favor of the new plan and engaged in victorious battle to prove it. Later young Trías was named governor, but General Pacheco was Díaz's chosen man in Chihuahua. Luis Terrazas discreetly retired, temporarily, from public office to make himself a fortune. Despite the rift and the icy feelings between himself and the new caudillo, he became thoroughly identified with the Díaz era. By their friends ye shall know them?

To TELL TRUTH from untruth, fantastic fact from flossy fancy, in the story of Luis Terrazas is virtually impossible. His biographers never have known objectivity.[65] His way of life, his tremendous fortune, the general times in which he lived made him an obvious target. Here was a criollo capitalist who personified the evils and the ills of the Díaz dictatorship. His defenders, strangely quiet during the passionate destruction of his kingdom, have been equally emotional in his glorification. Whether *ladrón* (robber) or leader, his greatest tragedy was outliving his epoch, an epoch thought romantic by the world. He outlasted his friends of the haciendas, the banks, the government. One son was kidnapped for ransom; another was brutally tortured; he lost his beloved wife. He lived to see the ruin of his homes and ranches with their luxurious furnishings and vast herds of stock, and to sense the paralyzing effects of a severe stroke. Even in death he was not to be allowed a funeral befitting an ex-general.

What of this ogre who lived on human misery, this man whose name became synonymous with the wrongs of the period? He was born, raised, and died on the frontier. A typically Mexican love of land burned in his soul. He grew to manhood in the difficult times leading up to the American invasion. Though he lived through that invasion, he seemingly bore no rancor for Americans. His father, proprietor of a butcher shop and a small business, was able to send him to the Instituto with the moneyed youths of the town, but he lacked the funds to provide further education. Anyhow, Luis felt he wanted a commercial rather than an academic life, so he joined the business of his father. He learned to buy lean, rangy cattle from small herders in the valley and to fatten them on family pastures on the bank of the Chuvíscar. He watched them butchering in the sandy river bed and came to know good meat from poor. He helped the *carnicero* hang a plain red flag over the shop doorway on days when fresh meat was available. And he developed an astuteness and skill at business which enriched him throughout his adult life. In 1849 his father died during the cholera epidemic which spread through the city. At the age of twenty-two, Luis was in business for himself.

From the beginning, young Luis seemed to have the God-given ability and the man-made desire to accumulate money. In three years he built a reputation for solvency, and then he married Carolina Cuilty Bustamente. Just as he would become rich in worldly goods, he became rich in children. He fathered fourteen. The Cuiltys were an old and large family, intermarried with the Zuloagas, Molinars, Campas, and Creels. All these connections would prove useful to Luis who determined to enter the highly unstable field of Chihuahua politics. He held positions as fiscal guard of the administration of rents, director of the ayuntamiento, and chief of the *cantón* Iturbide. In 1860 he was elected governor.

Tarrazas was frugal and energetic, two qualities too often absent in Mexican administrators. He was a campesino at heart. He arose at five, breakfasted at six, worked through the day with the drive of a Wall Street broker. He was plain in appearance and manner, considered bromidic by society leaders of the day. He cloaked himself and his family in dull respectability. There was none of the usual gossip of extramarital activities, of his being *muy macho* with a mistress tucked away in a suburban *casita*. Even though Terrazas had joined juarista condemnation of the unlimited power and wealth of the Church and had been in office at a time when it was the governor's duty to take over Church lands, he and his family attended mass regularly and gave freely of their money. Señora Carolina Cuilty de Terrazas donated the entire sum needed to build the second tower on the sanctuary of Nuestra Señora de Guadalupe, originally constructed in 1786, on a hill southwest of town.[66] Luis's amusements were those of the country—horseracing, tailing the bull, chicken pulls, and roping—but as a spectator, not a participant. He nursed a passion for the wide, tawny mesas and the sepia deserts reaching out to eternity. He was captivated by the violent, awe-inspiring thunderstorms of the wet seasons and the pirouetting whirlwinds of the dry. The lore of the *ganadería,* cattle ranch, with its two-hundred-fifty-year-old history in his state, appealed to him. In a sense, he was a Mexican drugstore cowboy. Certainly the economic potentialities of the raising of livestock were appreciated. His chance to begin buying up desirable land came at the end of the French intervention.

Terrazas and Enrique Müller, a Chihuahuense of German extraction, jointly had rented the lands of the old hacienda at Encinillas on the colonial highway to the north. At the end of the seventeenth century, when Santa Eulalia first was being exploited, some of the lands of Sauz and Encinillas were deeded to Benito Pérez de Rivera, whose heirs sold it in 1715 to Manuel de San Juan y Santa Cruz. San Juan had a brother, a royal customs agent at Vera Cruz, who acquired more debts than money, forcing the disgruntled Crown to take over the Chihuahua hacienda to pay off the debtors. In 1786 the government sold the property to the Conde de San Pedro del Alamo who enlarged it greatly until it contained thousands of square kilometers in the municipio of Ahumada. It was later purchased and leased to the partners from the city.

Its large lake and its extensive pastures of thick vega grass made the Encinillas valley attractive to travelers and cattlemen alike. It was also attractive to marauding Indians who periodically drove off large numbers of horses, mules, and cows, making Mexican occupation not only hazardous but profitless. However, Terrazas and Müller had risked their pooled capital in the hope that they would get enough from the hides and tallow of the cattle to at least pay the peons and the *patrón*.

The patrón, in this case, was Dr. José Pablo Martínez del Río, a wealthy, cultured gentleman, a British subject, who preferred the pleasures of continental travel and the refinements of his Paris home to living on his isolated Mexican ranch. He had rented out Encinillas for six hundred pesos annually and had gone to Mexico City to greet fair Maximilian. Don Pablo was present at the coronation of the figurehead emperor, from whom he accepted a diplomatic mission to the Sultan of Turkey and the King of Greece. When the French returned home and Maximilian to his Maker, Martínez del Río was considered a collaborationist. All his Mexican property was confiscated, including large holdings in Chihuahua. A lawsuit in his behalf was instigated immediately, but the Encinillas hacienda was sold to Müller. In 1868 Terrazas bought half of it, 386,235 hectares, or approximately 965,585 acres for 4,000 pesos![67] Don Luis was now a cattleman.

The tangled transaction, enmeshed as it was in confused legal proceedings and abrupt confiscation by Juárez, led many to believe that Terrazas had acquired the property as payment for services rendered the juarista cause, that somehow he had not come by it honestly. Added to that popular apprehension was the hotly debated adjudication of the baldíos, or public lands, and Church lands which had occurred during Terrazas's pre-Intervention term of office. There were numerous vague, suspicious rumors of his misusing his position on the inside track to gain land titles illegally. Accusations were many; proof, none. Either he was too cunning to be proved guilty, or he was guilelessly honest.

An empire within a state began to amalgamate, like a magnet drawing iron flecks to its poles. It was not the only hacienda-kingdom in Chihuahua, but it was the largest. One land title and then another was recorded in the Palacio de Gobierno in the name of Luis Terrazas.[68] In the years 1870, 1872, 1874, 1884, 1885, 1898, 1900, 1907—La Canada, San Lorenzo, San Miguel de Babícora, San Felipe, Labor de Trías, El Carmen, San Pedro, Tapiecitas, San Luis, El Torreón, Las Hormigas, San Isidro, San Diego . . . . Some were small, with a thousand hectares. Two thousand peons operated some. Others had two hundred workers. Encinillas remained the largest in area and in population. Don Luis, now, was not only a ganadero but a hacendado on the grandest scale ever known. By 1910 he owned *seven million acres* of the state* and livestock worth 25,000,000 pesos. To thousands of humble, barefoot folk, he was the most important entity in Mexico, next to God.

Terrazas's aptitude for business did not end with cattle raising. In 1871 he became an industrialist with the purchase, for 5,000 pesos, of a wool textile mill called La Industrial. Three years later he owned the first flour mill in Chihuahua. Just thirty years after inheriting the small butcher shop, Don Luis was able to join five other men in establishing the Banco Mexicano with a capital of 77,000 pesos. In 1884 he expanded his successful banking venture by founding the Banco Minero Chihuahuense, capitalized at 1,-000,000 pesos. His associates were Pedro Zuloaga, the old santanista conservative from a tremendous hacienda at the Lago de Bustillos, and Enrique Creel, his half-American son-in-law. This bank became one of the most powerful in Mexico. In one year it sent 5,000 five-peso gold pieces to Mexico City in care of Wells Fargo. By 1900, Terrazas and Creel together owned sixteen businesses with an investment of 27,350,000 pesos.[69] Don Luis had become the Midas of the midlands. Singular financial success was his in everything he tried. He was shrewd and adept, some said a parlor-bound robber, but there was much more involved than just his innate ability.

What were the conditions which permitted one man to own a

---

* As compared to the 900,000 acres of Texas's famous King Ranch. One story relates how once Terrazas was asked if he were from Chihuahua to which he replied, "No, Chihuahua is mine." (*México, Cincuenta Años de Revolución*, 1960, vol. III, 234.)

good tenth of Mexico's largest state? How could wealth be earned from plains enveloped in the shadow of death? The answers lay with the contradictory regimes of liberal Juárez and conservative Díaz and the termination of the scourge of the Indians out of the north. Terrazas had the great good fortune of being on the spot, cash in hand, at just the right time. He was eager to engage in ranching, an enterprise in which others had lost faith. Opportunity came and Don Luis was quick to seize it.

Juárez, through his proposed redivision of Church lands, village ejidos, and public "idle" lands, unwittingly created a new class of landowners. Ironically, it was substitution of one evil for another. President Díaz furthered these policies. All over Mexico, including Chihuahua, villages were stripped of land for which there was no clear legal title but only fragmentary Spanish land grants recorded in the foggy memory of each succeeding generation. It is uncertain as to just whether Terrazas himself aided this village disinheritance. If he did, he was following an accepted pattern (accepted by the landowners!) in use throughout the nation. Also his expropriation of public lands was not all through legal dodges but through purchase of established haciendas whose former owners already might have incorporated the adjacent ejidos.

It must be remembered that most of Chihuahua north and west of the capital lay abandoned and unused at the time Terrazas first acquired land. Apaches had scared off settlers completely. Land where it was yet impossible to produce crops or cattle was worthless. Many were eager to sell at any price and move, if they had not already done so, to the security of the city. But by 1880, or shortly after, the Indians had been subdued for all time. By that time, Luis already had bought almost half his domain at the same ridiculously low prices he had paid for Encinillas. No one else wanted the property. After the liquidation of the Indian threat, it was many years before ranchers would venture back to the islands of adobe settlements. It was as though they could not believe the nights would be safe from Apache terror, corrals and houses unviolated. Terrazas quietly continued collecting deeds.

With the peace enforced by the notorious mounted *rurales* (rural police force), who dispensed Porfirian justice at gunpoint, came a booming tide of prosperity. It was prosperity for the foreign interests (first welcomed by Juárez) and for the patrones. And Don Luis was the biggest patrón of all.

With Indians and rustlers fairly well under control, cattle and other stock flourished and multiplied on the expansive plains. Much of the terrain, however, was too arid and vegetation too sparse to support stock in any number. Holdings had to be enormous to accomodate herds of size. Was this not the largest of all states, with the least density of population? There was no need for confinement on a few hectares. As in neighboring Texas, in Chihuahua it was wise to think big and to act big. Ranches and haciendas grew larger and larger, cattle more plentiful and meatier, profits greater. Perhaps Quivira was animal, not mineral.

Díaz introduced certain forms of mechanization to Mexico. An ever growing network of railroads aided cattlemen and ranchers. For the first time, cattle could be shipped from distant ranches to market to be used for meat. The world's appetite for beef seemed insatiable. With the completion of the central railroad terminating in Ciudad Juárez and Don Luis leading the inaugural ceremonies, Terrazas became the nation's leading exporter. His horses and cattle poured north in cattle cars, as well as in drives, to be used for breeding and fattening purposes on Southwestern ranches. One often-repeated story concerning the size of his operations relates how an American buyer wired Luis's headquarters saying, "Can you supply five thousand head?" The terse reply was, "What color?"

For his time, Luis Terrazas must be considered progressive, to a degree. He studied the varied topography of his ranches and experimented with breeds of cattle suitable for existing conditions. He carefully chose the farming areas which were to furnish food supplies for his peons. He put down wells, raised windmills, dug stock tanks, and constructed hacienda houses meant to stand many lifetimes. But, together with other ranchers, Terrazas was an exploiter of human beings.

Mexico was a backward country with a tremendous pool of unskilled cheap labor. It was not to a landowner's financial advantage to mechanize. Too, Mexico was a country fettered by a deep sense of tradition and the heavy hand of custom. It was too difficult, too expensive, to overcome resistance to change. So, thousands of human backs and hands continued their toil at the same meager wages they had received for almost three centuries.

The hacendado had laborers bound to him through debt peonage and fear of trigger-happy rurales should they try to leave. They might bolt, but there could be no escape, for the system prevailed and steadily grew worse all over Mexico during the Pax Porfiriana. Terrazas undoubtedly was as guilty of perpetuating the general misery as his fellow landowners. But the fault was in the system rather than in the individual. Terrazas simply controlled more peons, not necessarily treating them any more harshly.

The Terrazas hacienda communities,[70] like those of other hacendados, were proudly self-sufficient worlds. Around them revolved a whole way of life, at slow tempo yet alive with constant movement. Within their shelter were the workers of the soil employed in sowing, tending, and harvesting of crops to feed men and animals. There were the master builders, the muddy-footed tampers of adobe bricks, the careful masons who chiseled out ponderous lintel blocks or delicately carved columns, the skilled carpenters capable of hewing rough rafters (vigas) or fine exquisite inlay, the creators of stone fences, tile floors, mosaic altars, bubbling fountains. There were their barefooted womenfolk who brought the buzz of gossip to cleaning, sewing, cooking, or serving in the master's house. Dirty children, in that brief, fleeting period alloted peon youth, scuffled in the windy lanes between row houses, playing the universal games of all children. In dark, shadowed, walled patios of the stables one could see surging red embers of blacksmith forges as sooty figures pounded on hot metal to make tools, hardware, or shoes for the horses. One could hear arrieros shouting orders to plodding lines of obedient beasts moving to and from dispatch points, the resounding riflelike crack of their long whips sharply punctuating the modulated hum of human life. Barebacked porters could be seen bent double as they dogtrotted under towering loads, their neck muscles roundly bulging at the pull of leather tumplines across sweat-wettened foreheads, doing the physical work of transporting materials in an ageless, inherited pattern. Beyond the quadrangle of feeding troughs and workshops in stonefaced corrals, one could watch the endless routine of currying and shoeing, or from the top of a wall look down to snubbing

posts where wild-blooded horses were tied firm to be gentled and
trained to ranch duties. This was a working community, each adult
with a specific task and fixed status. And during the daylight hours,
everywhere there was activity.

In the long, sweet hours of twilight when chores of the ranch
halted and a welcome breath of coolness swelled up from the
plains, life flowed from the block buildings of the workers' quarters. Groups of whiskered men, garbed alike in crudely woven
cotton trousers, full pullover shirts, and peak-crowned straw sombreros held secure by a band across the lower back of their heads,
lounged in the long shadows of the tenements for a precious smoke
or bit of conversation. Inside, their women crouched in the ruddy
glow of the corner cook fires as they stirred a cazuela of beans or
patted a few tortillas for the evening meal. Adolescent boys, with
the first longings of manhood awakened as the sun went down,
strolled about the lanes to seek out girls of their fancy for a play
of flirtation or illicit love. Giggles of clandestine happiness rippled
from dark corners. Sometimes a guitar could be heard being gently
coaxed to pour out a lamentation of forsaken love or of a hopeless
plight for which no peon could dare dream a remedy. Scrawny
dogs and grimy youngsters rolled together in the dirt, unmindful
of the dreary lot to which they both had been born. Darkness
staged a tableau of tranquility mocking the injustices being bred
by the hacienda scheme into which they, young and old, were in-
dentured.

An autonomous colony, it was knit together by isolation, ownership by a single family, and incalculable peonage. The hacienda's
grand commandant was head of that ruling family, the patrón to
whom all the residents were beholden. Usually he was a man of
extensive wealth and gachupín or criollo breeding. Traditionally
he was the proud patriarch—conservative, incurious, religious.
Often he was insensitive to the suffering inflicted by his system. He
operated his commissary, the infamous *tienda de raya* where employees were obliged to spend a considerable share of their meager
wages, with consummate greed. Need for staples and desire for a
rare luxury of a few widths of coarse cotton cloth or a stinging
swig of aguardiente accumulated debts to the point where neither
a man nor his children nor his grandchildren could extricate them-

selves. Thus, secure in his overlordship, the hacendado lavished time and money upon his home, making it a regal manor house upon the plains.

Chihuahua hacienda homes usually sprawled out across a knoll or a slight rise above the surrounding tablelands. If constructed during the days of Indian raids, a thick, protective wall encircled them. Enormous buildings, occasionally two-storied, often around a central courtyard, expanded as the family grew. New rooms, escutcheons, gates, walks, and portals were added constantly through use so that later a record of seventy-five or more years might be read in construction dates placed on renovations or improvements. Plastered adobe walls had corners, lintels, and portico columns of cut and shaped stone. Enormous beams to support the roofs were chopped in the sierra and hauled to the homesite. Doors, shutters, and furniture, crafted on the spot, were beautifully carved. Sundials, fountains, and walled gardens embellished the finer establishments.

For those who dwelt within, life drifted pleasantly along in a pall of self-gratification. The father and his older sons and sons-in-law saw to the ramified operations of the hacienda, finding pleasure in authority and in successful competition with tempestuous Nature. Their rewards came with the hectares of pale-green sprouts appearing in newly planted fields and the stone granaries later filled to capacity with golden grains, in the handsome horses outfitted with elaborate silver-mounted trappings, in the herds of fat cattle waiting to be driven to the slaughterhouses of Chihuahua. Younger brothers indulged themselves in horseflesh and the associated complex of fierce sports such as tailing bulls, wildly racing each other over the ranges, or whirling snakelike lariats at moving targets, learning in fun the various skills they would need when it came their time to join the ranch's management. Also, taking advantage of a recognized double moral standard prevalent in their society which allowed them a degree of sexual freedom while imposing a strict chastity upon their sisters, they concerned themselves too with human flesh, occasionally taking resigned servant girls who knew of no escape. The women of the family had to content themselves with tasks of the household, the large families they bore, and the care of the chapel, often incorporated into the hacienda compound. They had time to devote themselves to music, china painting, or embroidery. Life for them was secluded and dominated by their menfolk.

Typical of the Terrazas hacienda communities was Hacienda de San Diego south of the towns of Casa Grandes and Nuevo Casas Grandes, standing today in excellent condition though now in an ejido, occupied by sons of Don Luis's former vaqueros. San Diego sat on a small hill overlooking a fertile tree-dotted valley where the Piedras Verdes spilled its waters into the larger Río Casas Grandes. This rich bottomland on the eastern downslope of the Sierra Madre Occidental was completely, though primitively, cultivated to provide the beans, corn, squashes, chiles, onions, and other basic foodstuffs used by the six hundred peons who cared for the hacienda. The nearness of towns, only some six miles away, the Noroeste de México Railroad which skirted the property on its swing from the city of Chihuahua to Ciudad Juárez, the plentiful farm land with its river waters and bubbling hot springs, and the fine native grasses on the ranges made this a particularly valuable hacienda. Both Orozco and Villa forces operated throughout this section of the state in the later Revolution, and San Diego was the target for many raids.

The principal building at the headquarters was the home of Don Luis. He, and sometimes his family, made annual visits to the hacienda and expected the dwelling to be ready for occupancy at any time. At other times it was occupied by the *mayordomo,* Don Jacobo Anchondo. It was a long rectangular building of some forty rooms, built around a central garden patio. Over the main entrance projected an impressive portico faced with a pink stone quarried and shaped at an outcrop twenty miles distant and hauled to the site in large mule-drawn wagons. Above the central arch of the portico was a stone escutcheon reading "Hacienda de San Diego, LT, 1902." A carved stone cornice relieved the severity of an otherwise drab building. Long *portales,* or roofed porticos, flanked the central facade, their vigas supported by slender iron shafts set on stone. The building itself was constructed of adobe bricks, then plastered. The huge, rough-hewn ceiling vigas had been hauled from the mountains. Doors and lintels were elaborately carved. On the roof at the south corner of the facade tipped a sundial carved of stone. Furniture was the heavy, ornate European type admired at this period and was combined with native silver, leather, and fabrics loomed at the Chihuahua textile mills. Although elegant, San Diego was not as showy as many of the Terrazas establishments.

The large rectangular granary stood apart from the house and stables. It, too, was of adobe, of considerable height. The exterior corners were faced with the same cut stone as was used on the house. Drain spouts of stone dipped off the flat roof. Small, barred windows were placed very high, making entrance difficult. A doorway sufficiently wide to accomodate a wagon loaded with grain opened in the center of each long wall. The interior of the granary was divided by a series of four stone-faced arches grooved so that partitions forming grain bins could be slipped into place. The ceiling was of split cedar, covered by big beams, and topped with a thick layer of dirt. After withstanding the ravages of fifty years' time, sometimes violent weather, and war-bent men, the building still is dry and free of rodents.

Enormous stables and barns were needed to house the vaqueros' *remudas*, strings of ponies. At San Diego, one long building was separated into units built around large, open patios. Here animals were fed and shod, and the necessary blacksmithing and repair work was done on wagons and carts. The feed troughs were carved stone. Behind the stable were corrals with fences of piled river cobbles.

The peons at San Diego fared better, so far as housing was concerned, than they often did elsewhere. There were three long blockhouses, each with a central partition, containing about twenty rooms. There was one door, one window, one smoke hole per unit. A worker's family occupied one room, put its small altar with the garish paper flowers and warped candle in a corner, and hung its inevitable potted plants and bird cages on the exterior walls of the building.

San Diego was built after the Indian wars had faded into song and legend to be sung and told to small children. It therefore lacked much of the appearance of a fort that characterized other hacienda communities. There was no walled enclosure around the settlement. There were no barred doors. The water supply came from unprotected springs by the river. No one expected death to come swooping out of the night. San Diego sat serene and undis-

Cliff dwelling, Casa de las Ventanas, Garbato Drainage.

Cliff dwelling, Cave Valley, Chihuahua.

The Mogollones fanned out of southern New Mexico and Arizona, along both flanks of the Sierra Madre into the verdant drainages of the Bavispe, Piedras Verdes, and Aros, where they inhabited caves. As a result of influences from the north, they adopted an Anasazi architecture and the mountain caves sheltered cubelike houses.

About A.D. 1000, the Chihuahua mountain Mogollones forsook their elevated fastnesses and slowly spread down the eastern basins. Casas Grandes, with its large units of puddled adobe houses, was the zenith of the hybridization of Mogollon and Anasazi cultures. During the twelfth and thirteenth centuries, influences from central Mexico were responsible for the erection of stone-faced platforms and pyramids which were utilized in elaborate rituals.

Ruins of Casas Grandes.

One of the cobblestone-faced pyramids at Casas Grandes.

Jesuit mission of Tarahumara Alta, 1936 photograph. The missions brought European civilization to the Chihuahua mountains in the 16th, 17th, and 18th centuries.

ABOVE: The ruined haciendas of the Terrazas and the Zuloagas. Hacienda communities, with their mansions, walled patios, exquisite chapels, and peón tenements, sat grandly on the plains.

LEFT: Ruins of the Jesuit chapel of Santa Ana de Chinarras, founded in 1717, near the present town of Aldama, the only Jesuit mission outside the mountains.

Stock tank and corral in the northern country. With its wide plains and mild climate, Chihuahua is the cattle kingdom of Mexico.

German-speaking Mennonites have established a productive dry farming and dairy colony in the Bustillos Basin. They live in European-style houses, conduct business in Cuauhtémoc, but scorn the use of automobiles.

Gen. Alvaro Obregón, Pancho Villa, and Gen. John J. Pershing.
Photograph courtesy of Mac Howard.

The mausoleum of
Pancho Villa, Ciudad
Chihuahua.

Shrine of Guadalupe,
Ciudad Chihuahua. The
grave of Luis Terrazas is
in the churchyard.

The Cathedral and the Plaza, Ciudad Juárez.

turbed on her open hillock, productive and content in the cycle of warm winters, hot summers, and steadily rising beef prices.

THE LINEAGE founded by Carlos Zuloaga, although not as staggeringly wealthy as that of Terrazas, was nevertheless rich and powerful. It traditionally allied itself with rightist and Church groups, more often than not on the opposite side of political issues from Don Luis. Zuloaga sons—José, Pedro, Luis, Tomás, and Félix—all had been santanistas, tacubayistas, and *imperialistas,* depending upon the time.[71] One had been a governor of the state of Chihuahua, one an aide to the French military commander, and one a president of the nation. Behind their activities in government there always appeared the forceful hand of the clergy. One only needed to visit the Zuloaga-owned Hacienda de Bustillos to realize the great influence of the Church over the family.

Dominating the hacienda-fort settlement was one of the most handsome private chapels in the republic. Its single dome with a large iron cross and its arched exterior stairways leading into the lofts above the altar loomed above the crouched profile of dwellings and stables as one approached from either the murky lake of Bustillos or across the plains from the capital of Chihuahua sixty miles to the east. The chapel, constructed of shining blocks of pink-buff stone, stood on landscaped ground next to the Zuloaga house. Inside, shafts of soft light streaked from tinted windows across the floor of cool blue and white tile to the gleaming, white marble altar supporting massive, golden accessories. The care and money spent upon this tiny family-supported gem of church architecture pointed up the steadfast adherence of all the Zuloagas to the Chihuahua clergy. Their peons, crowded into unhealthy, dirt-floored row houses reeking with the combined strong smells of the stables and confined humanity, were given opportunity to worship in an exquisite stone, gold, and stained-glass structure.

EVERY LAND has many unsung heroes. In Chihuahua, none was more deserving of lasting recognition, or more overlooked, than Don Luis's cousin, Joaquín. He was lauded at the time and hailed by the cheering multitude—embraced, saluted, but then forgotten. Yet he, through his persistence and what some may have regarded as his treachery, opened the way for peaceful exploitation of the plains. He put an end to the menace to life and property that had gripped the northlands since the days of Tepóraca, Salvatierra, Retana, and the Caballero de Croix—he conquered the Apache. In Chihuahua the Mexicans who fought other Mexicans, those who committed barbarous crimes against people of their own race, who hit the pace of the gambler, lover, or thug, were the men who captured public fancy and left behind monuments of ribald stories and emotional ballads. Unlike the Western Indian fighter of the States, the Mexican, with all his skills of tracking, of outwitting a treacherous environment, of adroitly succeeding against overwhelming odds, is all but ignored in folklore and balladry. Joaquín Terrazas y Quezada is Chihuahua's forgotten man.

Like his cousin, Joaquín was enamored of the land. He saw sublime majesty in its sweeping bolsons and in the unbroken, deathlike silence which enveloped them. In rare years of peace, he had known the soul-satisfying rewards of the earth's fruitfulness when *tobosa* grass greened from showers and a mist of wild flowers blanketed the plateaus. Although he himself owned none, he gloried in the herds of sleek cattle grazing by scattered, trickling springs. Then, when he saw dry grass plains aflame, livestock slaughtered and left to scavengers, ranchos pillaged and spoliation everywhere, deep anger at the utter waste swelled within him. He knew he could not rest until these wrongs were righted, until the nomadic nightmare was dispelled.

The Americans had come and gone, and then the French. But always there were raiding Indians—before, during, and after. A man called to arms in the latter years of the century could remember back to his father's fireside tales of sorties against the Indians, and his grandfather's before that. It seemed to always have been so.

Nonetheless, time was running out for the American Indian. What could be more agonizing than the death of the proud spirit of a people born to a wild, unrestricted life, born to freedom to come and go at will. But the reservations were closing in on him, intending to convert him to a dull farmer, tied to crops. What possible outlet for expression could there be in such a life for a nation of warriors? Washington bureaucrats, however, decreed that Indians should be farmers.[72] Westward expansion of the white men, gaining momentum after the disruptions of the Civil War, steadily pushed the Apaches from their ancestral lands and drove away the wild game upon which they lived. They were being dislocated and dispossessed with increasing rapidity. These whites were heavily armed and not to be intimidated. The Indians fled in the only direction possible—to the south.

In that south there was a new resoluteness, a new dogged determination to see an end to this ancient, frustrating struggle. The man behind that will was Colonel Joaquín. He was a professional soldier, a man of action, but he was not the swaggering, egotistical gunslinger, the stereotyped Mexican warrior. He was neither a braggart nor self-effacing. In his simple honesty, he recognized the full potential of the enemy, but he knew his own inner strength. He would be patient. He would persevere. No sentiment would complicate his dedication. He knew he would be victorious.

The Terrazas crusade against the Apache, pushed by Luis as governor and Joaquín as military commander, started in earnest in 1880.[73] The year previous, residents of lonely Carrizal had been massacred by raiders galloping out of camps hidden in the sheltering Sierra de Candelaria. This was the final straw.

The Apache chieftain was Victorio. Rumors were that he was not an Indian at all but a renegade white man, which endowed him with an extra frightfulness to the Mexicans. The mention of his name was enough to send cold shivers down the spines of campesinos living at his mercy. He and his band were reported at widely separated localities across the expanse of northern Chihuahua. Colonel Joaquín and the security guard time after time rode off in hot pursuit, only to return empty-handed, without a battle, having seen no illusory Indians but only black buzzards funneling out of the cloudless sky to mark their butchery. The soldiers chased after them to the lagunas of Guzmán and Santa María where they had been reported hiding out. The Indians were gone by the time the army arrived. On to Corralitos, south to Namiquipa, back to El Carmen, east to Encinillas, out to Coyame . . . . The summer of 1880 was spent in crisscrossing the deserts, waiting under cover at water holes, circling the rocky hills known to be Apache strongholds, following each lead and each clue. Not until October 14 did they find the Apache.

Three hills of the Sierra de la Amargosa rose out of a wide plain. Victorio had selected the central one as a protected camp where his band, including many women and children, might rest. It was at dusk at Tres Castillos when Joaquín and Victorio finally came face to face. Three hundred fifty Mexicans from the area of Apache operations were under arms, a third from the vicinity of often-stricken Galeana under command of Juan Mata Ortiz and others from El Carmen, San Andrés, and Carrizal. As they rode toward the hills of the three castles, they formed into single file to give the impression, if they could, of a small guard on patrol duty through the desert. Indian fighters, knowing they had been seen, rushed down from their hillside hideout to engage the "patrol" to keep the shooting away from their women and children. In the first flush of battle, the notorious chieftain who had seemed invincible was brought down by two Tarahumara scouts, Mauricio and Rogue. In that second, the pause created by the death of their leader, there was vacillation and indecision on the part of the Apaches, allowing the Mexicans to seize command of the situation. Steadily the Indians were driven into the folds of the hills from which there was no escape. The fierce hand-to-hand battle continued long after dark until every Apache male lay dead in the desert brush and there were only the dependents loudly lamenting their fallen men.

The capital city greeted Joaquín as the "Hero of Tres Castillos" when the dust-coated and saddle-weary security forces forded the silty waters of the Chuvíscar and rode down Avenida Juárez into the plaza. Word already had swept through town that the Apaches had been defeated! Could it be true at last? Could the threads of old lives on the northern ranchos be picked up once more? Could there be peace and contentment where there had been only naked horror? At least, for the first time in a number of generations, there was a glimmer of hope. They owed thanks to Joaquín and his second-in-command, Mata Ortiz. Gone was their customary passiveness and unsmiling immobility. This was a victory which touched them all. They crowded the sidewalks and climbed lamp-posts to glimpse the victorious riders and the Indian women and children prisoners sullenly shuffling in chains behind them. They leaned from balconies above the street to yell, "Viva Terrazas! Viva Mata Ortiz! Bravo!" until they were hoarse. They drank and ate and joyfully celebrated—too soon.

One Apache leader had fallen, but there were others equally as bloodthirsty, as astute, and as determined to avoid reservation life in Arizona, to take his place. They now had an additional motive, revenge. Ju and Gerónimo led new incursions almost as soon as the news of the defeat of Tres Castillos reached them in Arizona. They crossed the border to burn ranches at Puerto de las Magueyes, Plan de Alamos, Torreón, Encinillas, and Galeana, and to ambush the *diligencias* (stagecoaches) traveling between Ciudad Juárez and the city of Chihuahua. Coach drivers, such as the Uranga brothers, José and Jesús, had to change routes often, had to bump over rocky flats and steep-sided arroyos in the dark, but attacks at Gallegos and the Sierra de Candelaria increased. Again a trail of freshly let blood reddened the Mexican deserts. When retaliatory forces mounted in pursuit, the Indians fled north of the international border. Ten times during 1881 Joaquín's men rode forth only to return to their garrison with nothing more tangible than fresh tracks of unshod Apache ponies and still smoldering ruins of former jacales. However, there was no sanctuary for the Apache in Arizona or New Mexico, where United States Army troops were seeking them out for enforced residence on the Fort Apache and San Carlos reservations. Ju and Gerónimo, with their followers, decided to migrate permanently to the Mexican sierra and to sue for peace. They asked to confer with Colonel Joaquín.

There had been a long history of treaties made between the Mexicans and the Indians, but the latter had no compulsion to observe the terms agreed upon unless it was to their advantage to do so. When they were hungry or tired or otherwise weakened, they had come to seek rations and nominal forgiveness. The Mexicans were glad enough for even occasional breathing spells. They handed out food and clothing with one hand and crossed themselves in prayer with the other. Joaquín, with his quiet determination to bring the Indians either to peaceful coexistence or complete annihilation, agreed to confer. Near Cases Grandes, site of pre-Hispanic "large houses" abandoned by peaceful Pueblo farmers, other Indians came to start anew.

Nothing came of two long parleys. The main body of Indians, suspecting a trap, stayed behind the dark pinnacles of the sierra while their chieftains talked. Not receiving the assurances they wanted, Ju and Gerónimo took the gifts of rations and departed. They found the United States Army on the border. They tried to cross over into Sonora but were bushwhacked in a surprise mountain attack. The realization that escape from their blood-soaked record was becoming increasingly difficult, if not impossible, forced them back to Casas Grandes and the indefatigable Colonel Joaquín.

Sorrowfully resigned to their doom but with childlike expectation of pardon, the Apaches made camp on the flat banks of the Río Casas Grandes, prepared to forswear their unacceptable mode of existence. They would promise Chihuahuenses to range quietly through the sierra madre where game and perpetual water would provide them a secure life, and when they could no longer resist the temptation of raiding expeditions, their victims would be Sonorans or gringos! Colonel Joaquín, however, was no longer in a mood of leniency. He had tried peaceful arbitration and had failed.

In the faint shafts of amber dawn light, two columns of Mexican soldiers fell upon the unarmed Indian camp. Time had caught up with Chihuahuenses too. They had sold their souls for peace upon the plains. The eastern Apache tribes never again would be able to offer the powerful resistance they had formerly. Ju escaped the massacre but vowed vengeance upon the fat Mata Ortiz. The next year his opportunity came.

Led into a trap while on the trail of the Indians, Mata Ortiz found himself with just a handful of men surrounded by a large whooping band of Ju's followers. One by one, snipers picked off the Mexicans until only unmounted Mata Ortiz remained. The Indians wrestled him into submission and threw him, alive, on to a lighted funeral pyre.*

Suspicion of motives and lack of trust on both sides of the border had hampered capture and punishment of the Apaches. Outrages committed against American settlers and travelers were frequent and just as gruesome as those perpetrated in Mexico, but when United States soldiers crossed the line of demarcation between the United States of Mexico and the United States of America, southern neighbors cried violation. American troops were forced to stop dead at the border, often to see the dust of fleeing Apaches drifting from dry trails to the south. The international border trouble

---

* Today a railroad settlement south of Casas Grandes perpetuates the memory of the Indian fighter of Galeana.

dated back to the 1840's when invasion of Chihuahua from Texas was an imminent possibility and from New Mexico a distasteful actuality. During a noticeable upswing in Indian activities after the Civil War, American soldiers on the Apache trail occasionally ignored orders not to penetrate Mexico. In 1879, twenty-five soldiers of Fort Bayard, New Mexico, crossed the desert south of Columbus as far as Ascensión, and then withdrew. They returned in September, their number increased to five hundred soldiers and Apache scouts, locating rancherías of other Apaches. Several years later American soldiers operated in the vicinity of the Sierra de Candelaria, while local Mexicans were torn between fear of the Indians and dread of another American invasion. Later the jefe of Janos was advised by Mexican agents that the Americans again were riding the trails of his territory with a supply train and a large contingent of soldiers supposedly in pursuit of Ju and Gerónimo. Mexican troops at their Casas Grandes headquarters were mobilized, and the Americans tactfully went north. Meanwhile, the Indians caught in the squeeze from both north and south were hurt by neither. The governments of the two countries belatedly recognized the necessity of compromise if a solution to the Indian crisis was to be reached. A treaty for mutual assistance was signed. American forces were to be allowed to cross the border, and vice versa, keeping only to unpopulated areas and only tracking down raiding Indians.

Ultimately it was the Americans who captured the outlaw bands in the crumpled mountain mass separating Sonora and Chihuahua. Four hundred Apaches were returned to reservation life in the White Mountains of Arizona. En route, Gerónimo fled for the last time. Ju was already dead of an accident. Gerónimo and a small group of rebels tormented Americans and Mexicans alike for three more years until at last the fires of rebellion were ashes, and they could not continue holding out against two great nations and the inevitable march of time. Gerónimo, a proud but broken man, surrendered voluntarily to General Miles in 1886.

This was not the death knell for the Apaches in Mexico. They continued to reappear spasmodically for a number of years, attack an isolated, unsuspecting dwelling, and vanish without trace. But their might was broken that infamous dawn on the banks of the Casas Grandes.

A few years later, Colonel Joaquín retired from military service into quiet oblivion, satisfied that the Apache troubles were ended forever. The way was opened for the economic evolution of northern Mexico. *Latifundistas*, owners of large landed estates, like his cousin, were about to create another inflammable situation with solutions even more cruel, more unreasoning, than his for the Apaches. The training the colonel's fighters had received in techniques of warfare by stealth, of sudden noisy attack and hurried scattering to the impenetrable mountains or deserts, would be proved and re-proved in the fluctuant campaigns of the Division of the North.

THE GLORIOUS Pax Porfiriana did not burst full-blown upon Mexico. Rather, it was a yoke growing heavier through many years which weighed down a tired people regarded universally as bigoted, ignorant, impoverished, and hopeless.

As a republic, Mexico had passed the half-century mark and never had known peace. The office of the nation's president had changed hands seventy times. In Chihuahua there had been eighty-two separate administrations divided among thirty-nine men![74] Genuine leaders capable of the intricate job of governing wisely were few, although many had tried their wings as political leaders and had failed to get off the ground. Caudillos had set themselves up with a rabble following which in time, usually a short time, turned traitor and revolted to join a new caudillo with a more appealing plan. Instability was becoming a national characteristic. As a result of Juárez's Laws of Reform, the Church was inept and greatly weakened, hence ineffective in its role as cultural and spiritual leader. Economically, Mexico was facing bankruptcy with tremendous foreign debts and no credit. Mines which once helped pay the bills of Spanish kings were closed because of lack of operating capital. Some mineowners further added to the financial chaos by issuing their own copper, aluminum, and paper currency, good only at company stores. Natural resources, such as oil and timber, stood untapped and uncut. Machinery, what little there was, suffered from rusty neglect. Ranches, employing only primitive techniques of operation, failed to produce enough food to meet the needs of a rapidly increasing population. Even the weather seemed to be against Mexican progress. "The year of yellow corn," 1877 was called, because a severe drought caused the loss of all Chihuahua crops. The only railroad in the country ran between Mexico and Vera Cruz on the Gulf, scant hundreds of kilometers. Cities were dirty, shabby, and unhealthy. Most of the people, victims of a vicious class system, were ragged and illiterate. The glowing dreams of the dedicated insurgents had faded but were, nevertheless, not forgotten.[75]

The Mexico of 1876 was ready for a strong man like Díaz, who, through repression, bribes, and an occasional shot in the back, brought order out of lawlessness and an outward appearance of peace and prosperity. To do these things, he relied upon two groups who were partly responsible in the end for his downfall, the rurales, or rural police, and the foreign investors. In Chihuahua, there were rich mines, vast timber resources and huge sawmills, lengthy railroads, and extensive ranches, financed and controlled by foreigners, intensifying the Mexican's resentment for outsiders. Added to this feeling was the residue of anger left from the war of 1846. And the cutthroats and guards who once wore the dove-gray uniforms of the rurales came to form the core of the forces for revolution.

Chihuahua mines, particularly those in the southern sector, were a frequent target for extortionists in the pre-Díaz days. Outlaws from the neighboring states of Sonora and Sinaloa crossed the snarled divide to mining settlements such as Batopilas, Urique, Guadalupe y Calvo, and Chínipas, imposed a "loan" of several thousand pesos or even took over operations of the mines for a time, and then dissolved back into the never-never land from which they had come. Capturing them was difficult because of terrain ideal for escape and because of the insufficient number and lackadaisical temperament of the enforcement officers.

Hacienda and ranch homes, removed as they were from centers of population, were open to brazen attacks by robbers and rustlers. Often such crimes went unsolved and unpunished.

Human flotsam set adrift by ground swells in both countries plagued the regions along the international boundary. Cattle were stolen in New Mexico and Texas and driven across to Mexico where United States officials had no jurisdiction. Outlaws rode out of the Southwest into Mexico to steal and to abuse, and escaped north out of reach of Mexican law. Border customshouses were robbed and plundered. At Ojinaga a fake religious cult headed by an American adventuress, who called herself Hermana María openly exploited suckers.

Under the Díaz regime this type of activity ended. The Mexican dictator, in order to get foreign investors to come to his country, had to guarantee safety of personnel and funds. Any crime committed against foreigners was more severely punished than if against Mexicans. Rurales were given better pay than the former unorganized public guard, remudas of spirited mounts, flashy uniforms with embroidery and silver trim, and a high prestige value. Dark specters of armed rebellion limited the size of each squad to not more than ten men. Following the adage "If you can't lick 'em, join 'em," Díaz recruited highwaymen, rustlers, murderers, and other assorted law violators to turn policemen and control their former allies. It was a successful experiment because the rurales, most of them with few scruples about shooting former companions, kept the peace as it had never been kept before.* Few dared raise a voice in protest at the methods, and those that did, cried out only once. The *ley fuga*, law of flight, was the law of the land. Rurales, organized by Ahumada in Chihuahua in 1895, had authorization to shoot anyone attempting to escape them, and, according to their word, that was almost one hundred per cent of their unfortunate prisoners. An example of Porfirian justice was the case of Cornelius Callahan. A boat in the west coast harbor of Manzanillo was assaulted by fifteen men in an attempt to capture 45,000 pesos belonging to this Irishman, a principal of the Chihuahua mining camp of Pinos Altos. The captured bandits, en route to a Chihuahua courtroom, were all shot through application of the ley fuga.

Life outside the rurales' concept of law was discouraged. Lonely roads through the empty plains were made safe from ambush. Isolated ranches and mines seldom were attacked. *Pistola* peace had come to Mexico, Pax Porfiriana.

WITH THE SETTLED conditions in Chihuahua following the end of the Apache depredations and the cessation (for thirty years, at

---

* "For four centuries robbery, banditry, and violence had characterized the land, affecting its travel, its business, even its architecture. Under Díaz Mexico became the safest country in the world without exception." Priestley, 1938, 393.

least) of internal struggles for leadership, attention was focused on some of the aims of the *Independencia* and the later *Reformación*. There was time for timid progress toward social goals such as the extension and improvement of education facilities, taken out of Church hands at the time of Benito Juárez. Chihuahua was the second state in the Mexican union (Jalisco was the first) to institute public education. In 1875 a new ruling decreed that everyone between the ages of seven and fourteen was to attend primary schools to be provided by the municipal governments and political authorities. Universal education remained an ideal, however, not a fact, although public primary schools spread over the state. One in the capital was for adults. However, most of the interest was in schools at this level for children. Six schools were authorized for the Tarahumara with a fund of 12,000 pesos put aside for their construction and maintenance. Hacienda owners were ordered to establish and maintain primary schools for the peons' children.

On the secondary level, the Instituto Científico y Literario continued as the main preparatory school for boys. That institution had received funds for further construction from the sale of merchandise confiscated from a Spaniard, José María de Nafarrando, who had smuggled contraband goods into Chihuahua during Doniphan's occupation. Its new structure faced the Plaza Hidalgo on the west. The curriculum expanded to include Spanish grammar, ancient history, Italian, French, English, cosmography, philosophy, mathematics, and law. The student body, with an increasing awareness of the strength of unity, revolted en masse against an unpopular director. Governor Ahumada listened to their complaints and replaced the school's regime, but told the boys he would close the school if they did not return to classes without further commotion.

A school of music had been attempted but had failed. There had not been much time for music for the Chihuahuenses. Late in the century, under the administration of that most able governor Miguel Ahumada, a school of arts and crafts was started in the building housing the government printing office, and an industrial school for girls offered business courses, Spanish, English, sewing, and physical culture. A private Methodist business college, Colegio Palmore, opened in 1890, to teach new courses in typing, business methods, and bookkeeping. A public library was established in the capital. Two schools of agriculture reflected the concern in some quarters for the need of training a nation of farmers to care for land rapidly being eroded away and to increase dwindling crops. One such school was started by a pair of engineer brothers in the fertile Juárez valley. It is still operating. The other was located in Aldama, the farm area which supplied fruits and vegetables to the city of Chihuahua.

Educational opportunities, although more diversified, were still largely for the upper-class young people. Rural schools were too few to make a dent in the general illiteracy.

A new awareness of their importance to the nation prompted Chihuahuenses to begin compilation of historical data pertaining to their state. Historical societies were organized in Chihuahua, Parral, Ciudad Juárez, and Guadalupe y Calvo.[76]

WHILE THE ARCHITECTS of government were trying to meet the challenges of chaotic conditions in public office and defeatist attitudes among its citizens resulting from a traditional default of moral and financial obligations, construction engineers with full backing of Porfirio Díaz began widespread beautification. Mexico City, with parks and massive buildings, came to be one of the western world's most handsome cities, if one did not look behind the marble-and-wrought-iron facade to the putrid slums.

Chihuahua's own building program started with the seat of government. Upon being given statehood status, a "palace of government" had been authorized by one of the early legislatures. Procrastination and endless distractions had delayed actual construction for over fifty years. A smaller "house of government" on Avenida Juárez housed the state government in crowded and unimpressive surroundings. In 1882, at the instigation of Governor Luis Terrazas who proposed the use of 60,000 pesos from the sale of the Compañía del Ferrocarril Federal, ground for the new building was broken. Nine years later Chihuahuenses had a block-square state capital looking east to the Plaza Hidalgo and west to Calle Libertad.* It had been designed by a member of one of the city's founding families, Pedro Ignacio de Irigoyen.[77]

---

* On June 21, 1941, this building was nearly demolished by a fire. What remained of the colonial archives was lost in flames.

A few years later, another block building of white marble quarried at Carretas enclosed the old Jesuit college and the tower of Hidalgo's confinement directly back of the capital. This was the Federal Palace. Commemorative plaques to El Padre de la Patria (father of the country) were set in the exterior walls and in the central corridor where the execution had taken place.[78]

On the northeast edge of the city, beyond the tree-lined drive to the chapel of Santa Rita, a new penitentiary was built to replace the dilapidated, towered jail, a crumbling relic of colonial administration. Up the Río Chuvíscar, a dam and water-filtering works were started in 1895 to provide potable water for a booming capital. It was completed by 1909 at a cost of 950,000 pesos. Governor Ahumada began a drainage project for the city. The streets, now lighted by arc lights, were being paved and widened to accomodate a trolley line. The first automobile in the state arrived in 1900 and was owned by Governor Ahumada. In 1906, a taxi stand on the plaza had two cars for hire. A new clock for the cathedral tower was imported from London. The Plaza de la Constitución was spruced up with a highly ornate European kiosk. A new hospital replaced the demolished Hospital Civil with more up-to-date facilities and imported equipment. A fire department, Cuerpo de Bomberos, was organized.

Distance and lack of communication with central Mexico had handicapped Chihuahua from the beginning. Great strides were made under the Díaz dictatorship to bring the outposts into the fold and to reduce the stagnation resulting from isolation. The first telegraph message was received in 1876 addressed to the Governor of Chihuahua. It read: "C. Gobernador. Progress comes. The electric current is in my home and carries to you a handshake. Viva Mexico!" It was signed by José Félix Maceyra, Governor of Durango. In 1888 a telegraph line stretched taut across mountains between Chihuahua and Sonora, where formerly neither man nor beast had been able to travel. Gradually, remote centers such as Urique, Cusihuiriáchi, and Chínipas were tied to the capital by telegraph wires. In May 1881, the first phone was installed in a Terrazas Chihuahua bank. Within three years, fifty others were in use in places of business.

Railroad expansion was the proudest project of President Díaz.

Five hundred miles of track in the nation when he assumed office were increased to fifteen thousand by the end of his tenure.

The need for access from the sea to expedite shipments from the south led to the first railroad concession within the state of Chihuahua, granted to Hipólito Pasqueir de Doumartin back in 1849, to connect the state with the Sonoran coast. The agreement was terminated because the terms of the contract were not met. Ten years later the English mint director, Potts, and the American trader, McManus, were granted a concession for a road to the west coast between the 29th and 31st parallels. Because of the knotted blockades of mountains and barrancas, surveys through the region were not completed, and that concession was terminated. In 1860, it was the turn of Angel Trías, the father. He proposed to construct a line from Ojinaga on the Río Grande to Guaymas on the northeastern edge of the Gulf of California in return for being ceded one half of the public lands one league on each side of the right-of-way. Who knew what riches lay buried in that ribbon over the Sierra Madre Occidental, or how much wealth could be realized from the stands of virgin pine and oak? Authorities in Sonora were equally anxious to obtain new markets in Chihuahua for products of the sea and the wide littoral and granted Trías the railroad concession through the Sonoran portion of his tentative route. Trías failed just as dismally as his predecessors because he was unable to get financial backing in the tight money market accompanying the French invasion. The next attempt to cross the barrier to the ocean was made by the Ferrocarril Kansas City, México, y Oriente, a line more pretentious in name than in operation.[79] It was to run from Ojinaga west to Topolobampo, Sinaloa. Work began in Chihuahua in 1902 with a subsidy from the state of one thousand pesos per kilometer with Enrique Creel as concessionaire, who expressed the wish of spending his fortune so that Oriental silks from Asian cargo ships could pass through Chihuahua daily en route to Chicago. However, his line finally petered out on the Conchos, having crossed the desert only as far as Falomir and Marquez, leaving Ojinaga stranded for half a century. The west extension terminated at Creel, and the old dream of uniting the Chihuahua plateau with the Sinaloan coast faded.

The most important railroad joined its northern limbs directly to the heart of Mexico. In 1880, Governor Terrazas got a concession for a line from Chihuahua to Cuidad Juárez. He drove the first spike in ceremonies held in Ciudad Juárez in 1881.[80] The construction company imported many workers into Chihuahua from the southwestern United States, among them large numbers of Chinese. It was the beginning of Asiatic immigration into this part of Mexico. Chinese came first as peons, but stayed as shopkeepers and cafe owners.[81] In Chihuahua, as elsewhere in Mexico, the Orientals quickly adapted themselves to Mexican life and were absorbed by the already Mongoloid mestizo. "Chinita" became a term of endearment; "China Poblana," Chinese señorita from Puebla, paradoxically the purely Mexican symbol of pulchritude.

The central railroad was inaugurated in September 1882, and was properly dedicated with prideful oratory and free rides for dignitaries and their ladies. A pullman ticket from Mexico City to Chihuahua cost seventy pesos.[82] The first iron horse puffed over plains which for centuries had known the pounding hoofbeats of Spanish ponies and Indian mustangs. Just as those earlier horses had carried civilization forward, so the new iron horse would mean opening up of resources, easier communication, and increased trade with the neighboring United States. The terminus, Ciudad Juárez, would become the state's largest center of population. With the railroad came a long bridge to join Mexico to the United States, replacing a ferry operated for many years by the Acosta family. The following year, 1883, a rail extension south to Jiménez near the Durango border was in use, and one more year saw its completion through to the Mexican capital.

At the end of the century another economically important railroad, the Noroeste de México, formed by fusion of two earlier companies, ran from Chihuahua west to Guerrero, then turned north to Babícora and Casas Grandes, and swung northeast to Ciudad Juárez. A valuable area of timber and mines thus was opened to more extensive development. Spurs cut off to the mines of San Pedro, Calera, and Cusihuiriáchi. This was the line to suffer most destruction during the next revolution.

In 1900, a one-hundred-kilometer road connected Parral with northern Durango, bringing new prosperity to those regions through promotion of agricultural and mining centers. Another line branched off the Ferrocarril Central to Sierra Mojada in Coahuila, one hundred thirty-three kilometers.

Was Chihuahua about to join the family? Would the North now be united in spirit with central Mexico as it was brought closer physically in fact? The answer can be no unequivocal yes or no. While the distant trend may have been in the direction of unification, the railroad that might have brought men together, brought them together in battle, speeding up movements of troops of the Revolution decade. *Villistas* on horseback were backed up by villistas entrained. With the puffing aid of Díaz's symbol of progress, the orphaned child turned renegade.

THE SOVEREIGN STATE of Chihuahua encompassed almost 95,000 square miles. Boundaries drawn sharply on a map at the time of statehood remained hazy and ill-defined in actuality. Disputes with neighbors sent border commissions to survey exact lines between Chihuahua and the adjoining states of Coahuila and Sonora. Sierra Mojada and its newly discovered ores went to Coahuila and the Sierra Rosales to Chihuahua. The vicinity of the northern Valle de San Bernardino was divided with Sonora. From colonial times the broad land of Chihuahua had been divided into individual property (*peonías* of one hundred by one hundred fifty feet and *caballerías* of five peonías) ; ejidos; the hacienda-rancho-latifundium type of holdings; and the baldíos. An ejido was designed as communal property, usually a square league. A hacienda was limited to 8,775 hectares (approximately 219,375 acres). A rancho was smaller, a latifundium larger. Baldíos were the lands of public domain. The process wherein the latifundia grew increasingly larger at the expense of the ejidos, and the baldíos passed to private ownership, created one of the discontents leading to the revolution.

Latifundia were consolidated, each over 250,000 acres. By 1910, seventeen persons owned two-fifths of the state—soil, water, and animals which fed upon it. Foreigners controlled vast sections. At a time when north of the border the wealth of the nation was being spread among more and more individuals, in Mexico it was becoming concentrated in the hands of fewer. Ninety-nine and five-tenths per cent of the residents of Chihuahua owned no land, indeed could not even possess an animal without consent of a patrón! Such was the staggering dislocation of property and wealth, the chimerical prosperity mistakenly admired by the rest of the world.

Luis Terrazas was the greatest latifundista of them all. Most of his lands lay north and west of the capital, although he did have several haciendas in the Florido drainage in the south. Four foreigners owned tremendous grazing latifundia: the mother of William Randolph Hearst in the Babícora basin in the municipio of Namiquipa and Temósachi, T.O. Riverside along the Río Grande between Ojinaga and Guadalupe, the Palomas Land and Cattle Company by the United States border in the municipio of Janos, and the Hacienda de Corralitos in the municipio of Nuevo Casas Grandes, owned by a New York firm. Other latifundia were those of Carlos Zuloaga on the wind-teased shores of Lake Bustillos, of the Tres Hermanos in Satevo, of Martínez del Río who retained areas in the municipios of Chihuahua and Ahumada, of Santa Clara in the municipio of Manuel Benevides by the border, of Santa Gertrudis in Saucillo, and of Dolores in Aldama near the capital.[83]

In the thirty year "peace" of Don Porfirio, Chihuahua, with the cooperation of an underpaid submissive peonage, a large, uniquely suitable terrain, and a clamoring northern market reached by train, became the nation's cow kingdom. The owners of this kingdom operated their crown colonies in absentia, preferring the bright lights of more cosmopolitan centers. The land was left to those whose bare feet trod in the dust, though they realized none of its material rewards.

The man who had received the first railroad concession, Hipólito Pasqueir de Doumartin, at the same time was granted first concessions of public domain in the sierra through which the railroad was to pass. In 1863, the Juárez government set 2,500 hectares (approximately 5,250 acres) as the maximum baldíos holdings one person could have, with a price fixed at twenty-five centavos per hectare. The Díaz administration established a grading system and price scale for public lands in Chihuahua—fifty-five cents for a first class hectare, thirty cents for second class, and twenty cents for third class. Prices rose to seventy-five cents, fifty cents, and thirty cents by 1887; to four pesos by 1909 under the influence of a Díaz-inspired land boom. Single companies acquired more than the legal limit of baldíos land through subsidiaries and formation of *compañias deslindadores.* Such companies disregarded earlier rulings that workers had to be paid in cash and not in merchandise from *tiendas de raya,* or company-operated stores. In the Madera and Temósachi regions the Noroeste de México Railroad held thousands of hectares of timbered land, the man behind the scenes being William C. Green. An American industrialist already involved in northern Mexico in the Cananea Consolidated Copper Company in Sonora, he spread his network of negotiations over the continental divide into Chihuahua.

In 1904 Governor Creel granted Green a chain of concessions to exploit the timber resources in the districts of Galeana and Guerrero. An investment was required of not less than 200,000 pesos, the land to be tax free for ten years. Green installed sawmills in the area of the new town of Madera, opened a paper pulp plant, a furniture factory, and lumberyards. His enterprises brought in the Noroeste de México Railroad and opened a new wagon road from Temósachi into the sierra near Ocampo. It was not long before his companies, with a capital of $7,500,000,[84] monopolized the various economic facets of the Chihuahua mountains. Thousands of families were dependent upon him and the success of his colossal operations. But giants, expecially industrial ones, are prone to stumble over their own tremendous feet. Green's giant collapsed with a roaring thud that shook the mighty mountains and sent shock waves over all of Mexico.

The world was feeling economic stresses prior to the outbreak of World War I, and the Cananea mines were suffering mounting losses as a result. Money from the Chihuahuan pockets was transferred to the Sonoran pockets until there was nothing left in either. Pay days for the workers in Green's various projects were becoming less frequent. There were rumblings and talk of strikes as uneasiness swept the cordillera. At last, $25,000,000 of Green's empire was lost, with outstanding debts still estimated at another six to eight million dollars. His Chihuahua sawmills and factories closed. A horde of unemployed families sat in their drafty cabins wondering what lay ahead. Where was the prosperity now, with no cornmeal or beans, even those to be bought on credit from the tienda de raya? Their dependence upon a foreigner angered them, and it seemed to humble peons that his bankruptcy had been aimed at them.

Another man interested in this section of baldíos was Weetman Pearson, a British magnate who had dredged the harbor at Vera Cruz, helped build the Tehuantepec Railroad, developed Tampico oil fields, and was involved in other grandiose projects for Díaz. He turned some of his attention and money to Chihuahua.[85] A few miles south of the Terrazas hacienda of San Diego, near Casas Grandes, he constructed what held promise of being a bustling industrial center named Pearson (now Mata Ortiz) which was occupied largely by Americans. Mammoth band sawmills, planing mills, drying sheds, and burners were designed to make Pearson one of the world's largest sawmills. Lord Cowdray (Pearson's title conferred for his financial successes in Mexico) was one of those who went down in the Atlantic disaster of the Titanic. He never lived to see his mills become stables for Villa's horses and soldiers or his flatcars loaded with dynamite and sent racing down cliffs to crash in thundering confusion on plains below.

The biggest owner of baldíos was Díaz's right-hand man and Secretary of the Treasury, José Ives Limantour, who with a partner was allowed to exchange relatively valueless land in Baja California and some offshore islands for 170,000 hectares, although the legal limit of individual ownership was but 2,500. Moreover, this land in the municipios of Guerrero and Bocoyna represented potentially the richest timber resources of the Tarahumara Alta. This shady transaction led to the Tomochi War, a local uprising to break out soon. In 1906 the disputed land was sold to the foreign-owned and -operated Cargill Lumber Company. The Chihuahua Lumber Company, also North American owned, ran another sawmill and lumber camp at Cuesta Prieta (modern San Juanito) in the same region.

The forests of yellow pine, Arizona pine, Douglas fir, and oak gave great fortunes to some men, but nothing was returned to the earth. Shade trees were planted around all the plains and desert towns, but the mountain forests were being destroyed. Slopes were denuded, left covered only with unsightly darkened stumps to rot away but not to hold the soil for long. The stripped sierra was not reforested. By-products of lumbering operations were discarded and wasted. Forests were further depleted by the railroads, whose engines used wood in gigantic quantities for fuel, and by the hungry furnaces of the mining mills. Indeed, the people themselves cut down their forest resources to burn in their kitchen cook fires. The *carboneros*, who converted raw wood into charcoal; the Indians, who cleared their fields by fire; the industrialists, who sought wealth in board feet of pine and clear oak never once thought of planting a young tree to replace what they had taken. To hell with posterity! Think only of present prosperity!

MINERAL WEALTH, the reason for the original colonization, through the centuries seemed inexhaustible and beyond calculation but hard to tap because of the rugged environment in which it was found. Mining, at best, was an expensive enterprise demanding a substantial reserve upon which to operate, the kind of financial resource difficult to find in the confused eras preceding the dictatorship. Díaz sought to help his country's desperate fiscal situation and to attract investment from abroad by a general revitalization of the entire mining industry. In laws of 1884 and 1892, he granted full subsoil rights to the owners of the surfaces. Rurales for protection and rails for transportation were added incentives. Also attractive was the low prevailing wage scale which operators, big and small, were not anxious to change. Foreign ownership of Chihuahua mines was not a new pattern, but a greatly enlarged one at the beginning of the twentieth century. Canadian, British, American, and even Japanese companies enriched themselves at the expense of Mexico. True, they employed large numbers of workers, which stimulated the sagging economy, and introduced new methods of pulverization and flotation, but the bulk of revenue went out of the country, not even leaving a residue of funds from taxation. By the time of the Revolution, over a hundred mineral districts in both the high sierra and the desert hills were being exploited by five hundred seventy mines to produce gold, copper, lead, mercury, coal, and silver.

Metallurgical plants opened in Aquiles Serdán (post-revolution name), Parral, Villa Escobedo, Jiménez, Lluvia de Oro, Calera, Cusihuiriáchi, and San Julián. The American Smelting and Refining Company (Asarco) built a mammoth plant on the plains of Avalos, seven kilometers from the capital, with a thirty-year exemption from taxation and a tienda de raya owned by Don Luis's son, Juan Terrazas.[86]

Subsoil wealth included oil. In 1901 the state offered a prize of 10,000 pesos to the person who drilled the first producing oil well within the state limits. Some scattered explorations were made in the vicinity of Ojinaga. To date, however, oil has not been found in any quantity in a state so rich otherwise in natural resources, but exploratory tests continue to be made along the course of the Río Grande.

Explorations for artesian water in the subsurface met with more results, the first well being at Ascensión.

THE FIRST LABOR STRIKE in Chihuahua was a miners' strike at Pinos Altos, a small camp high in the mountainous municipio of Ocampo.[87] In the beautiful, elevated Sierra Madre Occidental of Mexico, the national labor organization was born. In 1881, five years before the Chicago May Day strike which led to modern Labor Day celebrations, a serious dispute took place with Mexican miners fighting against their English management. Pinos Altos, an infant mining district only ten years old, had become a British holding after first being claimed by a Mexican *buscador,* or prospector. It represented a Devil's Island for a wayward son of an aristocratic English family who despaired of his scandalous escapades. Pinos Altos was about as far removed a place as could be found, and so it was to that forlorn spot that young John Hepburn was exiled. Not having the slightest desire to go to Mexico in the first place, or to understand the Mexican workmen at the family mine, Hepburn vacillated between authoritarianism and complete disinterest. He antagonized local officials by refusing to pay the required municipal "contributions." With no realization of the disruptions it would mean for people without reserves or without budgetary virtues, he arbitrarily ordered that pay days be at two-week intervals instead of the customary weekly period and that half the pay be spent at the company commissary. Angry at a long chain of unhappy edicts such as this, the men as a group appeared before Hepburn to request a restoration of the weekly pay. He refused to give them audience. The men, in turn, refused to work. A mob riot followed, and in the confusion, Hepburn received a fatal blow on the head. The next day after news of the accident reached Ocampo,

Carlos Conant, the municipal president, and twenty-five men rode to Pinos Altos to restore order. This was a most serious matter since a British subject was involved, and not only would protests be received from the British government but from an agitated Don Porfirio as well. The posse, anxious to please their president, stood four of the ringleaders against a wall and shot them before the jefe político arrived to put a stop to the violence.

That same year, workers laying the tracks for the new Ferrocarril Central to Ciudad Juárez grew bold enough to stage a strike because the director of the construction reduced pay from two pesos to one peso, fifty centavos per day. Throughout much of the world, May 1 became a holiday dedicated to labor. In Chihuahua's capital, as early as 1892 May Day was observed as Labor Day by three societies of workers, nascent labor unions.

Industry was expanding in Chihuahua, but it did not keep pace with other fields of activity. A textile factory to make cloth and thread opened at the Hacienda de Tabalaopa under management of Leopoldo von Kessel. Canuto Elias, Luis Terrazas, Carlos Zuloaga, Emilio Ketelsen, and Enrique C. Creel were its backers. Machinery for a large brewery was installed in the northern edge of the capital. In 1901, Creel founded a packing plant near the city to process meats from the state's herds. A cement plant owned by Juan Terrazas opened in Ciudad Juárez. Gas plants were built in Chihuahua and Parral, and a hydroelectric plant on the Río Conchos began operations.

ONCE A MEMBER of the Juárez camp favoring stringent control, even complete suppression, of the clergy, Díaz gradually allowed return of their power. He accomplished this by doing nothing. Quietly, without fanfare, the Church, without interference, regained its lands and its position of strength in government, education, and social life. Decrees from the Chihuahua governor's offiice ordered all business establishments to close after two o'clock in the afternoon on Sundays or face a hundred pesos' fine. The Sabbath was to be enforced. However, religious freedom also was enforced for the first time, and Methodists and Baptists openly gathered to worship. A Y.M.C.A. unit opened in an annex to the Teatro de los Héroes. A peaceful economic invasion by foreigners was to be matched by a religious one.[88]

Since 1620, Chihuahua had been attached to the bishopric of Durango, but in 1891, Pope Leo XIII saw fit to establish a bishopric of Chihuahua. A committee of devout Chihuahua Catholics, with Don Luis Terrazas as honorary president, was charged with planning a reception for Father José de Jesús Ortiz, first bishop of Chihuahua. The golden splendor of magnificent vestments and the beauty of the huge temple, the sensuous stimulations of mesmeric chanting, heavy incense, and flickering candlelight overawed the humble, ragged peasants gathered in the back of the great cathedral to witness the holy services, just as it impressed the fashionably dressed dons and doñas occupying front pews. For a few moments, rich and poor, highborn and illegitimate, pious and irreverent were drawn together in a unity of profound emotion. The Church and its myriad of shaded meanings to the individual and to the group, despite wrongdoings and transgressions, remained a fountainhead of strength and cohesion for the Mexican people. But the Church was in for trouble.

The trouble started at Tomochi. It was here that Tepóraca defiantly cursed his Spanish captors and refused the blessings of Catholic Christianity. It was here that Spanish armies were defeated time after time by native Indians fighting to retain their racial dignity. It was here that Zuloaga recruited tacubayistas, and Colonel Joaquín his Indian scouts and fighters. It was here that rebellion had become a bad habit and would flare again. Tomochi was in what the Mexican journalist Fernando Jordán called the Longitude of War, the 107th meridian, which in Mexico passes mainly through the mountains of western Chihuahua.[89]

The causes of the Tomochi War were both religious and economic, intermingled in the minds of the downtrodden who were struggling against injustices which confronted them on every avenue: *caciquismo, latifundismo,* and Pax Porfiriana.[90]

Tomochi was in the heart of the Limantour baldíos, which the inhabitants claimed had been stolen from them. They did not consider the fact that they had neither the capital nor the knowledge to turn the trees to money in the bank. Resentment further mounted when the sawmills paid such low wages that the men and their families could not sustain themselves on an already marginal standard. The men left the lumber camps and climbed the mountains to mines of the neighboring Rayón district where the pay was somewhat better. Díaz's political chief in the Guerrero sector had the rebels jailed as vagrants, which, of course, did not enhance his popularity. On November 30, 1891, the Tomochis, with their hair-trigger tempers, marched on the government office shouting angry protests, yelling that they would obey only the laws of God.

Unscrupulous priests had, at this same period, been milking the populace with exorbitant fees for the necessary sacraments of a Christian life—baptisms, marriages, funerals, even confession. Their bad example turned their congregations away from the organized church toward mystic and evangelical fanatics.

A bountiful crop of divine prophets, healers, messiahs, and claimants of holy visitations sprouted in the hills, like mushrooms after rain. One was called Teresa Urrea. She lived in the hamlet of Cabora, Sonora. A señorita no longer a girl yet not a woman, with a strong religious bent, a power of hypnotism, and a smattering of *brujería,* or witchcraft, and medical knowledge, she was credited with magical gifts and miraculous cures by superstitious peasants easily convinced of the fantastic. An autumnal wind before a storm, the fame of the Saint of Cabora crossed the mountain divide and swept through the high Chihuahua sierras. Some of the families of Tomochi had made the arduous pilgrimage to her shrine and returned home converted to her brand of religion. Among these was Cruz Chávez, the acknowledged head man of the village, whose very name had religious significance. He was accused later of having set up an idolatrous altar in his crude adobe home and of appointing priests and priestesses to conduct sacrilegious services. It is unlikely that the young saint was aware of her part in the death struggle about to erupt, but the use of her name as a call to the fray condemned her forever in the eyes of the clergy and Díaz.

Neither government nor Church felt inclined to accept such audacity. A battalion commanded by Captain Segundo Castro was dispatched to Tomochi. Cruz Chávez already had armed his village in anticipation of their arrival. Each man had been given a gun on whose butt was stamped a red cross and the platitudinous assurance that if he had faith, justice and right would win out. In battle, as they were being defeated, Chávez could only believe the Tomochis had fought with bad faith. The rebelling men were driven from the protection of their homes into the mountains where they found no refuge. They sought solace from their saint, only to be fired upon by Sonoran police. They slept through the bitterly cold nights without a fire to give away their whereabouts. By day they crept to isolated rancherías to beg for food, but there was little to share. In January, bone-cold and beaten, the Tomochis came home.

In return, the jefe político for Guerrero offered an "open" investigation of the causes of the discontent. Fearful of a trap and unused to fair treatment, the Tomochis refused. Again, government troops moved into the once peaceful valley. This time it was they who were defeated.

Tiny Tomochi, with a population of thirty or so poor families cut off from the world, then became a testing ground for the Díaz administration. More than twelve hundred government men from Guerrero and Pinos Altos were thrown into battle against a handful of brash mountain dwellers who kept alive through force of fanatical faith, skill in self-defense, and a great deal of luck. In a bit of trickery, some Tomochis dressed as women and advanced unmolested to within a few yards of the enemy to fire in a suicidal attack. Heavy losses were inflicted on the surprised troops as they were routed. At last, the soldiers gained a hilltop from which they raked the mud village with shells from their Hotchkiss machine gun. Five days passed before Captain Castro, Colonel Torres, and General Rangel let their forces open fire on the simple, white-washed church built by Father Glandorf, where Cruz Chávez's people clung to life. A Yaqui scout was sent forward to ask surrender. Chávez's insolent answer was to wave his own banner from the crumbling tower, a white flag with a large red cross in the center. The army with its well-placed cannon resumed bombardment of the church. Rain ate away the church walls. Finally there were just a half dozen men and one woman left inside, all wounded and without ammunition. As they wearily emerged in abject surrender, it was seen that the cacique of Tomochi, Cruz Chávez, was still alive. But not for long. The men were shot as traitors, leaving only the lonely old woman to remember all her sad remaining days the great bravery of the men of the Longitude of War.

It had taken a bloodstained month, a thousand men, and complete annihilation of all its men and boys to convince the Tomochis that Díaz was the "hero of peace," his way the best way. Peace and prosperity! For whom?

The Saint of Cabora, a girl of nineteen years, yet considered a monstrous threat to peaceful integration of Catholicism and dictatorship in the outlands, was exiled to Clifton, Arizona, where American heretics would know how to deal with her. She lived there for fifteen years, dying in 1906.

The reinstated Jesuits added a postscript to the religious history of the period with an archaeological expedition in 1907. Father Manuel Pinan, S.J., was to go to the pueblo of San Andrés de Conicari, Sonora, to attempt to find the earthly remains of two early seventeenth-century missionary martyrs, Julio Pascual and Manuel Martínez, for their possible canonization.[91] The town is situated at the junction of the Río Mayo and the Río del Quiriego, deep in the awesome Chínipas sector of the sierra madre. Church scholars came to believe it was the place where the two priests had been buried after a wild native uprising in 1632. Pinan was to find out. On foot and jogging burro, he crossed the scrubby Sonoran plains to the towering highlands and then, with the assistance of Tarahumara guides, wound through a confusing maze of castellated canyons to lonely San Andrés, which he reached after eighteen days. Beneath a mound of mud, rubble, and a modern cemetery, beside the present church, he was told there had been an ancient temple, perhaps the one for which he searched. Hopeful of the early success of his mission, Father Pinan applied to the *comisario*, or commissioner, for permission to exhume any bodies found. Then trouble came.

Red tape is a seemingly inexhaustible Mexican commodity and petty officials love to throw their weight around. This comisario hastened to point to a civil law prohibiting opening graves. He could only raise his shoulders in a gesture of resigned compliance, suggesting that perhaps the prefect of Alamos, many *jornadas*, or days' journey, across sheer cliffs and fast, rushing rivers, could grant permission. Quién sabe? An Indian runner was dispatched at once to Alamos to bring a legal document which the comisario could not read but upon which he would recognize the official seals of his state.

During his enforced wait, Father Pinan learned that the original townsite had been on the opposite bank of the river and that maybe his priests lay there. When permission to proceed finally arrived, fortunately with recognizable seals, Pinan read that he was limited to daylight excavation and that the comisario and the judge of the civil district had to be present. If any object of historic, artistic, or financial value be found, the padre was to present an inventory of same to the prefect. The dream of Quivira, fused with enchantment of buried treasure, lingered on. He directed a crew of peons to excavate a likely looking site where the ancient town was supposed to have stood. It was not long before an adobe paving was encountered, but exploratory trenches failed to reveal house or church foundations.

Much excitement was stirred up by the padre's diggings in a village almost asleep. The curious people came to stare, to advise, and to speculate. Putting bits of information together like a giant jigsaw puzzle, Father Pinan began to learn that in the foggy past a town had been projected where he worked, but because a Spanish miner wished to carry on operations there, contaminating the drinking water with his mill's tailings, the priest must have persuaded the entire pueblo to move across the stream and upriver. They had carted off adobe bricks and hewn beams to be reused in the new town. As the river rose in its annual time of high water, it flooded the bank and "paved" its borders with adobe silt. So back to his original mound went the black-robed archaeologist.

Distinct floor, corners, and naves of the decayed temple were soon found. Fervent whispers of "madre de dios!" and pious crossing of the breast were made by natives who had never known for sure of the church's existence and who now felt guilty of desecration. The accounts of the massacre had told of the priests having been buried side by side before the altar. Using this information as a starting point, Pinan's diggers trenched an area approximately where the original altar might have stood. Their efforts were rewarded when two coffins in parallel position were uncovered. With all the tense enthusiasm of treasure seekers (and archaeologists!) everywhere, the comisario, the judge, and the padre knelt in the warm dirt to examine the contents of the two boxes. There were bones which crumbled to the touch, as did the wooden boxes. Bits of black cloth, black braid, ornaments, copper thread, and hairs which seemed to be blonde were sifted from the fill. Definite proof of method of death, something archaeologists seldom find, was present. Two arrows, almost disintegrated because of the moistness of the soil but indisputable, rammed through the vertebrae of one skeleton. Neither skeleton possessed a head, but this did not surprise Father Pinan. Jesuit history told that the battered heads, decapitated by the Indians and spiked to a cross, had been sent to the Jesuit college in Mexico City for a nauseous exhibit, completely in character, of the pain inflicted upon missionaries in the heathen northlands.

A bizarre cortege rode down from San Andrés de Conicari, at last returning to their own the remains of two martyrs who had lain beneath a destroyed temple for two and three-quarters centuries.

THE VENEER of prosperity from increasing revenues from cattle, timber, mining, and new industries greatly stimulated cultural life in the capital. A theater became the entertainment center of town. It was called El Teatro de los Héroes in honor of the insurgent leaders of the revolt against Spain. A statue to them, dedicated by Angel Trías, the son, and financed by public subscription, was erected on the plaza on which the theater faced. The theater was a highly embellished structure designed by the English architect George King at a lavish cost of 655,000 pesos. Its gala opening performance was *Aïda* performed by a touring Italian opera company. Another opera company, starring María Tavery, gave four thrilling performances. Local reviewers in papers such as *El Pegaso* praised Miss Tavery but noted that all the troupe complained of the bitter cold wave then gripping Chihuahua. Plays by the troupe of Virginia Fabregas were applauded, especially one written by a Chihuahua lawyer turned playwright, José Muños Lumbier. The first movies were shown in 1899 in connection with the Treviño circus.

In 1896, a sporting event held at a frontier point between Coahuila and Texas attracted many Chihuahuenses. It was a prizefight between the world heavyweight champion, Bob Fitzsimmons, and his opponent, Pete Maher. The fight took place on a large, flat rock projecting from the Mexican side of the Río Grande while the audience sat in makeshift seats in Texas. A special train was run from Mexico City to El Paso, and a number of Chihuahuenses joined the gay crowd aboard the train as it moved through their state. Fitzsimmons won by a knockout in the first round.

That same year, 1896, the German colony of the capital celebrated the twenty-fifth anniversary of Emperor William I's coronation with a holiday and festive games. Two years later news of the sinking of the *Maine* and the imminent Spanish-American War was the subject of heated conversations at the early evening coffee time. Old animosities against both Spain and the United States were aroused, but only briefly. The assassination of the North American president McKinley in 1901 caused scarcely a stir. It was a familiar episode to Mexicans.

In the bullring by the Chuvíscar, where once American traders and troopers had camped, bullfights again were being enjoyed after a prohibition in effect since 1868. Vibrant "oles" and shrill whistles greeted the attempted artistry of matadors such as José Casanova—"El Morenito," Francisco Palomar—"Caro Chico," and Francisco Villegas—"Naranjito," who bravely faced ferocious bulls from the Terrazas Hacienda El Sauz.

A member of the Terrazas clan, Alberto, joined in partnership with an American, J. G. Fallansbee, to open a horse-racing track in Ciudad Juárez. Mexican admiration of horseflesh and the inherent love of the gamble made this a highly successful venture. One of the most ardent *aficionados* of this sport was Pancho Villa.

An annual religious holiday, May 22, was the fair of Santa Rita and the most joyous celebration held in the pre-Revolution capital.[92] Frame stalls with flapping canvas roofs were installed around the small plaza, where now there is a statue to the fallen hero of the French Intervention in Chihuahua, Manuel Ojinaga, to sell the brilliantly colored sweets of which Mexicans were so fond. Cantinas and gambling houses afforded the pleasure-bent citizens an opportunity to lose the new jingle in their pockets. Lotteries raffled foodstuffs, toys, and household goods. Small children, eyes wide with wonderment and excitement, crowded around the *tío vivo*, merry-go-round, with its bright whimsical seats made like tigers, lions, elephants, and prancing horses. Four husky boys pushed the merry-go-round's inner circular frame to make it whirl round and round in an exciting blur, twelve turns for three cents.

A military band under the skilled direction of José M. de la Vega held free morning concerts in the tree bordered park now called Parque Lerdo. A battle of flowers raged up and down the grass of the Paseo Bolivar. The phonograph made its first loud Chihuahua appearance in the Santa Rita fiesta of 1896.

Each fair time Señora Matilde Maceyra de Tavizón opened a cafe in an old building facing the plaza, which she decorated in streamers of colored paper, paper lanterns, large gilt-framed mirrors, and starched, white, lacy curtains. She called it "La Despedida" for it was next door to the depot from which carriages and coaches left for El Paso. Her specialities were tiny chicken tamales, fried chicken basted with piquant sauce, and rich ice creams of lemon and vanilla.

A unique feature of the fair was a contest in which prizes were given for the best-decorated carriages. A queen was chosen to ride in the flower-covered mail coach. The landaus, milords, and buggies of Eduardo Alfafull, Maximino Krakauer, or Howard Anderson were bedecked with colorful flowers, ribbons, and paper, and were driven around the plazas. The town's prominent young ladies, dressed in new hobbled skirts, organza flounces, and enormous picture hats, rode as giggling passengers, gaily throwing flowers to the barefooted spectators.

Peace on the prairies was enjoyed to the hilt—by the well heeled.

SUNBONNET met sombrero on the bleached Janos plains.[93] It was 1885 when Americans drove loaded wagons through the creosote and guayule of southern New Mexico, prepared to cast their lot forever with the Mexican nation. They came with their families— from St. George, St. Johns, Snowflake, Ogden, Salt Lake, Socorro, Panguitch, Provo. They were Allens, Cluffs, Eyrings, Hawkins, McClellans, Porters, Pratts, Romneys, Skousens, Spilsburys, Taylors, Woods. By vocation, they were cattlemen, farmers, saddlemakers, carpenters, tinsmiths, musicians, surveyors, millers, merchants, masons—and now immigrants. Bishop, Apostles, Elders, lay clergy—all were Mormons. They were fleeing what they regarded as persecution and infringement of religious and civil rights in the "land of the free." How troubled were souls who could dare hope for haven in a quick-on-the-draw country unsympathetic to re-

ligious dogmas outside the pale of Catholicism and traditionally
belligerent to Americans.

Three hundred years had passed since representatives of a Western brand of Christianity dignified by ages of consecration and
suffering fostered movement north, struck down almost unbelievable barriers to conquer a new realm, to settle it and shape it in
the image of Old Spain. Now, the infant Protestant sect of Mormonism, a mere half century old, was penetrating from the opposite direction. These Mormons had no desire to conquer and no
time to convert. They sought a home where they could continue
their church-sanctioned polygamous marriages.

Behind the desperate flight was a rising popular distaste for
plural Mormon marriages. A bill had been passed by the United
States Congress in 1862 for the suppression of polygamy, but it remained unsigned into law for twenty years. In 1882, violators were
disenfranchised and imprisoned. Many Mormons stubbornly refused to recognize the legality of the so-called Edmunds Bill. They
would not dissolve their marriages or leave their well-populated
homes. Troopers jailed some of those offenders, hoping the unhappy examples would persuade compliance. But rather than conform to the marriage law, many forsook their farms and shops in
Utah, Arizona, and New Mexico, loaded their plows and cook pots
into wagons, and charted a course across the Southwest to an adventurous life of exile among sometimes hostile neighbors. They
said their choking good-byes and there was no turning back.

Díaz, always an admirer of the foreigner, his money, and his
initiative, welcomed these latest colonists whose coming had been
announced by church officials in Salt Lake City. Only the year before, 1884, he had permitted a colony of Belgians to take land in
the arid municipio of San Francisco de Borja to introduce the raising of flax to Chihuahua. Later, in 1903, Díaz again opened lands
to foreign immigrants, a group of thirty-four Boer families. They
settled on the Hacienda de Humboldt in the municipio of Julimes,
near the wide confluence of the San Pedro and the Conchos. The
Belgians were disheartened by an unsuccessful battle against continued drought which withered their tender, sprouting crops year
after year. In contrast, the Boers were driven out by devastating
floods which washed roots of young fruit trees from the soil and

buried gardens in a crust of river silt. By the time of the revolutionary upheavals, Belgians and Boers had vanished from the Chihuahua scene. Only the Mormons had sufficient loyalty to a new homeland, enough stubborn tenacity, and a financial investment large enough to steel them to endure the tragic decade of 1910 to 1920.

Through efforts of Don Porfirio and his one-armed, one-legged Secretary of Foreign Relations and Governor of Chihuahua, General Carlos Pacheco, the Mormons were allowed to colonize on church-purchased land, to establish a polygamous island in the midst of a Catholic culture which would not even accept divorce, to import duty-free household and agricultural goods. In 1890, after the United States Supreme Court was given power to confiscate church property, President Wilford Woodruff of the Church of Jesus Christ of Latter-day Saints, as the Mormon sect is known officially, issued a manifesto to his people "to refrain from contracting any marriage forbidden by the law of the land." The reason for emigration was nullified. However, Mormons in Mexico continued polygamy after that date since they were not bound any longer by United States restrictions.

There was no mass entry of Mexico. Wagons, alone or in small groups, passed through a hundred miles of northern Mexican desert to the customs station at La Ascensión. It was here that others thirty-two years before had abandoned United States citizenship upon the inclusion of the border town of La Mesilla in the Gadsden Purchase and had re-established themselves south of the international boundary. The first Mormon colonist to arrive in Mexico, William C. McClellan, had been there before as a member of the Mormon Battalion which had blazed a precipitous trail across the Guadalupe Mountains. In the opening months of 1885, Mormon families converged on the camp at La Ascensión to await the purchase of land by scouts dealing with Mexican owners, and to attempt to untangle the bewildering knots of entry formalities. The customs station had to be moved north to Deming, New Mexico, to care for the steady movement of colonists and livestock. Had not the need for asylum been so great, the Mormon immigration would have ended before it had begun. Unsuitable lands and lack of water, doubtful title to lands, outrageous prices, brusque refusal to sell to Americans, delays and dilly-dallying thwarted the elders charged with site selection and purchase. While they dickered, the restless camp at La Ascensión grew and overflowed to Corralitos and Casa Grandes. Mormons stayed timidly by their wagons or wandered into the settlements to try to become acquainted with their new countrymen. Some studied Spanish in an effort to speed their adjustment, and others examined the loamy riverbank soil and felt the farmer's urge to get seeds into ground while the spring was young and receptive. All waited with daily mounting anxiety for word from their scouts that a deal had been concluded. Instead they were handed an ultimatum to leave Mexico within fifteen days!

Memories of some Mexicans were not so short but that they bitterly remembered other invasions of the northern frontier. When covered wagons packed with who-knew-what rolled into their towns and parked suspiciously along fifty miles or more of their river banks, was it not natural to become nervous of undeclared intentions? Officials at the capital had not made known to local jefes políticos the contents of the colonization permits. To them, this was armed invasion, and immediate expulsion was necessary. With the aid of impassioned propaganda prepared by a young Chihuahua lawyer touched by both the homeless plight of the refugees and by American dollars, a revocation of the expulsion order was secured. A subordinate, not yet indoctrinated with Díaz's "love thy neighbor—especially if he has money" policy, had been responsible for the curt demand to leave.

More months of waiting and praying followed. These were times of disappointment, of nagging suspicion that a return to former homes eventually would come. Faith and courage were being replaced by cynicism and low morale. Eleven months after McCellan's outfit had led the Mormon vanguard southward, word was received of purchase of fifty thousand acres of the Río Piedras Verdes and sixty thousand acres each in La Ascensión and Corrales. The homeless now had land and opportunity. Tap roots would penetrate deep, through the tough hardpan of Mexican resentment at their presence.

Eager to see at last their new homesite, camps quickly were dismantled and supplies crammed into wagons. The caravan of colonists bound for the Piedras Verdes settlement bumped south along the edge of the Casas Grandes River. At the junction of the

Casas Grandes and the Piedras Verdes, the lead wagons turned
northwest to follow the broad, flat river valley of the Piedras Verdes
for a half dozen miles. It was an unintentional re-enactment of an
early scene dear to their history, when a tired leader looked over a
bleak Utah basin and said, "This is the place." The colonists, tumbling from their wagon-homes to gaze at "the place" in Mexico, generally were pleased with the prospects of the choice made for them.
Sod dugouts were built along the river for protection through the
remainder of the winter. When spring came, these were replaced by
adobe homes of Mexican materials but American design. After a
townsite on the church-approved plan was surveyed, a communal,
stockaded meetinghouse was erected. A dam was thrown across the
river and a mile-long canal dug to reach trees and gardens planted
in the first flush of spring. On March 21, in ceremonies to which
local Mexican officials were invited, the settlement was named
Colonia Juárez, that being the patriot's birthday. A substantial
beginning, enough to inspire hope for the future, had been made.
But through a great miserable mistake, all the development had
been made on land which the Mormons did not own!

Gardens, canal, homes—all were on the property of the Rancho
San Diego. Some years later this land was incorporated into the
Terrazas' Hacienda de San Diego with headquarters at the junc-
tion of the two rivers. There was nothing to do but move.

Some of the men rode off into protected mountain valleys—
Strawberry, Hop, and Cave—to plant crops near the headwaters of
the river. This movement into the sierra led to formation of Colonia Pacheco, one of three such Mormon colonies more than 7,000
feet in elevation in Chihuahua. One, with the musical name of
Chuhichupa, was founded in 1894 at the headwaters of the Pacific-
bound Bavispe drainage. Colonia García in the "Top of the Mountain" meadows was established in 1898 by purchase of acreage from
the Garcia brothers. These colonies were compact clusters of wood-
en buildings in forest clearings, supporting themselves by dairying,
lumbering, and small-scale farming. Men who lived by agriculture
had returned to the area of first occupation in the state. Silent
Mogollon cliff dwellings looked down on productive Mormon settlements where farmers again found the earth good and the mountains a pleasant environment.

Other colonists had returned to the windswept plains of La

Ascensión where they laid out Colonia Díaz in square blocks and right-angle streets, with a two-mile, tree-lined avenue stretching out into desert dust. Springs afforded some water, pumped by twenty whirling windmills. In 1887, a candy factory was set up to provide a cash income. By 1891, over six hundred Mormons had made a new life for themselves in Colonia Díaz.

To have to move Colonia Juárez lock, stock, and barrel was bad enough, but onto land as rocky and as generally unpromising as the actual del Campo purchase was discouragement which almost drove the harassed settlers back across the border. They stood in mute, disconsolate company to scan their narrow valley compressed between grassy hills. Serious agronomists that they were, they held scant hope for productivity in the poor soil which trickled through their fingers. All felt most concern over the lowered water level of the river of green stones at the new location several miles farther toward the headwaters than they had been at Old Town. It was then, when hope was almost gone, that their Lord intervened and, in the manner of Old Testament miracles, brought about yet another. A mighty cataclysm cracked solid rock and fissured the earth's shell so that new waters could escape the inner womb, bringing life, fertility, abundance. Northern Mexico, in the birth of the year of 1887, heaved and convulsed in shuddering growing pains. In Bavispe, Sonora, every house crashed to the ground in a heap of dusty rubble. Arizpe, Aputo, Bacoachi, and Fronteras were damaged badly. Casas Grandes, Galeana, and El Carmen knew destruction and death. At Colonia Juárez chimneys toppled, furniture tumbled, animals fled in panic. Friction of moving boulders ignited a forest fire in the western mountains which blazed for days. Mormon farmers discovered new springs scattered along the entire course of the river bottom and an increased flow of water in the river proper. To these devout men, a religious interpretation was unavoidable. Omens were encouraging.

In that year of 1887, Utah was firmly implanted in the confined Chihuahua valley by the Piedras Verdes, and it has not left to this day. A leafy town grew along straight, wide streets, with names like Walnut Street, Snow Street, and Thatcher Street crossing Díaz Street, Pacheco Street, and Casas Grandes Street. Every house had its own large vegetable garden to produce the bulk of each family's food supply for the year, its flower arbors and beds where roses bloomed beside honeysuckle and pansies, and its trees for fruit, shade, and rope swings. Outbuildings to accomodate livestock and farm equipment stood behind. Irrigation ditches bringing river water to houses and gardens flowed bank to bank beside the lanes. Houses of brick, many of two stories, with steeply pitched shingle roofs, with door and window jambs imported from Deming, and with broad front porches inviting one to sit for peaceful meditation, recreated quiet rural villages behind the Wasatch. Children nurtured by each wife lived with her in a separate house but had access to the houses of other children sired by their common father. Usually, the extended family was grouped on the same block or across the street.

The cultural habits of food, dress, entertainment, language, and thought of the settlers were those of Anglo-Saxons, just as positively ingrained as blue-eyed blondness. They might forfeit their northern citizenship, but they could never shake loose their northern heritage. Wistful nostalgia for the past in the States equaled their confidence in their future in Mexico.

Along a two-mile stretch of the Noroeste de México Railroad north of the new Mexican tank town of Nuevo Casas Grandes, another colony was established in 1888 upon purchase of land from a German American. This was the beginning of Colonia Dublán, destined to figure prominently in the troubled war years. The railroad which it straddled would provide an escape. Water for the colony was supplied by a dam and intake on the Casas Grandes River. By 1912 the colony had a population of twelve hundred.

Three further colonies—Oaxaca, San José, and Morelos—were founded over the mountains in Sonora. The first of these, Oaxaca, was destroyed early in its history by a flood and was never rebuilt. Nine hundred people were residents of the remaining two outposts at the outbreak of the Revolution.

Colonia Juárez was the largest Mormon center and headquarters of the stake of the elaborately organized church. Its history echoes that of all the colonies. To people cut off from their own nationality, surrounded by unspoken suspicion and sullen hostility, it was of utmost importance that they "prove" themselves. They possessed a compelling drive and the financial necessity to become economically self-sustaining and to show their neighbors that they meant to become an asset to Mexico. Basically, all were farmers.

But many turned to other trades and enterprises to provide additional income. W. R. R. Stowell, the only colonist who personally had known Joseph Smith, opened a gristmill. Before the Revolution, flour was being shipped all over the Republic. John Walser and his boys operated a tannery. Later this expanded to include a shoe manufacturing business and harness shop. William McClellan found employment as a carpenter and builder. Henry Eyring opened a cooperative store patterned after the Zion's Cooperative Mercantile Institution (ZCMI) in Salt Lake, and by the Revolution had a stock valued at $10,000. John Harper, with his wife as cook, ran a small, comfortable hotel catering to traveling merchants and visiting relatives. Soon there was a butcher shop, schools, a lumberyard, a dairy. Cheese and milk products, eggs, and fruits were exported to Chihuahua and even on to Mexico City. Men and boys found jobs at the huge Pearson sawmills when they opened. Others did occasional work for the Hacienda de San Diego. For their part, Mormon homes and farms offered employment to Mexicans as servants and hands, paying wages higher than those elsewhere in the area. Both primary and secondary schools admitted Mexican children as well as Mormon children, teaching the same subjects as were taught in Utah, with the addition of lessons in Spanish language and grammar. They were housed in four buildings with a faculty of eighteen teachers.

Long canals were shoveled out, paralleling the river. Plumbing and lights were installed in homes. A phone service knit the community together and provided communication with the other colonies. Travelers, then as now, regarded Colonia Juárez as a virtual oasis. Skilled farmers and able technicians had made the desert bloom.

The colonists entertained with the same gusto with which they worked and worshipped. Mexican holidays, in addition to Pioneer Day, were celebrated with strict sobriety but robust vigor. Parades were organized, decorated carriages and floats depicted the aims and enterprises of the colonies. Eloquent speeches praised their benefactor, Don Porfirio, and the Mexican tricolor was waved with patriotic enthusiasm. The academy band eagerly played at such affairs, at weekly social square dances, and frequent school programs. Plays, recitals, musicals, and athletic events were occasions big enough to break the usual calm.

Abstemious as is the Mormon code, then prohibiting indulgence in alcohol, coffee, tea, cigarettes, and even in waltzing, their conduct seemed remarkable though unenviable to their Mexican neighbors. For the Mexicans, liquor frequently proved safer and more readily available than water, and coffee and tobacco were necessities of life. Through law-abiding behavior, self-sacrificing industry, and obvious sincerity in desire to be "Mexican," the hard-working Mormons made friends and wore down the cold reserve they had met from the beginning of their exile. They learned the language and accepted the mores. Mormonism, a proselyting religion of phenomenally rapid diffusion, began to gain converts among those who, for a number of reasons, had not found security in Roman Catholicism. The LDS church since 1880 had operated a mission in Mexico City; now new members were joining at the frontier. It began to seem as if the Mormons had been there always. They were further woven into the Mexican fabric through tragedy.

In the States, Mormons had prided themselves on getting along with the Indians. In all dealings they were determined to have peace with honor. In Mexico, everyone customarily carried firearms. To use them against mankind, however, was counter to church policies. From the outset the Mormons were warned of the Apache who understood nothing else, and who would be quick to take advantage of Mormon pacifism. The spurting flames which had consumed Mata Ortiz ignited wild fears among all *norteños,* "northerners." Mexicans had known too long the fiendish treachery, the screaming debacle, for quick forgetfulness. Supposedly Apache threats had been ended before the years of the Mormon arrival, but recurring rumors persisted of raiding bands stealthily moving through the pine-clad recesses, and with each fresh rumor a new series of tales of outrages were recounted to the newcomers. Painfully, rumor was confirmed when the Thompson family was attacked, two of its members ruthlessly slain.

On a crisp Monday morning in September 1892, Mrs. Thompson and three children were alone at their lonely cabin in Cave Valley, forty miles back in the mountains, while the father was at work in Colonia Pacheco. A small band of six Indians and a papoose surprised the children as they were walking to the fields to begin the week's chores, killing one teenage boy and severely wounding another. A six-year-old girl safely ran back to the house to sob to the mother details of the horrible affair, and as they foolishly darted from the house, the mother was shot. The girl, still unharmed, hid with her wounded brother until the looting redskins had departed. Then, true to the pioneer spirit which burned in all these people, the six-year-old child made her way to other Cave Valley ranches to seek help.

Frightened Mormon families from the still, and now strangely ominous, valleys called Hop, Strawberry, and Cave, moved back to the safety of the mother colony, Juárez.

Years passed without more than occasional loss of tools or supplies. Fears were forgotten, and the mountain valleys once more were plowed and proved productive. But another brush with the Apache came in 1900. A one-time Indian scout from Arizona had escaped authorities after having been falsely convicted of murder and for many years hid from United States troops in the Mexican mountains. His alleged murders and uncanny getaways, his elusive "now you see me, now you don't" techniques, shrouded him with legendary qualities and boosted the price on his head to 5,000 pesos. One November day in 1900, a mountain ranchería was robbed while the two families occupying it were at Colonia Pacheco attending church. Thinking the culprits were miners from nearby diggings, the men started after them to take back their property. But when they caught up with the bandits, they were Indians. In the fracas which followed, two of the fleeing Indians were killed. One was a woman and the other a beautifully garbed man. Because of his elegant attire, the Mormons felt they had killed the renegade Apache Kid. They had no positive proof of his identity and could not collect the reward money, although the president of the state did make a formal claim.

When rumblings of revolt actually burst into raging civil war, the Mormons were ripe for plunder. To disturbed peons, they were foreigners and they were rich. Also, they were, to their misfortune, near the eye of the Revolution hurricane which swept Chihuahua. They would know no peace or prosperity for a long time. Their benefactor, Don Porfirio, would know none either.

In the wake of facilitated worldwide travel, increased educational opportunities, and rising output of humming presses, thoughtful men of the late nineteenth century began to experience an unaccustomed curiosity about their fellow man. Scholars wondered about the relative status of societies of human beings; the impulses which furthered differentiation of language, racial stocks, social mores; the effects of environment upon cultural development; and the whys and wherefores of human origins. The discipline of anthropology was emerging into a ramified science dedicated to the study of man as a physical and cultural being. Concern was felt for the disappearance of primitive cultures through the processes of acculturation and the absorption of weaker groups by stronger neighbors. It was considered urgent to study and to record before it was too late. That was the motivation for the first archaeologic-ethnologic study made in Chihuahua.

A Scandinavian student of man, fresh from an exploring trip through Australia and a lecture tour of the eastern cities of the United States, was to spend five years in the Sierra Madre Occidental of northwestern Mexico reporting what he found. He hoped through his fieldwork to discover correlations and connections between pre-Hispanic northern Mexico and prehistoric southwestern Pueblo cultures, the latter just then becoming well publicized. The subject is one which still interests regional archaeologists.

Modern anthropologists and biologists are indebted to Carl Lumholtz for the first popular descriptions in English of archaeological ruins, living peoples, and biota within the northern mountains. The intervening sixty years since his work have seen relatively little change in the basic patterns of culture or in the plant and animal life which he reported, thanks to a barricading topography which, to a large degree, has shielded the region from European penetration. His volumes, *Unknown Mexico,* are fundamental background reading for any student of northern Mexico.[94]

Under sponsorship of the American Museum of Natural History and the American Geographical Society, and with blessings bestowed in a private interview with the *gran cacique* himself, Don Porfirio Díaz, the fall of 1890 saw Lumholtz's expedition on the border at Bisbee, Arizona, ready to strike through the sierra madre from its northern extension down into the heart of the nation. The trip was financed by Americans, many with names prominent in the Four Hundred of society—Carnegie, Dodge, Hyde, Marquand, Morgan, Vanderbilt, Whitney, Gould, Armour, Hearst. Anticipating a careful scientific survey, the party of thirty men included a geographer, an archaeologist, a botanist, a zoologist, and a mineralogist. There were Mexican cooks, guides, and packers to care for the physical needs of the scientists and the one hundred pack and riding animals.

Lumholtz led his men southward across the sere open country of northern Sonora to the outpost of Fronteras. Once a flourishing town of several thousand but almost deserted at this period because of repeated Apache incursions, it crouched in fear on a low mesa top hoping to sight enemies before their arrival. Although the last raid on Fronteras had been made in 1875, terrified Mexicans had not reinhabited scenes of bloody memory. Lumholtz, anxious to obtain Apache materials for museum displays, excavated in several localities where he had been told mass Indian murders had occurred and retrieved buried Apache accouterment.

Farther south, the expedition reached the Bavispe drainage where the waters of the Río Yaqui start their determined movement to the Gulf of California, then rode down to Opoto in a tropical depression of sugarcane, oranges, and figs, pushed east to the foothill escarpment, and finally moved up into the steep and rocky sierras of Huehuerachi, Bacadéhuachi, and the continental ridge. They passed through hills covered with oak thickets and maples brilliant in the breath of fall frost, and observed their first red-barked *madroños*. Upward travel was slow and dangerous. Pack animals often lost footing or their loads hit projections forcing them to lose balance and careen wildly down cliff faces.

Up in the pines at nearly 9,000 feet, the nights were sharp and penetrating. Water froze in camp buckets. Snow swirled around men huddled to warm their hands over blazing fires. Deer and wild turkeys were seen daily as the party moved across the mountains. Trout for food were dynamited from the streams. The expedition zoologist was enthralled with numerous opportunities to observe the world's largest woodpecker, *Campehilus imperialis*, a black and white plumed bird with a scarlet crest. This section of the Sierra Madre Occidental was his only know habitat. In the modern era, the big woodpecker has been victimized by the Mexicans who use his feathers in medical bundles, and by the Tarahumara who eat the young. The "Top of the Mountain" was found to be an inspiring series of narrow plateaus and jagged crests shadowing off in infinite succession of mauve, snow white, and deep forest green.

Everywhere after reaching the hills of Sonora were signs of ancient human occupation. Most numerous were *trincheras*, or rock-held terraces, cleared along watercourses or hillsides. Some low house walls of undressed stone were examined by the expedition archaeologist who speculated that a superstructure of thatch once had completed the dwellings. Pottery sherds scattered around the sites were of the crude, thick type which modern archaeologists might call Mogollon. Crumbling watchtowers stood on eminences near such houses. Other ruins still had traces of white plaster on exterior walls and therefore were known as *casas blancas*, or white houses, to the Mexican guides. Frequent signs of Apache camps and trails were encountered, bringing cold fear to the Mexicans in the group who knew the sound of echoing war whoops had been stilled but for a brief four years and felt ghostly Apache presence everywhere. A time span of a thousand years or more was represented by the remains of habitation and campsites seen by the Lumholtz party, showing the mountains to be an area where man successfully might search out the necessities of life and might find retreat from enemies.

Lumholtz crossed the difficult cordillera and came to the white settlement at Colonia Pacheco where sixteen Mormon families then were seeking their own brand of refuge. From them, Lumholtz learned of the spectacular caves and ruins of Cave Valley. So he determined to go down the Río Piedras Verdes to that valley and to set up camp for six weeks as a base for explorations. It was less than two years before the Thompson massacre, yet it seemed to Lumholtz that the green valley surrounded by its high, fawn-colored cliffs provided an idyllic setting for modern and ancient farmers, where man could happily be atune to his quiet environment, and to himself. The expedition probed house structures squatting in the shallow caves and discovered evidences of deplorable vandalism. They dug for burials in caves where signs of houses had vanished, and they trenched mounds on terraces above the river. When satisfied with their work, the men rode out of the mountains to the sun-soaked plains.

They camped for nine months at the Rancho San Diego, leased

by an American named Galvin, near the site of the original Colonia Juárez settlement. Over fifty mounds of prehistoric structures of varying size bulged along the valley bottom by the Piedras Verdes, rounded over by the combined action of wind and water until no clue of what lay beneath the adobe mantle could be seen from the surface. Lumholtz's group excavated in many such mounds, gathering samples of the fine Chihuahua pottery of the Casas Grandes complex, some in effigy and polychromes and all skillfully made. They visited with the Mormons at Colonia Juárez and found them interested in the archaeology of the area in the belief that its study would reveal confirmation of the section of the Book of Mormon which told of landings on the Sonora coast of American Indians emigrating from Asia.[95] With personal satisfaction, they saw trade with the coast growing as a result of the trail which they had blazed, which locals called *el camino del doctor,* the doctor's road.

Having completed reconnaissance of the Casas Grandes sector of the state, the expedition rode south along the broken foothills into the deep gashes of the Aros, Garabato, and Chico, and moved on to the plains of Yepómera, an elevated tableland with a thirty-foot-thick, horizontal, highly fossilized limestone crust. They observed, especially near Guerrero, numerous fossils of presumably extinct animals, some chunks being used as corral posts. Inhabitants were superstitious about these "giant's bones," grinding bits of them to include in potent medicine bundles.

Beyond Guerrero, the high savanah was gently hilly, with sparse stands of pines and oaks giving way to large tracts of arable lands. This region represented the northern extension of the Tarahumaras and the scene of their bloodiest uprisings under the leadership of defiant Tepóraca. Lumholtz traveled to the mines of Pinos Altos and the 980-foot waterfall of Basasiachi beyond Jesús María. Then he went down to Bocoyna, the Barranca del Cobre, and the Barranca de Batopilas, into Guachochi and Norogachi, over weathered pinnacles and forbidding slopes, from the tierra fría of the peaks to the tierra caliente of the canyons, through the hidden homelands of the lean-legged Tarahumara. For one year, he traveled, studied, and wrote to inform the scientific world of a fragment of Stone Age culture surviving in southwestern Chihuahua on the outskirts of civilization.

KNOWING THAT no demagogue can survive without control firmly in his own hands, that he cannot tolerate regional bosses that are too strong and too independent, Porfirio Díaz lost little time in taking over all the reins of government. Local caciquismo, or bossism, consolidated during Juárez times, disappeared. There was only one gran cacique, great chief. States were divided into districts (nine in Chihuahua), each with a chief responsible to the governor, who, in turn, answered directly to Don Porfirio. Mexicans, notorious for disorganization, now became thoroughly systematized. The unassailable power of the president was thrust into every dark crevasse and eroding plateau of Mexico.

Very often governors were handpicked. In Chihuahua, Díaz men generally were of a high caliber and helped bring about much of the outward progress associated with the era. Men like Carlos Pacheco, Lauro Carrillo, and Miguel Ahumada represented the best of the leadership of which Díaz was proud. Capable as some of the administrators were, they could not deflect the persistently growing current of discontent and criticism. Other men in office sometimes disgraced themselves and their country, and deepened the shadows stretching over the Pax Porfiriana. One such official was Angel Trías, son of the illustrious leader who for a quarter of a century was active in Chihuahua politics. He was removed from office because of alcoholism, gambling, and corruption.

A weak reconciliation was effected between Díaz and Terrazas in the early years of this century. Although Terrazas had been in and out of the governor's chair several times following Díaz's rise to power, the rift which came at the time of Juárez's death remained unhealed. Terrazas had prospered through application of Díaz policies, but there was no cordiality between the two. In a tour of the United States, Terrazas was hailed as a representative of Díaz prosperity and was accorded honors suitable to a famous personage. In 1903, the alliance between the two patriarchs became definite. Terrazas, for the eighth time, was elected Chihuahua's leading magistrate. Through the efforts of his son-in-law, Enrique Creel, this time he had the full public backing of the president. Thus it was that *terracismo* became identified with *porfirismo* in a rebellion-minded frontier. The upcoming struggle in the state would be more directly aimed at the powerhouse in the north than at the dictator in the capital.

The private fortune of Don Luis Terrazas was multiplying into incredible figures. His power was crushing in on all phases of life— political, economic, religious, social. Where his influence was not obvious, it was at least suspected. Many of the malignancies and overt tragedies of the times were laid at his feet. The Chihuahua press, fearing to attack him, gave him laudatory credit for superficial progress, but the *pelados* (penniless) remained glumly unconvinced. He was too rich, and they were too poor. He had all the lusty strength. They had none. Occasional high-handed conduct contributed substantially to a hot resentment of the strangulation hold the Terrazas empire had on Chihuahuan life. A robbery of one of the Terrazas-Creel banks led to imprisonment of innocent men and false confessions forced from them through brutal treatment. The citizens were angered by this regrettable episode, and after the Madero Revolution had succeeded, the nation's new president was called upon to intercede in behalf of Creel, who was being threatened with retaliation.[96]

Enrique C. Creel inherited the Terrazas mantle after the elder man retired from public office. He was born in 1854, the son of an American consul to Chihuahua. He married a Terrazas daughter and actively participated in the family financial affairs, and in time became the leading banking figure in the nation. One newspaper, *El Correo de Chihuahua*,* dared to question his right to the governorship because of his parentage, but despite such scattered opposition, he served as governor of the state from 1904 to the Revolution. Because of his fluency in English and his good education, he once had been Mexico's ambassador to Washington and Secretary of Foreign Relations. He was interpreter when Díaz met Taft on the international bridge in Ciudad Juárez.

For the second time in the Republic's history, in 1909 a national president visited the northern state of Chihuahua.[97] Juárez had come as a gravely worried refugee, but Díaz traveled as a proud, old warrior with a chest full of medals (one of which had been bestowed by the state of Chihuahua) and a blinding confidence in his own invincibility. The gran cacique, grey-haired idol of the foreign world and the cliques of reaction at home, moved in

---

* Edited by Sylvestre Terrazas who later became an official under Villa's regime.

triumph via his Central de México from pueblo to pueblo across the land. In Chihuahua, he was met at the Ortiz station by smiling dignitaries including Terrazas, he who once had ordered Díaz never to return. The aged goliaths, one eighty and the other seventy-two, shook hands and were ready to let bygones be bygones. Díaz rode through banner-strewn streets, greeting children on the curbs, nodding to their parents. He inspected exhibits at a fair of the state's products, including those of the Mormons, and toured the new public buildings. He was banqueted at an elaborate French dinner held in the Teatro de los Héroes. He stood bareheaded before an imposing statue of Benito Juárez at the intersection of Avenida Juárez and Avenida Colón, raised in commemoration of the hundredth anniversary of Juárez's birth. Two men who had molded Mexican destiny, one in stone and one in flesh, were now philosophical poles apart. The humanity of the president in stone was warmer than that of the president in the flesh. Díaz had lost touch with the common man.

Don Porfirio moved on north, leaving in the capital a dangerous mood of self-satisfaction and official acceptance of existent conditions. Disturbing whispers of insurrection momentarily were stifled. The following year, the Chihuahua legislature gave Díaz and his vice-president, Ramón Corral,* a rousing vote of confidence.

At Ciudad Juárez, where once the blood of Old Spain had surged and the histories of two nations had entwined, President Taft and President Díaz greeted each other with broad smiles and pledges of everlasting friendship.[98] After a twenty-one-gun salute, Díaz's party was escorted to the dingy Chamber of Commerce Building in El Paso where a brief interview took place. The exact topics discussed were never published, but rumor had it that the United States wished a concession for naval installations in Baja California. The following day, the American president was entertained on Mexican soil. After formal farewells, the presidents parted, and their trains chugged away from the Río Grande carrying each back

---

* Corral was once a resident of a Chihuahua mining camp and was the most detested man in Mexico because of his traffic in white women and Indian slaves.

to troubled capitals. In scarcely more than a year, Díaz's regime was to be shaken by a pitched battle in this same border town. Ciudad Juárez earlier had been the scene of an abortive plot against the Mexican dictatorship. The men behind the outburst were Enrique and Ricardo Flores Magón, two young anti-Díaz proletarian revolutionaries with a long record of arrests and jailings, raids and escapes. From St. Louis, Missouri, where they hid in exile, they outlined a program for needed change, and were in actuality the source of inspiration for the torrid pronunciamientos of the 1910 Revolution.* They spoke out against chronic re-election of Don Porfirio, the stifling power of the Church, the hopeless debt bondage, the dispossession of agrarians, and the exploitation of workers. In 1908, a *magonista* band breeched the border by trolley. All except two were captured. One drowned in the Río Grande, and Ricardo escaped to Los Angeles where the American government imprisoned him. They had made the mistake of taking the two military commanders of the Juárez *barracks* into their confidence and were given assurances that the garrisons stationed there would join with them in revolt. Instead, the spirited magonistas, charged with sedition, rebellion, conspiracy, threat to life and property, were handed stiff sentences to the frightful dungeons of the castle of San Juan de Ulúa in Vera Cruz harbor.[99]

More winds of rebellion blew over the rocky piedmonts and silty bolsons of the district of Galeana, impelled onward by the gusty oratory of magonista Praxedis G. Guerrero.[100] Some of his adherents fled through Palomas to the United States to escape arrest, but others joined the political prisoners at San Juan de Ulúa. Peace had been preserved.

The unruffled surface of calm prosperity, of imported culture and exported wealth, belied the deep turbulence that would roll the nation pell-mell toward war. All classes of society would be swept into that maelstrom of enmity, suffering, and license—tattered, barefoot peasants hopeful for release from biting penury, fine ladies with their silken, hobbled skirts and decolletage, their

---

* Writer Emilio Portes Gil, in *México, Cincuenta Años de Revolución*, 1960, vol. III, 492, calls the writings of the Flores Magón brothers the most important documents prior to the Revolution.

demimondaine sisters in form-revealing attire, elegant hacendados with their money-inspired arrogance and purchased aplomb, peace-loving, immigrant Mormons fearful for their homes and property, miners, priests, and newly rich, swinish officers as prone to banditry as to valor.

Out of the mountains galloped the legendary Pancho Villa. It was 1910.

FOUR

REVOLUCIÓN

1910 – 1920

By 1910 Mexico had been an independent nation for one hundred years. Although a decade-long civil war was to erupt in a mere two months, government authorities, seemingly unperturbed by mass discontent, set about to arrange centennial celebrations.

Mexico City had rushed completion of its marble Venetian post office, its ugly, ponderous Palacio de Bellas Artes, and the drainage of ancient lake beds into which the city was beginning to sink. Streets were widened and paved, flower beds in numerous parks were intricately manicured, buildings were scrubbed, and the poor and ragged were banned from public places. A glittering facade was demanded, concealing the primeval state of life off the shady boulevards with their statues. Engraved invitations were sent to diplomats around the world inviting them, all expenses paid, to this garishly showy and lavish feast. Díaz, pompous in pride of his "progressive" administration, was to display his Athens in the wilderness, his creation of civilization in the barbaric New World. Precious gifts, tokens of congratulation and esteem, flowed into Mexico from distant kingdoms.

Not to be outdone by central Mexico, Chihuahua had its own species of centennial festivities and back-patting. A new school building was inaugurated, and monuments to deceased heroes were placed in the plazas. Ojinaga, Pacheco, the victors of Tres Castillos, and the Juárez liberals were remembered in stone and bronze. With such expenditures officials seemed to forget the empty cazuelas or the habitual, haunting hunger in the outlying neighborhoods.

Don Porfirio was the "grand old man" to many citizens abroad but to a rapidly diminishing few at home. Especially since he had just had himself "re-elected."

To silence criticism directed against his repetitious "re-election,"

two years earlier Díaz had stunned his people with the announce-
ment that he would not run for office again, and he would welcome
political opposition! * For dictators voluntarily to give up power,
prestige, and profit is nothing less than sensational, no less astound-
ing than to allow free contest. Mexico rocked. Then, with brazen
face, he calmly dispatched word to the malleable masses that he had
heeded their "call" and could not desert. He again would be a
candidate. By this time, not all his children were fooled.

Díaz created faction through grooming unpopular Corral as a
successor and bypassing General Bernardo Reyes whom most favored. A rumor of a Reyes revolt was whispered through the land.
Clandestine meetings were held, speculators laid on odds, and
bandwagoners calculated their timing. There was no revolt however. Reyes chose exile in a diplomatic post and left undermining
of the Díaz administration to the more stouthearted. His followers, hopefully searching for dynamic leadership, swung in behind
Madero.

Francisco I. Madero was everything his adherents were not—aes-
thetic, theosophic, philanthropic, a physical weakling and vegetar-
ian, wealthy, indecisive, and timid.[1] That such a quixotic man
proposing only constitutional alteration could lead a revolution for
social reform is incomprehensible. The explanation lay in the
swelling, explosive strength of the movement itself. The proletariat desirous of labor unions, the students and political idealists
hoping for a change supercharged with opportunity for growth of
a middle-class balance wheel, the farmers wanting only a bit of
land to call their own, the tormented and fanatical—all sought an
embodiment of their varied ideals and a manifesto to express it.
They found it in a simple political tract (*La Sucesión Presidencial*)
written by Madero and with it tried to catapult him into the
presidency.

Upon receipt of the startling news that Don Porfirio would allow political opposition at the polls, open agitation for change
grew rapidly in Chihuahua. Such fervor centered in two clubs in
the capital, Electoral Ignacio Allende and Central Antireelecci-
onista Benito Juárez.[2] Their members traveled through the state

---

* Díaz's decision to withdraw as head of state appeared in the famous Creel-
man interview, *Pearson's Magazine*, March 1908. Brenner, 1943; Clendenen,
1961, 14; *México, Cincuenta Años de Revolución*, 1961, Vol. III, 496-97.

speaking against re-election. Further propaganda was disseminated through the anti-Terrazas-Creel newspaper, *El Correo de Chihuahua*, but the plea was for change in the mechanics of government rather than on the human grounds of social reform. Terrazas' shadow loomed menacingly in the background. A local delegation attended a national political convention in Mexico City of other antire-electionists to join in sponsorship of the ticket of Francisco I. Madero and Francisco Vázques Gómez. A heady breath of political freedom overcame common sense. They should have known they could not get away with it.

To an aroused puma in the presidential chair, it was time to pounce. Díaz men broke up Madero rallies, tore down antire-electionist placards, shot stray friends of the cause in the dark, and clapped Madero in jail. Chihuahuan *maderistas* yelled. They protested and shouted "tyranny" to no avail. The second Sunday in July, when all the Electoral College votes were in, cast and counted by Díaz men, Chihuahua was part of a landslide for the unconquerable gran cacique. Irregularities? Perhaps. A well-oiled dictatorial machine controlling courts, forts, and officialdom? Positively.

Madero escaped jail and, masquerading as a brakeman on one of Díaz's trains, fled to the States to raise forces and funds to pry the president loose from his deathhold on Mexico. The government retaliated by confiscating Madero family properties in Coahuila said to include an impressive array of cotton land, cattle, lumber, mines, distilleries, and banks. While Francisco's brothers were busy in New York making a deal with Limantour to protect their investments, the frail visionary was attempting metamorphosis, yet there was never a more unlikely warrior. In his Plan de San Luis Potosí, circulated in secret to his dispersed bands of sympathizers, he sent a call to arms. *Veinte de Noviembre* (November 20, 1910) was to be the day that David would confront Goliath.

Abraham González, outstanding figure in one of the opposition clubs of Chihuahua, was a leading organizer of the rebellion. He and his associates spread the word to solitary sierras and rolling tablelands where grim men stood ready. Prepare for Veinte de Noviembre!

Nervous Chihuahuenses were prompted to act prematurely by a border incident. A woman in Rock Springs, Texas, was killed by a Mexican. The Mexican was lynched by an angry Texas mob—a tragic incident unfortunately not unique along the border. In the Chihuahua capital, reaction was for vengeance, immediate and terrible. Angry men led by Instituto students milled before the American consulate, throwing bottles and insults with equal agility. The city's harried police broke up the demonstrations and sent the rioters off the streets, but anti-American feelings lingered.

This incident had no direct bearing on Mexico's internal troubles, but it served to concert feelings and raise them to the pitch of revolution. Outbursts of stirring peons had been made in the Yucatán henequen plantations and in the Sonoran copper pits, but it was the somber men of Chihuahua who successfully launched the Revolution, not on the Veinte de Noviembre but almost a week sooner.

At the historic village of Cuchillo Parado, a peasant uprising sparked the great revolt. There sixty-five villagers led by Toribio Ortega lashed out against their misery in a running skirmish with a gang of rurales.

This town of Cuchillo Parado, just south of the Texas Big Bend country, is notable for a number of fateful events. In 1715 natives stood there on the banks of the Río Conchos to proclaim allegiance to the King of Spain. Two hundred years later the name of Veinticinco de Marzo was given the pueblo to commemorate the defeat of French imperialists in Chihuahua on March 25, 1866. But Cuchillo Parado preferred its descriptive name of antiquity which means "stopped knife." Even after it was again renamed, this time for its Revolutionary leader, Toribio Ortega, it remained Cuchillo Parado to Chihuahuenses, the place where it all began.*

A second blow against the government was made three days later by armed men under command of Francisco Villa, across the state on the red altiplano of San Andrés west of the capital. They killed the mayordomo of the Hacienda de Chavarria and moved into the house and outbuildings. On the nineteenth, Pascual Orozco, the younger, closed up his shoe store in San Isidro, municipio of Guerrero, traditional birthplace of rebellion epitomized by Tomochi.

---

* Jordán, 1956, 346, gives a description of the modern village of Cuchillo Parado where thirteen of the sixty-five original insurrectionists of November 20 survived in 1956.

His band rendezvoused at the Rancho del Conejo and the following day marched on the headquarters of Guerrero.

On November 20, fires of maderista revolt were kindled by determined Chihuahuenses in scattered localities throughout the state—Baca and Gómez in Parral, Valenzuela in Témori, Luz Blanco in Santo Tomás, Brown in Morís, Guerrero and Salazar in Casas Grandes, González, Lometín, Cruz Sánchez in Ojinaga.[3] Through them, Madero, first a dreamy, political illiterate, then a critical candidate, and finally an exiled outlaw converted into a fighting revolutionist, was gripped by forces beyond his strength and understanding.

Norteños flocked to his cause. Their characters steeled through war-coated centuries would add immeasurably to his success on the field of battle. Their grievances basically were local. They were fighting against an evil in their own midst rather than decadence far away in Mexico City. Because of rabid anti-Terrazas feelings in Chihuahua, the national Revolution gained needed purpose and virility. Sinking Terrazas would pull the dead weight of Díaz under with him. There was no idealism, statesmanly leadership, nor long-range goals. The motivation was hatred focused on one individual as a symbol of excessive wealth and power. Objectives were immediate.

The Revolution to some meant chance to remedy frightful wrongs. To others it meant frijoles, supplied in return for gunplay, occasions to escape incidentless monotony and dragging poverty, to feel young again through wild charges into danger and dissipation, to gain personal status and longed-for spoils of war. Out of the tangle of men seeking to become bosses even on a small scale, out of the congested welter of reasons and motives, arose three men whose names would outshine others in annals of the decade—Abraham González, political thinker, cattle agent, and sincere devotee of the Cause; Pascual Orozco, small time shopkeeper ambitious for personal power; and Pancho Villa, brazen bandit who sought to burnish a thoroughly tarnished name.

To MANY on both sides of the Río Grande, Villa typified the Revolution. At the present time, when details of skirmishes and frequent liquidation of leaders are forgotten, the Mexican Revolution

to numerous North Americans means one man, Pancho Villa. As
he reared back atop his prancing horse, loaded cartridge *bandoleras*
crisscrossing his broad gorilla chest, and embroidered, silver-trim-
med sombrero pushed back on his head, he somehow embodied a
savage, free, reckless bravura envied by pedestrians of all nationalities. He was a violent contradiction of good and evil, kindness
and sadism, ignorance and crafty intelligence. Always the primitive, he had an insatiable lust for money, power, women, and life
itself. He was a born fighter, a blackhearted rogue, an archenemy
of the hacendado and gachupín, yet an openhearted, openhanded
friend of the peon. Don Luis Terrazas, on whom he spent his
wrath, represented a subtle, orderly, but stern formalism. Pancho,
however, explosively unpredictable himself, had nothing but contempt for such formalism. His violence was the very symbol of
revolt.[4]

Doroteo Arango was his name. His mother and the man with
whom she lived were an insignificant part of the army of peons on
the Hacienda Río Grande in mountain country of northern
Durango. There he learned the severe rigidity of the caste system,
saw through slit eyes the narrow horizon of the poor, and felt the
biting lash on naked flesh. When he bolted the ranch, he was
beaten. When he repeated, he was blacklisted by other regional
employers and thrown into a cell to nurture a consuming hatred
for the rich and a passion for vengeance. Out of jail briefly, he felt
frustration at reluctance in some quarters to give him work, he
whose name was known on rurales' records. The rape of his favorite
sister determined his future. In a blinding rage at the calloused
betrayal of family honor, the boy Doroteo, who was to become the
bandit Pancho, shot the hacendado's son who had forced himself
upon the ripening, dusky peasant girl. He dashed to the protective
sierra, leaving forever the degrading role of feudally molded peon.
A callow, naive youth passed into uncertain, suspicious manhood,
with the recurrent memory of his first murder to stay a lifetime. A
legend was born.

In the mountains the fugitive joined a notorious gang of out-
casts, changed his name to that of a former infamous outlaw, and
for some years rode the ranges one jump ahead of the rurales. From
his leader, Ignacio Parras, he learned the fine art of brigandage—to
pounce and vanish and strike again at an unexpected time and

place, to kill easily and fight readily, to forget in an exhilarating fog of sotol and erotic adventures in the night, to live off the land and its people. After Parras stopped a volley of bullets during an attempted holdup, the picaresque men rallied around young Villa to continue their wild depredations. Whatever else might be said of Villa, he possessed the intangible quality of leadership. Throughout his hectic career, he always was able to persuade others to follow him, sometimes through fear, sometimes through hope of reward, but often from honest admiration of his innate skills. A moustached Mexican version of Robin Hood, on sentimental occasions he was prone to share his loot with poor peons whom he encountered, thus creating a reservoir of hero worship upon which he could later draw. He was the incarnation of their wistful dreams of freedom and the sublimation of their repressed passion for vengeance upon full-bellied oppressors.

By 1910 Villa had a legal wife, María Luz Corral, in rural San Andrés and a large, black reputation. It was thought that his knowledge of the country, his flare for pyrotechnics, and his obdurate band of malcontents willing to risk fighting the government would be assets to the Cause. He was offered a captaincy in the maderista army and a cloak of respectability. He could rationalize his headstrong deeds of murder, robbery, and lust as all part of the internecine struggle. Now rapine had become patriotic and he could pursue his personal version of the Revolution, a formula as simple and uncomplicated as himself—a violent and immediate overthrow of the landed rich, no holds barred.

PRESIDENT DÍAZ at first failed to realize the power of the undertow of the inchoate movement in the north and considered it a purely local outbreak which could be locally contained. A small military reinforcement was sent to the state, under command of General Juan A. Hernández, who had helped bring Tomochis to their knees. But he was not to repeat his victory here on the Longitude of War, where martyred men of Tomochi lived on in the souls of others. Pascual Orozco, the younger, a general for Madero, took over tired village plazas one by one. Hoping the powerful influence of the Terrazas family could hold the cracking dike of the dictatorship, Díaz made a most disastrous blunder. He appointed a Terrazas son, Alberto, to the governorship. It was a maneuver which swelled the ranks of Revolution as nothing else would have done. Matters were getting out of hand.

Had Díaz thrown a large army into the fight on the Chihuahua plains, the Revolution might never have spread. Had he rejected Terrazas' partisanship, he might have quieted rumblings against the privileged. These were the two mistakes in strategy which cost him his reign. Too late did he relieve Terrazas by tossing his own friend, beloved Miguel Ahumada, to the wolves, gambling that his popularity would soothe the aroused people and save the day.[5] Terrazas left the Palace of Government by the back door, as Ahumada moved in the front. Alberto and his father fled south to Aguascalientes to wait the outcome of Madero's northern campaign. Ahumada stood powerless before the onrushing revolutionary tide.

On February 14, 1911, Don Francisco I. Madero, self-named Provisional President of the Republic, crossed the Río Grande downstream from El Paso, near Guadalupe, to lead an armed invasion on his own fatherland. Once again the wave of influence moved from north to south, but the impulse was Mexican. Three weeks later, having circuited the eastward-creeping dunes of Samalayuca, having wound through the barren ranges of La Magdalena and Arados, and having waded the turbid waters of the Carmen and Santa María, he challenged porfirismo at Casas Grandes. There he had his first taste of battle, was almost captured, hid terrified in a ditch until rescued by Máximo Castillo, and saw his bold men driven back in defeat. After regrouping his temporarily beaten forces at Galeana across a low divide, he marched them south through silent, pulverized basins to the Hacienda de Bustillos where a nucleus of partisans had gathered. Together they took Guerrero and the iron rails of the Ferrocarril Noroeste which were to provide a future, rapid movement to Ciudad Juárez. Even self-perpetuating Díazdom could no longer ignore the gathering clouds of total war.

Frantically a five-day truce was arranged so that the dispute with the revolutionaries, represented by Vázques Gómez (the defeated vice-presidential candidate), Pino Suárez, Madero's father, and the Jefe de la Revolución himself, might be settled peacefully. Since no terms other than abdication of Díaz and Corral were acceptable, settlement was left to gunpoint. Against Madero's wishes, General Orozco and Captain Villa pushed forward to open fire on the gateway to Mexico—brawling, rowdy Ciudad Juárez.

Weak, vacillating, incapable of quick decision, Madero hesitated, talked, delayed. The men who served under him, however, were men of action—and action they meant to have, in spite of the probabilities of disaster and Madero's requests to hold their fire. As he could not control his hotheaded army, there was little hope that he could manage his fiery nation. Fighting broke out in the Arroyo Colorado, near the mill upstream, raged through the streets by the great river, around the barracks walls rapidly becoming speckled with bullet potholes. City drinking-water supplies were cut off, and electric wires were downed. Excited Americans stood on top of freight cars in the railroad yards across the river to watch the birth of civil war. An "incident" could have occurred at any moment as stray shells whizzed in crazy disregard of the international boundary, killing more than a dozen persons on the north bank of the Río Grande.[6] After two days, General Juan Navarro of the Federal troops surrendered. The two maderista leaders, Orozco and Villa, who planned to cut off his head as reprisal for former shooting of rebel prisoners, were foiled by Madero who had to sneak his captive away from his own army and send him to safety across the river. A peace treaty was signed on May 21, and two days later Madero entertained defeated Navarro at a banquet. A battle unauthorized by Madero had toppled octogenarian government in Mexico and had placed this weakling in the hot seat of the presidency. Díaz sailed to Europe, where he died in France two years later. He gained a degree of posthumous fame for having left this world from natural causes, a feat unmatched by more than a decade of successors.

For those who made a career of being on the winning side, it was time to move. Recruits clamored to join Madero's army. Now was the chance for old-line revolutionaries to brush desert dust from their trousers and strut in the streets and sing in the cantinas. This was the moment to pour numbing aguardiente on parched tongues, to weep large saline tears for fallen comrades, to hail a new jefe. *Viva la Revolución! Viva Madero! Viva México! Viva* the bright new future!

Governor Ahumada resigned. He moved to El Paso, to witness from the sidelines the rivalries, betrayals, and brutalities which would tear apart the nation he had served for fifty years. He died in voluntary exile in 1917.

The man who followed Ahumada into office was no less noteworthy—one of the most outstanding yet least known of the northern revolutionary leaders. Abraham González had been active in Madero's presidential campaign, later had raised men in the vicinity of Ojinaga to strike on the historic Twentieth of November, and had accompanied Madero to the battle of Casas Grandes. For his loyalty to the Cause, he was made governor, as his grandfather before him, elected to serve the four-year term from 1911 to 1915. Actually he was in office only from June to November. After Madero's inauguration, he was given the cabinet position of Secretary of Government. During his brief tenure, he revealed himself as a capable, thoughtful administrator with a sincere desire to solve the infinitely complex economic and social problems of his state, within the channels proposed by Madero. Neither he nor his jefe, Madero, advocated wholesale indiscriminate splitting up of the latifundia or blacklisting of foreign capitalists. He did demand that such enterprises be subject to just taxation. He worked for recognition of labor groups and impartial arbitration of their problems, even traveled to the remote pueblos of the sierra to talk with groups of miners and lumberjacks. Gambling was made illegal in hopes of restraining some men from sinking deeper into the morass of hopeless debt.

Although Madero had won the first round of the Revolution and Díaz had been dethroned, peace did not follow. Once stirred to angry action, Chihuahuenses were not quickly quieted. Victory had been too easy. If the entrenched dictatorship of seven terms in office could be ousted with show of force and several skirmishes, other less fortified caudillos could be vanquished in the same manner. Treason became merely a point of view, revolution a habit, and enemies changed with shifting allegiances.

Before his inauguration, the chief of the Revolution made a return visit to the state which more than any other was responsible for his obtaining high office and high responsibility. Enthusiastic maderistas cheered their leader, slight in physical stature but an embryonic giant among revolutionists. Viva Madero! Viva le Revolución! But, they asked with hurt tone of disillusionment, why was Vázques Gómez, the vice-presidential candidate of 1910, dumped? Why was the vocal young newspaper man from Yucatán, Pino Suárez, to be second-in-command?[7] In vain, the stammering ineffectual president-elect attempted to soothe ruffled feathers of his strutting gamecocks. "Pino, no! Pino, no!" they chorused, not willing to accept feeble, red-faced explanations. But Pino Suárez stayed. Many of the discontented began to seek out unscrupulous, ambitious Orozco and to figure their chances.

The Cause was being sniped at from all directions. A maderista officer, Antonio Rojas, committed excesses in western municipios without regard to protests of municipal authorities. Trouble came from another malcontent in the same region, Blas Orpinel, who was spreading anti-Madero propaganda. Both troublemakers were apprehended by one company of rurales and sent to the penitentiary in the capital city, only to be released. On the border they gathered three hundred followers and waited. Magonistas, or followers of the Flores Magón brothers, felt called upon to express their unhappiness with the general state of affairs by yet another plan, that of Santa Rosa named for a cemetery in the capital. They were driven to the northeast by overworked rurales.[8]

Ciudad Juárez, scene of Díaz's downfall, continued prominent in the vicissitudes of revolution.[9] At the end of January 1912, a barracks revolt was staged in the local garrison. In February the town stirred because of an "invasion" of several dozen American soldiers who, upon seeing the alarm their presence caused, retreated back across the international bridge without incident. Four days later a group of Orozco's men, led by disgruntled magonistas of the Galeana area—José Inés Salazar, the Ponce brothers, and Enrique Portillo—and the waiting rebels with Rojas and Orpinel, took the border town after Orozco had countermanded Madero's orders and had dispatched federal troops to the city of Chihuahua. Orozco himself had "retired" to his private business at San Isidro. It was his former comrade-in-arms, Villa, who brought him back to public limelight.

Abraham González, staunch Madero supporter, returned to Chihuahua and the governorship. Despite recognized slippage in his state toward a revolt within a revolt, he urgently proposed to seek an immediate loan of 6,000,000 pesos from the federal government to help resolve some of the agricultural and educational problems of the state, to bring about the program which he (but not his leader) visioned would come from the upheaval. His clarion call to knuckle down to work on the basic aspects of the Mexican social illnesses fell on unlistening, unready ears. Chihuahuenses, like the Mexican nation in general, were unripe for reform. They could not yet rise above personal jealousies, self-seeking ambitions, fallacious grievances. And they felt betrayed in the matter of Pino Suárez. Orozco, thought to have been angered at not having been selected Minister of War,[10] embroidered disharmony upon the fabric of popular resentment toward the little jefe in Mexico City.

With the keen suspicions naturally cultivated in revolutions, Governor González was hypersensitive to the way the hot wind of rebellion was blowing. He sent for a man he knew who had remained doggedly loyal to Madero, that bad man from the hills, Pancho Villa. Villa raised auxiliary forces from Satevó and Zaragoza and marched them toward the capital. Now was Orozco's hour. He struck and left no doubt about it. The city of Chihuahua was his, to protect the capital from being sacked by Villa, so he said. Behind him stood the total force of the rurales; it was a bloodless coup. González fled for his life and was replaced by an Orozco puppet, Ing. Felipe R. Gutiérrez. Salazar, Rojas, and Orpinel moved in from Ciudad Juárez to the packing plant at Nombre de Dios and waved a banner of *Reforma, Libertad, y Justica* to give a social character to an otherwise sordid affair.[11] The Colorados, as Orozco forces were called, enjoyed a series of rapid military triumphs and brief hours of licentious glory. Federalists, led by General Victoriano Huerta, a doughty, rum-cured Díaz soldier retained by Madero, came north by train to crush the rebels at Conejos, Jiménez, Camargo, Bachimba, and finally the capital. By July 7, González was in again, and Gutiérrez was hiding north of the border. Orozco's humiliated army licked its wounds at Casas Grandes and made trouble for the Mormons.

JUNIUS ROMNEY, president of the Juárez stake of the Church of Jesus Christ of Latter-day Saints, had little choice but to comply when General José Inés Salazar ordered the Mormons to surrender all their firearms to the rebel army. It was no use to protest that the Mormons had no guns because possession of firearms was universal. But Romney felt there was hope of outsmarting the crafty general if his followers voluntarily surrendered their guns rather than submit to a house-to-house search. He issued the order for guns to be brought with the greatest promptness to the bishop in Dublán and to the Colonia Juárez bandstand, where rebel officers would be waiting to receive them. In return, he demanded a safe conduct to allow all women and children to take the Noroeste de México to Ciudad Juárez, knowing that with conditions so seriously degenerated, they might be subjected to all sorts of indignities and to real physical danger. This was the beginning of the Exodus, always referred to with a capital letter, from which the Mexican Mormon colonies would never recover. The high-water mark of expansion and prosperity in their adopted homeland had been reached. The tide had turned, and with it flowed the dreams of Mormon Zion below the Río Grande.

On July 26 and 27, 1912, a thousand worried, saddened women and children rode away from their comfortable homes. Some could remember back across a busy quarter century when they had followed husbands south seeking a new homeland. They could count numbers of their men, their sisters, their babies lying now in the warm Mexican earth. They had known the trials of living far from other members of their families, the inconveniences of "making do," the satisfactions of facing stern tasks and succeeding. Some of them had been born right here in the once peaceful hamlets on the Casas Grandes and the Piedras Verdes. To them, Mexico was the only home they had even known.

Now they were being driven out by a political turmoil in which they strove to remain nonpartisan. All felt the situation would ease soon, and they could return to normal living. As a result, they took with them only a few essentials for their welfare. In their brick houses, rich with the scent of heavy bowers of summer blooms, they left behind the treasures of their households—the tatted sofa doilies worked by the fireside in wintertime, the crocheted afghans with gay colors delicately interlaced, the darkened tintypes of Utah relatives, the rows of variegated jams and jellies and spicy pickles on the cellar shelves, the slingshots and dolls and homemade toys of lazy summer leisure hours. Like those ancient dwellers of Casas Grandes, they abandoned the raw plains with the pocketed green vales and migrated to safety back up the Río Grande.

As the refugees spilled from the stifling, overcrowded train in El Paso, the extent and tragedy of their plight became all too apparent. They were stranded in a country they now considered "foreign," with no financial resources and no place to go. Temporarily housed in crude sheds in a lumberyard and in army tents loaned by Fort Bliss, and with the full human-interest treatment by the press and news photographers, these proud people felt the shameful misery of being public wards. The United States Government, from which they once had fled, appropriated $20,000 for their aid. They settled down to wait for the shooting to stop and, in a vexing dearth of news from the colonies, to fear for beloved menfolk.

For months Mormon leaders in Mexico felt they were walking a tightrope and that any slip at all would be in the wrong direction. They determined to follow soft-spoken policies of strict neutrality, to ask protection and friendship from whomever was in regional control. Their well-known popularity with ousted Díaz, their affluence as compared to the stark poverty of the campesinos living around them, their extraterritorial connections and dissimilar objectives made them stand apart. They sensed that any rash act would license trouble from federalists and rebels alike. Continued guerrila warfare ate at Mexican respect for law and order. Natives who had been friendly and polite turned insolent. Requests for needed horses, food, and pesos changed into firm demands and unabashed robbery. Ringleaders in the assault on Mormon property were Demetrio and Lino Ponce, a couple of unprincipled fire-eaters from Galeana who were using Orozco's rebellion as a cover for their own illegal activities, and Enrique Portillo, once a student at the Juárez Academy. Promises of protection against looting seldom were kept. When they were, results frequently were rapid execution of culprits, without a hearing, without mercy. Unsympathetic treatment of Mexicans by Mexicans appalled them. Mormons could not have such violence on their consciences, nor did they relish being held responsible, directly or indirectly, for such brutal murders.

A shooting in defense by one of their number assigned the ticklish job of arresting a known local robber had placed Colonia Juárez on the dangerous brink of racial strife. Mormons and Mexicans involved had been jailed, and glowering crowds of natives milled before the tithing office, tense and threatening, eager for a riot. The Ponces had suddenly galloped into town to personally investigate the killing, had been dined by the Mormons at the Harper Hotel, and had ridden back over the hill to the Tinaja Wash and Casas Grandes without doing anything to quiet the mob but much to increase the general feeling of uneasiness among the colonists. The Mormons had sent appeals for aid to an American freebooter, Captain Creighton, with the rebel forces at downriver Pearson, who despite suave assurances of help, did nothing. Because of rumors of a night attack on all the houses in Colonia Juárez, they posted well-armed guards to stand watch throughout the night. No fight developed. The prisoners had been removed to Casas Grandes at the very time of Madero's disastrous battle there, and in the confusion of the rebel route, they had escaped. Later, when he had become more successful, Madero exonerated the Mormons of blame in the death of the Mexican and officially ended the incident. But for the aroused peons, it was not ended. Sooner or later they meant to have their revenge. And the Mormons knew it.

Although proud of their reputation on both sides of the international line for being law abiding, the Mexican Mormons turned to smuggling guns from the States to provide themselves with a needed armory for protection in a situation daily growing more chaotic and ominous. Their first attempt to bring long-range rifles and ammunition in through Columbus, New Mexico, failed as alerted United States secret service men confiscated the forbidden shipment. Later they were successful in their desperate gunrunning. These guns were hidden carefully for the day when a last ditch stand might have to be made. The Orozco-Salazar Red Flaggers, or Colorados, had no idea of the number of guns and rounds of ammunition they missed when they had accepted Romney's voluntary surrender of guns and had failed to search the houses.

After women and children left the settlements, looting and rapine steadily increased, carried on by bands of rebels operating independently of each other but all desirous of stocking up on horses and supplies while they could. Colonia Dublán, because of its open site and nearness to the new railroad town of Nuevo Casas Grandes, suffered most. Rebels entered stores and confiscated or destroyed their stock. Pantries were raided. Those precious preserves meant for johnnycake and light soda biscuits sweetened steaming tortillas and fried brown beans. Clothes were pulled from hangers; furniture was hauled off. Soldiers under one leader and then another, all praising La Revolución but caring little for its meaning, swept in and out of Colonia Juárez using the school buildings and tithing office for garrisons. When excited rebel bands received reports brought in by rebel scouts that federalist General Blanco was on his way over the divide from Sonora, they took all the stock they could find in the barns and fields and made their getaway. The colonists decided it was also their hour of departure.

The call went out to the mountain settlements of Chuhuichupa, García, and Pacheco, to the farming colonies on the plains. Every man of them was to come to an appointed rendezvous spot in the mountains. They locked up their houses and barns, entrusted them to the care of loyal Mexican friends, and rode away without looking back. Many would never return. With unanimity the council voted to return to the United States and their families until such time as repossession in quieter conditions could be accomplished. They organized themselves along military lines. On August 8, less than two weeks after they had put their women on the northbound train at Pearson and Dublán, they were on the march. With them they took three hundred eighteen guns, twenty-six hundred rounds of ammunition, and five hundred horses which the rebels had failed to capture. Under a white truce flag the group crossed to United States soil three days later near Hachita, New Mexico. From there, the colonists took the train to El Paso and tearful reunions with their families.

September saw a small number of Mormon families back at Colonia Juárez in time to harvest the fruit and put the cannery into operation. Pearson was under control of Blanco's federal troops, but Casas Grandes was still held by Orozco rebels. A summary rebel execution of a Mexican intruder into an occupied house precipitated a second Exodus to El Paso of most of the Mormons. Some of the bolder ones chose to stay on through the winter, caring for property in Dublán and Juárez. During this time the other colonists did not attempt to return to Mexico.

Then at the end of January 1913, sixty-five persons climbed off the train at Columbus, New Mexico, and into wagons to ride south to home in scarcely easier conditions than the original migration in 1885. Several days after they had passed through deserted Colonia Díaz, that settlement was burned to the ground by the wanton rebel, Antonio Rojas. Every home and place of business was completely wiped out. In the colonies of the Casas Grandes vicinity, the Mormons were relieved to find homes much as they had been left. It was with deep emotion that they accepted handclasps, embraces, and kindly "Bienvenidos, amigos!" from their Mexican friends and neighbors. They had come home, and they meant to stay. For seven more difficult years, the war and its protagonists came and went, but no Mormon again mentioned or even thought of leaving.

During the trying period of exile in El Paso, many of the men, in order to support their large families, accepted jobs in other towns. Some moved farther north to be closer to kinfolk in the States. With the entry of the United States into World War I, some were channeled into military service. Families became relocated, readjusted. Many felt unready to return to disturbed conditions in Mexico. When the Revolution finally did drag to a halt with the election of Obregón in 1920, life was gone from enterprises which had flourished in the pre-Revolution colonies. Reconstruction was too expensive and too unsure. The need for foreign residence had long since been erased; now there was no desire. The revolutionary decade had placed an unplanned curb on Mormon expansion in Mexico.[12]

AT THE END of 1912, El Paso sheltered another troubled exile. Once-swaggering Pancho Villa, recently escaped from jail where he had been flung by Huerta on charges reported variously as horse stealing or insubordination,[13] dejectedly sat alone in a dingy, threadbare hotel room in the Chamizal or "Little Chihuahua" district. He did not like being outcast. He missed those zestful, ego-building days of being in power when compliments, money, and women were easily obtained. And he fretted about how to proceed with his vague plans to liberate those *pobrecitos*, "poor little people," of Chihuahua from the sharp heel of hacendado oppression. Pancho probably convinced himself that those peasants needed him. Certainly he needed them, for unquestionably all his ambitions for regaining power and prestige depended upon peon support. From his outpost he secretly began to seek their aid.[14] His opportunity to rejoin the fray came in early spring.

In what Mexicans call the Ten Tragic Days (La Decena Trágica) of February 1913, Madero and Pino Suárez were assassinated by a Huerta-led coup d'état. To Pancho Villa this shattering event provided a cause, a point around which he could arouse followers. To do away with the sleek landowners, yes. To return property stolen from the villages and to fatten lean bellies, yes. But first, get Huerta —that terrible traitor who had not only betrayed the whippet president whom Villa had admired, but who had stripped Pancho of his glory and had plunged him into a black nadir. Throughout his remaining revolutionary career, Villa's uncomplicated cause was devoid of any loftier political philosophies or goals. Illiterate and sometimes childishly direct, he lived, fought, and governed by instinct. This simplicity of purpose was the key to his success with the masses who likewise had little concern for the intangible problems of Church and State but who only wanted revenge on patrones and their own stomachs and pockets filled.

Sincere as Madero had been in his heart-bleeding for the Mexican people, this was the point where he lost them. He talked, and he wrote. But to the impatient men in the villages and the hills, he did not act. Their ardor noticeably cooled. Furthermore, he kept Díaz officials and army officers in power, gave political plums to his relatives, and incompetently pussyfooted his way around the wreck of dictatorship rather than ruthlessly clearing away the wreckage. The tragedy of the way in which his regime collapsed was of little consequence as compared to the calamitous events which followed. The nation fell victim to inflammatory demagogism, militarism, and insatiable hungers for power and prestige; the people stood ready for personal sacrifice, but their leaders did not. Never before had the lack of wise leadership been so apparent. In Chihuahua, through a blind groping for direction, the peasantry found tumultuous voice in Francisco Villa.

A self-anointed "general" with an army of eight vaqueros, Pancho, despairing no longer, charged over the border, dug biting spurs into horseflesh in eagerness to embrace his destiny.[15] In March 1913, he captured the telegraph office at San Andrés (modern Riva Palacio) to wire a threat to Huerta. For the next two years he would be the flamboyant gran jefe of northern Mexico, the idol of the rabble. The roar of the lion of the desert would be carried clear to the Zócalo of Mexico City and into the emptying halls of the federal palace.

After word of Madero's murder reached Villa in El Paso, he had dispatched word to the deep barrancas and the denuded hills, to the silently waiting pueblitos wooed and won. *Venga a la presa!* Come join the fight! Don't let Huerta get away with this! *Muerte a huertismo!*

From out of the tawny earth arose an Amerindic army such as only

Mexico could produce. Like a newborn geyser, it bubbled and boiled up in the mountains and out of valleys and sterile sands. *Venga a la presa!* Men, women, and children responded to the call, for this was a fight for everyone, old and young, like the character of the nation itself. They rode to Villa's rendezvous on mounts stolen anywhere possible. Corrals and fields were stripped of horses as they passed. When necessary, they trudged on foot over the gritty hills, carrying whatever weapons they could find or take. By the hundreds, with their few worldly possessions on their backs, they poured into the treeless valley by the dam on the Chuvíscar, looking more like applicants for Red Cross aid than an army on the march. They squatted on thin haunches in the dirt to warm a few tortillas over smoky fires, stretched out in the warm sun to puff a strong cigarette or snatch a quick siesta, fingered well-worn gun stocks, wondering just where and when it all would begin and end. That Pancho, *ay, ay, ay!* He was some man! He would lead them a merry way, *verdad!* Maybe good things would come of this fight. Maybe . . . well, frijoles and meat and boiling coffee, a new gun to strap on the hip, a horse of spirit, a nod of recognition on the streets—who could ask for more? *Vamonos con Pancho Villa!* (Let's go with Pancho.)

By the time General Villa arrived, three thousand men had thrown in their lot with his. He again had followers and very soon would be back on top.

Although Chihuahuenses were moved to action by the murder of their national leader, they were more firmly bound to prosecution of the rebellion by the traitorous death of the political leader of their own state. Abraham González had been arrested after Huerta's usurpation of the presidency. En route to Mexico City with a military escort, in the Bachimba Canyon he was suddenly executed. Chihuahuenses, with the exception of the diminishing forces of Orozco, would not stand for that crime.

The jargon of the Mexican Revolution grew as orozquismo was replaced by huertismo. Troops formerly defeated by Victoriano's army now joined him. Numerous unorganized groups took to the field against them and spread the curse of internal war over the map of the state. Angry bands rode through the countryside taking on all comers and each other. Moral standards were tumbling. Everyone felt like fighting, but the ideological purposes lay buried beneath suffocating pettiness. It was one grand dogfight. A state was running amok. In southern sectors—at Santa Bárbara, Parral, Camargo, Jiménez—men like Pablo González, Manuel Chao, and Tomás Urbina R. seized control; in the northwest, Villa's growing army captured Guerrero, Bustillos, and Nuevo Casas Grandes; on the northeastern border, the man who had fired the first shots of the maderista revolution almost three years earlier, Toribio Ortega, took Ojinaga and went on to Monclova, Coahuila, to join in the Plan de Guadalupe with the so-called First Chief (*Primer Jefe*) of the Constitutionalist army, Venustiano Carranza. In July, Ortega and Villa combined efforts, and in defeating the huertista column at San Andrés, captured their first artillery. Now realizing that victory was possible only through joining forces, the leaders of all the scattered bands agreed to recognize Pancho Villa as their standard-bearer. The bandit from the hills was master of the plains as well. He was undisputed chief of Chihuahua revolutionaries. *Mi jefe* once, now *mi general*. Later would it be *mi presidente*?

Villa's Dorados scrawled their mark upon the pages of Chihuahua history, and a terrifying mark it was. Handpicked by Villa for skill at shooting and riding, for reckless courage and ferocity, this mounted band of three hundred guerrillas recreated all the old horrors of the Apache campaigns. The sudden, wild, night charges amid deafening noise, the ability to attack places where their presence never was suspected before battle and then to disperse as suddenly as they had come, the total lack of predictability, compassion, and fear, the acts of brutality done in the name of the Revolution—these were surrounding the Dorados with a reputation for bloody invincibility. Mere rumor of their approach was enough to create panic. Folk imagination had been captured by the thunder of racing hoofs, the blaze of guns, the readiness to kill, and the willingness for heroism. Villa's vices became his virtues. Guerrilla warrior or bandit, for the peons he was wreaking fierce vengeance.

In November the revolutionaries flexed their bulging muscles and reached for the prize, the beautiful city of Chihuahua. Entrenched troops of Huerta held firm, and Villa's men were pushed southward, beyond the city streets. Then with bold initiative, the wily general sent a telegram to Ciudad Juárez giving a false location of his troops, loaded them into train cars, bypassed the city, and sped to the border. Here they quickly enveloped the surprised federal garrison whose chief, General Francisco Castro, scurried across the river. This was the choicest plum of all, and one about which Villa had dreamed during his long period of hiding in El Paso. That night of victory, Ciudad Juárez saw some of the most riotous, debauched celebrating of the entire Revolution. Villa coldly witnessed the execution of seventy-five federal officers.

Huertista governor Mercado, shocked by Villa's brawling triumph, dispatched chameleon José Inés Salazar (magonista, orozquista, huertista) to retake the border town. In a pitched battle sixteen kilometers from the Juárez plaza at Tierra Blanca, Villa vanquished his enemies, routed them completely.* Salazar found it convenient to become a villista. And a frenzied evacuation of the isolated capital began. Not only were the professional huertistas pulling out, but the compromisers, the critics of the Revolution, the innocent bystanders who felt no safety in neutrality. Prominent in the hegira was Luis Terrazas.

FATE was hard on Terrazas. He was a man trapped by his own success, whose fortune was used to erase him and his kind from the face of the land. In November 1913, things looked grim, and Don Luis did not realize just how complete would be his ruin.

Once Madero had taken office, Terrazas returned to his Chihuahua home confident that order would be restored. Publicly, he had taken no sides in the incubation of the Revolution. Although he was considered in the Díaz camp, never did he raise a finger to help the drowning dictatorship. When the newspapers denounced him and aligned him with Don Porfirio, he said nothing. Once his son was relieved of the governorship, he quietly shipped sixteen sealed boxes of deeds, titles, and financial papers to Mexico City and chose to sit out the uprising at Aguascalientes. In the worried months of the activation of the Plan de San Luis Potosí in late 1910, he had given firearms to workers on his haciendas in a vain effort to stop the wave of rustling and vandalism which was thinning down drastically the size of his herds and destroying his settlements. Turncoats among his peons used the guns for further robberies. Terrazas found himself indirectly responsible for the maderista successes in

---

* A popular march entitled "Tierra Blanca" commemorated the victory. Puente, 1957, 84.

the state as his cattle were slaughtered to feed rebel troops or sold across the Río Grande for ready cash.

When uneasy peace settled over the plains, Terrazas filed claim with the Madero government for damages wrought by rebels. Interwoven governmental red tape blocked payment, and then it was too late. Máximo Castillo, a general who acquired power through orozquismo but functioned thereafter as a one-man army, preaching division of the lands, naturally chose to go to work first on the limitless latifundia of Don Luis. Under his sponsorship, with no legal claim or authority other than his ready guns, peons moved onto the Galeana district haciendas of San Luis, San Diego, San Lorenzo, El Carmen, Santa Clara, and San Miguel de Babícora. At the same time, Castillo, knowing he had Terrazas in a bad spot, resorted to extortion. He demanded a 15,000-peso monthly "retainer" on threat of dynamiting fields and buildings and running off the cattle if Don Luis did not pay.

With Castillo's questionable prosperity, it became open season on the Terrazas family. No revoluntary leader passed up the opportunity of taking at least verbal potshots at them. Huerta and Villa found themselves in agreement on one issue: Terrazas. Huertistas condemned him in the national legislature. To Villa, he was the incarnation of all the evils of the despised aristocracy. Orozco, who in the early phases of his counterrevolt had implied he was being fed Terrazas pesos to overthrow Madero, brazenly helped himself to whatever supplies he wanted.* He sanctioned theft of food and clothing from the tiendas de raya and wanton killing or stampeding of livestock. He ordered farm machinery, cars, furniture, grain, and hides removed from Terrazas haciendas and shipped to Ciudad Juárez for resale. Dirty troops moved into carpeted salons, scratched plaster from the walls, and fed their horses from marble-topped tables. At the elegant town house named Quinta Carolina for the señora, orozquistas forced entry and, in rampaging through the spacious building, roughly pawed gowns and suits hanging in the closets, tramping on the garments they did not want.[16] In Ciudad Juárez, one of the sons of Terrazas was kidnapped and held for

---

* Cumberland, 1952, 195, states that Terrazas, together with other hacendados, paid part of the expenses of Orozco's revolt to keep agrarian reforms from being undertaken.

ransom. Terrazas was forced to secure large loans in hopes of riding out the storm.

As Villa's burly column steamrolled southward from Ciudad Juárez, Don Luis and his family knew the time had come. They must run for cover. For Luis, who had clung tenaciously to his land through many years of strain, it was a difficult decision. He was eighty-four years old, and he knew the chances of his return were slim. He felt the restraining tug of deep roots, but safety for his large family had to come first. Hurriedly they packed a few belongings, said their hasty good-byes, and drove to the edge of town where an excited mob was gathering about mounted government troops.

The Terrazas family joined almost five thousand Orozco soldiers and nonpartisans in a mass migration toward the northeastern border.[17] Three hundred miles of uninviting desert lay between them and peace. Mothers with sucking infants, skittish, barefoot children, owners of small city shops, well-dressed businessmen, persons who had spoken too loudly and too recently of the disgrace of the bandits and riffraff, all these and more were united in the struggle to escape what promised to be certain disaster. The frightened train moved on horseback, on foot, and, although there were no roads, by car.

Terrazas's driver bounced erratically over rocky flats, gingerly circumnavigated clumps of sotol and mesquite, and jounced his passengers wildly from side to side. He was forced to stop periodically in order to allow blinding clouds of dust to drift away from ruts cut by the lead cars. At one of these pauses, Don Luis chanced to see several priests wearily making their way on foot with obvious discomfort. Politely hailing them, he gave them use of his boiling automobile and athletic chauffeur and he, the old campaigner of fifty years of military experience and one-time opulence, trudged over the barren plains beside the common folks. Out of respect for his great age and kind generosity toward the tired priests, someone soon offered him a horse to ride. After days of travel, he forded the Río Grande at Ojinaga. From there he made his way to that haven of other dislocated Chihuahuensese, El Paso.

His troubles were far from over. In the years which followed, he was caught in a squeeze between Villa and Carranza. Each accused the other of accepting Terrazas' aid while they both robbed and vilified him. Villa, obsessed with his hatred for Terrazas as a symbol, went out of his way to destroy everything reminiscent of the old man. He had troops torture a Terrazas son in an unsuccessful attempt to gain information about a suspected cache of money and jewels. He completed the ruin of the Terrazas empire begun by maderistas.

FOR TWO YEARS, the Dorados and camp followers of Villa reigned in the plazas of Chihuahua, a period of primitive debauchery. Villa's hysterical regime began December 8, 1913, when he became provisional governor, appointed by a junta of constitutionalist generals.[18] Among his first appointees was Silvestre Terrazas, no relative of Don Luis but long known for his newspaper editorials condemning him.

An unschooled outlaw with no working knowledge of the machinery of government, Villa soon floundered beyond his depth in the Palace of Government. But while his flow of naïve directives horrified economists and amused politicans, he endeared himself still further to the peons. He needed money in order to sustain his troops. So he printed it, 435,000,000 pesos, all unsecured. He authorized duty-free importation of necessities from the United States. At villista meat markets in the Mercado Juárez, the poor could purchase meat from freshly butchered, freshly stolen cattle at fifteen cents per kilogram for chunks without bones and ten cents with bones. Justification for such low prices was that it had come from enemies of the Revolution who deserved no profit.[19] In a surprising move he extended amnesty to huertistas still under arms, but he confiscated their property. With that impounded security, he directed foundation of the Bank of Chihuahua to aid agriculturalists to whom he gave plots of land. Harking back to the period of the first throes of independence, he expelled all Spaniards from the state, claiming they backed Huerta.[20] One, a small boy, is alleged to have become the movie actor Gilbert Roland.

Now that he was the chief of state, he set about building a home for his First Lady, María Luz Corral de Villa, one of a reputed score of wives he acquired in the course of his other campaigns. In a shabby neighborhood on the northeast slope, he had a fifty-room mansion constructed after his own plans. Half home, half fortress with watchtowers and secret passageways, by any standards it was a drab structure. Each room was decorated with a different decor but all were gaudily furnished with Victorian bric-a-brac from the States. To a man born in a one-room mud hut and haphazardly reared in mountain caves, city brothels, and makeshift quarters wherever obtainable, the house on Tenth Street looked palatial. He felt drunk with an exhilarating, new sense of social status. He turned his attention toward providing a palace for the Hereafter.

He who took other lives so casually made elaborate precautions for preserving his own with a loyal bodyguard of sizable proportions and a tight tongue about his exact movements. Being realistic enough to know that his own death could be just one bullet away, he meant to come to final rest not only in peace but in splendor. He ordered construction begun in Panteon de la Regla of an impressive mausoleum of highly ornate, colonnaded, neoclassic style said to have cost some 200,000 pesos.[21] Beneath the dome's bell tower was an elaborate stone altar adorned with ornamental Grecian urns. Above, carved in grey stone, were bleeding hearts. And later buried nearby were the bodies of two of his most reliable generals, Trinidad Rodríguez and Toribio Ortega.[22]

It did not take long to give Pancho his fill of governmental administration. At a desk in a drafty office he lost his luster and verve, just as some of his glamour evaporated when he dismounted and stood bowlegged on the ground. He turned the actual reins of governorship over to General Manuel Chao with stern warning that he, Francisco Villa, commander of the Division of the North, was still jefe, and galloped full tilt through the desert to Ojinaga to push remnants of the huertista adhesion over the river into Presidio, Texas. He was back in his element at the head of troops, blossoming in the roar of artillery and the stench of death, his tooled-leather leggings hugging a horse's belly, his immense disk of sombrero pushed back on his reddish, kinky hair, his horsehair *reata* (rope) ready for action.[23]

In January 1914, all the state of Chihuahua was under control of the Villa counterrevolution.

THE YEAR 1914 was a big one for Villa—and for Mexico. It was the year he was tendered the presidency, and realizing he was hopelessly outclassed, humbly declined it. Before his unprecedented refusal, Villa had barely survived capsizing rivalries and near disasters. In northern Mexico, three strong men were pulling out ahead. In Sonora there was Obregón; in Coahuila, Carranza; in Chihuahua, Villa. With so many prima donnas, upstaging was inevitable.

Carranza, declaring himself Primer Jefe, had passed through the southern sierra near Guadalupe y Calvo to organize forces in the western coastal states, and in March had returned to the central plateau via the northern Púlpito Pass. He was received by the Chihuahua puppet governor, Chao, with the courtesies he considered his due, and was feted at the old Teatro de los Héroes. While he was still in the state, United States marines landed at the port of Vera Cruz in a bluff to force Huerta's ouster. Carranza was native of a state once swept by American soldiers, and he lost no time in sending a vehement protest to Washington. Villa, with many American friends in strategic government and military posts, hastened to publish his pro-Yankee views. Perhaps this was to protect his munitions supply line through Texas, or he may have been making amends for the unfortunate "Benton Affair," recounted below. At any rate, Chihuahuenses by tradition had been anti-American. To them, American troops anywhere in Mexico smacked of 1846. Governor Chao, put into office by Villa, refused to let the general pull strings any longer. He took only Carranza's orders. That insubordination quickly put the forthright governor before a villista firing squad. Carranza interceded, demanding Chao's release.[24] Proud Pancho, cock of the walk but nonetheless aware of the displeasure his hasty move had caused, backed down. From that moment he added a new name to his multiplying list of enemies, Venustiano Carranza. Chao, thankful to be alive, gave his unhealthy job to Silvestre Terrazas.

Many observers north of the border considered Pancho a liberator for the pepole of Mexico, albeit a rowdy one, and cheered his victories. "Viva Villa!" rang through the deserts on both sides of the river. Wilson's government, in refusing to recognize Huerta, offered unofficial "neutral" assistance to strong challengers of that authority. Villa's brother, Hipólito, was allowed to go to New York to purchase military supplies. Guns flowed through customs with no questions asked. Señora Villa rented a house in El Paso to be out of range of buckshot, and peddled candies to get funds for her husband's cause. American mercenaries and adventurers, including the later well-known actor, Tom Mix, were sprinkled through the villista ranks. In Ciudad Juárez, Pancho made friends with Black

Jack Pershing and General Hugh Scott of Fort Bliss; went on hunting trips with them to the sierra madre. A United States State Department man, George Carothers, accompanied his forces. Lincoln Steffens sent home pro-Villa dispatches. Photographers and cameramen from the States, particularly John Reed of the Mutual Film Company, hitched onto the villista trains and ground out photographic records of some of the Dorado charges. Pancho, barely able to read or write himself, had tremendous respect for the influence of the printed word. Early in 1914, he basked in the aura of a uniquely favorable American press. In February, this international relations deteriorated through the careless shooting of an Englishman.

Revolutionary fires swept along the routes of the Díaz-built railroads, particularly in the north where distances were great and the climate sometimes was enervating. Trains packed to overflowing moved the troops, as well as their horses, women, and supplies. When the cars were filled, soldiers of both sexes sprawled together on the rooftops or clung to the train exterior like the flies on the beef in the market. William Benton, a British subject but longtime resident of Mexico and known for a quick temper, owned and operated a hacienda spread at Sueco, a short distance north of Gallegos. It was traversed in the early days by the Camino Real going from Chihuahua to El Paso del Norte, and after 1882, by the rails of the Ferrocarril Central. This placed Mr. Benton's outfit right in the path of the various tides of rebellion which spread alternately north and south. As the trains chugged through the property, soldiers shot grazing cattle or horses for the sheer pleasure of target practice. Or the trains stopped while rebels packed off whatever they saw that they wanted. Fences were cut or destroyed. Mrs. Benton, daughter of a Mexican hacendado, had been threatened with violence or worse if she refused to hand over money and food. Finally, Benton had enough. He went to Ciudad Juárez to see Villa.

Stories of what took place are varied. But it was an undeniable fact that Benton was murdered. Some say that after hearing Benton's accusation against his soldiers, Villa made the fearless Britisher dig his own grave and then shot him. Another account has the killing done by several Villa henchmen who thought Benton was drawing a gun as he reached for a handkerchief.

After the hacendado was dead, Villa called a council to review the facts and vindicate the killing, which it immediately did. It was claimed that Villa, or his men, had acted in self-defense. Besides, Benton himself was accused of committing crimes against the Revolution with the aid of that old boogeyman, Terrazas!

The American Department of State, acting on request of the more distant British government, asked for security for Benton. After word leaked out that Benton had been killed, American officials demanded Benton's body. Villa haughtily refused, ignoring all such requests. A mass meeting protesting the killing took place at an El Paso movie house. It looked for a time as though Villa might lose his trappings as the liberator in the American press. To set himself up as judge, jury, and executor over his own people was one thing, but to deal this way with Anglo-Saxons was, for American readers, quite another. Villa sought to reinstate himself by loud praise of his neighbors to the north. Time and new conquests partially effaced the unpleasant memory of the high-handed shooting of Benton.

In this year of 1914 Americans in the northwestern part of Chihuahua had reason to fear another of the revolutionary generals more than Villa: Máximo Castillo. Extortioner, thug, self-made power, Castillo ruthlessly reigned through terrorism. He and his band flashed through the basins and ridges at the eastern skirts of the Sierra Madre Occidental, sweeping up possessions and loot like so much flood-borne detritus. Mormon colonists armed themselves psychologically against Castillo's men who seemed to have unlimited appetites for horseflesh. On occasions they entertained him at Academy programs, trying to impress upon him their fast intentions of drilling the best of Mexican ideals into their children, hoping he and other rebels would come to identify them with Mexico and not the United States. Sporadic attacks and unreasonable demands were met with clear-eyed bravery but never armed resistance. Finally, as the stripping of Mormon property became more complete, Castillo left the colonies alone.

Others, however, suffered at his hands. At Pearson, potential heart of the new sawmill industry, his men burned and pillaged, and in ignorance and greed destroyed the fruit of foreign technology and investment in their part of the state. Saws were broken, parts scattered and smashed. Buildings were set on fire. Railroad cars were blown to bits. And all the officials, mostly Americans, were lined up and shot. Castillo then shortsightedly sought to destroy the Noroeste de México Railroad which linked the northwest to the border. His band, waiting in ambush for a train loaded with over fifty passengers to enter the Cumbre Tunnel south of Pearson, ignited dynamite charges at both entrances. All the people on the train were killed from burns or suffocation from the clouds of black smoke which clogged the passage. Many of the victims were Americans engaged in the sierra lumbering operations.[25]

Near hysterical protests at such insensate slaughter came from Mexicans and Americans alike. Castillo, challenged by no lesser man than Villa, made quick escape into humiliating exile. He died in Cuba in 1919.

The Division of the North, trained by generations of guerrilla warfare and touched with the fire and swashbuckling fervor of its leader, moved on to the south. Held in control by an iron discipline, an ardent personal adhesion to Villa, and sometimes a persistent fear of its own commanders, the Division was tutored by strategists like Felipe Angeles and Raúl Madero. In April when Villa gave the orders, the rabble wave surged to the outskirts of the Coahuila city of Torreón. One of the bloodiest battles of the Revolution was fought in the alleys and narrow streets of the city, leaving dead over seven thousand men and women.[26] After Torreón, came triumphs at Paredón, Saltillo, and Zacatecas. The lusty power of the Division of the North threatened to mold the destiny of the Mexican nation.

That July, Carranza's constitutionalists were in power. Bibulous Huerta, fenced in by the frolicking northerners—Carranza, Villa and Obregón, and by Zapata in the south—gave up and fled to Texas. There he died in jail in 1916, planning a comeback. Already having envisioned himself as Primer Jefe, Carranza at once set about staking his claims, naturally engendering an ill-concealed resentment in the cartridge-strapped breast of his competitor from Chihuahua. Most of the friction between the two men developed over relative trivialities as each tried to fill the whole circle of public limelight. Villista general Toribio Ortega held up movement of a train on which Carranza was riding. Carranza refused to send Coahuila coal to fuel Villa trains. Bad feeling between the two camps grew, undermining the unity which should have followed Huerta's abdication. After a peacemaking convention with Carranza at Aguascalientes, Villa and his Dorados rolled on south to Mexico

City to find themselves wildly, and not a little fearfully, acclaimed as heroes of the people.

For five months Villa and Zapata traded presidential office. Neither chose to remain, although either might have established a dynasty. Feeling restive and strangely introspective amid the chill, green highlands, Villa headed for home and the ruinous storms of 1915.

Gray-bearded Carranza carefully moved into strategic position.

As THE NEXT two years progressed, Villa's enemies became stronger and abler and he was outmarshaled, outfought, and outdone on every front. But ignoble surrender was not in his makeup. He determined to make all possible trouble for his enemies. That enemy list grew at an accelerated pace with increasing defeats. When Carranza outsprinted him in the race for control, his name was added. When Obregón sided with Carranza, he became an enemy. Then when the United States recognized Carranza as the true leader of Mexico, Villa defied an entire nation and any force it chose to send against him. To Villa himself and to numbers of loyal peasants, he was and always would remain the *gran hombre,* the leading actor in the pageant of the north. Let them have their colorless wishy-washy Carranza or their smooth-spoken, smooth-operating Obregón. Strong men of Chihuahua liked their idols forceful, devilish, and devastating.

The gradual military eclipse of Pancho Villa began in 1915. His army was routed at Celaya, León, and Aguascalientes by constitutionalists under Obregón. Villistas were pursued into the Chihuahua mountains where at Tasajera, Creel, and Batopilas they again tasted bitter defeat. It was a taste to which Villa's army would have to become adjusted, for there were no more glorious aguardiente-soaked victories ahead, no more carousing bursts of "Adelita" or "La Cucaracha," no more opportunities to push others aside. Wilson's United States Government, seeing that Villa had lost control, withdrew support in October.*

---

* Many prominent Americans felt this action on the part of the United States Government to be unfortunate. Schuster, 1947, 176, quotes General Hugh L. Scott, "The recognition of Carranza had the effect of solidifying the power of the man who had rewarded us with kicks on every occasion and of making an outlaw of the man who had helped us."

Cornered, persecuted, and stirred by deep resentment at the loss of American patronage, the gran hombre re-entered the ancient role of *gran bandido*, cleaning the regions through which he passed of everything of value. He especially enjoyed terrorizing all foreigners, demanding at gunpoint payment of large *mordidas*, or bribes, by mine operators and "protection" money from cattlemen.[27] For some inexplicable reason, he avoided the Mormon colonies although he often used nearby Casas Grandes as a base of operations. The Chinese population, dating from the railroad construction days, suffered tragically because of an intense hatred Villa had for the *chinos*, claiming that they had withheld money from him when he needed it most. The Dorados became more brutal, more malicious than ever. Soon the government of the state placed a price upon their heads. Then the desertions, intrigues, and doublecrossings began. Fear kept many men in the ranks, but the motivating spirit of success was no more. Villa was forced to hang an old companion, Tomás Urbina, for hiding loot taken in a series of bank robberies.[28] He was losing *compañeros* as well as *soldados*. Breakers of moral indignation were swelling into crushing strength, pushing Pancho toward the reefs, as Chihuahuenses would tolerate him no longer.

As in the past, Pancho tried to recapture his glory through new military victories. Against the advice of his knowledgeable general Angeles (director of the military academy under Díaz), he pushed his army through the narrow Púlpito Pass on to the broken tableland of northern Sonora. Torrents of rain had turned arroyos into boiling rivers. The troops mired down and became fatigued and thin. Villa the guerrilla had never mastered logistics, and it was to be his undoing. At Agua Prieta and Naco on the Arizona border, *carrancista* general Calles had received arms through the United States border, and constitutionalist troops had been transported through United States territory. Dorados, villistas, and Yaqui Indians, high on marihuana, were slaughtered in a sanguinary battle lighted by American searchlights and witnessed by Americans living in the Arizona desert.[29] Thoroughly angry at this unexpected aid to his enemies after he had returned millions of dollars worth of property to Americans in Mexico, Villa vowed retaliation for what he could only regard as dirty dealing.

In January 1916, southwest of the Chihuahua capital near the hamlet of General Trías (then called Santa Ysabel), villistas Pablo López and Rafael Castro halted a train bound for the mines at Cusihuiriáchi. They dragged fifteen Americans to the mesquite-covered bank of the railroad bed, shot them, and mutiliated their bodies.[30] All had come to Cihuahua under a safe conduct authorized by the governor. El Paso became hysterical when news of the atrocity arrived. Martial law was ordered to keep Americans from swarming over the river to take revenge on innocent Mexican residents there. López later was captured and in June was executed at the penitentiary in Chihuahua.[31] A movie of the execution was sent for showing at El Paso.*

Two months passed while Villa nursed his pride and plotted. Weary and disillusioned, the rabble army had melted back to the red earth from which it had sprung. Only those irretrievably committed remained. With those few, he hoped to embarrass Carranza with the United States and force armed intervention, while at the same time shooting a few more new American enemies. Samuel Rabel, supplier of contraband arms who had accepted Villa's money and then refused to deliver the goods, was a special object of his wrath.[32] Another enemy on the list was John Johnston who was said to have robbed him during the Sonoran campaign.[33]

Some reports had Villa bound northward for a conference in Washington with Wilson. Others said he had pledged himself to kill ten Americans for every one of seventeen Mexicans who had been burned to death accidentally in a disinfectant vat at the El Paso customs station.[34] At any rate, whatever the motive, and it may well have been personal revenge, as March winds commenced to blow up cold puffs of prickling sand, scouts brought word to the commander of the Juárez garrison that Villa was marching again. This time he was headed toward the border.

COLUMBUS is a name bestowed upon a sprinkling of towns and cities across the breadth of the United States, but in March 1916 the only Columbus of which Americans were thinking was Columbus, New Mexico.[35] A lethargic, little village straggling unhappily

---

* After the Revolution, a Special Claims Commission declared Mexico not liable for this murder. Dulles, 1961, 318.

across a sere plain several miles north of the border, it was at an intersection of the deeply rutted wagon road running north-south from Deming, New Mexico, to Guzmán, and the El Paso and Southwest Railroad running east-west. A few stores, a bank, a hotel, the customs house, and the railroad station made up the center of town. Most of these buildings were of frame construction with wide front porches to deflect the intense rays of the relentless summer sun. Across the railroad tracks were placed buildings needed for the small garrison of troops of the Thirteenth Cavalry assigned to guard the sixty-five-mile long uninhabited line of the border from Noria to Hermanas. Barracks, mess shacks, hospital, quartermaster storehouse, and stables spread out into dust-covered mesquite. Most of the officers and their families lived in houses dispersed throughout the town. Some quarters were adobe and therefore bulletproof; others were not.

Life at the Columbus outpost drifted quietly along, with today much the same as yesterday and little chance that tomorrow would be different. Soldiers lay on their cots to enjoy sweaty dreams of periodic furloughs to the bustling metropolis of El Paso with its many bars and night spots where one could fritter away six months pay in a few congenial hours. Civilians resorted to thoughts of a cool, leafy paradise far beyond the Chiricahuas. The only rapid movement was the passing of the "Golden States," eastbound each morning and the westbound each afternoon, and that occasioned by the chance encounter of rattlers who slid from hot sand to hot floor without regard to ownership, or in the swirling clouds of gray dust seeking to restore the desert to its primal state.

Then suddenly there was excitement. From Brownsville to Nogales there were whispers of impending trouble. There had been trouble before as the Mexican war had seethed across the frontier. Protests from Washington had been duly lodged with the *de facto* government of Mexico and had as duly been ignored. Orders had gone to United States posts along the boundary to strengthen forces, take precautions against raiding Mexicans, but to preserve peace at all costs. Rumors were rife, but, as nothing had developed of a nature serious enough to bring two nations to war, tensions slowly had eased back into complacency.

But now it was different. By that mysterious invisible communications system which Mexico possesses, a strong feeling that Villa plotted trouble for the gringos permeated the settlements of the desert, finally reaching El Paso. General Pershing at Fort Bliss dispatched warnings to Colonel Slocum at Columbus.[36]

Alerted patrol riders jogged uneasily along their routes east and west. Sometimes they mounted in chill, star-strewn night when each creosote bush looked like a crouching human form, but daylight patrols looked out upon a sweeping horizon of leached lands and folded eminences empty of any indication of approaching disaster. No soldier could cross over into the forbidden land to observe at firsthand what might be brewing in the purple distance. Upsetting reports persistently filtered through the carrancista-held border gate of an amassing of villistas south of Palomas. Two American cowboys from a line camp on the Palomas Land and Cattle Company holdings unfortunately verified the rumors.

McKinney and Corbett had spotted a motley band of some four hundred men making camp on the Cases Grandes River and they foolishly had ridden into their midst. Promptly they were surrounded by a threatening mob and, upon orders from Villa, were killed.* A Mexican helper, Antonio, who had been with McKinney, had refused to accompany his foreman and had run as fast as his pony would go to Colonel Slocum at Columbus. That was March 7. For twenty dollars from the United States army, all the following day Antonio hid in the hills to spy on the movements of the villistas. Later accounts of Antonio's information vary. Some had Villa headed for Columbus, and some had him going south away from the border. The army for a reason never made clear felt no immediate alarm.

According to Mexican writer Calzadíaz Berrera, Villa had been quartered at the hacienda of San Jerónimo in central Chihuahua when he conceived the idea of the Columbus attack. Gathering together some four hundred followers under command of generals Pablo López, Jesús Manuel Castro, Francisco Beltrán, and Candelario Cervantes, he had ridden north to San Miguel de Babícora, then into the protection of the sierra for two weeks. Finally he

---

* Calzadíaz Berrera, 1960, 37, places the blame for this killing upon one of Villa's generals, Candelario Cervantes.

arrived at Boca Grande just below the border. There, McKinney and Corbett were executed as they interrupted the Mexicans killing cattle for food.[37]

The next day plans for the raid were completed. Cervantes and ninety-eight men from Namiquipa were to find and kill Rabel and to set his hardware store and hotel on fire. Castro's force was to rob the bank and then burn the building. Beltrán was to fire on the military camp, while López was to storm the railway station and cut the telephone and telegraph wires.[38]

The young hours of March 9 were moonless and black. Small groups of stern-faced, sombreroed riders silently crossed the international boundary three miles west of the border gate, guardedly united at the slopes of a rocky knoll, and directed their ponies north across the plains until they were about a half mile from the New Mexico settlement. Then columns forked, one moving on foot south of the black outlines of buildings of the town to slip into the garrison stables and cut loose the horses and the other walking west to prepare to attack and loot the army camp and sleeping Columbus.

Nervous requests made by Colonel Slocum for street lamps and oil for illumination previously had been denied. So now, in the moment of desperate need, Columbus was without a lighting system and lay swathed in immense darkness so impenetrable that sentinels found it impossible to see twenty feet beyond themselves. A kerosene lantern flickered weakly at the railway station, and small lamps created yellow pools of light in the two hotel lobbies. The Columbus Theater, the bank, Dean's Grocery Store, and Miller's Drug Store were dark. Huarache-shod Mexicans met no obstacles as they hugged along the sides of buildings and stole into the heart of the village. There was only the rhythmic creaking of a blotchy sign whose dimmed lettering read "Commercial Hotel, A. L. Ritchie, Prop." as it gyrated in the incessant, droning wind.

At four-thirty in the morning Private Fred Griffin, Troop K, sentinel on duty at the regimental headquarters, was shot down as he challenged an approaching Mexican. At once, like coyotes barking at the moon, "Viva Villa" echoed and ricocheted from all parts of town. Red-eyed shouting men, guns blazing, excitedly raced through the dirt streets shooting into open windows, breaking down doors, setting fire to anything that would ignite, creating hell for the half-wakened, stunned residents. Samuel Rabel, for whom angry Mexicans searched, had gone to El Paso, but his business house was destroyed. A night which had begun in doleful silence was ending in a gigantic uproar.[39]

Officers' quarters were surrounded by howling villistas trying to prevent aroused inhabitants from joining the troops. In retrospect, it was all too obvious that spies for the invaders, posing as traders from Palomas or vaqueros from scattered ranchos on both sides of the border who were dependent upon the Columbus railhead for supplies, surely had located these dwellings in advance as there was no outward sign of just which homes were those of the military. Several besieged families scurried out back entrances as the front door was being torn apart. One family crowded in an outhouse until the Mexicans left. Another squatted amidst mesquite growth beyond their yard, hardly daring to breathe for fear of giving themselves away. Inky darkness was their sole protection.

Hungry Mexicans broke into well-stocked army kitchens hoping to find food, only to be met with scalding water showered on them by fearless Negro cooks or forced to flee whirring swishes of meat cleavers and wickedly sharpened axes.

The officer of the day, Lieutenant Castleman, got his troop into action at once. Two other unmarried lieutenants, Stringfellow and Lucas, lived in camp and were on hand to join in the disorganized opening phases of the fighting. One reported later that in his hurry to repel the enemy, he had run from his house without his shoes, and as he had fought several hours barefooted, it took six months to rid his tender feet of the accumulation of thorns and goat burrs. Machine guns were set up quickly at strategic locations. Afterwards, the American press criticized these weapons for jamming. But Lucas's four guns used five thousand rounds apiece in an hour and a half and were an important factor in bringing about the Mexican withdrawal.

Ultimately, American soldiers were able to drive the raiders from the camp into the small, centrally located blocks of business houses where they were trapped in vicious cross fire. Confusion caused by the darkness was lessened when Villa's men set the hotel afire. They then were silhouetted against the angry flames and were easy targets for soldiers crouching back in the shadows. As the time of the arrival of the eastbound morning train approached, a retreat of the invaders was called. Almost two hundred villistas* were left dead in Columbus streets or in the desert brush around. Twenty-four Americans were killed; seven wounded. The train's conductor pulled some fleeing Americans aboard the incoming train and, on learning of the raid, telegraphed the news to Fort Bliss.**

The escaping Mexican column reached its horses and struck for safety south of the wire fences of the border. Major Frank Tompkins, who had been isolated in his home during the thick of battle, mounted up a pursuit troop.† In twenty minutes, thirty-two men rode from camp hoping to overtake the villistas. On reaching the border, they cut the fences and charged down on a Mexican hilltop patrol trying to guard the rear flanks of the retreat. Tompkins at once dispatched a courier back to headquarters asking permission to carry the fight onto Mexican soil. The request was granted and additional troops were dispatched. Tense and angry soldiers traveled fast after the churning column of dust which marked the southward bandit flight. Mexicans were forced to fight four separate rear-guard actions as the cavalry progressed fifteen miles into Chihuahua.

Fearful of getting beyond reach of supplies, Tompkins swung his column back to the garrison. As they trotted north, sagging dejectedly in their saddles after an eight-hour ride, they watched thin spirals of smoke snake upward from the smoldering ruins of the hotel, the drugstore, and scattered homes. They saw their wounded being carried on stretchers to a train waiting on the sidetracks, and they watched men of the town probing the embers of destroyed property. Solemnly they rode past huddled women and children whose tear-streaked faces still told of the hideous terror of the early morning. Dismounting, they had to announce the escape of the raid's ringleader.

Some prisoners had been captured by the Americans. Later one of these was hanged at Deming, New Mexico. Another was given a life sentence which was commuted. Suspects were captured after-

---

* Schuster, 1947, 221-31, claims no more than fifty villistas were lost. Salinas Carranza likewise doubts the two hundred figure. (1936, 104)

** Aboard the train was Luis Cabrera, later one of the Mexican representatives to the Altantic City settlement meeting. Puente, 1957, 138.

† On September 11, 1934, Tompkins received a medal for valor in the action at Columbus eighteen years previously.

wards in the Mexican campaign, but by protesting their ignorance of being in the United States and with the excuse of a soldier's acknowledged duty to follow his commander's orders without question, eleven were freed by the governor of New Mexico.[40] But Villa was never taken. His romantic biographers protest he had not been involved. One wrote that the general, lying prone in an irrigation ditch out of town, had held the reins of some of his men's horses, an action totally out of character for the unquellable Villa. Another stated that Villa was in Casas Grandes or Palomas at the time of the raid and had no knowledge of the senseless shooting until it was alarming history. However, it seems quite certain now that Villa had been in full command at Columbus, although presumably he actually took no part in the fighting.[*] He had thrown from four hundred to a thousand followers[**] into battle against two hundred sixty-six men of the Thirteenth Cavalry and an unarmed sleeping town.

Interestingly enough, March 9, 1916, the day of the attack, was the sixty-ninth anniversary of the American attack on Vera Cruz.

MANY THOUGHT President Wilson's Mexican policy bordered on thinly veiled intervention.[†] Behind him ranted a vociferous Ameri-

---

[*] The distinguished Mexican lawyer and Minister of Hacienda under Carranza and a member of the Atlantic City peace conference, Luis Cabrera, wrote, "The assault on Columbus by Villa was a deliberate act aimed at producing an international complication." Salinas Carranza, 1936, 16.

[**] Calzadíaz Berrera sets the Villa force at 403 (1960, 28); Puente says villistas numbered 240 (1957, 137); Salinas Carranza gives the two forces equal size (1936, 102); General Funston reported to Washington that 1,000 to 3,000 men were involved (Salinas Carranza, 1938, 116).

[†] A series of incidents substantiated such beliefs: the rejection of Huerta on the grounds of murder but acceptance of Villa, a figure known to be ruthless in use of his firing squads; the bombardment of the port of Vera Cruz by U.S. Marines; the passage of arms across the border if they were assigned to U.S.-approved revolutionists; and the assignment of envoys to Mexico who knew little of Mexico and nothing of the language. McCullagh, 1928, 86-100. Senator Henry Cabot Lodge on March 17, 1916, stated, "The responsibility for conditions in Mexico rests largely on the government of the United States. The present administration found Mexico and Mexican relations in bad condition. They have made these conditions infinitely worse." Schuster, 1947, 177. Mexicans regarded the Punitive Expedition as an attack and a basic error of American international policy.

can press. Villa must be captured and killed or his bands so completely dispersed as to be impotent thenceforward. Mother Mexico,
it seemed, was unable to discipline her wayward offspring. So Uncle
Sam would do it for her.

Obregón sped to the border to initiate a program of smiling delay and what Americans considered behind-the-scenes treachery.
Mexico and the United States, he said, should join in a plan of
mutual assistance such as brought results in the 1880's. Then, he
acidly reminded General Scott and General Funston, it was from
the northern side of the boundary that trouble came pounding into
Mexico on the backs of Indian ponies. If an incident such as occurred at Columbus should be repeated, Carranza's government
would be happy to have United States forces come to Mexico to aid
in ending the border disturbances. In the meantime, the Mexicans
could deal with Villa. It was an old refrain which had underlain
all of Mexico's relationships with the United States: proud, sensitive, steadfast determination to solve her own problems in her own
way without Yankee interference. General Luis Gutiérrez, in Chihuahua, was to take twenty-five hundred men in pursuit of the
Columbus raiders. However, sensing that the deliberate mires of
diplomacy were allowing them to escape, Wilson ordered Brigadier
General John J. Pershing, of Fort Bliss, El Paso, to Columbus at
once to chase Villa in Mexico. It was "Villa, dead or alive."

Intoxicating infusions of self-importance, righteous indignation,
and excitement overnight transformed Columbus. Gone was tedi-
um and in its place, high adventure. Everywhere there was an unaccustomed sense of urgency as the Punitive Expedition outfitted.
Waves of army personnel arrived by trail and by train to create a
bustling cantonment around the garrison. Barracks, hospital, and
mess tents were sowing a white forest in a treeless land. Horses were
brought in from as far away as Fort Oglethorpe, Georgia, to be
drilled and sleekly curried in hastily constructed stables. Trucks,
and even airplanes, were shipped to the border to be assembled.
Then appeared the professional camp followers, the soldiers of
fortune, the newspapermen, the chronically restless.

"Villa, dead or alive."

Regimental colors unfurled, rippling softly in the wind, as the
men of the Thirteenth Cavalry galloped across the border on March
15, bound on a mission which Mexicans said was "buscar el gato en

el garbanzal" or like looking for a needle in a haystack. Nine days
after the treacherous raid, an American army entered Chihuahua
for the second time in seventy years. The mounted column, determined to follow Wilson's orders to proceed despite Mexican resistance, rode over the desert through Palomas, a scattering of
thirty squalid, unplastered adobe houses around a seeping spring.
Being on the alert for trouble, with rifles tucked into the saddle
skirts under their leggings, the troopers anxiously scanned horizons
for approach of natives. Although the jefe of Palomas sent word to
Pershing that he would resist the Americans with force, Palomas
had been abandoned to the care of one old couple. The southbound
cavalry moved out at a steady trot.

An eastern column composed of the garrison at Columbus and
reinforcements from Nogales and El Paso was to drive south to
Ascensión where it would be joined by a western column coming
from Fort Huachuca, Arizona, via Hachita, New Mexico. A change
of orders en route forced the western unit to march without sleep
for two days and two nights and move directly to Colonia Dublán.
There they were met by General Pershing and his aides, one of
whom was a young first lieutenant who years later would become
one of the most colorful and controversial generals in the army's
history, George S. Patton, Jr.

The era just prior to World War I still belonged to the cavalry.
Few realized that the horse and the mule were going to be replaced
in warfare by the truck and the tank, and even fewer anticipated
the military value of the airplane. Yet the Mexican campaign was
to hurry out the old and usher in the new. Thereafter the "old"
army would be no more.

Many of these cavalrymen had been born into the regiments in
which they served, as had some of their fathers. As youngsters they
had played soldiers-and-Indians through army corrals at remotely
located garrisons sprinkled over the western plains. Almost from
infancy they had learned well the hard game of riding and fighting
and surviving, of reading the telling signs of bent twigs, horseshoe
prints, warm embers of a forsaken campfire. They had grown up to
take to their souls the mighty extensions of sweeping land and sky,
to place first before oneself the love and care of horseflesh, to absorb
the mingled odors of saddlery, the smoke of open fires, and the
strong sweat of physical exertion of men and beasts. They had cul-

tivated a blasting lingo into high art until the expression "to swear like a trooper" became an accepted phrase of Americana, requiring no explanation. More fundamental than any other attribute, bred into them in years of witnessing the mounted army at work, was the cavalryman's great sense of unfaltering, chivalrous loyalty to his outfit and his comrades.

Fifteen thousand American soldiers had become involved in the pursuit of a handful of Mexican bandits. Troops from the Second, Fifth, Sixth, Eighth, Tenth, Eleventh, Twelfth, and Thirteenth Cavalry rode south across Chihuahua deserts. In case of battle they were to be supported by infantry and field artillery. Engineers followed up to turn trails into roads. Signal Corps men strung telegraph lines along the routes of march. Most ironic, scouts employed to aid the invaders were Apaches whose ancestors had been enemies of both Americans and Mexicans. Wagon companies and mule packtrains with their necessary saddlers and blacksmiths kept the materials of war moving to the front columns. Behind them roared newly created companies of trucks and a squadron of aircraft, baffled by their infinite lack of knowledge and thwarted by improper equipment but learning rapidly the intricacies of supply and reconnaissance under war conditions and unideal terrain. For the very first time, thanks to horseman Pancho Villa, mechanization on land and in the air was being tested by the American army.

Colonia Dublán, only partially repopulated after the Exodus, offered advantages as a base of operations. Located astraddle the Noroeste Railroad and on a telegraph line direct to the border, its residents promised an invaluable supply of guides and interpreters. The selected scouts quickly learned that Villa's men were rounding up supplies south of Casas Grandes at the once lush Terrazas hacienda of San Miguel.

The chase was on. Three pursuit forces took to the field immediately even though some already had traveled more than several hundred miles without rest. One column rode eastward to Galeana, El Valle (San Buenaventura), and from there were to ascend the sierra slopes to the rolling plateau on which San Miguel lay. Two parties were to go south by train, one getting off at Rucio and moving on horseback to San Miguel and the other continuing to Las Varas to cover the regions south of Babícora. It was necessary to prevent Villa from escaping over the cordillera into Sonora on the west or from reaching the central railroad on the east. And it was hoped he could be cut off to the south before he had opportunity to reach the mountains beyond Guerrero.

Because of Mexican refusal to allow use of their railroad cars, Pershing wired El Paso to request the Southwestern and El Paso line to furnish his army some rolling stock. When it arrived, it was in deplorable state and required a great many time-consuming repairs. Holes in the floors were patched, but others for ventilation had to be cut in the walls of box cars. There was no fuel to feed the boilers. Stock pens at Dublán and San Diego were torn down and thrust aboard for tinder. At San Diego the engineer had to uncouple his engine, go ahead to Pearson for water, and return in reverse. He had been fearful of stopping at the water tank of Nuevo Casas Grandes as the train passed through because of the well-known villista sympathies of the people living there. When the switchbacks south of Pearson were reached, it was obvious that the troop train was too long and too heavy. Although the caravan was divided into two sections, the pull was slow and tortuous, the engine furnace coughing up great fumes of black smoke in the mighty effort. At the Cumbre switchback, two cars loaded with men, horses, and equipment plunged wildly from the tracks down a steep embankment. The first casualty of the Punitive Expedition was a young cavalryman killed amid the careening debris of this accident. Eleven others were injured. An American foreman on one of the Hearst ranches in the area made a two-day trip on a railroad hand-car carrying the hurt back to Dublán.

For an interminable month of alternating hot days and freezing nights when a temperature change of as much as ninety degrees shook both men and horses, of heavy whirling snows, hot prairie fires, and gagging sandstorms, of indistinct rock-lined trails, misleads, and misfortunes, the army steadily forged into the wilderness of Chihuahua.

Each soldier carried field rations and a mess kit. He was his own cook. At the end of a long rough ride, after his horse had been watered and fed some of the oats from a grain bag strapped across the pommel or handfuls of native corn so mixed with pebbles that the horses' mouths were getting sore, he had to rustle up firewood, get a blaze going, and prepare his monotonous meals. As the army continued to move farther away from the border, supplies became exhausted, and the cavalcade of trucks was unable to reach them until the engineers made passable roads. The men were then forced to live off the land which had been stripped quite thoroughly through the years by other armies and other hungry men. They learned to know pinole, tortillas, and chile-flavored jerky and looked forward to a boiler of steaming beans or an occasional slice of fresh beef. It was soon discovered that the command should have been supplied with a great many more Mexican silver pesos. The villagers, already resentful of American presence in their state, were reluctant to give up foodstuffs they sorely needed themselves in return for a quartermaster's draft which might be lost in the depths of military channels between Chihuahua and headquarters at San Antonio, Texas. Hard cash was something as rare and savory as peace itself, and the sight of it brought forth a few dirty eggs here, a sack of corn there, a bit of pungent coffee from a secret hiding place. Officers found it necessary to dip into their personal funds in order to feed their men.

Spring brought no softening to Chihuahua but high, penetrating winds to split a man's lips and impregnate his bones with chill. The parties scouting the mountains through Cave Valley to Pacheco and sacked Chuhichupa tramped through deep snow. Each morning they found their canteens of water frozen solid and icicles dripping from their whiskers. All learned to dig narrow trenches just wide enough for two, build a roaring fire in them to warm the sod, scrape the ashes away, cover the pits with their issued shelter halves, and lie stiffly together through the long nights. Sometimes they had to ride over the difficult terrain in darkness; sometimes dismounted and leading the horses, hoping not to become separated from the group. Other times, in spite of the cold, the fatigued lay down on the ground, and holding horse reins in their grip, fell asleep for a brief rest.

Hunger, cold, and weariness were things which the troopers could understand. Suspicion, deception, and polite misinformation were not. Mexican government forces were their nominal allies, but very often the Yanks learned they had been deliberately sidetracked, put off, or misguided by those allies. Why? Why had the carrancistas not made a real effort themselves to take Villa when his whereabouts were well known? How could a people find in themselves the desire to cheer an outlaw simply because he eluded the Americans? Yet this was the bitter fact. Down through the villages along the Santa María, those towns known as *pueblos de los indios,* where men had been recruited on the way to Columbus and impressed on the return, townsfolk were quick to accept American tips and give false leads. "Sí, señores, Villa has been here. No, señores, not recently. Maybe he rode to Santa Clara or Madera or Chihuahua. Quién sabe?" Villa seemed to be everywhere, yet he could not be found.

In reality, at this time in late March, Pancho was scarcely one jump ahead of his pursuers. After the retreat from Columbus, he and his weakened band had pounded back to the central basins of the state. Casas Grandes received news that the desired intervention had come, but not exactly as Villa had plotted. Now he was a renegade sought by two countries. It was a role to give suitable test to all his adroitness, skill at the fantastic dodge, force of leadership, and the sentimental loyalty of the peons. The odds were in his favor, although his army was greatly outnumbered, for he seemed to have spent a lifetime preparing for this moment. There was not a crevice or water hole or cave in the entire region which he did not know. And he felt secure in the knowledge that his reputation with the simple peons woud now pay off in aid and concealment. Experience had taught him too that where his people would not help him willingly, they could be encouraged to do so with a gun at the temple. So Villa was in his flamboyant glory as he rode into villages one by one—San Miguel, Namiquipa, Bachiniva, and then Guerrero. He harangued the gathered inhabitants, aroused them against the detested *americanos* who were invading Chihuahua once again, and accompanied by rousing "Vivas" took all supplies and manpower available.

By 1916 not all rebellious men in Chihuahua were sympathetic to Villa. Blind obedience had been undermined first by a feeling of futility and then repugnance. Villa, unseeing when he needed clairvoyance, operating as always on emotion and not logic, overstepped himself. During a running skirmish with Carranza troops, he was wounded in the leg by a bullet which may have been fired intentionally by one of his own men.*

---

* Salinas Carranza, 1938, 137, states Villa was hit by a stray bullet during the retreat of government forces from Guerrero. Schuster, 1947, 223, is of the opinion that the gun accidentally discharged while being cleaned.

Word of Villa's disablement was relayed quickly to the oncoming American columns. One, under command of Colonel Dodd, pushed hard southward toward Guerrero, covering a particularly rugged section by a forced night march, hoping to capitalize on the Mexican jefe's incapacity. After Guerrero was taken by the Americans, it was learned that the villistas had been holed up in the town. Those that escaped scattered to the four winds and, according to General Pershing's reports, were never again able to reorganize. But the sought-after leader had vanished.

In the middle of the night, General Villa, running a high fever and in great pain after having been treated by a Yaqui in his command, had bounced out of town on the floor of a jolting wagon bed, escorted by fifty of his most die-hard followers. Had Dodd taken a different route to Guerrero, he would have encountered his prey. By sheer luck, Villa continued free. Dodd had his moment of victory, however, when he was cheered in the halls of Congress and promoted to brigadier general for his part in the Mexican campaign.

The two other prongs of the American southward thrust came down through the rolling hill country of the Hearst property of Santa Ana*, Chavez, and Babícora. Hearst's general manager was Maximiliano Márquez, later a carrancista officer, and, according to Tompkin's account of the campaign, one of the few Mexicans encountered who seemed genuinely sincere in his desire to aid the Americans. He obligingly made welcome quarters available for the weary riders and offered the services of fifty of his men as scouts.

As penetration into Mexico deepened, army headquarters moved forward from Namiquipa to San Gerónimo to San Antonio de Arenales, the latter Zuloaga land attached to the Hacienda de Bustillos, east of Guerrero on the trail and railroad to Chihuahua. To keep in touch with his troops, Pershing rode in one of the three Dodge touring cars at his command. With him went the builders of communications—the engineers to blast roads where none existed, the signal corps men to stretch tight the valuable telegraph wires and then guard them, the pilots to shortcircuit time and terrain, the truck drivers to keep the army fed and shooting.

---

* Gutted by Villa a month before the Columbus raid.

On land, elephantine lines of White ton-and-a-half trucks gouged out prairie roads; broke axles and springs in vast *ollas*, or chuckholes; sat stalled for hours when rains turned dry basins to soupy lagoons. Although many of the drivers had earned their positions through written examinations and not driving ability, they learned to cope with Chihuahua. In their raucous, swearing stride they took the Ascensión sands where it was necessary to travel in low gear for over fifty miles, the marshes near Ojo Frederico where lengthy detours sometimes were demanded, the treacherous arroyos north of Namiquipa where sudden flash floods could sweep away an unprotected truck, the steep winding grades on the approach to Las Cruces where backing up was required in order to negotiate some curves. They looked forward to a bath in the stream by Las Cruces and a cool drink at one of the roadside stands set up by Chinese who seemed to appear from out of nowhere. Or if they were lucky enough to be passengers instead of drivers, they could join the rowdy crap game which went on daily in the kitchen truck. In the training ground provided by the Punitive Expedition, the handful of men engaged in the truck run from Columbus to Namiquipa, came to know more than any of their contemporaries the techniques and problems of supplying an army in alien territory through the use of wheeled vehicles. They could advise their government of the need for interchangeable parts and standardization of both equipment and tools. They could direct the establishment of motor pools and could train mechanics and operators. With loud jeers and good fun, they could noisily salute the plodding mule trains bringing forage to the cavalry mounts, little realizing that in their own success they were spelling the doom of the traditional beasts of war.

For the air, birds were hatched—sky jinks to set afire the imagination of countless generations yet to come. Eight light biplanes and eleven pilots under command of Captain B. D. Foulois formed the United States' first active air squadron.* On March 16, the day after ground troops crossed into Mexico, a reconnaissance flight was made south from Columbus. For the first time soldiers

---

* Earlier Villa had purchased five planes and hired five pilots to aid in his original conquest of Chihuahua, but there are no records of their participation. Schuster, 1947, 135. Obregón is said to have had three planes in 1915. Almada, 1955, 410.

on the ground looked up enviously at the soldiers in the sky. Three days later, all eight planes were ordered to the newly established headquarters at Colonia Dublán to be put into courier and reconnaissance service. The beginnings of military aircraft duty were inauspicious as one plane immediately developed engine trouble after takeoff and had to return to Columbus, and the seven others, being overtaken by darkness, became separated. Four managed to land at Ascensión but one came down at Ojo Caliente, one at Janos, and a third was wrecked in landing at Pearson. The pilot of the last, abandoning the plane, walked back to Casas Grandes. The others arrived the next day.

Man's longtime dream of flying was still very young. Only thirteen years after the flight at Kitty Hawk, eleven men on the Mexican border were called upon to prove to the world the military value of the airplane. They bravely took their cumbersome, flimsy planes, correctly and affectionately called "crates," over most of the central Chihuahua corridor, kingdom of fabled horsemen. Two goggled men rode in each plane, one to pilot and one to either observe or experiment with operation of the army's first automatic aerial camera. Daily they calmly risked their skins in those flimsy, underpowered kites, picking the gaps in the spiky sierra they could not have possibly surmounted—caught occasionally in downdrafts which flung them to within twenty feet of sudden death. In the open cockpits they were buffeted by icy winds, rain, or hail. It was not uncommon for pieces of the planes to be torn off by wind pressure; the feeling of complete disintegration at any moment lurked inside each pilot. Because of limited carrying capacity, no extra food or clothing could be stowed aboard. In the event of a crash or forced landing, if they were not killed or taken prisoner, the fliers could only look forward to hitching up their leather leggings to trudge back to headquarters and the chance of going through it all again—as long as the planes lasted.

In April, two planes were sent from San Antonio to Chihuahua to deliver dispatches to the American consul stationed there. The planes caused much excitement as they approached the city and landed simultaneously, Lieutenant Dargue putting his "crate" down on the south side of town and Lieutenant Carberry on the north. Captain Foulois, observer in Dargue's plane, immediately went on foot toward the consulate to deliver his papers. Before he had gone far, he was rudely stopped by rurales and placed under arrest. A yelling mob of several hundred crowded around as he was pushed and manhandled to the cárcel. Although frightened at the tense situation, Foulois was able to signal to an alert American in the throng. He, in turn, notified the military governor, General Gutiérrez, of what was taking place. Quickly Gutiérrez demanded Foulois's release and eagerly offered florid apologies to avoid provoking retaliation.

Meantime, the other airmen were having trouble. Dargue had flown his plane across town to join Carberry and was fired upon by rurales enroute. After he landed, numerous curious, insolent men pressed in around the planes, burning holes in the wings with lighted cigarettes, slashing the thin cloth with pocketknives, and removing nuts and bolts. The two pilots, feeling helpless in the swarm of the growing rabble and knowing their planes were in danger of being wrecked, determined to fly six miles out of town to the safety of the American Smelting and Refining Company plant. Carberry got his plane away safely. Dargue took off in a shower of rocks. No sooner was he up than the top section of the fuselage flew off, damaging the stabilizer. The unhappy lieutenant landed back in the crowd which was now bolder than ever. It was in this unenviable predicament that Foulois found him.

Dargue's difficulties with the city did not end there. During a later flight over town, made for the purpose of photographing entrances to the capital, his plane crashed. He set fire to the wreckage and with no little exasperation plodded the seventy miles back to San Antonio. With all its hazards, flying was more to his liking than walking.

By April 20, with two of the eight original planes remaining, the squadron was ordered back to Columbus. Four more planes were waiting there. Having been tested only in the moist regions near sea level, they soon were found to be unsuitable for service in the arid, elevated Chihuahua theater. Appreciable help from the air ceased.

ACT ONE of the Mexican campaign ended with the battle at Guerrero. Act two further developed the theme of flight and pursuit, accompanied by swelling overtones of animosity between the two nationalities involved. The Americans were growing nervous lest some overt act set off an unfortunate chain reaction.

New parties were formed to follow Villa's hot trail toward Durango, spearheaded by a small, mobile detachment under command of Major Tompkins. Tracks of one of Villa's leading henchmen, Pablo López—perpetrator of the Santa Ysabel massacre—led straight east across the altiplano to the once populous Hacienda de Bustillos where his aged parents continued to occupy one of the longhouse rooms. He rode an American horse which had thrown a shoe, making his trail an easy one for the scouts to follow. It was known he had been wounded at Columbus, and it was hoped that in his suffering he might unwarily lead the troopers to his ailing jefe. But at Bustillos there were only the wide-eyed, blank looks and the dismissive shrugs of the shoulders. No one had seen López. No one could account for the three-shoed tracks. At a trot the cavalry spun around the fountain, which once had brought the sensuous sound of gurgling water to the arid tableland, and rode out of the walled Bustillos garden. Although Tompkins noticed that all the buildings were heavily marked with depressions of bullet shells, he saw too that the Zuloaga church remained unharmed.

At Cusihuiriáchi the Tompkins party was informed by the carrancistas that Villa was dead. But Villa was very much alive. His escort hurried on day and night in a southerly direction moving as rapidly as the general's condition would allow. The bullet which shattered the leg below the knee brought not only a creeping gangrene to threaten Villa's body but a terrifying fear to destroy his spirit. Never before in a life fraught with imminence of violent death had he known what it was to be afraid, not only of his enemies but of his friends as well. From his crude bed in the wagon, he deliriously roared out orders to speed along, to take care to avoid the bumps, to make for the hills. Hurry, hurry, hurry! Looking at his leg hourly getting blacker and more swollen, he groaned and ranted. He steeled himself to wrathful agony, yet his fat jowls grew thin and his robust face turned ashen. Maybe this was the end.

But no, they would not take him alive, those damned Carranza lovers or weak-bellied gringos! He knew just the right hiding place

—a cave deep in the sierra just a few more days ahead. If only his leg would stop throbbing, if only he could trust the fickle ones not to give him away for the growing price on his head. Who was loyal and who was not? He would allow only his brother-in-law, Manuel Corral, or his most trusted men to approach the wagon. Through parched lips he whispered to them his plan.

Moving by wagon was too painful and too slow. And the group was too large. A simple litter of poles and rope was made, and a detail of sixteen close associates was assigned to carry it in relays. Corral led the jefe's empty-saddled roan pony. On the litter device the wounded man was carried gently over ground made slippery by late spring snows. They struggled up steep grades where gaining firm footing was difficult, back into the uninhabited, abrupt-walled canyon west of San Francisco de Borja. High on the face of a stony cliff was a large cave whose dark, yawning mouth was completely concealed by oak trees and a well placed rock fall. Villa was bedded down carefully near the cavern's entrance where he could glimpse patches of sky and feel the cold mountain air on his hot brow[41]

Tompkins' party had followed the Villa route south, at times only two days to the rear. They found the overturned, abandoned wagon and at Cienguita were informed that Villa, being carried on a litter, had come through that village a few days before, on April 1. No one could tell the scouts just where the Villa men went from there. It was felt they were still in the general vicinity but were working their way south. Actually, Villa had been carried west into the mountains, and the main column of his men had traveled on south as a decoy. The Americans passed along the foot of the cliff which sheltered Villa, once even camped near enough so that the two Villa guards could hear their voices.

The United States troops and their horses were showing signs of the strain of the pressure of long rides without rest, the altitude to which they still were not adjusted, the lack of forage and water. Horseshoes for which there were no replacements were breaking; Mexican shoes were too small. The men themselves were dirty, shabby, and worn. But all of them felt Villa's capture was nearing, for how could he get away in his present state? None believed the widely circulated rumor that Villa was dead. He must be cut off

at Parral, an old-time haunt of the bandit's and the last town before the mountains of Durango.

Although a government captain assured the Americans they
would be well received at Parral—might even find a place to buy
a hot bath, a cold beer, or an evening's entertainment—the man in
charge, General Lozano, appeared haughty and hostile. With an
uncomfortable feeling that he might have taken his men into a
trap, Tompkins withdrew the troopers to the outskirts, trying to
avoid an open clash yet demanding the delivery of promised supplies. Scornful civilians crowded the narrow streets shouting, "Viva
Villa." The American soldiers kept a sharp eye on their Mexican
"allies" gathering on a nearby hillside. Suddenly the shooting began. Presumably it was a mob action and not a military maneuver
by the four hundred Mexican soldiers stationed at Parral. In the
first burst of gunfire an American was killed. His body had to be
left, in the rapid but orderly withdrawal north toward Santa Cruz
de Villegas. A constant rearguard action kept the Mexicans at a
distance.[42]

Once at Villegas, the horses were placed under cover; sharp-
shooters lay on the rooftops. The wounded were tended. Barri-
cades were set up. Patrols encircled the town. Soon Tompkins'
men welcomed another American column coming down from San
Antonio de Arenales. In a few days the remainder of the pursuit
forces arrived at Villegas.

Two Americans had been killed in the April twelfth Parral
fight, as opposed to Mexican losses estimated at forty-two, but the
expedition officers were apprehensive lest these be the opening
shots of a war. At the moment their main problem was in supplying the seven hundred men and their mounts now at Villegas, in
a region of no grass and little feed, one hundred eighty miles south
of headquarters at San Antonio, beyond the reassuring reach of
truck and telegraph. Disgusted with the twists of fate and the
kinks in Mexican psychology, knowing they probably would never
again have a chance at Villa, they realized that they must pull back
their current southerly penetration. The Mexican de facto officers
sent denials of responsibility in the trouble at Parral, claiming that
a vengeful young girl whose brother had been killed by Lozano
had stirred up the mob in hopes of embarrassing the general. Al-

most parenthetically, they relayed the government's orders that the Americans not be allowed to continue their march in any direction but back to the north and out of Mexico. No attempt would be made by the government to flush Villa out of the hills nor would it permit the Americans to do so.

After taps for its two fallen comrades who lay in cross-topped graves beside an adobe wall, the small American army turned north to windy San Antonio de Arenales. From there, patrols rode through the Namiquipa, Bustillos, Satevó, San Francisco de Borja, and Guerrero districts, hoping to further disperse villista remnants. On Easter Sunday one patrol fought a band led by Cervantes in the ancient center of rebellion, Tomochi, leaving thirty Mexicans dead beside a fresh American grave.

Thus, American intervention handed Villa another ready-made cause. Instead of becoming weak and ineffectual, the size of his force steadily grew in number as government troops revolted to join his ranks. After two months' recuperation in the mountain cave, Villa's body and spirits rebounded, for his was the amazing resurgence characteristic of his often betrayed but never defeated nation. Again he was spoiling to get at his adversaries, and he found he had a willing army waiting.

ACT THREE of this farcical invasion opened with talks at Ciudad Juárez between representatives of the two governments. Generals Scott and Funston again faced Obregón. According to the Mexican, Villa was dead. The need of American troops in Mexico no longer—indeed never had—existed. Even as he spoke an audacious villista band struck across the border at Glenn Springs, Texas, where it carried out the usual practices of murder and pillage. In the avalanche toward serious trouble, the United States secret service men obtained startling information that Carranza was plotting to drive a large armed force between Pershing and the border to cut him off from aid or escape and to win lasting glory from his people by annihilating all the Americans. A neat bit of double play if he could pull it off.

Without further ado, for the first time in the history of the United States, a civilian army of National Guard troops was called to the colors. In May, units from Arizona, New Mexico, and Texas moved in to stand watch on the border. During the next several months they were joined by adventure-seeking men from New England, Ohio, and Michigan. By the end of July, one hundred eleven thousand guardsmen were occupying four congested camps along the border, one of which was in El Paso, and numerous small garrisons spotted over the desert. All had arrived expecting to see action in a war with Mexico. As the monotonous months went by without conflict, the minor physical discomforts of sandstorms, flies, and summer heat became exaggerated and unbearable. Civilians chafed to go home. To hell with Villa and all his greaser brothers!

In Chihuahua, "Villa, dead or alive" was heard no more. Pershing had retrenched to Colonia Dublán where he set to work putting his command through an intensive training program. The National Guard up on the border lived in luxury compared to the Punitive Expedition. Lying out in the flats as it did, Pershing's camp was in the path of frequent high winds bringing either freezing cold or strangling dust. When the torrents of late summer arrived, the adobe huts built by soldiers formed waterlogged islands in a lake of brown ooze. Men sloshed around in the mire cursing the ill luck which had brought them to this hole. Although their days were occupied by the tasks of army life, their leisure activities aside from poker were limited to hunting for souvenir pots in the surrounding Indian ruins, sampling fiery tequila, or tom-catting in Casas's back alleys.

Scouts brought in accounts of increased activity of carrancistas along the central railroad. Ten thousand men were reported at Villa Ahumada with others spreading through the northern depressions. Captain Charles T. Boyd, with a company of Negro troops from the Tenth Cavalry, was ordered to make a reconnaissance toward Ahumada but to do nothing to bring on a fight. At the Santo Domingo ranch sixty miles east of Colonia Dublán, Boyd's company was joined by another which had ridden from Ojo Frederico. They were cautioned by the American foreman at the ranch not to march through the crumbling presido of Carrizal which lay across the road to Ahumada. It was occupied by a sizable government force and was a deathtrap. Boyd, however, stubbornly refused to go around the town and ordered his troops to pass through the center of the settlement.* Both he and the Mexican general, Félix U. Gómez, were killed in a brush which quickly turned to a disastrous route of the Americans.⁴³ They were murderously attacked from every direction and were driven back into the sands west of town. For several days afterward dazed survivors wandered through the mesquite trying to find their way back to Dublán. The Americans lost twelve soldiers. Within ten days after the battle, a few prisoners and a good deal of equipment taken by the Mexican forces were sent by train to El Paso where they were met by an escort from the Eighth Cavalry stationed at Fort Bliss. June 21, the date of the defeat of Carrizal, became a Chihuahuan holiday. Sacramento had been avenged at last.

Now a new conference was called, this one at New London, Connecticut, away from the prejudicial atmosphere of the border. As it opened in September, invincible Pancho Villa, quite alive and unbowed, entered the city of Chihuahua. For several hours he and his men held the penitentiary (where he liberated two hundred unbelieving prisoners), the Federal Palace, and other government buildings. When he left town, he departed with sixteen carloads of arms and ammunition and more followers than he had had when he came. Only after he was out of the city did the *carrancista* commander fire his artillery! In rosy, familiar triumph Villa galloped east to San Andrés, the countryside flocking to his cause. It was a monstrous bitter joke on the gringos.

At three in the afternoon of February 5, 1917, the last of the Punitive Expedition rode through the border gate south of Columbus. Behind them trailed five hundred wagons of Americans and Mexican allies who feared reprisals. At once Carranza granted amnesty to all outlaws who had participated in the Columbus raid eleven months before. Ironically, in years to come many Americans would remember Carranza with distaste but Villa would be transformed in popular memory to a forgivable rogue.

Had the expedition failed? Not completely. Soldiers had been toughened, machines and equipment tested, mechanized and aerial warfare baptized. Leaders of two World Wars, Black Jack

---

* Students of this conflict are uniformly of the opinion that the battle could have been avoided if Boyd had not been rash. The interpreter Spilsbury absolved Mexicans of blame. Salinas Carranza, 1938, 303.

Pershing and George Patton, had won their spurs even though Pancho Villa was still at large.[44]

IN 1917, the American army went home; Zapata was assassinated. The Constitution of Querétaro, said to be the most radical social document of its day, was adopted, and quasi-sincere labors toward peaceful solution to the economic, social, and political problems of the nation were begun, at least on paper.

But in Chihuahua conditions were more alarming than ever. Villa's forces, morale bolstered by the Pershing fiasco, created complete chaos, dealing out inhuman punishment to those who had aided the Americans, killing foreigners, robbing and threatening Mexicans. Federalists, under General Murguía, sent to capture them and to restore order were as guilty of misconduct as the villistas. Murguía, despotic and arbitrary, refused to recognize the authority of the state's governor and ultimately had to be relieved of his post as military chief. The result was the organization in each municipio of Defensas Sociales to oppose flagrant abuse. With no indication of help from any source, every family head lived with a gun within reach to protect his home and property. A 50,000-peso reward was offered for Villa, dead or alive. Later this was increased to 100,000 pesos. The biggest surprise of the entire prostrate era was that no one betrayed him.

Someone did betray Villa's fickle general, José Inés Salazar, he who was responsible for the Mormon Exodus. He had staged a raid on Colonia Juárez only a few days after Pershing's withdrawal. Shortly after that, he was ambushed and killed by vaqueros as he traveled alone through the desert.

As if Chihuahuenses did not have enough to bear, in 1918 the worldwide influenza epidemic reached them too. No accurate count of the deaths was made, but estimates were that there were over five thousand white deaths. Thousands more unprotected Tarahumaras had succumbed.

Señora Terrazas died in El Paso in 1919. She had lived to see her homes and way of life wiped out and her husband a broken man. It was the year when Villa for the third time in his career attacked Ciudad Juárez. This time he sought to make it appear an international conflict by deploying some of his troops north of the river. American soldiers chased them far down into the northern Chihuahua desert, and then the Americans withdrew at the request of the Juárez garrison commander who feared gringos more than Villa. The year 1919 also saw Villa's former right-hand man, General Felipe Angeles, captured and executed in the city of Chihuahua as he sought to stir up a new revolution for return to the Juárez constitution of 1857.[45] Pleas to spare his life because of his military genius poured into the National Palace, but Carranza had no compassion.*

The following year another rebellion was more successful. Started in Sonora by the governor, Adolfo de la Huerta, a new political plan was formulated in Agua Prieta, obregonista in character. Whole states slid to the new banner. Barracks revolts took place in Parral, the city of Chihuahua, and Jiménez. In May, according to a now firmly established method of changing leadership, Carranza was murdered en route to Vera Cruz, de la Huerta became temporary president, and Professor Abel A. Rodríguez was named governor of Chihuahua. In 1920, too, occurred a tremendously important event for the peace and stability of the state of Chihuahua: Pancho Villa, for a price, made his peace.

Villa was to meet with Federalist General Enríquez (a governor of Chihuahua at the time of Villa's worst depredations) in the southern town of Allende to discuss his submission to the new government. Shortly before the meeting was to take place, impulsive Pancho disappeared. He turned up later in Sabinas, Coahuila, captured some Federal soldiers and three trains and demolished miles of train tracks.[46] He wired de la Huerta of his willingness to negotiate but not with Enríquez. Another general was ordered to Sabinas, where, on July 28, a nation expressed its gratitude for Villa's years of military service, tacitly forgiving his barbaric past. The federal government gave him a hacienda with clear title in the state of Durango, just across the state boundary south of Parral. He was to receive pay established for the rank of general and to retain at government expense an armed fifty-man bodyguard. Amnesty was extended to his followers who also received one year's mustering-out pay. Doroteo Arango, the embittered peon from

---

* The remains of Felipe Angeles later were transferred to a shrine at Pachuca, Hidalgo.

Durango, trod the full cycle to become Francisco Villa, the hacendado from Durango. He rode to his new home, where he had once waged a successful battle, as a conquering hero traveling through his land, acclamations wildly ringing in his ears, full of glowing dreams.

Other villistas were given land at the Río Conchos village of Falomir. Blind hero worship of Villa lingers on today in escapist memories of sons and grandsons of his fighters. With characteristic Chihuahua irony, the town where they dwell now bears the name of Maclovio Herrera, a villista who deserted and became an enemy, whose father and brother Villa hanged.

And so it was that the Chihuahua revolutionary fires sputtered and went out. More decisive than any other factor was the deal with Villa. With that "general" in the saddle, there could be no permanent peace. Perhaps it was wise to consider the cost of Pancho's "retirement" and a great dose of pride-swallowing cheaper than the human and moral cost of a new civil war certain to erupt if he were captured and jailed or perhaps executed.

THE BLOODY DECADE of 1910 to 1920 was not without accomplishment. It had created a spirit of nationalism and pride in Indian ancestry. It had toppled the feudal system, and it had cast off some of the bondage of inherited debts, class stuffiness, foreign ownership of resources and industry. It had produced a liberal constitution and a determination to prevent dictatorship through rigged re-elections. But these gains were intangible then, only to bear fruit in the future. Outwardly, it seemed the results had been negative and ruinous.

Where once herds of fat cattle and horses browsed and handsome haciendas stood, there was nothing but barren plains—no stock, no crops, no windmills, no homes or furnishings. In the towns, businesses were closed, their windows blackened with metal shutters. Small factories lacked usable machinery; commerce was at a standstill. Families sat cold and hungry. The patróns were gone. Men who had been born into slavish security would have to learn to stand alone, precariously but free. From 1900 to 1910, the population of Chihuahua increased from 328,000 to 405,000, but in the ten years of Revolution it had dropped to nearly 402,000, despite a tremendous tide of refugees which flowed from the interior to the border town of Ciudad Juárez. Stubborn remnants were predominantly rural, overwhelmingly illiterate, unemployed, and mightily concerned for the future. It was hard to see just how a state in a condition of bankruptcy, without elected leadership for over seven years, shackled by the sorrows and hatreds of a war of brother against brother, exhausted emotionally and physically could find the strength and courage to look to the future and the wisdom and patience for rejuvenation. Much of the past had been obliterated or degraded. The present was dispirited and dismal. Only the future offered promise. Stoic frontiersmen, having withstood centuries of onslaughts of Indians, Americans, and Mexicans, now found themselves unified through desperate need—and a small measure of timid hope. It was time to pick up the pieces.

FIVE

RECONSTRUCCIÓN

From 1920

AFTERMATH OF WAR often demands more than war itself. There was a wide gap between feudalism and modern industry and agronomics to bridge. Fortunately, Chihuahua, among her soldiers and civilians, found the men to bridge it. For some years, however, military-minded presidents only waved banners and made speeches loudly heralding *La Revolución* but never acted toward fulfillment of its grand pledges. However, resolute Chihuahuenses began work on the harassing problems of land redistribution, public education, and labor organization. In the relatively short span of forty-five years, these men and the inherent determination of its people have moved the state toward leadership of the Republic in economic wealth and exciting prospects for the future. The Revolution is considered by Chihuahuenses to be continuing to the present day though the fighting is done.

The first elections since the outbreak of the civil war were held in 1920. The Querétaro Constitution was ratified. Orderly government was reaffirmed. But all was not calm. Regional rebellion of diehards addicted to violence continued to break out. In 1922, General Murguía led a small riot in Ciudad Juárez halfheartedly aimed at overthrow of Obregón. He was captured and shot at Tepehuanes. Again, in 1929, another border disturbance, this one against President Portes Gil, was the last gasp of armed political resistance. Its perpetrators fled the state via the Púlpito Pass.

With civil war over, the nation divided still further and more bitterly in a religious war. For more years, government and agrarians fought devout Catholics and priests. "Viva Villa" gave way to "Viva Cristo Rey." Again the dusty charges across the basins, the noisy splatter of spraying bullets on adobe walls, the lifeless bodies hanging from the trees. Again bigotry, hatred, brutality, and evaporating dreams. Again El Paso offered refuge for deported clergy

and their fanatical followers. This time airplanes piloted by new
World War I aces like Roberto Fierro* representing an anticlerical faction headed by Plutarco Calles dropped bombs on encamp-
ments of the cristeros or clerical group.[1] But, as in former years
and former wars, somehow the dogged Mexican people managed
to garner strength enough to rise again. Cristeros and callistas together came to grips with the problems of peace.[2]

One hundred years had passed since the granting of statehood to
Chihuahua. In 1924 the state briefly halted its renaissance to celebrate its original birth. Northerners in their new maturity could
appraise their past and find purpose and confidence in their future.
A civic fiesta, the first for many years, was ordered. All the state
buildings were decorated with the brilliant colors of the Mexican
flag. Special parades accompanied by the city's band marched
around the Plaza de la Constitución. Names of members of the first
legislature and the first governor were inscribed on a plaque in
the Salon of Sessions, and a solemn program was held in the Teatro
de los Héroes. It was time also to acknowledge leaders of the decade just ended.

Following a decree of the Chihuahua governor that all place
names with a religious connotation be eliminated, the state's revolutionaries were recognized by renaming a dozen or so pueblos
after them. The state map now shows names like Félix Gómez,
Francisco Portillos, Manuel Benevides, Aquiles Serdán, Belisario
Domínguez, Ignacio Valenquela, Benjamín M. Chaparro, Praxedis
G. Guerrero, and Toribio Ortega. One town on the central railroad was christened Villa González after the governor killed by
huertistas, but citizens petitioned return of its former name, Villa
Ahumada, to honor Miguel Ahumada, porfirista but a credit to
his state.

The capital street names, like street names throughout the land,
underwent transformation, and Venustiano Carranza and Veinte
de Noviembre became the names of two main thoroughfares. But
it was only recently that a new broad boulevard was named División del Norte, the sole tribute in all the Mexican rash of name-
changing to Villa or his army.

---

* In the late twenties Fierro was acclaimed in Mexico for nonstop flights
from Mexicali, Baja California, to Mexico City and from New York City to
Mexico City. Dulles, 1961, 498-9.

Those two implacable enemies, Terrazas and Villa, each symbolizing an era in northern history, died almost at the same time in 1923. Each met death in a manner befitting the way in which he had lived.

Four years before his death Don Luis had suffered a severe stroke which had left him a bedridden invalid. His sons took him from his home of exile in El Paso to southern California where they hoped the sea air might prove beneficial. But the old man was a son of the scrubby desert, and the ocean did nothing for his spirits or his health. As soon as conditions were sufficiently stabilized, he demanded return to Chihuahua. There he was greeted with respect and mercy. Young people who knew him in name only stared in curiosity as members of the family and a few servants who had remained loyal through the long revolt helped the pathetic, helpless old patriarch through the atrium and into the cathedral's hushed incensed interior. He had come home and wanted to give grateful thanks to his Lord. Gone were his properties and money, his way of life on its supremely lavish scale. His wife, other members of his family, and many of his friends were dead. He had outlasted his golden age. Never having understood the causes nor the forces of the upheaval, he did not belong in the new era of mechanization and the vocal proletariat, labor unions and cooperative farms. He died in June at the age of ninety-four. His life had coincided almost exactly with that of the state of which he had been master. Requiem mass was sung in the cathedral, attended by a large number of men who had helped bring his epoch to a bloody conclusion. Although the chief of the Chihuahua military district asked for a funeral suitable for an old warrior who, within the limits of his conscience, had served his country well, the new government flatly refused the request.[3] He had been a symbol of the enemy for ten years, and he would remain one in death. His body joined that of his wife beneath a large, white marble cross in the sanctuary of Guadalupe on a hill south of town. Graves of his friends of the old days—the Müllers, Ketelsens, Ahumadas—lay near in friendly, understanding silence.

One month later Pancho Villa was murdered.

After the government granted him amnesty, irrepressible Villa had cast off his outmoded role of guerrilla fighter. Straightway he had molded himself into a firm but benevolent hacendado and serious gentleman farmer. Money in great quantities from the de la Huerta Office of Haciendas and from his horde of war spoils was expended upon the latest combines, tractors, plows, and trucks from the States. An American farm expert, Jimmie Caldwell, was employed to oversee the operation of the hacienda, to develop long-range plans of crop rotation, fertilization, construction of water tanks, and contour plowing. With all the drive once devoted to battle, Villa worked to make the Canutillo hacienda into a model, profitable agricultural community.[4] Rumors were rampant that treasures which he had cached during the turbulent years were being tapped, not only to improve his ranch, but to give his two sons an education in a private school in Texas, to keep his brother, Hipólito, in fancy cars and fancy women, and through philanthropies among Parral's poor, to build up a new, devoted following.

No one wanted Villa to again take up the chilling battle cry. Cliques around Obregón were pushing for position. Villa was still someone with whom to reckon. How great a factor would he be in a contest between Calles, whom he hated for the disaster at Agua Prieta, and de la Huerta, whom he favored and to whom he owed his present peaceful magnificence? There were some conspirators who thought him a good deal safer dead than alive. Villa only turned a deaf ear to such rumors.

One hot July morning after spending the night in his hotel in Parral, Pancho, his secretary Miguel Trillo, and Ramón Contreras, former head of the Dorados, climbed into the Dodge he had bought in Ciudad Juárez to return to Canutillo. Before they had crossed the last bridge out of town, all were dead. A blinding yellow burst of gunfire from a group of seven men hidden behind the thick walls of a house flush with the sidewalk had brought an abrupt end to their lives. The threat of Villa had been too great. Incredibly, Villa was only forty-five though he had seen more of life than a hundred men, had been praised and profaned, and perhaps was on his way to becoming civilized. Perhaps, but there was the risk.

Scarcely were the bodies cold than the bloody death car was on exhibit for a fee, and for extra centavos peddlers offered gruesome postcards of the scene of the murder and Villa's disemboweled body with its forty-seven wounds.

Villa was buried in a humble grave in the municipal rock-walled cemetery at the northern entrance to Parral. Modern travelers stopping at the gas stations at the junction of the highway and the road into town may gaze at the sea of crosses and wonder just which marks his grave. But without close inspection, they cannot be sure, for Villa's is indistinguishable from the hundreds of peon graves surrounding it. The stormy parvenu had returned to his own. The embellished mausoleum in Chihuahua, with its symbolic bleeding hearts, stands empty despite Señora Villa's attempts to have his body transfered. Nor is his skeleton complete. Three years after his assassination, someone opened his grave and stole his skull. An American adventurer then in Parral, Emil Holmdahl, was arrested, accused of the desecration, but released because of lack of evidence.[5] The head never was found.

The treasures which no one doubts Villa possessed never have been found either. Some say he buried gargantuan caches of stolen gold and jewels deep in the mountain caves from Santa Bárbara to Mount Franklin behind El Paso and along the banks of the Río Grande. Rumor has it that he always returned from these "banking" trips alone, after having killed the men who dug the pits and transported the loot. When he died, his secrets died with him. The compelling lore of their telling, these mysteries of the picaroon of the prairies, has been added to the Southwest's literature of lost mines and hidden Spanish treasure. Quivira has taken on another form. Seldom has one individual, even within his own lifetime, had such an impact on the folklore of his people as did Pancho Villa.

Soon after Villa's fatal shooting, a young fanatic from Durango, Jesús Salas Barreza, was charged with the crime and sentenced to twenty years in the state penitentiary. After serving six months, he was pardoned by officials who apparently felt a gesture at punishment was sufficient. A commission named to investigate the political undercurrents of the murder wrangled over the upcoming election and got nowhere. In 1951 Salas Barreza on his deathbed denied that Calles had been implicated in the plot.

Brother Hipólito and Manuel Chao sought to incite a war of revenge. Governor Enrique promptly ordered the government troops at Canutillo to headquarters in the city of Chihuahua and had Hipólito placed in jail in Durango. War-wary leaders knew by now how to deal with the firebrands. Chihuahua was saved for the battle of rebirth.

EVERY MEXICAN LEADER since Madero has found it expedient to speak of agrarian reform, which has become a political catchword if not a mystique. In a nation of landless farmers, land was, and is, all important. The demographic facts that much of Mexico's terrain is unsuitable for farming, that population is unevenly dispersed, that in some areas soil erosion is advanced, and that 82.69 per cent of the total surface of the nation falls either in arid or in semiarid zones have heightened this problem.[6]

Land ownership was the single aim of *zapatistas* in the south and of many villistas in the north, because at the Revolution's inception, 97 per cent of all property was under the control of eight hundred thirty haciendas.[7] Article 27 of the Querétaro Constitution dealt specifically with this enormously complex problem. On the state level, agrarian commissions of federal agents, state agents, and representatives of the campesinos were created, and further bodies were organized to check and double-check their planning and results. The halls of the Palace of Government became lined with delegations of men from the country trying to settle their official questions. Four types of ownership were recognized: ejido (communal village lands), *colonias agricolas* (agricultural developments) and ganaderías (cattle ranches) created from the division of the latifundia, and private ownership. Restrictions as to size, capital required for acquisition and sale were numerous and involved. A National Bank of Ejidal Credit and a National Bank of Farming and Stock Raising Credit were founded to carry on a program of reclaiming land and financing and subsidizing farmers.

President Obregón began actual redistribution with the division of nearly 120,000 hectares scattered throughout the nation. In the period 1930 to 1950, 30,549,248 hectares were allotted campesinos. The allotment is continuing. The first agrarian colonies in Chihuahua were established after Madero came to power in 1913, two years before a national agrarian law. Their development necessarily had to await more settled times. After 1920 lands and waters and forests were returned to ejidal ownership upon proper petition and proof that the villages once had possessed title. Under later administrations, ejidos were granted to villages on basis of need as well. Over 3,500,000 hectares (approximately 8,750,000 acres) in the state now have been given in 415 ejidos controlled by 48,000 people. Almost 9,000 colonists live in 194 colonias agrícolas.

A judgment on the effectiveness of the land reform movement is not within the realm of this book. Suffice it to say that politicking with the issue has been inevitable. Chihuahua, like the nation, has a long way to go. But like Sonora and Sinaloa, though unlike much of the nation, Chihuahua holds tremendous promise. However, many consider the program thus far to have been a failure. They point to the fact that over the years the banks giving credit to the ejidos and colonias agrícolas have been able to collect only 60 per cent of their investments. The lack of solvency on the part of the small farmers in Chihuahua has been due to a combination of factors such as the initial expense incurred in preparing the land, obtaining seed, and acquiring a few tools; the unavoidable farmer's gamble with weather and plant and animal diseases; the infertility of much of the soil and the cycles of erosion progressing in large areas; the prevailing ignorance of scientific agricultural and animal husbandry practices; the difficulties imposed by terrain and inadequate means of transportation in reaching markets; and above all, the lack of water. In arid Chihuahua, lying as it does in the zone of the world's great deserts, this last aspect of the problem has been most restrictive. The inability to master their farm dilemma has not been due to lack of industry on the part of campesinos. There are many students of the agrarian problem who are quick to remind critics that what returns do come from the land now go into thousands of pockets instead of one.

Splitting up of the twenty-nine Chihuahua latifundia was begun in the early reconstruction period. Immediately Terrazas property became embroiled in a heated dispute. An American promoter, Arthur McQuatters, had signed a contract with the Terrazas heirs for acquisition of their extensive acreages for 20,000,000 pesos. When news of the transaction reached the public, there was strong reaction against its consummation. Foreign ownership and exploitation was one of the very evils against which the Revolution had been directed. Telegrams of protest swamped President Obregón's office. Demonstrations were held in scattered towns. Newspapers warned of the dangers and called the sale antipatriotic. The government had to step in and take over the Terrazas latifundium in the name of the Caja de Ahorros. The heirs were paid 13,000,-000 pesos in settlement. Orders were given to proceed with the land's subdivision. Today agrarians occupy the remaining buildings as squatters, carry on limited farming, and many barely eke out an existence. They have neither the knowledge nor the capital to return to full-scale operation.

A second McQuatters subdivision of the loamy banks of the Río Conchos had to be abandoned in view of the outburst caused by the Terrazas contract. This area later came under control of a highly successful government irrigation project.

Another latifundium dissection which came in for a good deal of publicity was that of the Zuloaga family in the western municipio of Cuauhtémoc. Then began one of the most unique programs of colonization in the state's history. One foreigner had been denied, but Obregón welcomed others. An area which had provided haven for South African Dutch war refugees, for Belgian flax farmers, for a persecuted, polygamous, American religious sect, and for temporarily ousted Mexican politicians now opened its doors to some old-fashioned Germans. Mennonites, five thousand strong, came to the broad basins of Bustillos.[8]

Early in 1921 agents of the Mennonite sect traveled to Mexico to confer with President Obregón, wishing to secure permission to arrange emigration en masse for members of a colony then residing in Canada. They were prepared to buy farmland and had sufficient funds to sustain themselves until crops could be brought into production. Except for climate, the expansive plains of Chihuahua were not too unlike those of central Canada where they had been farming, and they came into the picture at an opportune time when the latifundia which formerly had owned those lands were being partitioned. Obregón gave them a receptive ear. In the face of all the deafening uproar over privileges for foreign residents of Mexico, he granted new ones. The pacifist Mennonites demanded exemption from military duty on religious grounds, release from any obligation of swearing allegiance, the right to enter and leave the country at will, and the authority to establish and conduct their own schools and churches without interference from Mexican officials. The government unaccountably made all these concessions. Once more, foreigners were to enjoy the fruits of Mexican citizenship without its duties. Mennonite agents bought 100,000 hectares of land from the Zuloaga latifundium for 600,000 pesos and went back to Winnipeg to arrange for the move.

The reason behind the emigration was one which had driven Mennonites from western Europe over the face of two continents: persecution. Persecution had pushed them from their native Holland to Poland in the late 1500's, had moved them into the Ukraine between 1788 and 1820, finally had driven them from the Old World to the prairies of North America between 1874 and 1900. In Canada they had refused to participate in World War I, and the Canadians then applied strong sanctions and social pressures against them. Again they chose to pack up and move on, hoping someday to find a spot where they could successfully shut out the modern world and pursue life in their own highly antiquated, unrealistic way. In this, they have found Mexico a reasonably good home, for much of the past lingers on, especially in its rustic areas.

Almost everything modern has been rejected by members of this sect which remains conservative in the extreme. Life is as hard and unyielding for them as it was for their predecessors a hundred years ago. No luxuries or laborsaving devices make living easier or more enjoyable. As a matter of economics they have come to the use of farm machinery. But for their own transportation, they still rely on horsedrawn buggies and wagons, those only recently made a bit more comfortable with the addition of rubber tires. Their hardworking women still bend over washboards, crank churns, and mop floors on their hands and knees. In dress, they seem to have stepped from story books of the last century. Women wear long, full skirts of black or other somber colors, emphasizing their native plumpness. Black or flowered shawls are wrapped around their shoulders. High-topped, flat-soled black shoes and black cotton stockings, suitable for farm women who have to walk through freshly plowed fields, do little to enhance their appearance. Their only bow toward personal adornment are the bright red and pink ribbons which they tie to practical broad-brimmed straw hats. No cosmetics or jewelry are permitted. Their men wear bib overalls, black coats, and straw hats. Children are miniatures of their parents.

The spring of 1922 found long trains loaded with these fair-skinned people clearing border inspection at Ciudad Juárez and rolling on to the capital city. From there they took trains west to San Antonio de Arenales. This settlement of the flowing name they found to consist of a water tank, a few mud huts tumbled along the railroad tracks, and a shell of a huge warehouse built by the house of Zuloaga when it was master of the altiplano. On arrival, the migrants stood in quiet groups beside the dirty cars into which they had been crowded, and their blue eyes scanned the broad, flat valley. They saw its dusky-colored vastness, unsevered by fences of any kind, rippling up to rocky, treeless hills and found it fitting. They appreciatively felt its stillness and oppressive majesty, its loneliness. Farmers that they were by a four-hundred-year tradition, they stirred with spring eagerness to root young seedlings and put the plow to the deep soil never before cultivated. Quickly, but with the orderliness which came through repetition of a familiar pattern, they settled down to redecorating the municipios of Cuauhtémoc, Namiquipa, and Riva Palacio.

As communal enterprises they have taken native materials of adobe bricks and stone and have built in a style reminiscent of European or Canadian rural areas but unfamiliar to Mexico. Schools and churches are simple, rectangular structures without towers or bells. Clusters of unbeautified two-story houses are placed across the basins in communities called "camps." To these camps (fifty-seven in Chihuahua) they have given names like Blumenfeld, Eichenthal, Grosweide, and Ofterwick. Beyond lies the table-like sweep of thousands of hectares planted to wheat, oats, barley, and flax. This is dry farming on an elevated plateau of six thousand feet, with a normal annual rainfall of twenty inches. In cyclic droughts the Mennonites suffer. Only at the campsites are there wells and windmills to produce household water and water for irrigation of the orchards of fruit trees and the plots of vegetables and berries. Where under Mexican direction the land had been given over to the pasturing of beef cattle, the Mennonites specialize in dairying. A complex of industries formerly unappreciated by Mexicans has developed around the milk and milk products of the hundreds of imported cows. These foods never have been characteristic of the Mexican diet. Their growing popularity in the current nutrition-conscious period is largely due to Mennonite and Mormon influence. Cheese and butter factories are in operation. Smokehouses turn out hams, bacons, and German-style sausages. Large numbers of chickens are raised. Advertising agents in the cities plug Mennonite products which now are shipped to all parts of the Republic.

Even though the Mennonites cannot be called socially enlightened, they are progressive in the matter of agriculture. They constantly endeavor to improve their crops and their stock. New breeds of cattle have been tried, new types of seed, new methods of planting and fertilizing. Armed with almost unbelievable capacities for sustained, backbreaking toil, an inner peace requiring few diversions, and a skill developed by centuries of devotion to the soil and its fecundity, these people have created an agricultural breadbasket in a region once considered suitable only for pasturage. A grateful Mexican government has recognized their work by bringing farmers from all over northern Mexico to see what has been accomplished at the Mennonite *granja* (farm) .

The slumbering village of San Antonio de Arenales, quieter than ever after Pershing's departure, has been gently awakened by the tread of many German-speaking strangers in its single rocky street at the foot of the hill of the bird, Cerro de Pájaro. The town changed its name to that of the last Aztec emperor, Cuauhtémoc, as if in attempt to retain an unfaltering Mexican identity in this sea of Europeanism, and in the boom of business it grew to over four thousand souls. Cuauhtémoc is a Mexican town catering almost wholly to Mennonite needs. Its new buildings are ugly and its plaza characterless. But money tinkles in its cash registers, and it bustles with restless energy which is beginning to characterize other settlements of the "new" Chihuahua. At the terminus of a paved, seventy-mile highway from the capital, Cuauhtémoc stretches confidently over the lower slopes of the Cerro de Pájaro, sure of today and of tomorrow.

Mennonite frugality, industry, and ability have made the municipio of Cuauhtémoc one of the richest in the state, not only through productivity and the lucrative revenues the government has gained by taxation and duties but through the subsidiary businesses which are dependent upon them. Mexicans recognize this fact. But they resent Mennonites as un-Mexican with supra-Mexican privileges. Mennonite self-imposed isolation causes further irritations. Unlike Mormonism, this Anabaptist cult is not prose-lyting in desire or performance but is introspective and with-drawn. Its members have made no attempt at acculturation with the single exception of learning the Spanish necessary to their en-terprise. They allow no Mexican children in their schools, no Mexican adults in their churches. No Mexicans are employed as household servants or farm hands. Their only contact is in the stores and shops of Cuauhtémoc and occasionally the capital. They can never be assimilated into the main stream of Mexican life under these conditions. Furthermore, no restrictions were placed upon the size of the colony nor the lands which it could buy. Their original number has doubled, and they have acquired an additional fifty thousand hectares. Dangerous encroachments upon the Mexican campesinos are feared if curbs are not made upon their rapid expansion. This, in turn, might lead to another exodus.

As LATE AS 1939 another colony of foreigners was established on Chihuahuan plains.[9] This one came more prepared culturally and linguistically than any of the former colonists. They were Spanish Republicans fleeing the Franco regime. When defeated in the Spanish Civil War, they had gone into refuge in France. Then, they were forced to move on and turned to Spanish-speaking countries of Latin America. In Mexico, Cuba, and Santo Domingo they were welcomed with kindness and understanding. Some mer-chants were able to re-enter business. Many of the fancy grocery stores of the cities owe their foundation to this Spanish emigration. Others were farmers and sought resettlement outside urban cen-ters. At the encouragement of Chihuahua's governor, two thou-sand of these refugees purchased 140,000 hectares of land from the old hacienda of Santa Clara in the mid-state municipio of Namiquipa. A state which one hundred ten years earlier had ex-pelled Spaniards now gave them sanctuary. In time it is presumed that because of a basic similarity of culture they will be absorbed.

DESPITE mandatory division of the latifundia as decreed by the Querétaro Constitution of 1917 and the statutes prohibiting for-eign ownership of land in a several-hundred-mile band around its borders (softened by not being applicable to titles obtained be-fore 1917), Mexico postponed action against two American holdings in Chihuahua until the early 1950's. No government felt strong enough to stand up to the journalistic power of William Randolph Hearst. Even Cárdenas, who expropriated the oil fields, did not give in to pressures from the north to confiscate Hearst land. Hearst did lose oil rights he had in the vicinity of Ojinaga, but until his death in 1952, he retained the title to the hacienda of Babícora.

This latifundium, located in the Babícora basin at the flanks of the Sierra Madre Occidental, he had inherited from his mother.[10] Hearst himself was said to have visited the ranch only three times in his manhood, but through a Mexican manager, he maintained a strong hold on its operation. An unimposing ranch house, but furnished in the grand old manner of luxurious haciendas, stood ready for his infrequent occupancy. A larger home was on the architect's drawing board at the time of his death. By tradition the 350,000 hectares in the basins of Babícora, municipio of Temósachi, were devoted to cattle. This had been the outskirts of Tarahumara country in the late 1600's when Franciscans and Jesuits clashed for rights of missionary activity, and the padres of both Orders had recognized its value to the development of stock raising in the province. In moist years when the snows accumulated drifts in the wilderness of the sierra madre and late summer rains pelted persistently down across the steppes, grass cushioned lushly, and animals thrived and fattened. There were other uncertain years when stock had to seek out miry sinks cupped in basin depressions and had to browse into sheltered rincons to find protected patches of tough grama grass. In the fifty-year period of Hearst ownership, the ranch was exploited to the fullest possible extent and improved with stock tanks and wells. Its pastures supported over twenty thousand registered Herefords, twenty thousand sheep, and more than five hundred horses.

After some scandalous conduct on the part of Hearst's manager and dishonest public officials, in 1953 the administration of Ruiz Cortines concluded purchase of the Babícora 263,000-hectare latifundium for $2,500,000.[11] The cattle were sold, and the sheep were taken elsewhere. In 1954 government agronomists decided that at least 50,000 hectares of the old latifundium could be converted into agricultural lands, following the example of the neighboring Mennonites. Plots of 20-hectare size were sectioned off, and hopeful farmers were transplanted to the basins. Thousands of shanties, fences, and rutty roads are everywhere across the once empty land. Unfortunately Babícora farmers began the new life during a dry period. Perhaps the bold venture will end in failure. It is too soon to know. Man in this part of the world still has little control over his environment.

Another latifundium untouched until recent years straddled the bleak borderlands of the municipio of Ascensión. The Palomas Land and Cattle Company controlling some 700,000 hectares had run a huge cattle operation there since the turn of the century. Mexicans protested its presence, claiming it blocked development of the region. As this is a part of the bleached Chihuahua desert, as uninviting to human occupation as any spot in the state, Mexicans presumably did not covet the land; they merely did not want the Americans there. So expropriation came during the tenure of Miguel Alemán, again encumbered with grafters hoping to make a dishonest peso even at the expense of their own countrymen.[12] Now the land belongs to the campesinos.

Not all farming in Chihuahua is of the dry-farming pattern of Bustillos and Babícora. There is a growing development of irrigated farms. It has been Chihuahua's misfortune that although the mountains have given birth to the churning Yaqui, Mayo, and Fuerte rivers which have so greatly stimulated agricultural development of Sonora and Sinaloa, the eastern plateaus have not benefited from their waters. River systems traveling east out of the sierra are not so large nor do they carry the volume of water. This shortage of life-giving water in the past has placed definite limits on farming in Chihuahua. Where land could be watered, yield was rewarding, for the basins lie flat, are easily cleared of their scanty native plant covering, and the soil is rich. Skinny threads of river valleys have been cultivated from earliest time, but beyond the reach of the water there was sterility. Along the Ríos Florido, Allende, and Parral in the south, the San Pedro, Chuvíscar, and Conchos girdling the midriff of the state, and the Casas Grandes, Santa María, Carmen, and Río Grande to the north, men of the soil from earliest times have created farms. Before the Revolution, the waters of the Casas Grandes and the Piedras Verdes were diverted into an intricate irrigation canal system built by the Mormons of Colonia Dublán and Colonia Juárez. To the south of the city of Chihuahua some irrigation developed along the Río Conchos as a result of La Boquilla dam constructed at the end of the Díaz regime. Elsewhere artesian wells and the springs were utilized by farmers in diverse localities.

Now, with the aid of heavy equipment and latest technology there is an increasing network of dams being thrown across rivers as Chihuahua boasts one hundred twenty-seven small irrigation projects in operation.[13] A 1960 governor's report claimed a total of 8,000,000 pesos going into construction of dams in the municipios of Matamoros, Temósachi, Janos, Ojinaga, Madera, and Ascensión.[14] Successful well drilling from Sauz to Jiménez has added to water sources. Water is being found in volume beneath the arid, unpromising surface rind of many bolsons. The loudly resounding noise of forty new pumps is Chihuahua's blatant symphony of prosperity. Desert and plains are coming into bloom, offering not only hope of substantial monetary returns and replenishment of Mexico's dwindling home-produced food supply, but new, uncongested regions for resettlement by peasants from overcrowded, overtilled lands of central Mexico. The state's population has more than doubled since 1920 and has increased 3.8 per cent in the last ten years partly as a result of a movement of farmers to the north.[15]

Three government-controlled irrigation projects are the heart of the agricultural economy of the state—system number five on the Conchos, number forty-two on the San Buenaventura, and number nine on the Río Grande.

System number five is in a wide, flat basin lying along the San Pedro and the Conchos. It was established as one of the nation's first seven irrigation distribution districts in 1926 with the creation of a National Irrigation Commission. Since that time other projects of enlarging and cleaning the canals and drains have been undertaken. More than 53,000 hectares are watered by a series of dams on both rivers and a deep canal of one hundred forty-six kilometers length.[16] A happy combination of an assured water supply behind the reservoirs of La Boquilla, Francisco I. Madero, Rosetilla, and Colina, fertile soil, warm climate, and Chihuahuense determination has produced a verdant Chihuahua oasis. Lacking the first factor, the land is a mesquite- and creosote-bushed prairie beyond the extension of the ditches. Wind breaks of cottonwoods, tamarisks, and poplars surround well-kept fields of cotton, alfalfa, wheat, vegetables, and grapes. Cattle, goats, horses, and fowl are raised. White-stuccoed homes with their red-tiled roofs are set in spacious grounds amid the fields. The air of well-being on these granjas blows through the towns of the Conchos region. Busy Delicias in particular epitomizes the new era with its white cement buildings and wide paved streets, its lack of a Catholic temple dominating the skyline, its cotton gins and brandy and wine distillery, and is indeed a new town dating from 1933. Here the Stetson-hatted man in the pickup truck is king. He eats steak and refried beans at the local hotel, smokes Raleigh cigarettes,* drinks Nescafe and Cruz Blanca beer, and worries with Stetson-hatted neighbors over the current price of bales of cotton, the threat of untimely frost, the need of more insecticides. Success has made him smiling and confident. He is often a trained farmer, a graduate of one of the agricultural colleges of the southwestern United States or of Mexico. If necessary, he can drive a tractor, irrigate a field, wean a calf. Usually he is keenly interested in affairs north of the border because, through yanqui example of practical, arid climate farming, through northern markets, and through American investment in the district's enterprises, these have a bearing on his own future. He is the new, energized aristocracy of his state, one which not only directs but labors. Having no choking monopolies, he shares with numbers of ejidatarios and small landowners** the prosperity and the work of the project.

The Valle de Juárez project, worked between 1929 and 1934, amplifies the area and production of the river-silted Juárez valley, near the old town and down river, to settlements of Zaragosa and Guadalupe. Some 15,000 hectares are included in this project.[17] Mexicans and Americans both are benefiting from international treaties controlling the waters of the Río Grande. The Americans, however, have a larger amount of the river bottomlands. Towns such as San Elizario and Socorro, once on the Mexican side of the river, are in the United States because of a change in the river's course.

---

* American company which also packages in Mexico.

** 4,397 current users of system number five's waters. Secretaría de Recúrsos Hidráulicos, 1956.

In the central river valley of San Buenaventura sixty-five hundred hectares were brought under irrigation during the Alemán administration. Here, as in the two districts discussed above, the project has reached the fullest possible development. Government interest now has turned to new areas for development. Large projects have been initiated in the municipios of Guerrero, San Buenaventura, and Ojinaga at a cost 33,500,000 pesos.[18]

As a result of these various works, Chihuahua is producing cotton, grapes, alfalfa, corn, wheat, and peanuts in commercial quantities. Nationally the state, once considered an unconquerable desert, ranks ninth in amounts of corn produced, fifth in beans, sixth in wheat, and sixth in cotton.* This is the product of mechanized agriculture which makes use of the latest kinds of farm machinery.

To the east of Delicias and on both sides of the line of the central or Juárez-to-Mexico City highway lie the anguished lands of the desert. This is the territory of Chihuahua's traditional agricultural wealth: cattle.[19] A native vegetation of drought-resistant black grama and tobosa grasses and such browse plants as mesquite and screw beans have provided excellent stock feed since the days of the first colonization, although to a casual observer the land might appear desolate. Occasional columns of dust mark the passage of an automobile over a distant, two-rutted road leading apparently nowhere. But beyond the somnolent hills, here and there huddle squalid jacals where men fight a one-sided battle against environment. Here live the vaqueros who tend the cattle of ganaderos, many of whom live not on ranches in this forsaken area but in fine houses in town. These owners, too, have pickup trucks, western hats and boots, and can parley in educated, agrarian vernacular. They easily could pass unnoticed in the lobby of a San Antonio hotel as they do in the coffee shop of the Palacio Hilton** in Chihuahua. These are modern-style, southwestern cattlemen sharing a culture which is Mexican at root. They have gone a long way toward rebuilding the cattle industry which was virtually wiped out by the Revolution.

---

* Mexico is now the second cotton-producing country in the world. James, 1959, 651.

** First of the Hilton Hotel chain outside the United States. The old Palacio Hotel on the same site was a Terrazas holding.

In a thirty-year period between the end of Apache raids and the 1910 Revolution, Chihuahua became the number one state in the Republic in stock raising. There were almost four million animals worth 98,000,000 pesos grazing the Chihuahua plains. By the Revolution's end, there was scarcely any vestige left of all this wealth. After a semblance of order was restored following Villa's "retirement," the ganaderos again returned to their old haunts and their old way of life. Their numbers, however, were greatly increased. According to the Agrarian Code, the maximum amount of land any one individual could possess for grazing was 40,000 hectares. The division of the latifundia provided space for many persons who, by 1961, were raising 1,400,000 head of cattle, 100,000 head of sheep, and 100,000 head of horses, mules, and burros. Of these, 200,000 animals yearly were being shipped out of the state. The general area called "the north," of which Chihuahua is a large part, has come to rank first in the Mexican Republic in horses, mules, and goats, and second in cattle, pigs, and sheep.[20]

Limitations on size of holdings forced several improvements. Owners had to seek new or additional sources of water for their herds. Wells had to be drilled, and whirling windmills and metal stock tanks became familiar sights throughout the cattle empire. Also the quality of the animals demanded improvement. Formerly all Chihuahua cattle were criollo, as intermixed as the people themselves. Now recent studies indicate 65 per cent of Chihuahua stock is Hereford, 3 per cent is Aberdeen Angus, .5 per cent is Cebu, and the remaining 31.5 per cent is criollo.[21]

World War II and the resultant meat shortage in the United States were a boon to Chihuahua cattlemen. Thousands of head were driven to loading pens along the Central and Noroeste railroads and sent to El Paso to be sold northward for feeders. American dollars coming into Chihuahua brought with them new stateside luxuries of RCA radios, GE refrigerators, Buick and Cadillac cars, Catalina sweaters, and Van Raalte nylons. At home, meat still remained a rare treat on many Mexican tables, but consumption and demand were increasing steadily. Once more Chihuahua was the backbone of Mexican cattle business. This time it brought money to many families.

In 1946 the bubble of American-supported prosperity in the cattle business burst. There were two reasons: first, the war ended, and second, highly contagious hoof-and-mouth disease (*aftosa*) was discovered among Mexican herds farther south. Immediately the border was closed to shipment from Mexico, and the pens in the Juárez stockyards no longer smelled of the stench of confined cattle. For six years no beef could be admitted through Chihuahua; the ban lifted in September 1952. Although many ganaderos were suspicious of the reasons behind the American embargo, suspecting the main one was unwelcome Mexican competition, they turned their loss of market to some advantage. Nineteen meatpacking plants were established throughout the north, six of them in Chihuahua. In Ciudad Juárez, Nuevo Casas Grandes, and Chihuahua the new industry developed and expanded. Empacadora de Chihuahua developed to a stage of being able to process fifteen hundred head in twenty-four hours and to produce canned meat products such as tasty stews or meat in red or green chile sauce, to be exported to the States and all over Mexico. Industrializadora del Cerdo, capacity operation of three hundred head per twenty-four hours, was established to make sausages, lard, and other products for export. Exporpac confined its activity to canning horsemeat for dog food.

A statewide cattlemen's organization now has forty-five hundred members, with twenty-seven locals. It aids in operation of one hundred thirty-nine radio transmitters to outlying ranches and thirty-nine meteorological stations to distribute weather data. It further works in improving the range, in eradicating *alfombrilla* (a toxic plant harmful to cattle), in bettering breeding stock through artificial insemination. On four occasions the Unión Ganadera Regional has sponsored a livestock exposition. In 1960 as part of the observance of the fiftieth anniversary of the Revolution, the Chihuahua ganaderos were invited to join in such an exposition at the national capital. In competition with exhibitors from the states of Chiapas, Mexico, Durango, Aguascalientes, Nueva Leon, Coahuila, Sonora, and Sinaloa, the Chihuahua group took three championships and seven first place ribbons.[22]

As further indication of the importance of stock raising to the economy, the government operates a range experimental station in Chihuahua, and the state university successfully maintains a school of stock raising to train her young men for this old and honored profession.

However, life for the vaquero of the north has remained grim. He works for the "new rich" ganadero but shares little of the boom. Now he sometimes has a scrawny cow or two of his own, and if he lives near the border in some orphaned area like Ojinaga, engages in contraband. His family relies on gathering *candelilla* for extraction of wax, despite a monopoly claimed by Coahuila interests, and lechuguilla for fibers. Occasionally he manufactures small quantities of sotol from the desert plant of the same name. He lives in squalor and poverty on the backwash of society. He is a leather-faced man of the wind and weather, solemn, taciturn, and dejected. More than that, he is disillusioned on realization that La Revolución to which he contributed so much has returned him nothing.

Almost one half of Chihuahua's people are rural.* Yet it cannot be said that either the hurrying irrigation-project dweller or the vaquero, resigned to dusty life amid the sagebrush, is completely characteristic. The essence of the Chihuahuense may be found in quiet country towns spaced along the watercourses or on the alluvial fans and downhill slopes. Here are random groupings of dark-colored mud houses forming an effective backdrop for a simple, whitewashed chapel. Here are unmortared fences of piled boulders arching over ridges and down gravelly draws. Here are yellowing corn stalks piled on top of brushy *ramadas*, or arbors. Here are burros and chickens and pigs grazing by the roadside. So far, these farmers have little to sell. They concentrate on providing the necessities of life for their own families. Corn, beans, oats, potatoes, and a few other vegetables are their main crops. Their fortunes are regulated by simple, seasonal rhythms of sun, soil, and harvest.

Here there is a muted harmony between man and nature, not quite trustful—for how can trust come from unreliability?—not relaxed or joyful, for the struggle has been too long and too bitter. But here is valor, resoluteness, deep hope, and a fascinating glimmer of the knowledge that after four hundred and fifty years, the central government is at last realizing the value of their northlands. They are beginning to feel important. In their newfound pride,

---

* According to *México, Cincuenta Años de Revolución*, 1960, v. I, 112, 48% of the population of the north is rural as compared to a national figure of 55.4%. 1950 census figures show that of 257,897 persons of working age in Chihuahua, 141,920 were engaged in agriculture. *B-SCEH*, 1953, 650, v. III, no. 3.

they are redoing their settlements, redesigning ancient plazas, re-
painting and replastering houses, paving roads, digging wells for
drinking water, setting out ornamental shade trees, and obtaining
rural electrification projects. They are throwing off the inertness
of the past and are eager to take on the twentieth century.*

EVEN MORE EAGER to update themselves are the few cities of Chihuahua. The capital, two hundred fifty years old in 1959, in a
burst of building, now has a number of new, attractive structures
which house banks, hotels, and shops. The twin towers of the cathedral which used to stand high above one-story block-shaped
buildings of the eighteenth century, now are dwarfed by fifteen-
storied edifices facing on the green plaza. New, modern school
buildings erected under Plan Chihuahua, an ambitious school
construction and education betterment program initiated by the
administration of Governor Teofilo Borunda, are located in the
outskirts. A new state university, founded in 1954 by former
governor Soto Maynez and planned to meet the specific needs of
its youth, has graduated its first classes. Streets have been resur-
faced or paved for the first time. Drinking water for the city's
residents has been increased by five hundred liters per second in
the last four years through the drilling of new wells. More household water will be obtained through the utilization of a new dam
upriver on the Chuvíscar. The old riverbed of the Chuvíscar has
been confined in a cement-lined canal as it courses through town,
is crossed by five bridges, and has appropriate flood drains. An

---

* *Informe de Gobierno*, No. 4, 1960: 565 km. of new roads were laid between 1956 and 1960, new bridges were installed, and new seal coats spread
at a cost of 71,500,000 pesos from government, state and private funds (Informe de Carreteras y Caminos). In the period 1956-1960 works to provide potable water and sewerage were installed in 33 towns in the state and were being
completed in 12 more. Total cost: 41,000,000 pesos. Total number of persons
benefited: 681,328 (Informe de Agua Potable y Alcantarillado). Five electrification projects to benefit 21,188 inhabitants were completed in the same period,
and five others to benefit 11,399 persons were begun. Four additional projects
were realized by the Cía. Electrífica Mexicana del Norte, S.A., to reach 10,655
persons. Total number of inhabitants aided by these works is estimated at
43,252 at a cost of more than 10,200,000 pesos. Areas to receive special attention
were La Junta in the municipio of Guerrero, Namiquipa, Madera, and Nuevo
Casas Grandes (Informe de Electrificación).

area of some one hundrd fifty square meters of hovels which used to border the banks has been cleared, subdivided, and lined with mercury lights in preparation for a new housing and urbanization project at a total expenditure of 50,000,000 pesos, planned not only to eliminate an unhealthy situation but to beautify the city. Cautiously guarding a reputation of being one of the cleanest urban centers in Mexico, Chihuahua has launched other efforts at slum clearance as numerous multi-unit structures of modern style are being readied for occupancy by families of low income.[23] Located on the perimeter of the city is a ring of busy industrial plants which testify to the present stability of the political situation. A city which differs in appearance from those to the south through the lack of colonial buildings and cobblestone streets, its spirit too is different as bustle, prosperity, and pride of achievement characterize its citizens. These are norteños at their best.

Ciudad Juárez, with a population of one hundred fifty thousand, claims to be Mexico's fourth largest city and Chihuahua's largest. Many thousands of Americans never have penetrated Mexico beyond the limits of this town, but so many have crossed the international bridges there that it is now the biggest port of entry in the United States. Three hundred five million dollars were spent along the Mexican border in the one year of 1957, much of it in Ciudad Juárez.

In addition to the flood of pleasure seekers crossing the Río Grande and returning after a few hours, American officials are swamped controlling the movement of laborers coming north to work under an international agreement, apprehending illegal entrants (wetbacks), and keeping check on Juárez residents who work in El Paso. A million persons pass through the port each year.

This river town has had an appeal for Americans for over a century. Its young ladies early had a reputation for being pleasantly responsive to American overtures, its vineyards productive of a good, light wine and potent brandy, its winter climate warm and sunny. Through the period of the Mexican-American caravan trade, the California-bound argonauts, and the coming of the railroads, Ciudad Juárez, like her sister across the river, became more and more a melting pot where cross currents met and were fused.[24]

Two events occurred late in the epic decade of the Revolution which sent a section of Ciudad Juárez down the primrose path. Thousands of uprooted refugees spilled into the border town during the late stages of the fighting. These were people shaken by civil war, frantic in their need for readjustment and new opportunity. For many, that opportunity came in 1918 with the advent of prohibition in the United States. The Mexican border sopped in alcohol. Much of it was smuggled into Texas and New Mexico. Bars and saloons found a treasure of which the conquistadors never had dreamed. A foreign distillery moved to Ciudad Juárez and is still in operation. Mexican and European liquors by the thousands of gallons were rushed to the Río Grande. With the liquor came prostitution, lewd shows, dope parlors, undercover gambling, and open violence. Juárez's reputation grew increasingly black. Mexican police were unable or unwilling to curb the rowdy atmosphere. It was New York's Eve in Chicago Gangland every night of the year. Thrill-bent Americans loved the risks, and business boomed. The street of the cabarets and curio stalls, Avenida Juárez leading to the out-bridge, *was* Mexico to countless Americans. They came to buy a shot of whiskey or tequila, to have their pictures taken on a wooden horse with their shoulders draped in a gaudy Saltillo serape and their heads crowned with a sombrero bearing the large letters of MEXICO on the upturned brim, to buy an ashtray shaped like a hat, to see a girlie show, to eat a few red enchiladas, to send home a postcard from Old Mexico picturing a smoking volcano.

In 1933, repeal of prohibition brought about the closing down of many liquor houses. Nonetheless, Mexican prices on bottled goods, far below heavily taxed American liquors, remained enough lower to entice yanqui buyers. The United States limited the quantity which could be imported to one gallon per person per month, and Texas gathered tax money on every drop. In the autumn of 1965 this duty-free import was reduced to one quart.

Then emphasis was placed upon shops of another nature. The perfumes, tooled handbags, handwoven tablecloths, embroidered blouses, tinwork, and blown glass began to draw the customers. Ciudad Juárez became, and has remained, one of the leading centers of the curio business in Mexico with sixty such shops lining Avenida Juárez. Customshouses flanked both sides of the river. A million-dollar export-import business grew up as craft items went north and American appliances, canned goods, and machinery went south in steadily increasing volume.

Protests from American officials spurred Ciudad Juárez to clean house. The cabaret street remained "Mexico" to many sightseers. The bars and night spots flourished, providing stout drinks, tender steaks, and indifferent entertainment. Prices were high by Mexican standards, low by American. American currency is used almost exclusively along the thoroughfare. The climate became more respectable than formerly. But this part of Ciudad Juárez was, and is, atypical. It was neither Mexican nor American but often a blend of the worst of both.

Away from the street of the dancing girls and noisy hawkers, Ciudad Juárez now is like other urban centers of northern Mexico. It has an air of newness, in this case partly because of a disastrous fire in 1904 which destroyed most of the old downtown section, and the Revolutionary battles which finished others. Its grassy plaza spreads out in front of a mammoth, double-spired cathedral whose yellow-tiled dome catches the sunlight. It is a town anxious for industrialization and modernization, progressive in attitude, full of admiration for American ways and American luxuries. Many of its residents are English speaking. They, or their children, have attended schools in the States. Quite a few are Protestant. All are oriented toward the north rather than toward the south from which they are separated by distance, topography, and tradition. To travel to Los Angeles, or Albuquerque, or San Antonio is for many a more real desire than to go to Mexico City. There are the off-color jokes about their rich Anglo neighbors and the mutterings of discrimination and resentment, but imitation of the American goes right on.

Commerce in Ciudad Juárez revolves around two distilleries, a brewery, refrigeration plant, soap factories, cotton gin, wheat mills, clothing manufacturing plants, tile factory, retail clothing stores, groceries, and so on. A powerful radio station broadcasts in Spanish and in English, with singing commercials and disk jockeys. The railroad yards provide employment for many. Chihuahua's only street cars operate through the city and across two Río Grande bridges. It has an important air terminal. A large corps of government customs officials are needed to man the customshouse. And the army maintains its barracks, remembering too well the border uprisings of the Revolution.

Out beyond the settlement are the farmlands, rich and productive as they were when Zebulon Pike first saw them. Río Grande waters keep the well-ordered fields green with cotton, alfalfa, grapes, corn, and wheat. Up on the dry bench above river level, there is new agricultural development through water supplied by wells. The line of human occupation extends downriver to rural hamlets of Zaragoza, Guadalupe, and Banderas. Seven of the twenty-three international bridges spanning the Río Grande are in the Juárez valley. South and east of this thin line of life lies the sunbaked expanse of Chihuahua desert.

The brown, mud-thickened waters of the Río Grande, sometimes called "silvery" by poetic balladeers, officially had become a line of demarcation in 1847. What lay north was the United States. That to the south was Mexico. Then nature played a monstrous joke on the Mexicans. From time to time, turbulent river waters swelled from their low banks to cut off meandering loops and create new ones. Throughout most of the course of the river this shifting action was not too important. However, in 1868 in puckish humor the mighty river left its channel right at the site of the international twin towns and described an arc more southward. What had been *mexicano* overnight became *norteamericano*. Socorro and Isleta, hamlets created after the Pueblo Revolt of 1680, were left to the States. Those in El Paso who wished to retain Mexican citizenship gradually sold their property in the stranded Mexican neighborhood of Chamizal. It was an act of God which was considered inconvenient but not cataclysmic. The Juárez government made no protests to Washington.

But twenty years later matters had changed. The Central de México Railroad ran from Mexico City north to Ciudad Juárez. An international bridge connected Mexican rails with the Southern Pacific Railroad. El Paso, on a strategic junction of rails and roads began to be a thriving trading center, drawing business from an ever increasing radius in west Texas and the New Mexico Territory. Added to legitimate trade was a lively international contraband activity. The town of El Paso expanded down the river bottom and up the terraces. Chamizal lay between Mills

Street in the heart of town and the river. It developed as an area of office and commercial buildings as well as a district of Mexican homes and small industries. Its value in a few years was many times what it had been in 1868, estimated at more than $400,000. The Mexicans began to eye the Chamizal and demand return of the land to their jurisdiction. A chunk of worthless land lost was one thing, but the guts of a growing city was another. The United States refused to recognize Mexican claims. Maybe the matter was one discussed in the private discussions of Díaz and Taft. At any rate, in 1911 both parties agreed to arbitration.[25]

A three-man commission—one Mexican, one American, and one neutral Canadian—sat down to re-examine the claims and rebuttals. In the end, the Mexican and Canadian outvoted the American and recommended that that portion of the Chamizal which had been lost through the violent river action be returned to Mexico. Unsettled conditions in Mexico precluded any serious efforts at forcing Washington's hand, and the United States Government quietly ignored the whole affair. Possession and investment were American. But on July 19, 1963, President Kennedy and President Lopez Mateos of Mexico officially announced an agreement that would rechannel the Río Grande to follow its old course, thereby returning the Chamizal to Mexico. The new channel will be lined with permanent concrete for a width of 270 feet and a length of 4.3 miles, forestalling future quirks of nature.

Subject to ratification by the U.S. Senate, Mexico was to receive 630 acres of El Paso, the United States, 193 acres of Mexican-owned Córdoba Island a little downstream. For the United States, this meant relocating 3,500 Americans, compensating owners for 500 single dwellings, 7 tenements, 60 plants and commercial buildings, 1 school, 4 bridges, Border patrol buildings, part of the El Paso sewerage disposal plant, as well as approximately 400 acres of agricultural land. Though reactions were mixed, even in El Paso many thought the ultimate effect would be good economically and agreed that it was certainly in the spirit of international amity to heal this festering sore. The official transfer occurred in September.

Córdoba Island, named after two brothers who operated a flour mill there, was cut off from Mother Mexico in 1899 by the capricious river. Parcels of this land were bought up by speculators, but later the Mexican government took over the entire marooned island and formed a colonia agrícola there in 1922. Today this bit of Mexico north of the Río Grande lies surrounded by a high, barbed fence and American industry. It is cultivated by a few farmers living in squat adobe houses. Nearby, along a wide thoroughfare rushes El Paso traffic. Towering above the scene was a high border-patrol lookout, now no longer necessary, guarding against illegal entrance into the United States.

THE MOTHER MOUNTAINS of Chihuahua stand vigilant along the western border, jealously protecting wide tracts of the interior from the sea. Only at their crests can one feel the salty moisture and the enchanting odor of the Pacific far toward the haze of the horizon. Between the central tableland and the shore is a lost world of row on row of forested crags and sawtoothed pinnacles, twisted, fathomless canyons slicing through strata of reds and yellows into the earth's hot interior, blind channels etched by angry, frothy waters seeking outlet, silent, grassy meadows whose heaven stillness is disturbed only by frisky, white-tailed deer and the murmur of wind against trees. Some of this mountain kingdom knows perpetual snow and frozen soil, bitter sharp cold that drives man away. At the foot of such peaks can be found the humid tropics of the mosquito and the *jejéne*, the slithering snake, the orange, banana, and pineapple, the wattle-and-daub house with its thatch roof, the naked children. In between these two extremes—the tierra fría and the tierra caliente—are thousands of square miles where hot sunshine is mitigated by elevations of 8,000 feet and snows come only in the winter. Here is found one of the cold poles of Mexico, the headwaters of streams which in their course to the Gulf of California to the west and the Gulf of Mexico to the east build into mighty rivers gouging canyons equally as awesome as Arizona's Grand Canyon. Here are Mexico's highest waterfall, one of the world's greatest mineral districts, and majestic forests of virgin pine. Here dwell three distinct socioeconomic groups of Chihuahua: the miner, the lumberjack, the Indian.

Although by its very nature mining is an enterprise which exhausts a nonrenewable natural resource, mineral deposits sought and discovered by the conquistadors and their heirs still are being exploited in modern Chihuahua. When one considers the fact that all of Mexico is highly mineralized with only the limestone platform of the Yucatán peninsula having no significant mineral areas, Chihuahua's high position in mineral yield assumes even greater importance. With 50 per cent of the national mining income derived from Chihuahua, the federal government annually accrues 270,000,000 pesos in mine taxes and 1,382,788,177 pesos in profits.[26] This northern state leads the nation in its output of silver, lead, and zinc, is second in amount of copper produced (surpassed by western neighbor, Sonora), and is third in gold (exceeded by southern neighbors, Durango and Zacatecas).[27]

Parral, Santa Bárbara, and San Francisco del Oro, the original big three of Chihuahua's mining districts, remain the core of the mining industry. The high point of gold production was reached there in 1910, the high point of silver in 1929, of copper in 1956, of lead in 1938, and of zinc in 1955. At these mines, gold and silver remained the principal metals sought throughout the early periods, but with the post-Revolution industrialization of Mexico a shift of emphasis gave new importance to the metals basic to industry. The American Smelting and Refining Company (Asarco) operates establishments at Parral, Santa Bárbara, and Aquiles Serdán. The latter is said to be the world's largest lead smelter. Santa Eulalia, whose discovery led to the founding of the city of Chihuahua and whose silver helped pay for the cathedral, now has assumed new importance as a producer of lead and zinc. San Francisco del Oro Mines, México, Ltd. runs the production at that town and is creating new mountains of tailings to creep out upon the red plains. All these smelters use coke from Coahuila and power from the hydroelectric plant at La Boquilla dam on the Conchos.

Elsewhere on the plains sector of Chihuahua, the mines of the Los Lamentos district, in the desert east of Villa Ahumada, opened up just before the Revolution, ship their ores to the big smelter at El Paso. In the northwest near Janos, Ascensión, and Casas Grandes, deposits of manganese and tungsten are profitable at present and offer hopes of potential reserves. East of Aldama some desert regions are thought to contain workable deposits of uranium, but these as yet have not begun to be exploited.

The towns at these eastern mines are company towns, often built with the uninteresting uniformity of company towns everywhere. Those with old roots have more personality. Management lives in cheerful, modern quarters surrounded by a bit of grass and a few trees. Social improvements are noticed in the airy, well-equipped schools and hospitals. A watchful government enforces minimum wage laws and workmen's compensation. In general, the men who work the mines are better paid than those who work the fields.

It is in the sierra that Chihuahua mining has almost died, although all these highland municipios have had mineral deposits worked in the past. At Chínipas, Guazápares, Urique, Cusihuiriáchi, Batopilas, and elsewhere, work has been suspended through a series of misfortunes, the most insurmountable of which is their location.

During the Díaz dictatorship seven hundred forty-six claims were registered, 1892 being the year of greatest activity. Most of these claims were located in the mountains and were exploited by foreign concerns who were set above the law of the land with exemption from taxation and other prerogatives. Mexicans could not compete. Subsurface wealth, which had initiated the original exploration and colonization, flowed out of the country. Natives were left only the physical diseases of lifetimes spent in black pits for paltry pay and a corrosive rancor at their exploitation.

At first revolutionaries seemed afraid to tackle the powerful mining trusts, but with success they grew bolder. Operators were forced to pay big bribes to gain protection from successive waves of rebel bands who rode through the sierra. With the continuation of the fighting for so many years, the mines were paralyzed by dearth of manpower and destruction of means of transportation. Many never were revitalized. Others recovered with the end of hostilities, and exploitation continued as before except that the new constitution proclaimed the nation's ownership of subsoil rights. Taxation of mines was enforced. However, lack of native capital kept the Mexicans out and the foreigners in.

The worldwide depression of the 1930's hurt Chihuahua mining companies because of their dependence upon foreign markets. Mexico went off the gold standard, but this was not effective enough to pour new life into mining. The slump succeeded in permanently shutting down some mines which had survived the Revolution. Others found the difficulties of terrain and transportation too much to overcome. In the sierra madre there was widespread misery as scores of men set aside their carbide-lanterned hats. Some took up picks to rework abandoned veins or to prospect for new outcroppings. Others panned for gold along the gravelly river banks. None made more than the meagerest living, but all were sustained by the miner's eternal hope of bonanza.

With man's inexplicable determination to stay within his known environment, many of the miners and their families clung to the jumbled mountain communities to watch stoically the creeping decay and collapse of large-scale mining industry within the sierra. They stayed on in their dreary settlements perched crazily on steep slopes or rocky canyon floors, places which seemed always to have had a tenuous air about them as if ready to dissolve when the bonanza ended. With each day they mired deeper into debt with the regional general store. Numberless houses stood empty until roofs caved in and rafters were carried off. Soon there was little left but the telltale ore dumps and gaping shafts and a stump-dotted clearing. From the Tarahumara Alta in the north to the Durango border, at Guaynopa, Bocoyna, Urique, Guazápares, and Guadalupe y Calvo, there was a gradual cessation of activity.

But now once again a few Mexican nationals with money have begun to reinvest in mines and smelters. More than twenty-six hundred concessions have been recorded for the state.[28] At Ocampo, Pinos Altos, El Pilar, and El Madroño, all in the central mountains, bold businessmen are sitting on the threshold of revival. Their companies are not large nor their techniques and equipment the last word. Old *haciendas de beneficio* have been mucked out and grinding mills and mules work the ores much as they did in the time of Nueva Vizcaya. But they are working again, and the miners feel a better day is just ahead.

Thousands of square miles lie stranded along the continental divide. Whole municipios contain not a single motor vehicle. The only passable road penetrating the southern sector is that to Batopilas. Beyond there, out of this world into the one of the fantastic barrancas, communication between the dying mining camps and plateau civilization is by man's oldest means—the burro, or his most recent—the airplane. It is the latter which is keeping some villages from succumbing altogether.

Lindbergh year, 1927, was a big one for Chihuahua. In that year a passenger airplane blazed the first air route from north to south en route from Ciudad Juárez to Mexico City. Two years later, the first flight across the mountains was made to Chínipas. In a matter of a few years landing strips were cleared near many mountain- and canyon-bound camps. With the daring aid of a war-trained clan of American daredevil hedgehoppers who fanned out over all of Latin America, Mexicans were propelled from the Neolithic to the Air Age. Mines which were weeks away by ground could now be reached in a few hours. Regular flights were inaugurated to transport officials and concentrates. A new school of Mexican avia- tors flew from the capital to the sierra with a casual deftness bely- ing their recent initiation into the cult of the machine. Air travel was, and remains, expensive, impractical for many of the small op- erators. With the juxtaposition of the ancient and the modern so characteristic of Mexico, planes overhead carry out the products of some mountain mines while products of others are packed on muletrains over grueling narrow trails.

MEXICO has wasted another of her great natural resources of the mountains, her forests. Each year has seen thousands of trees destroyed, burned by fires ignited by man or lightning, chopped down, or riddled by insects. Not until 1958, with the passage of a good forestry law, did the government finally secure funds and sanction to go to work on this problem with all the diverse forces at its command.

Although isolated and largely unpopulated, the forests of Chi- huahua have suffered the same fate as those elsewhere in the na- tion. There, the Indians have been accustomed to burning off their fields before planting, and frequently fires set for such pur- poses have blazed out of control, blocking trails as well as ruining the timber. Other forest fires started during the wicked lightning storms centered over the mountains often have burned undetected and always uncontrolled. It has been estimated that, for a long pe- riod of time, some one hundred sixty fires each year have black- ened Chihuahua mountains. Furthermore, in the vicinity of the mining areas the hillsides early were stripped for mine cribbing and household fuel. Unrestricted grazing in the forests has ham- pered natural reforestation because cattle and sheep understand- ably have a fondness for tender, young shoots. Thus a number of activities in the mountain watershed have led to quick erosion of the soil, a change in ecological balance, and a gradual ruination of the timber resources.

These are things which have been going unchecked for several hundreds of years, but it was only with the arrival of this century that another unfavorable factor became an important part of the diminution of the stands of trees in Chihuahua. That was ruthless commercial exploitation whose goals embraced nothing as foresighted as conservation. With the Noroeste de México Railroad and the western spur of the Kansas City, México, y Oriente to haul out the lumber, several large companies set to work cutting over large tracts of pine, oak, and madroño.[29] Fortunately, the Revolution ended their activities before total destruction was accomplished. It was not until 1952 that commercial lumbering enterprises on a large scale again resounded through the mountains. Now the industry operates under strict government control.

A group of Chihuahua industrialists bought up the defunct Compañia Madera, S.A., one of the Díaz-blessed corporations which worked the eastern slope of the sierra madre in the vicinity of the town of Madera (quite appropriately the Spanish word for wood). This group, which calls itself Grupo Industrial Bosques de Chihuahua, with the aid of private and government capital seeks to make forestry as important to Chihuahua's welfare as are agriculture and mining. They are on the way to success.[30]

With an investment of 470,000,000 pesos and some eighty towns dependent upon various activities associated with lumbering, Chihuahua has seven major, primary lumber companies employing six thousand workers who receive a monthly payroll of 750,000 pesos. Bosques de Chihuahua is the largest of these. Industrias de Madera, Maderas de Pino Industrializados, and Industrias Conexas each employ two hundred fifty or more men. Directly associated with the processes of cutting and using fallen trees, there are in the state some fifteen sawmills with band saws and forty-nine with circular saws. In at least six localities, there are creosote plants to prepare railroad ties and telephone poles. Factories or mills turning out boxes, door and window casings, furniture, and construction materials represent secondary industries.

On the shores of Lago de Bustillos, midway between two isles of nineteenth-century culture—the Zuloaga Hacienda de Bustillos and the Mennonite colony—three lumber-connected enterprises of tremendous significance have come into being. The most outstanding of these is a concern called Celulosa de Chihuahua, S.A.,[31] which began as an Italian project with Italian architects, engineers, and money. Its many glass-walled, domed, and stilted buildings reflect the best of modern Italian architecture. Clean-lined facades, done in brilliant Venetian tile mosaics with piercing blues, yellows, reds, and greens, flash in the sun and stand proud against the brush of swirling winds. Most eye-arresting is a tile panel on the front of the headquarters building where Romulus and Remus find themselves in bizarre association with the eagle and the serpent and a dead tree stump.

This is a plant for the manufacture of wood pulp. With the three necessary resources at hand—wood, water, and power—and with a magnificent plant built, the Italians found that they had the theoretical process for operation but not the technical competence. After several years of discouragement they withdrew, leaving the floundering plant to Mexican partners who were just as unsuccessful in manufacturing satisfactory pulp. Kimberly Clark, makers of Kleenex, distressed by the poor quality of pulp available for their Mexico City factory and with the blessings of Celulosa de Chihuahua, assigned four Canadian and American engineers to the job of getting the difficulties of production corrected. After two years the plant was returned to a corps of twenty-eight Mexican chemical engineers trained in technical colleges of Mexico City and Monterrey.

Celulosa de Chihuahua now manufactures some of the world's finest pulp, a difficult task using as it does only dead wood. The paper rolls off gigantic revolving presses in large sheets and is packed into four-hundred-pound cartons which are shipped by train to Mexico City and by truck to Monterrey. For the first time since William Green's pre-Revolution pulp plant, residual products of the lumbering operation are being utilized. However, the plant represents more than its products. A thousand men, organized into a strong union, find employment in the new industry. They live in a town of pastel-colored houses called Anahuac which has modern schools, hospitals, hotels, and playgrounds.

Some Italian interest remains in a second neighboring plant called Viscosa de Chihuahua where rayon is made. This is an operation on a much smaller scale than Celulosa de Chihuahua but is also helping the local economy through the employment of another two hundred fifty men.

The third plant in this industrial nucleus, which has grown up on the windy tableland, is a factory devoted to the manufacture of plywood.* Here five hundred workers find jobs.

Fire prevention and fire fighting have assumed new importance in the wake of the growth of a lumber industry in Chihuahua. Backed by national law, all-out efforts have reduced the number of annual fires by half. A dozen steel lookout towers spotted through the mountains, thirty-two radio-telephone stations, and four motor brigades are new evidences of the determination to guard this resource. Every person who works in the forests has the legally prescribed obligation of fighting fires as do all the personnel of the Fifth Military Zone. The subsidiary industries aid in reduction of fire hazards. Planned reforestation projects for the first time in history are being carried out in certain sectors of the sierra.

IF THE WHITE MAN is not a miner or a lumberjack, he does not survive in the Chihuahua mountains. But Tarahumara (population estimates vary from 20,000 to 45,000) and a smattering of other Indians have mastered that demanding environment.[32] Perhaps it would be more correct to say they have adjusted to the environment. It is a delicate balance to be sure, but it has been successful enough to allow them to survive and increase their numbers. In part, their residence in the Sierra Madre Occidental was forced upon them. Mostly, it was their own choice. This was their ancient hearth, but there was a time when they spread out of the mountains into the foothill basins. With white pressures and sometimes fraudulent acquisition of Indian lands, they gradually moved deeper into the sierra and farther southward where topography was more inhospitable but, by the same token, more protective.[33]

After the late 1600's and the savage battles directed by Tepóraca, the Tarahumara warlike spirit and complex of war traits which they had shared with the Yaqui and other west coast tribes disin-

---

* Spelled "playwood" in a phonetic Spanish adaptation of an English word.

tegrated. They came to the realization that physical resistance to the Spaniards was hopeless. Therewith they became some of the greatest pacifists of all time, practitioners of a sort of nonviolent resistance. Quietly, in small family groups, they withdrew, both physically and psychologically. They avoided all possible contact with the Europeans. Only at the missions did they enter into a sphere of Spanish influence. After the expulsion of the Jesuits and demoralization of missionary activity, neophytes deserted the settlements to go back into the mountains. Outposts in the heathen realm, founded with so much self-denial and sacrifice on the part of the padres, crumbled into decay, their goals of Europeanization of the natives largely unobtained.

The Tarahumara walked into the mountains to the most remote, unvisited areas, and where they found a small meadow or patch of ground suitable for meager farming, they settled down. The limited size of these plots necessitated their use by a single family unit. Another spot adequate for farming might be several miles distant. Thus the environment forced its most overwhelming characteristic on its inhabitants: its isolation. This was isolation not only of Indian from white, but Indian from Indian.

Until recently there have been no Tarahumara towns, except those established by missions. There are no groupings of houses. There are no elaborate clan or moiety systems as in many other so-called primitive groups. Furthermore, they do not farm along main trails but prefer to remove themselves as completely as possible from all chance encounters. They have accepted the yoke of isolation and have found comfort in it. As a result, they are one of the least Mexicanized native entities in the country.

Nonetheless, on an unelaborate agricultural base of pre-Hispanic times there have been European modifications. Thanks to missionary work—Jesuit, Franciscan, and parish Catholic and, in the post-Revolution era, Protestant—the Indians are Christians. The church rolls no doubt would include their number among the record of converts. Realistically viewed, however, the conversion of the Tarahumara is superficial. Some have learned portions of Catholic ceremony to chant in Spanish although they neither speak nor understand the language. It is estimated that almost ten thousand of them speak only their Uto-Aztecan tongue. They go through ritual and observe feast days such as Easter and Christmas. Beyond that, there is little, if any, grasp of the dogmas of the Church.

In the realm of government, they operate democratically through elected governors and trials for wrong-doers. They can resort to aid from the nearest Mexican municipal president. By and large, the mestizos refrain from interference in Indian disputes unless a mestizo is involved.

Important contributions to the economic life of the Tarahumara have been domesticated animals, metal tools, and firearms. The cow is of vast importance, not so much for the meat, as for the by-product of manure. This has enabled the Indians to fertilize a soil pitifully shallow and infertile and to raise crops where, without fertilization, it would be impossible. Sheep have provided wool for blankets needed against mountain cold. These animals have imposed a seasonal nomadic existence upon their owners, and the great care they demand has made stock raising a family enterprise. Animals cannot be turned loose to graze for there are the high cliffs, the preying coyotes, the boring ticks, the numbing cold, so that constant attention to his herd is the lot of the Tarahumara stockman and his family. Primitive farming can be carried on only a third of the year because of the early frosts and snows which come with the elevation. Other months must be spent moving the animals from one sparse range to another. At this time many of the mountain dwellers leave their crude plank houses to migrate to the warm barrancas. Here they occupy numerous shallow caves worn into the cliffs, and one sees the Neolithic close at hand.

Metal-tipped plows, as well as wooden ones, pulled by oxen work the soil in the two ecological regions occupied by the Tarahumara, the barrancas and the mountains. Steel machetes in the lowlands and steel axes in the highlands have enabled the Indians to better control their environment. The machete hacks away exuberant, spiny growth flourishing in the canyons. In the heights the ax splits boards, beams, and fence posts from the large-cone pines, helps make musical instruments, bowls, and spoons of ash, or roughs out plows of oak. Indians hunt with bows of mulberry in the upper Río Conchos region. This is the source of the photo-

graphs of the half-naked, wild-looking Indians assuming the arch-
er's classic stance. Elsewhere Mauser rifles gained during Revolution sorties allow Indians to shoot deer which they formerly had
to wound or stun with well-aimed rocks or arrows and then run
down.

To overtake a deer on foot might seem to approach the impossible. Not for the Tarahumara men who from infancy are trained
for long-distance running. In the colonial period Indian runners
carried the mail from the capital of Chihuahua to Batopilas, a
distance of two hundred fifty rugged miles, in three days, rested
a day, and made the return run in three more days.[34] The reasons
for the emphasis on running are strictly social. Foot races, sometimes in the form of kick-ball games, are big events and a part of
almost all Tarahumara gatherings. For that reason a Tarahumara
foot race was part of the two-hundred-fifty-year anniversary of the
founding of the city of Chihuahua celebrated in 1959. It seems
incredible that Indian athletes suffering diet deficiencies and
breathing the thin air of high altitudes can run for sport up and
down mountains for whole days and nights without stopping—incredible but true! Tarahumara backs are weak but Tarahumara
legs are strong. And those who are not running are drinking cop-
iously and wagering on the outcome of the races. The worried
cocktail party hostess who frets to see her gathering lingering long
after hours should witness the *tesgüinadas* of the Tarahumara
which drag on for delirious days! Alcoholism and tuberculosis
among all age groups are bringing rapid physical decline, in spite
of a well-earned reputation for fleet-footedness.

Contact with other Mexicans is limited. More meetings occur in
the lowlands because of the mines and the mestizo population
which they have attracted. A few other mestizos live among the
Indians as blacksmiths or as itinerant traders exchanging thread,
needles, cloth, soap, and salt for Indian corn and beans. On occasion the Indians have hired out as porters, packing mule loads
on their backs. Others have hewn railroad ties with a skill and
precision Mexican laborers envy. Government reports indicate
that in this employment they have been victimized again. Standard
wages for tie splitting among the mestizos is fifteen cents per tie,
but Indians are paid in overpriced goods. Some make a practice of

carrying crates of fruit * to Mexican settlements of Creel, Nonoava, Batopilas, or Bocoyna. Crudely woven serapes of natural-colored, hand-carded wool are brought to the city stores. Other Indians walk several hundred miles from the tierra caliente to Mexican markets to peddle small packets of wild medicinal herbs gathered in the warm barrancas. Many come "out" just to see the sights. Often they travel as family groups, carrying their supplies in small bundles on their backs. Youngsters walk beside their parents, unconcerned at the long distances to be covered. Babies ride on their mothers' backs wrapped in a once-white *cobija* sling. They can be seen, dirty and expressionless, peering into shop windows and cafes of the capital. Young and old sometimes knock on doors for a handout from their ancient enemies.

Children of the mountains, the Tarahumara reflect the somberness of their peaks, the quiet grandeur of their canyons and much of the barrenness. They are a colorless, passive people but are not unlike the swift mountain deer—delicate, timid, quick to vanish. They dress without the display of color of many aborigines. Men wear white cotton breechclouts or more rarely pants such as blue jeans. They have adopted loose, white, homespun shirts. Many still wear their hair long, foreheads wrapped with a headband. Others have begun wearing a western-style straw hat.[35] Women wear unfitted blouses and full skirts of white or red manta cloth which become heavily impregnated with dirt as they drag mile after mile over the trails. They have no craft tradition which might enliven their drabness, no embroidery or beading or brilliant featherwork. Women make undecorated utilitarian pottery, mostly large ollas to contain the intoxicating tesgüino. They weave a poor-grade blanket without character. Centuries of oppression and abuse from white neighbors have made them distrustful and cautious.

As the years of independence accumulated, so did the feelings of superiority of whites over Indians. Many students of the matter felt it was a social rather than racial discrimination. With the evaporating strength of the Church in the mountains, the Indians were left without protection against dishonest neighbors who coveted their farm and forest holdings.[36] Officialdom felt sporadic

---

* The knowledge of fruit culture is attributable to Jesuit missionaries.

pangs of conscience at the dispossession of the Indians, but all efforts at Indian betterment were a matter of deluding rhetoric not put into practice and were a part of an indigenist social movement for racial justice dating from the days of Las Casas and Quiroga.[37] The problems of the Tarahumara were those of other marginal groups of Mexico—the desert vaqueros, for instance—extreme poverty which the slightest undesirable fluctuation in climate could turn to famine, disease and death rates of alarming proportions,* complete illiteracy, and lack of vocational skills which might enable them to better their standard of living and to move into creditable columns of Mexican economic life. After the Revolution when sincere men did begin to come to grips with staggering nationwide problems, naturally the Indians had to wait their turn, and, as usual, their turn was last.

Just how is the incorporation of the Tarahumara into national life going to be accomplished? The arguments wax loud. The proposals are many. Some students want to make the mountain municipios where the Indians dwell a reservation, excluding all whites and so end white malpractices. The Instituto Nacional Indigenista wants to work with big groups to get big results. They want to bring the Indians together in Mexican-style settlements with modern sanitation and comforts; teach them to read, write, and speak the Spanish language; instill in them a sense of belonging to a great nation which incorporates not only their own group but hundreds of other Indians as well; help them develop crafts or simple skills on a large scale; show them how to farm larger areas more productively; create co-operatives to enable the Indians to benefit from lumbering. They recognize the urgent need of land to farm and propose restitution of ancient holdings. To further these efforts the Instituto has founded a Co-ordinating Center. Jesuit missionaries, back in the field once more, choose to work with smaller numbers brought into a mission community, indoctrinating the very young with Christian ideals and concepts, suppressing the escape into alcoholism, developing technological skills and knowledge of healthful homemaking in the period of puberty, and continuing contact throughout life.[38]

There is much to be said for and against both approaches.

* Eight out of ten Tarahumara babies die in their first years.

Fundamental to the success of either is overcoming Indian mistrust and nonviolent resistance. That will depend entirely upon the good will, understanding, and persuasiveness of the people sent to do the job, as well as upon the determination of the government to end exploitation of the natives. Government schoolteachers, social workers, and clerics are in a position of making a lasting impression which will either lead toward acceptance or rejection of the whole idea of acculturation.

The Tarahumara of the past have not taken to community living. They have preferred dispersion. Misguided efforts to transplant them en masse might end in failure. However, a small trial of this technique is being made at Guachochi on the southern cliffs of the Río Urique barranca, at Norogachi, and at Cieneguita. Both vocational and agricultural training are being offered to "interned" Tarahumara youth. The boys have their hair cut, are taken out of breechclouts and put into bib overalls. The girls are dressed in clean white dresses. Both sexes are exposed to a sample of Mexican life. They learn to play band instruments, to operate foot-treadle sewing machines, make shoes, care for babies. The idealists hope the Tarahumara youngsters will be dissatisfied to return to miserable preschool conditions and will strive to change the mold. The realists only hope that when the children do go home, they will at least be a bit better able to cope with the trying conditions.

For anxious bureaucrats the missionary method is too slow and limited in its scope. But dedicated churchmen are developing such communities as Cárichi at the edge of the mountains, Chinatú and Guadalupe y Calvo in the stranded southern municipio of Guadalupe y Calvo, Chínipas in the tierra caliente near the Sinaloa border, Cerocahui on the headwaters of the barrancas of the Río Fuerte, and Norogachi in the central uplands. At Cerocahui a simple yet inspiring chapel built by Father Salvatierra in 1680 is being restored and embellished. Headquarters of the mission network is at Sisoguichi, not far from Creel at the end of the old Kansas City Railroad, now called the Chihuahua al Pacifico. Sisoguichi, founded in 1676, now in the municipio of Bocoyna, has had rebirth and boasts a hospital, schools, shops, and stores surrounding a new church. It is an Indian town governed by a Catholic priest. Communication with the other missions is carried on by radio as there are no connecting roads. The devotion and service demanded of these isolated priests is in the twentieth century as great as it was in the seventeenth. Their labors are making some small inroads in the paganism and ignorance of the Indians, but not enough to bring any immediate remedy to the Tarahumara's plight.

During the past decade the Mexican government finally has simplified administrative complications to begin serious and expensive campaigns of attracting fringe Indian elements into the sphere of national development. Alfonso Caso, distinguished Mexican anthropologist, heading the Instituto Nacional Indigenista, after considerable experience with Indian groups to the south, proposed a concerted drive of aid for the Tarahumara. By presidential decree on June 4, 1952, the Tarahumara Co-ordinating Center was opened under the directorship of a longtime champion of the Tarahumara, Francisco M. Plancarte.[39] Located at Guachochi, two hundred kilometers west of Parral, its immediate goals were focused on health and welfare, education, and the economic situation.

Medical units were established at Guachochi, Tonachi, Cusárare, and Baquireachi with four doctors and Indian nurses trained by them. Their small crew of helpers traveled hundreds of miles via jeep to bring medicines and care to the ailing, and where roads were nonexistent, they rode horses or walked. During a flu epidemic in the spring of 1960, some of the medical team hiked eight hours to carry in antibiotics to the ill.[40] Digging wells for drinking water, promoting personal cleanliness, persuading natives of the efficaciousness of medicines, overcoming old superstitions, and giving vaccinations were part of their assignment.

Some fifty native men and women, called cultural promoters, all bilingual in Spanish and Tarahumara and with primary education, set to work getting schools in operation. After a year, three hundred youngsters were enrolled. Besides the task of teaching the Indians the language of their motherland, the writing and reading of their own tongue, simple arithmetic, and historical and geographical information about their nation, the schools helped in the planting of five communal apple orchards of three thousand trees, introduced a species of wheat suitable for the mountains and led experiments in sixteen varieties of vegetables and fruits, constructed a meteorological station, and provided barber equipment, personal hygiene material, and agricultural tools.[41] The number of teachers trained in the specific problems of their charges has continued smaller than desirable but is increasing.

Two dozen *trojes*, or communal barns, were built to aid in the saving of any surplus crops and to make loans of corn, beans, and seed to needy individuals. From these sources, and as outright gifts, over three tons of corn were distributed during a near-famine in 1961.[42] More than three hundred kilometers of new roads were constructed in the mountains including one from Parral to Guachochi; four hundred eight kilometers of trails were improved. A landing field was cleared. An old abandoned electric plant was reactivated, but because of the dispersal of Indian population, it remains unlikely that individual homes will have this service.

The most impressive project begun by the Instituto Nacional Indigenista on behalf of the Tarahumara is one aimed directly at the sensible exploitation of the main resource of the mountains, the forests. Work began at the ejido of Cusárare which had been granted to the Indians in 1930, part of the thirty thousand hectares having been the property of Astolfo Mendoza who had established the first sawmill in the Tarahumara Alta and part the ancient concession of Asunsola del Río. Prior to establishing this ejido, men of the area had made a meager living cutting wood for the boilers of the Kansas City, México, y Oriente Railroad. In 1943, the Secretary of Agriculture took charge of the ejido which had not progressed because of lack of capital and technical knowledge. Under government supervision, co-operatives were organized, sawmills constructed, and a program of operation outlined. Unfortunately control fell into the hands of a mestizo family whose high-handed methods ruined the budding enterprise. After the Co-ordinating Center came into existence, the Indians petitioned to have a new lumbering enterprise organized for them.[43]

This action required a large loan from the Banco de Crédito, whose officers were skeptical of the Indians' ability to make the venture pay. However, after one year, these Indians who, by themselves, under a single outside administrator, were responsible for the functioning of the entire process of felling trees and getting them through the mills, realized a profit of 115,000 pesos. Jubilant over their success, they bought out the local store, danced in the clearings, and toasted Alfonso Caso, Instituto chief, whom they now venerated as a saint. The second payment to the Cusárare ejido was up 5,000 pesos, and the figures have continued to mount each year. Because of this new wealth, many Tarahumara families have made the long pilgrimage to the city of Chihuahua, but now instead of begging on the streets, they come to enter shops, go to the movies, have a sweet treat, and see some of the sights.

On the basis of the Cusárare example, other lumbering co-operatives are being tried in the mountains. At Norogachi, Sama-chique, Choquita, Caborachi, Guauachique, Rocheachi, and Papa-jichi, forest ejidos are making money for their members, estimated at 3,000,000 pesos yearly.[44]

Those who doubted the Indians' ability to cope with finances or to plan for the future were in for a surprise when, from the first return of the lumber businesses, the participants voluntarily voted to invest in improved school buildings, road repair, meals for school students, medical stations, fruit trees, fertilizers, barbed wire, laundry equipment, insecticides, granaries, and scales, as well as repayment of the loan. At Cusárare the amazing phenomenon of the first Tarahumara planned town became fact as stone houses with glass windows, wooden floors, stoves, and doors with lock and key were constructed near the new school and clinic. Another good which came from the Indian interest in lumbering was a new respect for the forests. The slash-and-burn practice of clearing fields presently is controlled rigorously as the natives realize they may be their own worst enemies in this regard.

Thus, for the first time in four centuries, there appears great promise for the successful incorporation of the Tarahumara, not only because of a raised economic status and a fair certainty that it will increase, but because of a newfound sense of responsibility and an earnest desire for improvement. A stirring phrase uttered at the Fifth Tarahumara Congress meeting in Creel in 1958 which claimed that the Tarahumara "have as their only patrimony hunger, alcohol, and suicide"[45] may no longer be quite as true as it once was. The ramified problem of integration is by no means solved. But at least the government, local and national, is awakened to the fact that all-out exertions in that direction must be made, for humaritarian reasons, certainly, but also for economic ones. A nonproducing, nonconsuming block of the population can only impede progress. The Indians must be helped as much for the sake of the white Chihuahuenses as for themselves.

The southern mountains shelter three other native groups whose problems and way of life are much the same as those of the Tarahumara. About two thousand Tepehuanes dwell along the Durango border in the municipio of Guadalupe y Calvo, living as they did when Father Fonte came among them in the early 1600's. Down in the hot barrancas along the Sonora border near Chínipas are two hundred Varohíos. In southwestern portions of the municipios of Urique and Batopilas and western Morelos, are scattered Indians whose ties prehistorically were with the Tubaris. All these people are culturally and racially impure, although many speak Indian dialects and consider themselves Indian. To the north in the area of Temósachi and Madera are to be found about five hundred Pima Bajo who have strayed over from Sahuaripa, Sonora.[46]

Also, it is estimated that approximately twenty-five Apache families still wander through the no man's land of mountains between northern Sonora and Chihuahua.[47] A new outburst of Apache terror in the 1920's revived old horrors long forgotten. Under leadership of a man called Indian Juan, a fierce band preyed upon ranchers and prospectors, striking in the too familiar pattern of sudden, screeching attack, looting and murdering at will. In an effort to trap Indian Juan, the Mexicans instead captured a beautifully dressed young girl who claimed to be Gerónimo's granddaughter. She stayed with a Sonoran family, took Catholic vows, changed her name to Lupa, and forsook her Indian past.

During a trip to Bavispe, Sonora, in 1927, a Mexican family named Fimbres was attacked by Apaches. The mother was killed and the boy kidnapped. An angry, heartsick father vowed vengeance. For three years he roamed the northern mountains, driven on by agonizing desire to find his son and to make the Indians pay for the death of his wife. At last he and several friends met the band. Indian Juan was killed in the fight, and so was Fimbres' son.[48] Then Sonoran ranchers of the downslopes declared relentless war on the Apaches. They rode into a camp of squaws and heartlessly killed them all. One young girl managed to escape but was captured by an American two weeks later. She was taken to the jail at Casas Grandes where she was the object of curious inspection from everyone in town. Ultimately she died of malnutrition because she would eat nothing offered her and was buried in the Casas Grandes cemetery.

TURISMO, catering to tourists, has become a big-time, lucrative business in Mexico that in a twenty-year period has increased 700 per cent.[49] Almost forty-four million persons entered that country in 1959—94.6 per cent of them Americans. Hotels and auto courts, restaurants and bars, curio and handicraft shops, tour and guide services, entertainment houses and lines of transportation have reaped tremendous profits, with more promised for the future. The Bank of Mexico has estimated that in 1959 tourism brought $636,000,000 to the nation.

Mexico, eager to guard this twentieth-century Quivira, has gone all out to sell itself to the traveling public. She has dramatized her Indian heritage, with all its brilliant pageantry, folklore, and folk crafts, its archaeological monuments among the world's most impressive. The "quaint," the "charming," and the "exotic" have been emblazoned on travel posters. Magazine articles and Sunday supplements have dwelt on the great amount of local color for a little amount of money. A national tourist bureau has provided tons of maps and border regulations to stateside travel agencies. Supreme efforts have been made to offer the physical comforts which travelers, particularly Americans, expect. Unquestionably the campaign to increase tourism has paid off.

The paramount reason for the tide of American tourists to the south has been the highway construction program which now has brought four main paved arteries from central Mexico to the border. Americans are a people on wheels, and where roads go, they go. More than half the visitors to Mexico go by private car. Added inducements to travel in Mexico are the favorable rate of exchange, which helps stretch dollars, and the abrupt entrance into a totally different cultural atmosphere the moment the border is crossed.

Chihuahua, sitting right next to the States, was unable, except at Ciudad Juárez, to tap that tourist resource until the late forties. The road to the interior was too poor and exhausting to attract any but the most hardy travelers. Going to the city of Chihuahua was not a pleasure jaunt but an expedition, and Americans did not care that much. Those tourists who got beyond the borderland bistros seldom stopped off anywhere else in the state. Planes and trains carried their passengers straight through to Mexico City. Even Mexican tourists were not lured to Chihuahua, so far from centers of great population or from the seacoasts.

The highway south from Ciudad Juárez to the Chihuahua capital, virtually retracing the colonial Camino Real, was completed about 1948. Its extension to the Durango border came several years later. Even then, the northern Durango mountains slowed down construction, and for a long time remained the final area to be breached in a planned highway connecting Mexico from border to border. Sightseers from the United States' west coast and central states began to roll south beyond Ciudad Juárez through Chihuahua. Wise men made plans, for swimming-pool worship was about to reach the Chihuahua desert.

Motels and hotels with stylish pools sprouted along the highway, enough by 1960 to make Chihuahua seventh in the nation in number of hostelries.[50] The city of Chihuahua, where one motel was built at the site of the old bullring, where Americans of an earlier time were accustomed to stay, became the main stop.

In general, Chihuahua tourism, termed an industry without chimneys, has remained devoted to travelers en route to somewhere else. Chihuahuenses, who see precious dollars being carried away, now are analyzing local assets in the tourist field in the effort to decide what to do about it. They point to the beauties of the mountain scenery with the high waterfall of Basasiachi; the peaks of Romurachi in the central cordillera and Mohinera to the south with perpetual snow on its head, and palms at its feet; scattered Indian settlements and colonial missions; and vast canyons such as Oteros, Tararecúa, Cobre, and Urique. Because of the similarity of terrain, comparison between these mile-deep gashes and the Grand Canyon of the Colorado is inevitable, and contrast of the Sierra Madre Occidental's isolation to the accessibility by road, train, and plane to the Grand Canyon is sharp. The tourism developers call attention to numerous other physiographic features such as many caves and thermal springs which might be exploited but are not. They praise the climate which is not too unlike that found in tourist spots just north of the border. In an attempt to create interest in the state, the tourist bureau has organized regional fairs, jeep excursions, and a syle show of Tarahumara costumes modeled by socially prominent mestizo girls. The government has provided several points of interest in an archaeological and historical museum in Chihuahua and a newly opened archaeological zone at Casas Grandes.

Historical places in the capital, aside from the plaza, aqueduct, and cathedral, include the old San Francisco chapel where Hidalgo's urn was kept (next door to what is presently an ultramodern, new Sears Roebuck store) and the gloomy tower of Hidalgo's confinement. But Papá Hidalgo is an unknown to most Americans and therefore uninteresting. The one name which rings a bell with almost all travelers is that of Pancho Villa.

Since September 1956, an impressive statue of General Villa, seen at his best—astride a prancing horse—greets the traveler at the new northern approach of the city. He and his horse rear over a reflecting pool around whose rim are the names and dates of Villa conquests: San Andrés—August 28, 1913; Ciudad Juárez—November 15, 1913; Tierra Blanca—November 25, 1913; Ojinaga —January 10, 1914; Torreón—April 2, 1914; San Pedro de las Colonias, Paredón—May, 1914; Zacatecas—June 23, 1914. These are names and dates which have little meaning for outsiders but had a wealth of significance for norteños who were bursting feudalistic molds. Villa's home at 3004 10th Street on the northeastern slope of town has been opened to public tours, and one may meet his widow, María Luz Corral de Villa. And if the traveler cares to, he may go to the Panteón de la Regla to see where Villa wished to be buried. For a small contribution for the upkeep of the cemetery, a boy will guide one to the mausoleum which dominates the grounds and will shove aside planks covering a deep, and empty, subterranean crypt. Villa was romanticized in his lifetime by the peons. Now the upper class are joining in. Such is the power of turismo.*

Of tremendous significance to the tourist trade, and even more important to the general economy, has been the completion of the railroad from the northeast border town of Ojinaga through Chi-

---

* In New Mexico, Villa likewise has received recognition in a new state park at Columbus to mark the point of his raid and to call attention to the last hostile action by foreign troops within the United States.

huahua and the Sierra Madre Occidental to the Gulf of California. Such a transportation route has been a dream dating from the 1880's when Díaz granted Robert Owens the concession to put in a railroad from a socialist utopia he planned to establish at the bay of Topolobampo on the Sinaloa coast east through the mountains to connect with another set of rails planned from Chihuahua west. Owens' project failed. Creel abandoned his Chihuahua enterprise after reaching a station established at the edge of the sierra, and the Revolution wiped out hopes of any completion of a trans-sierra railroad. Gradually it came to be regarded as an impossible feat because of the roughness of the country.

In 1940 the Mexican government bought up the old Noroeste line which skirted the eastern slopes of the sierra north to Ciudad Juárez and the two spurs of the Kansas City, México, y Oriente line, one of which went from the city of Chihuahua east to Ojinaga (completed in 1928) and the other west to the station of Creel. The line was christened the Chihuahua al Pacífico. Engineers began to revive plans of traversing the mountains by rail as actual work on the line was begun in 1944. Because of chronic shortages of funds and the difficulties inherent in the route, progress was slow and work gradually ceased altogether. Then in 1952 President Ruiz Cortines decided to pour millions of pesos* and thousands of man-hours into finishing the railroad. Finally, eighty years after the original concession was granted, on November 21, 1961, President López Mateos rode with an official party from Chihuahua to the sea. The Chihuahua al Pacífico would stand as a monument to the men of the Revolution whose spirit, steadfastness, and brilliant engineering skill had made these rails a work of art.

Two hundred fifty-five kilometers of mountain country is crossed by the new line. Forty-five of these are through seventy-two tunnels, one of them at 1,823 meters being the longest in all of Latin America. Several of the tunnels are curved and there are many stretches of track sheltered above from rockslides, destructive during the rainy season. Twenty-seven bridges span chasms to

---

* Estimated total cost, one billion pesos. *México, Cincuenta Años de Revolución*, 1960, vol. II, 469.

connect neighboring mountains. The bridge over the Río Fuerte
is 500 meters in length, that over the Río Chínipas is 300 meters.
Some of the spans of steel and concrete are 150 meters high.[51]
Hairpin curves, switchbacks, and arcing loops are commonplace as
one drops off the plateau escarpment and goes down to sea level.
At the settlement of Temoris, three levels of track are visible from
one location. The tracks pass within fifty meters of the Divisadero,
an overlook on the Urique where six gorges may be viewed at
once. To accomplish these amazing works dozens of firms were involved. Some were engineers who contracted for the bridges or
tunnels, some supplied and creosoted ties, some operated the machinery. For the first time in the New World a new method of laying track, called vía electrica, was tried. Most of the materials used
in construction of the road and in manufacture of the railroad
cars came from Mexico.

The value of the Chihuahua al Pacífico cannot be accurately
known yet. At the present time, two freighters of a hundred cars
go in each direction biweekly hauling lumber, corn, and wheat
down to Sinaloa and bringing fruits and vegetables up to Chihuahua. Two other passenger cars make the run on alternate days
carrying tourists and mail. The tourist bureau has turned out
reams of publicity about the new attraction, with the result that
passage must be booked in advance. Undoubtedly when full-scale
utilization of the line is achieved, the iron route through the
sierra will have a profound effect on all of northern Mexico as
markets of the industrial eastern United States are made accessible
through a connection with the Atchison, Topeka, and Santa Fe
in Texas. There is agitation for making both Topolobampo on
the coast and Ojinaga on the Río Grande free ports to enable duty-
free goods to pass into the United States.[52] Within Mexico, the
railroad will link the industrialized northeast area of Mexico to
the agricultural northwest for their mutual benefit. And a tide of
travelers will come from the midwestern and southwestern United
States, bringing their precious dollars with them. For many, a train
ride will be a novelty; for all, this particular one will be unique
as it descends from the meseta central, through virgin mountains explored by only a few white men, into the gorge of the Río
Septentrión and out onto the cactus-covered Sinaloa foothills,

terminating on a great landlocked bay of the Pacific. Its completion commemorates almost exactly four and a half centuries of European occupation and influence.

Also Chihuahua is building highways in the knowledge that such improvements will aid both regional development and attract tourists. A new paved highway cuts southeast from Jiménez out across the Bolsón de Mapimí to Torreón, and another connecting Ojinaga to the capital will be completed in the near future. A road is planned from Nuevo Casas Grandes direct to Ciudad Juárez, and a second one from this region will follow the old Pershing Highway north to Columbus. In the mountains, lumbering roads, construction roads used during the building of the Chihuahua al Pacífico, and others penetrating the Indian realm are beginning to lace the once impenetrable massif.

With the furtherance of a system of automobile roads and railroads, Chihuahua will become enriched from tourist dollars. Americans will have the opportunity of seeing one of the most interesting and diversified Mexican states of the twenty-nine. Through such contact and intermingling, the scars of a century of misunderstanding may fade and the turbulence in this storehouse of storms may be solely climatic.

NOTES

NOTES TO CHAPTER ONE

1. Lister, 1958, 15-22, 112, records in detail the earliest man-made tools yet known in Chihuahua. For discussions of cultural content and distribution of the Desert Culture, see Jennings, 1957. For a historical interpretation of the archaeology of North America, see Willey and Phillips, 1955.

2. Lister, 1958; Mangelsdorf and Lister, 1958. Similar finds of corn-using cultures which presumably predated ceramics have been recorded at Bat Cave, New Mexico, and in the Mexican states of Tamaulipas and Puebla.

3. Dick, 1952, 158-63.

4. Mangelsdorf and Lister, 1956; Mangelsdorf *in* Lister, 1958, 96-108.

5. Lister, 1958. Mogollon culture north of the border is defined in Haury, 1936; Martin and Rinaldo, 1950, 1952, 1954; and Wheat, 1955.

6. For a résumé of architectural features of the Toltecs of central Mexico, see Marquina, 1951, and Peterson, 1959.

7. Under the direction of Charles C. Di Peso, the Amerind Foundation of Dragoon, Arizona, excavated at Casas Grandes from 1958 through 1961. The results of this work are now being prepared for publication.

8. Tribal distribution maps for northern Mexico are to be found in Beals, 1932, and Sauer, 1935. Both are limited in scope and do little to aid in placement of aboriginal Chihuahua peoples prior to white contact. Almada, 1945, 100, merely lists a sampling of tribal names. A map in Forbes, 1960, 31, gives the distribution of Apache peoples along the northern border of Mexico. Other references are Mecham, 1927, 13-18, and Pérez, 1942, 204-07.

9. Kelley, 1947.

10. Kelley, 1955.

11. Forbes, 1960, xix.

NOTES TO CHAPTER TWO

1. Almada, 1955a, 26-32; Bancroft, 1886, 102-11; Forbes, 1960, 42-47; Jordán, 1956, 33-43; Mecham, 1927, 58-133.

2. Mecham, 1927, 159-73.

3. Mecham, 1927, 223-25; Saravia, 1941, 204, 273-93.

4. West, 1949, 10-14.

5. Forbes, 1960, 49-55; Hammond, 1927, 7-8; Horgan, 1954, 153-54; Jordán, 1956, 46-51; Mecham, 1926a, 265-91.

6. Forbes, 1960, 4.

7. For a description of these conflicts, see Horgan, 1954, 113-36.

8. Forbes 1960, 55-65; Hammond, 1927, 8-9; Horgan, 1954, 154-57; Jordán, 1956, 51-52; Mecham, 1926b, 114-38.

9. Forbes, 1960, 76-106; Hammond, 1927, 13-95; Hammond and Rey, 1953, 42-336; Horgan, 1938, 3-27; Horgan, 1954, 160-66; Jordán, 1956, 53-64.

10. Hackett, 1923, 227-29; Hammond, 1927, 19; Hammond and Rey, 1953, 42-57.

11. Hammond, 1923, 78; Hammond and Rey, 1953, 1032-34.

12. Villagrá, 1933, 99-103.

13. Villagrá, 1933, 110.

14. Villagrá, 1933, 129-37.

15. Decorme, 1941, and Dunn, 1944, are the two best sources for biographical data on the Jesuits in northern Mexico. Both writers are themselves Jesuits and their treatment therefore is sympathetic and perhaps biased. Bolton, 1939, presents a more objective appraisal of the order and its accomplishments in missionization of the natives and in holding the political frontier.

16. Bancroft, 1886, 319-24, 328-29; Saravia, 1954, 45-73, 169-215.

17. Bancroft, 1886, 331.

18. Jordán, 1956, 74-78; Terrazas, 1940, 314-17, 340-51.

19. Rocha, 1938a, 42-45; 1938c, 214-16, 238. For a map of the Parral mining area, see West, 1949, opposite 5, text 12-13.

20. Porras, 1952, 599.

21. Forbes, 1960, 34. Jordán, 1956, 93, mentions slaves being taken in the Conchos district. West, 1949, 49, indicates that some Concho worked the mines under encomienda.

22. Jordán, 1956, 95.

23. Bancroft, 1886, 346.

24. Schmiedehaus, 1946, 46-49.

25. Bolton, 1939, 182-89.

26. For a detailed study of the religious and secular trade of the seventeenth and eighteenth centuries between central Mexico and the north, see Bloom, 1937, and Moorhead, 1958. Horgan, 1954, 229-30 discusses the Franciscan freight service.

27. Forbes, 1960, 36.

28. Bancroft, 1886, 350; Rocha, 1939c, 53; 1939d, 166-73, 193.

29. Forbes, 1960, 141-43, believes the Nueva Vizcaya rebellions may have triggered rebellion in New Mexico.

30. Almada, 1955a, 65-69; Bancroft, 1886, 352-60; Saravia, 1954, 265-330, describe various Tarahumara uprisings of the last half of the seventeenth century.

31. Jordán, 1956, 102-106.

32. Jordán, 1956, 107-14.

33. West, 1949, 54-55.

34. Almada, 1955a, 73-74; Saravia, 1954, 331-58.

35. Terrazas, 1940b, 375-77, 408-11.

36. Rocha, 1942, 197-202.

37. Bolio, 1956, 874-75; Schmiedehaus, 1942, 14-17; Valdéz, 1941, 70-73.

38. Porras Muñoz, 1947, 120-26.

39. Forbes, 1960, 200-206.

40. Archives of Hidalgo del Parral.

41. Bancroft, 1886, 371-72; Jordán, 1956, 151-53.

42. Horgan, 1954, 304.

43. Forbes, 1960, 211-16; Underhill, 1953, 241-51.

44. Forbes, 1960, 24, 281, doubts that the Apache were predatory prehistorically.

45. Forbes, 1960, 149.

46. Almada, 1939e, 5-15; Chávez, 1939b, 399-405; 1955, 815-20; Jordán, 1956, 179-89.

47. Bancroft, 1886, 582; Jordán, 1956, 168.

48. Almada, 1938a, 6-10; 1943, 419-30; 1955a, 89-92; Jordán, 1956, 154-63; Lozano, 1955, 843-46; Ramírez Caloca, 1952, 10.

49. Bancroft, 1886, 670-71; Terrazas, 1938, 148-49, 158.

50. Hernández Rodríguez, 1939c, 395-98, 423.

51. Arellano Schetelig, 1939g, 256-63.

52. Arriguanga y Peón, 1955, 793.

53. Archives of Hidalgo del Parral.

54. Bancroft, 1886, 585, 598; Ramírez Caloca, 1952, 37.

55. Bancroft, 1886, 680.

56. Rex Gerald, of the Texas Western Museum, El Paso, has made a recent archaeological survey of the northern presidios in which he has located and mapped eleven stations. Personal communication.

57. Almada, 1938b, 36-41; Bancroft, 1886, 670-71; Jordán, 1956, 190-207.

58. Barri, 1941, 91-94.

59. Almada, 1955a, 115-20; Arellano Schetelig, 1938b, 116-23, 131.

60. Archives of Hidalgo del Parral.

61. Cordero y Bustamante, 1944, 112-23, 148-60.

62. Beltrán, *et al*, 1960, v. I, 46.

63. For a description of mining and processing of ores in colonial Nueva Vizcaya, see West, 1949. For picture of *arrastre*, see Twitchell, v. II, 89. Gregg, 1954, 294-97, gives a good description of colonial mining as he observed it in northern Mexico.

NOTES TO CHAPTER THREE

1. Arellano Schetelig, 1939e, 60-64; 1939f, 98-101, 144.

2. Arellano Schetelig, 1938a, 74-84, 94.

3. Almada, 1955a, 137.

4. Almada, 1955a, 149-50.

5. Almada, 1955a, 146-47; Arellano Schetelig, 1939b, 332-35; Fernandez Perea, 1938, 134-39; Jordán, 1956, 211-18.

6. Almada, 1955a, 145.

7. Lozano, 1949a, 225-27; Rasura, 1955, 870-72.

8. Almada, 1944, 80-84; 1955a, 154.

9. Almada, 1944, 178-83.

10. Almada, 1944, 178.

11. Arellano Schetelig, 1938c, 159-65.

12. Almada, 1944, 220-25.

13. Almada, 1955a, 190.

14. Arellano Schetelig, 1939d, 408-12.

15. Ramírez Caloca, 1952, 10.

16. Kendall, 1929, 579.

17. Almada, 1939a, 289-90; Arellano Schetelig, 1939f, 136-43, 151; Ramírez Caloca, 1952, 13.

18. Almada, 1938d, 108-11.

19. Hernández Rodríguez, 1939d, 65-67.

20. Pattie, 1905, 154.

21. Underhill, 1953, 257.

22. Almada, 1939e, 10.

23. Bieber, 1937, 357-58; Connelley, 1907, 388-89; Kendall, 1929, 57.

24. Almada, 1955a, 139; Hollon, 1949, 147; Horgan, 1954, 396-99.

25. Hollon, 1949, 149-57; Horgan, 1954, 403-18.

26. Connelley, 1907, 630-31; Gregg, 1954, 9-21, 264-78, 297-314, 331-45; Horgan, 1954, 495-504.

27. Bloom, 1938, 215.

28. Bieber, 1938, 31-37.

29. Gregg, 1954, 303-304.

30. Falconer, 1930; Horgan, 1953, 569-85; Kendall, 1929.

31. Connelley, 1907, 129-220; Horgan, 1954, 116-36.

32. Webb, 1931, 179-278.

33. Hafen, 1950, 123-59.

34. Gregg, 1905, 307.

35. Gregg, 1905, 306-308.

36. Almada, 1955a, 224-25; Connelley, 1907, 360-486; De Voto, 1943, 381-85, 391-400, 402-407; Gibson, 1935, 321-63; Horgan, 1954, 736-53, 768-69; Jaurrieta, 1950, 413-20; Jordán, 1956, 231-242; Priestley, 1938, 309.

37. Hughes, 1848, fn. 115-16.

38. For photograph of flag, see Gibson, 1935, 301.

39. Hughes, 1848, 115-16.

40. Fulton, 1944, 79-130.

41. Bieber, 1937, 358.

42. De Voto, 1943, 376.

43. Connelley, 1907, 360-486; Cooke, 1938, 65-240.

44. Jordán, 1956, 243-44.

45. Horgan, 1954, 784-87.

46. Bieber, 1937, 356.

47. Bieber, 1937, 159-206, map; Evans, 1945, 43-144.

48. Almada, 1955a, 236.

49. Almada, 1955a, 241-42; Jordán, 1956, 249-50.

50. Ramírez Caloca, 1944, 245-60; 1952, 38.

51. Escobar, 1944a, 104-105.

52. Jordán, 1956, 257-58.

53. Jordán, 1956, 260.

54. Jordán, 1956, 261-65.

55. Fuentes Mares, 1954, further expounds the belief that Juárez was not genuinely concerned with the problems of the norteños.

56. Almada, 1955a, 269.

57. Ayala, 1942, 131-34; Jordán, 1956, 266-74.

58. A description of this affair is given by Juan de Dios Peza in his Memorias and is reproduced in Boletín, SCEH, III, 7, 1941, 88-91.

59. Almada, 1955a, 277-80.

60. Almada, 1947, 90-99.

61. Ramírez Caloca, 1952, 21.

62. Ramírez Caloca, 1952, 62.

63. Briones Martínez, 1942, 212-15.

64. Almada, 1939d, 391-94; 1955a, 296.

65. Fuentes Mares, 1954, gives an impassioned defense of Terrazas.

66. Irrab, 1938a, 11-16.

67. Almada, 1955a, 131-32.

68. Fuentes Mares, 1954, 279-83.

69. Valadés, 1948, 239, 223.

70. For a contemporary photograph of a Terrazas hacienda, see Brenner, 1943, plate 38.

71. For a biography of Luis Zuloaga, see Ahumada, 1939f.

72. Underhill, 1953, 247.

73. Almada, 1939e, 14-15; Chávez, 1939a, 336-40, 346; 1939b, 361-67, 376-77; 1943, 437-57, 481-504; Escobar, 1944b, 216-17; Jordán, 1956, 273-89.

74. Almada, 1955a, 167-71.

75. Valadés, 1948, 20.

76. Almada, 1955a, 328.

77. Irogoyen, 1942b, 188-96.

78. Ramírez Caloca, 1952, 12.

79. Almada, 1945, 333-34; Valadés, 1948, 303-304.

80. Ramírez Caloca, 1952, 43.

81. Almada, 1955a, 331.

82. Valadés, 1948, 307.

83. Almada, 1945, 264; 1955a, 335.

84. Valadés, 1948, 258.

85. For photograph, see Brenner, 1943, plate 24.

86. Almada, 1955a, 375.

87. Almada, 1955a, 329-30.

88. Almada, 1955a, 338.

89. Jordán, 1956, 290-308.

90. Fuentes Mares, 1954, 215-27.

91. Saravia, 1954, 272-76; Terrazas, 1940a, 340-51.

92. Arellano Schetelig, 1941, 109-14; 1943, 471-76.

93. Almada, 1945, 123-24; 325-26; Hatch, 1954, 1-158; Jordán, 1956, 385-88.

94. Lumholtz, 1902, v. 1.

95. Lumholtz, 1902, v. 1, 79.

96. Almada, 1955a, 372.

97. Fuentes Mares, 1954, 231-33.

98. Almada, 1946, 1-4; 1955b, 862-64; Schuster, 1947, 33-35.

99. Almada, 1955a, 370-71; Ramírez Caloca, 1952, 43.

100. Almada, 1955a, 371; Briones Martínez, 1955, 852-53; Lozano, 1949, 333-41.

NOTES TO CHAPTER FOUR

1. Brady, 1955, 92-93; Priestley, 1938, 394-410.
2. Almada, 1955a, 378-79.
3. Almada, 1955a, 381.
4. Beals, 1932; Brady, 1955; Brenner, 1943; Clendenen, 1961; Herring, 1955; Muñoz, 1931; Pinchon, 1933; Schuster, 1947; Terrazas, 1944, 1946, 1949, 1950, 1952, 1953, 1954, 1955; Quirk, 1960. As controversial a figure as Villa inspired many conflicting stories and interpretations. Our picture is based upon a composite taken from sources both Mexican and American and hence reflects the biases of each.
5. Almada, 1955a, 383; Fuentes Mares, 1954, 246.
6. Schuster, 1947, 74-86.
7. Priestley, 1938, 403.
8. Almada, 1955a, 392-93.
9. Almada, 1946, 1-17; Ramírez Caloca, 1952, 43-44.
10. Clenenden, 1961, 18.
11. Almada, 1955a, 395.
12. Hatch, 1954, 159-227.
13. Brady, 1955, 95-96; Clendenen, 1961, 23-25; Schuster, 1947, 95.
14. Schuster, 1947, 104-107.
15. For the names of the eight companions, see Puente, 1957, 69.
16. Fuentes Mares, 1954, 251, 267.
17. Fuentes Mares, 1954, 256.
18. Lozano, 1949, 176-80.
19. Almada, 1955a, 404.
20. Terrazas, 1944-55 (1950), 362-65, 377-81.
21. Schuster, 1947, 132; Terrazas, 1944-55 (1952), 561-64.
22. Puente, 1957, 93.
23. For a photograph of Villa leading a mounted charge, see Brenner, 1943, plate 86.
24. Campobello, 1940, 63-73.
25. Schuster, 1947, 138.
26. Quirk, 1960, 27.
27. Quirk, 1960, 283-84.
28. Puente, 1957, 127.
29. Brady, 1955, 112-27; Clendenen, 1961, 209-14; Quirk, 1960.
30. Clendenen, 1961, 225-27; Salinas Carranza, 1936, 80-81.
31. Campobello, 1940, 133.
32. Calzadíaz Berrera, 1960, 17-19.
33. Almada, 1955a, 414.
34. Muñoz, 1931, 174.

35. Brady, 1955, 128-45; Calzadíaz Barrera, 1960, 7-177; Horgan, 1954, 904-34; Muñoz, 1931, 176-278; Schuster, 1947, 213-31. Tompkins, 1934, gives the official U.S. Army version of the attack and pursuit, and his account is the basis of this review.

36. Salinas Carranza, 1936, 92.

37. Calzadíaz Barrera, 1960, 34-37.

38. Calzadíaz Barrera, 1960, 39-40.

39. Salinas Carranza, 1936, 101-11.

40. Calzadíaz Barrera, 1960, 153-75.

41. Salinas Carranza, 1938, 316.

42. Campobello, 1940, 131-32; Porras Muñoz, 1953, 637-38; Salinas Carranza, 1938, 164-66.

43. Pérez, 1955, 865-67; Schuster, 1947, 224.

44. Clendenen, 1961, 294-95.

45. Almada, 1955a, 423; Cervantes, 1960, 41.

46. Dulles, 1961, 68.

NOTES TO CHAPTER FIVE

1. Almada, 1955a, 411.

2. Lara, 1954.

3. Fuentes Mares, 1954, 257-58.

4. Brady, 1955, 153-55.

5. Brady, 1955, 161.

6. *México, Cincuenta Años de Revolución*, 1960, Vol. I, 102.

7. *México, Cincuenta Años de Revolución*, 1960, Vol. I, 99.

8. Almada, 1945, 124-28; 1955a, 430-31; Jordán, 1956, 369-73, 463-70; Schmiedehaus, 1939, 241-46; 1947, 131-33.

9. Almada, 1945, 81, 128.

10. Jordán, 1956, 378-81.

11. Jordán, 1956, 380.

12. Jordán, 1956, 459.

13. *México, Cincuenta Años de Revolución*, 1960, Vol. I, 352.

14. *Informe de Gobierno*, No. 4. Irrigación, 1960.

15. *México, Cincuenta Años de Revolución*, 1960, Vol. II, 4.

16. *México, Cincuenta Años de Revolución*, 1960, Vol. I, 350.

17. Almada, 1945, 269-70; James, 1959, 619; Jordán, 1956, 352-53; *México, Cincuenta Años de Revolución*, 1960, Vol. I, 350.

18. *Informe de Gobierno*, No. 4. Irrigación, 1960.

19. *México, Cincuenta Años de Revolución*, 1960, Vol. I, 126-28.

20. *México, Cincuenta Años de Revolución*, 1960, Vol. I, 134-36; *Turismo*, January 1961, 83-84.

21. *Turismo*, January 1961, 83-84.

22. *Turismo*, January 1961, 4-5.

23. *Informe de Gobierno*, No. 4, 1960. Pavimentación y Luz Mercurial, Vivienda Popular y Pensiones, Educación, Presa Chihuahua.

24. Jordán, 1956, 356-59.

25. Almada, 1955a, 389; Cardona, 1949, 342-53.

26. *Turismo*, January 1961, 84.

27. *México, Cincuenta Años de Revolución*, 1960, Vol. I, 60.

28. *México, Cincuenta Años de Revolución*, 1960, Vol. I, 56.

29. Almada, 1945, 279-84.

30. *Turismo*, June 1960, 20-24, 27-31.

31. Jordán, 1956, 373-76.

32. Almada, 1945, 102; 1955a, 14-16; Bennett and Zingg, 1935, 355-83; *Boletín Indigenista*, Vol. XII, No. 3, 1952; de la Peña, 1946, 503-18; Gonzalez, 1953, 107-17; Schmiedehaus, 1940, 370-74.

33. Basuri, 1940, 299-352.

34. Brandt, 1948, 394.

35. For a picture of a modern Tarahumara male, see the cover of *Natural History*, November 1948.

36. Almada, 1945, 110-15.

37. For a discussion of the indigenista movement over all of Mexico, see Beltran, *et al*, 1960, Vol. II, 163-202.

38. Almada, 1945, 116-22; Jordán, 1956, 415-28.

39. *Acción Indigenista*, No. 98, 1961; Aguirre Beltrán, 1955; *Boletín Indigenista*, Vol. XX, No. 1, 1960; Vol. XIX, No. 2, 1959; Vol. XII, No. 3, 1952.

40. *Acción Indigenista*, No. 98, 1961.

41. *Acción Indigenista*, No. 87, 1960.

42. *Acción Indigenista*, No. 99, 1961.

43. *Acción Indigenista*, No. 97, 1961.

44. *Acción Indigenista*, No. 96, 1961.

45. *Turismo*, January 1960, 47.

46. Almada, 1945, 102; 1955a, 16.

47. Almada, 1945, 102; 1955a, 17.

48. Ramírez Caloca, 1946, 30-35.

49. *México, Cincuenta Años de Revolución*, 1960, Vol. II, 292.

50. *México, Cincuenta Años de Revolución*, 1960, Vol. II, 300.

51. *México, Cincuenta Años de Revolución*, 1960, Vol. II, 468-69; *Turismo*, August 1960, No. 116, 5-25.

52. *Turismo*, October 1961, No. 119, 105-11.

GLOSSARY

adelantado: office and title given to conquerors of new lands; governorship granted by the King to rule over conquered territory

agujón: sighting device in Colonial period, now a hatpin

alcalde: mayor

alfombrilla: toxic plant harmful to cattle

alhóndiga: granary

altiplano: plateau

anda: move along

arriero: muleteer

arroba: Spanish weight equal to 25.36 pounds

ate: fruit paste

audiencia: highest judicial tribunal during the colonial period

ayuntamiento: municipal corporation

baldío: public land

bandolera: bandoleer

barra: bar or ingot of gold or silver

barranca: canyon

blancos: whites

blanquillos: whitish: name given the provincial dragoons because of the white facings of their jacket lapels

bonapartista: partisan of Napoleon Bonaparte

brujería: witchcraft

buscador: prospector

caballería: tract of land given to a soldier in a conquered area

caballero: nobleman; gentleman

cabildo: municipal council

caciquismo: bossism

callista: partisan of Plutarco Calles

campesino: countryman; rural

candelilla: Euphorbia antisyphilitica: characteristic plant of the Chihuahua desert yielding a pale green milk used in candle making

cantón: region or district

carbonero: charcoal maker

cárcel: jail

carnicero: butcher

carrancista: partisan of Venustiano Carranza

carreta: long, narrow cart

casa consistorial: town hall

casa de gobierno: government building

casas blancas: white houses

casita: little house

caudillo: dictator or boss

cazuela: earthen pan or crock

cédula: decree

charrada: country dance

charro: Mexican cowboy who wears showy or flashy clothing

chinos: Chinese

Chihuahuenses: people of Chihuahua

ciudad: city

cobija: shawl

colonias agrícolas: agricultural developments

comandancia: district or province of a commander

comandante general: commander general

comisario: deputy; commissioner

compañeros: friends

compañías deslindadores: boundary companies

compañías patrióticas: patriotic companies

corregidor: magistrate of a city or territory

corrido: song

cristeros: a priest-led group who rebelled in retaliation to President Calles' anti-clerical steps in 1926

cuartelada: military coup d'état

denuncia: miner's claim

Día de la Raza: Day of the Race; celebration of Columbus' discovery of America, October 12

diligencia: stagecoach

ejidatario: owner of an ejido

ejido: communal land granted to a city or village

el camino del doctor: the doctor's road

empanada: meat pie

encomienda: grant of Indians within a specified area with the obligation to Christianize them and defend them and the right to demand labor or tribute from them in return

fernandino: partisan of King Ferdinand VII

fierro: brand

gachupín: a person of Spanish blood born in Spain

ganadería: cattle ranch

gran bandido: great bandit

gran cacique: head man or chief

gran hombre: great man

granja: farm

grito: shout; cry of rebellion during the Revolution

guía: permit or letter of safe conduct proving that the carrier had paid customs and duty at the customhouse

hacendado: owner of a hacienda

haciendas de beneficio: reduction works

hechicero: sorcerer

hectare: a surface measurement equal to 2.471 acres

hijo: son

Hispanidad: a spirit of cultural unity with Spain

huapango: dance

huertismo: Huertism

huertista: partisan of Adolfo de la Huerta

huisache: botanically, a sponge tree; in northern Mexico, used as a general term to indicate thorny desert plant growth

jacal: hut made of a wickerwork of poles plastered over with mud

jefe: chief

jefe político: political chief

jején: gnat

jornada: journey

juarista: partisan of Benito Juárez

ladrón: robber

latifundismo: the occurrence of many landed estates

latifundista: owner of a large landed estate

lechuguilla: Agave lechuguilla; very abundant in the Chihuahuan desert and prized for its tough fibers

ley fuga: law of flight; political prisoners during the Díaz period were shot on the pretext they were attempting to escape

maderista: partisan of Francisco I. Madero

madroño: an evergreen tree with red berries

magonista: partisan of Ricardo and Enrico Flores Magón

maíz: maize or Indian corn

marco: unit of weight for gold and silver equal to approximately eight ounces *mayorazgo:* entailed estate

mercado: market

meseta central: central plateau

mole: pungent sauce made of chile, chocolate, ground raisins, and many spices, usually served on special feast days

mordida: bribe

muerte a huertismo: death to Huertism

municipio: municipality

muy macho: very masculine

norteño: northerner

Nueva Viscaya: New Biscay; the area comprising the states of Durango, Chihuahua, and portions of Sinaloa and Coahuila.

obregonista: partisan of Alvaro Obregón

ojo: spring (water); eye

olla: clay jar; colloquially it can mean chuckhole

orozquismo: Orozcoism

padres prietos: name given the Jesuit priests (the Franciscans wore brown)

parroquia: parish church

patrón: landlord or owner

Pax Porfiriana: the "peace" of President Porfirio Díaz

pelado: penniless

peonía: tract of land given to a soldier in a conquered area

pepita: pumpkin seed

peso: Mexican dollar

petate: palm or rush mat

pinole: a drink made of ground parched corn, water, and sugar

pobrecitos: poor little people

porfirismo: domination by Porfirio Díaz

portal: roofed portico

Primer Jefe: First Chief

pronunciamiento: pronouncement, sometimes proclaiming insurrection

pueblos de los indios: Indian towns

punche: a plant resembling tobacco

Qué lástima: what a pity

Quién sabe: who knows

quintal: Spanish weight equal to 220.45 pounds

ranchería: settlement

rancho: ranch

real: Spanish coin equal to twelve and one-half cents

real de minas: mining district

repartimiento: distribution of Indians for working in Spanish settlements

rincon: narrow valley

rurales: rural police force

sacerdote: priest

santanista: partisan of Antonio López de Santa Ana

sierra madre: mother mountains. In northwestern Mexico the cordillera which separates the west coat from the high central plateau is called Sierra Madre Occidental. Paralleling this range to the east is the Sierra Madre Oriental.

soldado: soldier

tacubayista: partisan of Félix Zuloaga and the Plan of Tacubaya

tecomaca: herb used to cure sciatica

tepache: a slightly fermented pineapple drink

terracismo: control by Terrazas

tesgüinadas: a party at which tesguino is served

tesgüino: an intoxicating drink

tianguis: herb used for fever

tienda de raya: master's store on the hacienda where employees were compelled to buy their necessities

tierra caliente: hot land
tierra fría: cold land
tierra templada: temperate land
tío vivo: merry-go-round
travesía: crossing
trinchera: rock-held terrace
troje: barn
turismo: tourism

valle: valley
vara: measurement equal to thirty-three inches
vega: meadow
veinte de noviembre: November 20
veinticinco de marzo: March 25

venga a la presa: come to the dam
verdad: true; isn't that so?
villa: town
villista: partisan of Pancho Villa
visitador: inspector-general

yanqui: American (United States)
ya vienen: they are coming
yerba del oso: herb used to break a fever
yerba de San Nicolás: herb used for snakebite

zapatista: partisan of Emiliano Zapata
zócalo: public square

BIBLIOGRAPHY

Abert, J. W.
 1848   *Report of J. W. Abert on his Examination of New Mexico in the Years 1846-47.* 30 Cong., 1 Sess. Ex. Doc. 41. Wendell and Van Benthyusen Printers, Washington.

Acción Indigenista (Monthly Newsletters, Instituto Nacional Indigenista)
 1960   September. No. 87.
 1960   December. No. 90.
 1961   January. No. 91.
 1961   February. No. 92.
 1961   June. No. 96.
 1961   July. No. 97.
 1961   August. No. 98.
 1961   September. No. 99.

Aguirre Beltrán, Gonzalo
 1955   "A Theory of Regional Integration: The Coordinating Centers," *América Indígena,* Vol. XV, No. 1. México.

Alegre, P. Francisco Javier
 1841   *Historia de la Compañía de Jesús en Nueva España.* 3 vols. Imprenta de J.M. Lara, México.

Almada, Francisco R.
 1927   *Diccionario de Historia, Geografía, y Biografía Chihuahuenses.* Chihuahua.

 1937   *Apuntes Históricos de la Región de Chínipas.* Chihuahua.

 1938a "La Fundación de la Ciudad de Chihuahua," *Boletín, Sociedad Chihuahuaense de Estudios Históricos* (hereafter cited as *B-SCEH*), Vol. I, no. 1.

 1938b "La Comandancia General de Provincias Internas," *B-SCEH*, Vol. I, No. 2.

 1938c "El Archivo de la Comandancia General de Provincias Internas," *B-SCEH*, Vol. I, No. 3.

 1938d "La Imprenta y el Periodismo en Chihuahua," *B-SCEH*, Vol. I, No. 4; pt. 2, Vol. I, No. 5; pt. 3, Vol. I, No. 7; pt. 4, Vol. I, No. 8.

 1938e *La Rebelión de Tomochi.* Chihuahua.

 1939a "El Aniversario del Instituto," *B-SCEH*, Vol. I, No. 9.

1939b "Lista de Alcaldes de la Villa de San Felipe el Real de Chihuahua," *B-SCEH*, Vol. I, No. 10.

1939c "Etimología de la Palabra Chihuahua," *B-SCEH*, Vol. I, No. 10.

1939d "La Batalla de Tabalaopa," *B-SCEH*, Vol. I, No. 12.

1939e "Los Apaches," *B-SCEH*, Vol. II, No. 1.

1939f- "Gobernadores del Estado," B-SCEH, Vol. II, No. 1, No. 3,
1942   No. 4, No. 5, No. 6, No. 8-9, No. 12; Vol. III, No. 1-3, 1940; Vol. III, No. 4-6, No. 7, No. 8, No. 9, 1941; Vol. IV, No. 3, No. 5, 1942.

1939g "Archivos Perdidos," B-SCEH, Vol. II, No. 7.

1941 "El Grito de la Independencia, 1810-1941," *B-SCEH*, Vol. III, No. 12.

1943 "Los Primeros Pobladores de Santa Eulalia y San Felipe de Cuellar," *B-SCEH*, Vol. IV, No. 11.

1944 "Sucesos y Recuerdos de la Independencia en Chihuahua," *B-SCEH*, Vol. V, No. 2, No. 3, No. 5, No. 6.

1945 *Geografía del Estado de Chihuahua.* Chihuahua.

1946 "Ciudad Juárez al Través de la Revolución Mexicana," *B-SCEH*, Vol. VI, No. 1.

1947 "El Presidente Juárez en el Villa de Paso del Norte," *B-SCEH*, Vol. VI, No. 3.

1949a "Las Víctimas de Pinos Altos," *B-SCEH*, Vol. VI, No. 7.

1949b "La Capilla de Santa Rita," *B-SCEH*, Vol. VI, No. 9.

1954 "Etimología de la Palabra Chihuahua," *B-SCEH*, Vol. VIII, No. 7.

1955a *Resumen de Historia del Estado de Chihuahua.* Chihuahua.

1955b "La Entrevista Díaz-Taft," *B-SCEH*, Vol. IX, No. 6.

Amador y Trias de Norena, Teresa

1940 "Algunas Notas Bibliográficas del Gral. Angel Trías," *B-SCEH*, Vol. III, No. 1-3.

Archives de Hidalgo del Parral. (Unpublished). Parral, Chihuahua.

Arellano Schetelig, Lorenzo

1938a "El Brigadier Comt. Gral. Don Nemesio Salcedo y Salcedo. Bendiciones Nupciales en 1806," *B-SCEH*, Vol. I, No. 3.

1938b "Jesuitas," *B-SCEH*, Vol. I, No. 4.

1938c "Los Restos de los Primeros Caudillos de la Independencia," *B-SCEH*, Vol. I, No. 5.

1939a "Bautismo del Insurgente Don Pedro Elias Bean," *B-SCEH*, Vol. I, No. 8.

1939b "Los Prisioneros en Chihuahua en Julio de 1811," *B-SCEH*, Vol. I, No. 10.

332 CHIHUAHUA

1939c "Juegos Prohibidos," *B-SCEH*, Vol. I, No. 11.
1939d "Don Melchor Guaspé," *B-SCEH*, Vol. I, No. 12.
1939e "Chihuahua en 1810," *B-SCEH*, Vol. II, No. 2, No. 3.
1939f "El Instituto Científico y Literario del Estado," *B-SCEH*, Vol. II, No. 4, No. 5, No. 6.
1939g "La Catedral de Chihuahua. Altar Mayor y Colaterales," *B-SCEH*, Vol. II, No. 7.
1940a "Las Elecciones de Alcaldes en 1740," *B-SCEH*, Vol. II, No. 10-11.
1940b "A Propósito de un Centenario," *B-SCEH*, Vol. III, No. 1-3.
1941 "Las Fiestas de Santa Rita," *B-SCEH*, Vol. III, No. 8.
1943 "Origen, Tradición y Leyenda de la Feria de Santa Rita," *B-SCEH*, Vol. IV, No. 12.

Arreola, Victor M.
1961 "The 'Chihuahua al Pacífico' Railroad, a Gate to the Sea," *Turismo*, No. 119.

Arriguniga y Peon, Joaquín
1955 "Estudios Etnográfico-Social de la Ciudad de Chihuahua, Durante la Colonia," *B-SCEH*, Vol. VIII, No. 12; Vol. IX, No. 1.

Ayala, Manuel
1942 "Algo sobre la Peregrinación del Presidente Juárez y sus Ministros en el Estado de Chihuahua," *B-SCEH*, Vol. IV, No. 4.

Bancroft, Hubert Howe
1884 *History of the North Mexican States and Texas, 1531-1800.* A. L. Bancroft and Company, San Francisco.
1889 *History of Arizona and New Mexico, 1530-1888.* The History Company, Pub., San Francisco.

Bandelier, Adolphe F.
1884 *Final Report of Investigations Among the Indians of the Southwestern United States.* Vol. II. Papers of the Archaeology Institute of America.

Barri, Leon
1939 "Documentos sobre la Fundación del Colegio de los Jesuitas en Chihuahua," *B-SCEH*, pt. 1, Vol. II, No. 1; pt. 2, No. 2; pt. 3, No. 4.
1941 "Introducción al Bando del Caballero de Croix," *B-SCEH*, Vol. III, No. 7.
1942 "Acta de la Fundación de Chihuahua," *B-SCEH*, Vol. IV, No. 1.

Basauri, Carlos
1940 *La Población Indígena de México.* Tomo I. Secretaría de Educación Pública, México.

Beals, Carleton
1923 *Mexico, an Interpretation.* B. W. Huebsch, New York.
Beals, Ralph L.
1932 "The Comparative Ethnology of Northern Mexico Before 1750," *Ibero-Americana,* Vol. 2. Berkeley.
Bennett, Wendell C., and Robert M. Zingg
1935 *The Tarahumara.* University of Chicago Press, Chicago.
Bieber, Ralph P., ed.
1937 *Southern Trails to California in 1849. Letter and Journal of John E. Durivage.* The Arthur H. Clark Company, Glendale, California.
1938 *Exploring Southwestern Trails, 1846-54. Cooke's Journal.* The Arthur H. Clark Company, Glendale, California.
Blackiston, A. H.
1905 "Cliff Dwellings of Northern Mexico," *Records of the Past,* Vol. IV.
1906 "Cliff Ruins of Cave Valley, Northern Mexico," *Records of the Past,* Vol. V.
1909 "Recently Discovered Cliff Dwellings of the Sierra Madres," *Records of the Past,* Vol. VIII.
Bloom, L. B.
1937 "The Chihuahua Highway," *New Mexico Historical Review.* July.
Boletín Indigenista (Unsigned articles and statements of progress)
1952 Vol. XII, No. 3.
1959 Vol. XIX, No. 2.
1960 Vol. XX, No. 1.
Bolio, Clemente
1956 "Nuestra Antigua Parroquia de Guadalupe," *B-SCEH,* Vol. IX, No. 7.
Bolton, Herbert E.
1939 *Wider Horizons of American History.* D. Appleton-Century, New York.
Brady, Haldeen
1955 *Cock of the Walk, the Legend of Pancho Villa.* University of New Mexico Press, Albuquerque.
Bradt, George McClellan
1948 "The Tarahumaras, Twentieth Century Cave Dwellers," *Natural History,* July. New York.
Brand, Donald D.
n.d. The Historical Geography of Northwestern Chihuahua. Ph.D. thesis, University of California, Berkeley (1933).

1937 "The Natural Landscape of Northwestern Chihuahua," *University of New Mexico Geological Series*, Vol. 5, No. 2. Albuquerque.

1943 "The Chihuahua Culture Complex," *New Mexico Anthropologist*, Vol. VI-VII, No. 3. Albuquerque.

Brena Ponce, Guadalupe

1956 "Monografía de la Isla del Córdoba," *B-SCEH*, Vol. IX, No. 7.

Brenner, Anita

1943 *The Wind That Swept Mexico*. Harper and Brothers, New York.

Briones Martínez, Esteban

1942 "¿Cuando se Erigio en Ciudad la Villa de Paso del Norte Tomando el Nombre de Ciudad Juárez?" *B-SCEH*, Vol. IV, No. 5.

1955 "Praxedis G. Guerrero," *B-SCEH*, Vol. IX, No. 5.

Brondo Whitt, E.

1940 *La División del Norte (1914)*. Editorial Lumen, México.

Call, Tomme Clark

1953 *The Mexican Venture*. Oxford University Press, New York.

Calzadíaz Barrera, Alberto

1960 *Villa Contra Todo Y . . .* Editorial Libros de México, S.A., México.

Campobello, Nellie

1940 *Apuntes sobre la vida Militar de Francisco Villa*. Edición y Distribución Ibero-Americana de Publicaciones, S.A., México.

Cardona, Manuel L.

1949 "El Chamizal," *B-SCEH*, Vol. VI, No. 12.

Cervantes, Federico

1960 "Felipe Angeles," *Turismo*, No. 116.

Chávez, José Carlos

1939a "Extinción de los Apaches," *B-SCEH*, Vol. 1, No. 10.

1939b "Clamor de los Papigochis del Siglo XVIII por los Constantes Ataques de los Apaches," *B-SCEH*, Vol. I, No. 12.

1943 "Peleando en Tomochi," *B-SCEH*, Vol. IV, No. 11-12.

1947 "The Coat of Arms of Chihuahua," *B-SCEH*, Vol. VI, No. 3.

1949 "La Ciudad de Chihuahua a Mediados del Siglo XIX," *B-SCEH*, Vol. VI, No. 5.

1955 "Los Apaches en Chihuahua," *B-SCEH*, Vol. IX, No. 2.

1956 "Juárez," *B-SCEH*, Vol. IX, No. 9.

Chávez Franco, Ignacio

1939 "Don Miguel Ahumada," *B-SCEH*, Vol. II, No. 5.

1941 "Guadalupe y Calvo," *B-SCEH*, Vol. III, No. 4-6.

Clendenen, Clarence C.

1961 *The United States and Pancho Villa: A Study in Unconventional Diplomacy.* American Historical Association, Cornell University Press, Ithaca.

Connelley, William Elsey, ed.

1907 *Doniphan's Expedition and the Conquest of New Mexico and California.* Bryant and Douglas Book and Stationery Company, Kansas City, Missouri.

Cooke, Philip St. George

1848 *Report of Philip St. George Cooke of his March from Santa Fe, New Mexico to San Diego, Upper California.* 30 Cong., 1 Sess. Ex. Doc. 41. Wendell and Van Benthuysen Printers, Washington.

Cordero y Bustamante, Antonio

1944 "Los Apaches a Fines del Siglo Dieciocho. Notes by G. C. Muñoz," *B-SCEH*, Vol. V, No. 3, No. 4, No. 5.

Cumberland, Charles Curtis

1952 *Mexican Revolution.* University of Texas Press, Austin.

Decorme, Gerard

1941 *La Obra de los Jesuitos Mexicanos Durante la Epoca Colonial, 1572-1767.* Antigua Librería Robredo de José Parrua e Hijos, México.

De la Peña, Moises T.

1946 "Ensayo Económico y Social Sobre el Pueblo Tarahumara," *B-SCEH*, Vol. V, No. 12; Vol. VI, No. 1.

De Voto, Bernard

1943 *Year of Decision, 1846.* Little, Brown, and Company, Boston.

Dick, Herbert W.

1952 "Evidences of Early Man in Bat Cave and on the Plains of San Augustin, New Mexico," *Proceedings*, 29th International Congress of Americanists.

Dulles, John W. F.

1961 *Yesterday in Mexico: A Chronicle of the Revolution, 1919-1936.* University of Texas Press, Austin.

Dunne, Peter Masten

1944 *Pioneer Jesuits in Northern Mexico.* University of California Press, Berkeley.

Duran, Francisco R.

1961 "Rumbo al Mar, Una Obra Gigantesca al Servicio de México," *Turismo*, No. 119.

Dutton, Bertha P.

   1963   *Sun Father's Way*. University of New Mexico Press, Albuqer-
que.

Emory, W. H.

   1848   *Notes of a Military Reconnaissance, from Fort Leavenworth, in
Missouri, to San Diego, in California*. 30 Cong., 1 sess. Ex. Doc.
41. Wendell and Van Benthuysen Printers, Washington.

Escobar, Rómulo

   1943   "Memorias de Paso del Norte. Los Uranga, Los Canoeros
Acosta," *B-SCEH*, Vol. V, No. 1.

   1944a "Memorias de Paso del Norte. La Linea Divisoria con los Estados Unidos," *B-SCEH*, Vol. V, No. 3.

   1944b "Memorias de Paso del Norte. El Coronel Don Joaquín Terrazas," *B-SCEH*, Vol. V, No. 5.

Espinosa, Conrado

   1961   "Del Pacífico al Altiplano Continental," *Turismo*, No. 119.

Esquer, Manuel R.

   1961a "La Zona de las Barrancas en el Futuro Económico de Chihuahua," *Turismo*, No. 118.

   1961b "Chihuahua y sus Perspectivas Turisticas," *Turismo*, No. 118.

Evans, George W. B.

   1945   *Mexican Gold Trail; the Journal of a Forty-niner*, The Hunt-
ington Library, San Marino, California.

Falconer, Thomas

   1930   *Letter and Notes on the Texan-Santa Fe Expedition, 1841-42*.
Dauber and Pine Bookshops, Inc., New York.

Fernández Perea, Octavio F.

   1938   "El Proceso y Ejecución del Padre de la Patria," *B-SCEH*, Vol.
I, No. 5.

Fierro, M. Rosario

   1961   "Chihuahua, Estado Revolucionario, Recibio al Señor Presidente," *Turismo*, No. 117.

Forbes, Jack D.

   1960   *Apache, Navajo, and Spaniard*. University of Oklahoma Press,
Norman.

Fuentes Mares, José

   1954   *Y México se Refugio en el Desierto: Luis Terrazas: Historia
y Destino*. Editorial Jus, S.A., México.

Fulton, Maurice Garland

   1944   *Diary and Letters of Josiah Gregg*. University of Oklahoma
Press, Norman.

Gardner, Erle Stanley
1954   *Neighborhood Frontiers.* William Morrow and Company, New York.
Gandara, José F.
1961a   "The Fabulous Canyons of the Tarahumara," *Turismo,* No. 118.
1961b   "The Grand Canyons of the Urique," *Turismo,* No. 119.
Gibson, George R.
1935   *Journal of a Soldier Under Kearny and Doniphan, 1846-47.* The Arthur H. Clark Company, Glendale, California.
González, Filiberto
1953   "Las Tarahumaras, el Grupo Etnico Mexicano mas Numeroso que aun Conserva su Primitiva Cultura," *América Indígena,* Vol. XIII, No. 2. México.
Gregg, Josiah
1905   *Commerce of the Prairies.* In Thwaites, Reuben Gold. *Early Western Travels: 1748-1846.* Vol. XX. The Arthur H. Clark Company, Glendale, California.
Guzmán, Martín Luis
1930   *The Eagle and the Serpent.* Translated from the Spanish by Harriet de Onís. Alfred A. Knopf, New York.
Hackett, Charles Wilson
1926   *Historical Documents Relating to New Mexico, Nueva Viscaya, Approaches Thereto, to 1773.* Collected by Adolphe F. A. Bandelier and Fanny R. Bandelier. Carnegie Institution of Washington, Washington.
Hafen, Leroy R.
1950   *Ruxton of the Rockies.* University of Oklahoma Press, Norman.
Hammond, George P.
1927   "Don Juan de Oñate and the Founding of New Mexico," *Historical Society of New Mexico, Publication in History,* Vol. II. Santa Fe.
1932   *The Conviction of Don Juan de Oñate, New Mexico's First Governor in New Spain and the Anglo-American West.* Historical Contributions Presented to H. E. Bolton, Vol. I. Lancaster Press, Lancaster, Pa.
Hammond, George P., and Agapito Rey
1953   *Don Juan de Oñate, Colonizer of New Mexico, 1595-1628.* University of New Mexico Press, Albuquerque. 2 vols.

Hatch, Nelle Spilsbury
1954 *Colonia Juárez*. Desert Book Company, Salt Lake City.
Haury, Emil W.
1936 "The Mogollon Culture of Southwestern New Mexico," *Medallion Papers*, Vol. XX. Globe, Arizona.
Hernández Rodríguez, Pedro
1939a "Epidemia en 1807," *B-SCEH*, Vol. I, No. 8.
1939b "Pregón y Subasta de la Plaza de Toros en 1800," *B-SCEH*, Vol. I, No. 10.
1939c "Bando Colonial 1728," *B-SCEH*, Vol. I, No. 12.
1939d "Leyes de Policía y Buen Gobierno en 1828," *B-SCEH*, Vol. II, No. 2.
Herring, Hubert
1955 *A History of Latin America*. Alfred A. Knopf, New York.
Hodge, Frederick Webb
1912 *Handbook of American Indians*. Bulletin No. 30. Bureau of American Ethnology. Washington.
Hollon, W. Engeue
1949 *The Lost Pathfinder, Zebulon Montgomery Pike*. University of Oklahoma Press, Norman.
Horgan, Paul
1939 *The Habit of Empire*. Rydal Press. Santa Fe.
1954 *Great River: The Rio Grande in North American History*. Rinehart and Company, New York. 2 vols.
Hughes, Anne E.
1914 "The Beginnings of Spanish Settlement in the El Paso District," *University of California Publications in History*, Vol. I, No. 3. Berkeley.
Hughes, John T.
1848 *Doniphan's Expedition*. Cincinnati.
Informe de Gobierno
1960 No. 4. Administration of Teofilo Borunda:
Agua Potable y Alcantarillado
Carreteras y Caminos
Educación
Electrificación
Irrigación
Pavimentación y Luz Mercurial
Presa Chihuahua, Canalización y Urbanización del Río Chuvíscar
Vivienda Popular y Pensiones

James, Preston E.
1959   *Latin America.* 3rd ed. The Odyssey Press, New York.
Juarrieta, Rómolo
1950   "Batalla de Sacramento, 28 de Febrero de 1847," *B-SCEH*, Vol. VII, No. 4.
Jennings, Jesse D.
1957   "Danger Cave," *University of Utah Anthropological Papers*, No. 27. Salt Lake City.
Johnston, A. R.
1848   *Journal of Captain A. R. Johnston, First Dragoons.* 30 Cong., 1 Sess. Ex. Doc. 41. Wendell and Van Benthuysen Printers, Washington.
Jordán, Fernando
1956   *Crónica de un País Bárbaro.* Associación Mexicana de Periodistas. México.
Irigoyen, Ulises
1942a   "El Problema Económico de las Ciudades Fronterizas," *B-SCEH*, Vol. IV, No. 2, No. 3.
1942b   "El Palacio de Gobierno y el Arquitecta Don Pedro Ignacio de Irogoyen," *B-SCEH*, Vol. IV, No. 5.
1943   "El Coronel Miguel Ahumada, Gobernante Educador," *B-SCEH*, Vol. V, No. 1.
Irrab, Noel
1938a   "Documentos Sobre el Santuario de Nuestra Señora de Guadalupe en Chihuahua," *B-SCEH*, Vol. I, No. 1.
1938b   "Efemerides Chihuense," *B-SCEH*, Vol. I, No. 1, No. 3, No. 4, No. 7, No. 8, No. 10; Vol. II, No. 1, No. 2, No. 3, No. 5, No. 6, No. 7, No. 8-9.
Kelley, J. Charles
n.d.   Jumano and Patarabueya: Relations at Junta de los Ríos. Ph.D. thesis, Harvard University (1947).
1955   "Juan Sabeata and Diffusion in Aboriginal Texas," *American Anthropologist*, Vol. 57, No. 5.
Kendall, George Wilkins
1929   *Narrative of the Texas-Santa Fe Expedition.* The Lakeside Press, R. R. Donnelley and Sons Company, Chicago.
Kidder, Alfred V.
1939   "Notes on the Archaeology of the Babícora District, Chihuahua," in *So Live the Works of Men.* Albuquerque.
Lara, J. Andrés
1954   *Prisionero de Callistas y Cristeros.* Editorial Jus, S.A., México.

Life
1950   "Into the Depths of a Hidden Canyon." September.
Lister, Robert H.
1939   "A Report on the Excavations made at Agua Zarca and La Morita in Chihuahua," *Research*, Vol. III, No. 1. Albuquerque.
1946   "Survey of Archaeological Remains in Northwestern Chihuahua," *Southwestern Journal of Anthropology*, Vol. 2, No. 4.
1953   "Excavations in Cave Valley, Chihuahua, Mexico," *American Antiquity*, Vol. 19, No. 2.
1958   "Archaeological Excavations in the Northern Sierra Madre Occidental, Chihuahua and Sonora, Mexico," *University of Colorado Studies, Series in Anthropology*, No. 7. Boulder.
1960a   "History of Archaeological Field Work in Northwestern Mexico," *El Palacio*, Vol. 67, No. 4. Santa Fe.
1960b   "Closing the Gap," *Desert Magazine*. December.
Lozano, Jorge Davo
1960a   "Un Viaje por El México Desconocido," *Turismo*, No. 114.
1960b   "En Medio del Desierto, en Cd. Anahuac, Chihuahua, Florence la mas Audas de las Industrias Creada en México," *Turismo*, No. 114.
1960c   "La Industria Maderera de Chihuahua," *Turismo*, No. 114.
Lozano, Jesús J.
1949a   "Francisco Villa, Gobernador del Estado de Chihuahua," *B-SCEH*, Vol. VI, No. 5.
1949b   "Edicto de Excomunión en Contra del Padre de la Patria, Don Miguel Hidalgo y Costilla," *B-SCEH*, Vol. VI, No. 7.
1949c   "Precursores de la Revolución Mexicana de 1910, Praxedis G. Guerrero," *B-SCEH*, Vol. VI, No. 12.
1951   "José Esteban Coronado," *B-SCEH*, Vol. VII, No. 7, No. 8.
1955   "La Fundación de la Ciudad de Chihuahua, 12 de Octubre de 1709," *B-SCEH*, Vol. IX, No. 4.
1959   (Editor) *Chihuahua, Ciudad Procer.* Publicación de la Universidad de Chihuahua, Chihuahua.
Lumholtz, Carl
1902   *Unknown Mexico.* Vol. I. New York.
Magoffin, Susan Shelby
1926   *Down the Santa Fe Trail and into Mexico.* Yale University Press, New Haven.
Mangelsdorf, Paul C., and Robert H. Lister
1958   "Archaeological Evidence on the Evolution of Maize in Northwestern Mexico," *Botanical Museum Leaflets*, Vol. 17, No. 6.

BIBLIOGRAPHY

Also in Lister, 1958, University of Colorado Studies, Series in Anthropology, No. 7.

Manzano, Carlos F.

1961a "Promoción Industrial de Chihuahua," *Turismo*, No. 118.

1961b "Cuauhtémoc es el Emporio Industrial del Estado de Chihuahua," *Turismo*, No. 118.

Marquina, Ignacio

1951 *Arquitectura Prehispanica*. Memorias del Instituto Nacional de Antropología e Historia, México.

Martin, Paul S., and John B. Rinaldo

1950 "Sites of the Reserve Phase, Pine Lawn Valley, New Mexico," *Fieldiana: Anthropology*, Vol. 38, No. 3. Chicago

1952 "Mogollon Culture Continuity and Change," *Fieldiana: Anthropology*, Vol. 40. Chicago.

1954 "Caves of the Reserve Area," *Fieldiana: Anthropology*, Vol. 42. Chicago.

Martínez, Francisco

1961 "Se Realizará el Aprovechamiento de las Aguas de la Cascada de Gusarare," *Turismo*, No. 118.

McCullagh, Francis

1928 *Red Mexico*. Louis Carrier and Company, New York.

Mecham, J. Lloyd

1926a "The Second Spanish Expedition to New Mexico," *New Mexico Historical Review*, Vol. I. Santa Fe.

1926b "Antonio de Espejo and his Journey to New Mexico," *Southwestern Historical Quarterly*, Vol. 30, No. 2. Austin.

1927 *Francisco de Ibarra and Nueva Viscaya*. Duke University Press, Durham.

México, Cincuenta Años de Revolución.

1960 Vol. I, *La Economía*. Vol. II, *La Vida Social*. Vol. III, *La Política*. Prologo de Adolfo López Mateos. Fondo de Cultura Económica, México.

Molina, Reynaldo P.

1960a "La Urbanización de Ciudad Delicias," *Turismo*, No. 114.

1960b "Chihuahua Necesita Mayor Propaganda Pro-Turismo," *Turismo*, No. 114.

Muñoz, Rafael F.

1931 *Vámonos con Pancho Villa*. Esparacalpe, Madrid.

Muñoz Ochoa, Lucila

1949 "Resumen del Origen de la Civilización Christiana y de la

Historia Cultural en el Estado de Chihuahua," *B-SCEH*, Vol. VI, No. 5.

Parra, Lorenzo
1942 "Breve Resena Historia de Coyame," *B-SCEH*, Vol. IV, No. 6.
1961 "Chihuahua Será Grande por sus Centros Turisticos," *Turismo*, No. 118.

Pattie, James O.
1905 *The Personal Narrative of James O. Pattie of Kentucky*. In R. G. Thwaites, *Early Western Travels: 1748-1846*. Vol. 18. The Arthur H. Clark Company, Cleveland.

Pérez, Baudelio
1942 "Las Tribus Aborígenes de la Región de Ciudad Juárez," *B-SCEH*, Vol. IV, No. 5.
1946 "Casas Grandes en la Historia Nacional," *B-SCEH*, Vol. VI, No. 2.

Pérez, Pedro
1955 "El General Félix Uresti Gómez," *B-SCEH*, Vol. IX, No. 6.

Peterson, Frederick A.
1959 *Ancient Mexico*. George Allen & Unwin Ltd., London.

Peza, Juan de Dios
1941 "Cumpleanos de Juárez en el Destierro." *B-SCEH*, Vol. III, No. 7.

Pinchon, Edgecumb
1933 *Viva Villa!* Cassel and Company, London.

Porras Muñoz, Guillermo
1946a "Origen de Saucillo," *B-SCEH*, Vol. V, No. 12.
1946b "Datos Sobre la Fundación de Ciudad Jiménez," Vol. VI, No. 1.
1947 "Las Tropas de El Paso en 1684," *B-SCEH*, Vol. VI, No. 3.
1952 "Hidalgo del Parral," *B-SCEH*, Vol. VIII, No. 1, No. 2, No. 3, No. 4.

Priestley, Herbert Ingram
1938 *The Mexican Nation, a History*. Macmillan Company, New York.

Puente, Ramón
1957 *Villa en Pie*. Editorial México Nuevo, México.

Quirk, Robert E.
1960 *The Mexican Revolution, 1914-1915*. Indiana University Press, Bloomington.

Ramírez Caloca, Jesús
1944 "Ascensión," *B-SCEH*, Vol. V, No. 6.
1946 "El Ultimo Apache," *B-SCEH*, Vol. VI, No. 1.
1952 *Nociones de Geografía del Estado de Chihuahua*. Chihuahua.

Rasura, Salvador
1955   "La Muerte de Hidalgo." *B-SCEH*, Vol. IX, No. 6.
Reed, John
1914   *Insurgent Mexico*. D. Appleton and Company, New York.
Rocha, José G.
1938a   "El Descubrimiento de Parral," *B-SCEH*, Vol. I, No. 2.
1938b   "La Primer Fundación Española en Territorio Chihuahuense,"
        B-SCEH, Vol. I, No. 3; pt. 2, Vol. I, No. 5.
1938c   "Parral, Capital de la Nueva Viscaya," *B-SCEH*, Vol. I, No. 7.
1939a   "El Descubridor de Parral Murió en la Pobreza," *B-SCEH*,
        Vol. I, No. 8.
1939b   "La Imprenta y el Periodismo en Parral," *B-SCEH*, Vol. I, No.
        9, No. 10, No. 11.
1939c   "La Fundación del Primer Hospital en Tierras de Chihua-
        hua," *B-SCEH*, Vol. II, No. 1, No. 2.
1939d   "Campana de los Gobernadores de la Nueva Viscaya Contra
        los Indios Rebeldes," *B-SCEH*, Vol. II, No. 5; Vol. III, No. 1-3;
        Vol. IV, No. 1.
1942   "El Fundador del Primer Mayorazgo Instituido en Tierras de
        Chihuahua: Valerio Cortés del Rey," *B-SCEH*, Vol. IV, No. 5.
Romero, Manuel
1949a   "Incidentes de la Revolución," *B-SCEH*, Vol. VI, No. 5.
1949b   "El Epopeya de Pascual Orozco," *B-SCEH*, Vol. VI, No. 8.
Salinas Carranza, Alberto
1936   *La Expedición Punitiva*. Ediciones Botas, México.
Saravia, Atanasio G.
1938   *Apuntes para la Historia de la Nueva Vizcaya*. Vol. I, *La Con-
        quista*. Instituto Panamericano de Geografía e Historia. Pub.
        35. México.
1941   *Apuntes para la Historia de la Nueva Vizcaya*. Vol. II, *La Ciu-
        dad de Durango*. Instituto Panamericano de Geografía e His-
        toria. Pub. 35. México.
1954   *Apuntes para la Historia de la Nueva Vizcaya*. Vol. III, *La
        Sublevaciones*. Instituto Panamericano de Geografía e Historia.
        Pub. 35. México.
Sauer, Carl
1932   "The Road to Cibola," *Ibero-Americana*, Vol. 3. Berkeley.
1935   "Aboriginal Population of Northwestern Mexico," *Ibero-
        Americana*. Vol. 10. Berkeley.
Sayles, E. B.
1936   "An Archaeological Survey of Chihuahua, Mexico," *Medallion
        Papers*, Vol. XXII. Globe, Arizona.

Secretaría de Recursos Hidráulicos
1956   *Distrito de Riego de Delicias, Chihuahua.* Dirección General de Distritos de Diego, México.
Schmiedehaus, Walter
1939   "Los Ruso-Germanos en México," *B-SCEH,* Vol. II, No. 7.
1940   "El Pueblo Escondido," *B-SCEH,* Vol. II, No. 12.
1942   "Datos Complementarios Sobre la Fundación de Paso del Norte, hoy Ciudad Juárez," *B-SCEH,* Vol. IV, No. 1.
1946   "¿Cruces Precortesianas en la Sierra de Chihuahua?" *B-SCEH,* Vol. VI, No. 2.
1947   "Colonias Mennonitas," *B-SCEH,* Vol. VI, No. 4.
Schuster, Ernest Otto
1947   *Pancho Villa's Shadow.* The Exposition Press, New York.
Schwartzlose, Richard A.
1955   "La Repoblación de la Sección Montanosa del Noroeste de Chihuahua," *B-SCEH,* Vol. IX, No. 3.
Simpson, Lesley Byrd
1952   *Many Mexicos.* University of California Press, Berkeley.
Terrazas, Silvestre
1938   "Los Primeros Colonos de la hoy Ciudad de Chihuahua y sus Cercanías," *B-SCEH,* Vol. I, No. 5; Vol. II, No. 7; Vol. III, No. 9.
1939a   "Confirmación y Juramento de las Primeras Autoridades Habidas en la Villa de San Felipe el Real de Chihuahua," *B-SCEH,* Vol. I, No. 12.
1939b   "Mineral que Produce mas de 80 Milliones en Oro," *B-SCEH,* Vol. II, No. 6.
1940a   "Los Martires de la Tarahumara," *B-SCEH,* Vol. II, No. 8-9, No. 10-11.
1940b   "El Gran Sabio y Santo Padre Glandorf en Chihuahua," *B-SCEH,* Vol. II, No. 12; Vol. III, No. 1-3.
1941   "Los Primeros Blancos al Norte de la Nueva España," *B-SCEH,* Vol. III, No. 4-6, No. 9, No. 12.
1942a   "La Arqueológica Zona, Madre de América." *B-SCEH,* Vol. IV, No. 3.
1942b   "¿Está Surgiendo Una Enorme Zona Arqueológica al Nor-Oeste de Chihuahua?" *B-SCEH,* Vol. IV, No. 4.
1943   "Apoteosis del Sr. Gral. D. Felipe Angeles." *B-SCEH,* Vol. IV, No. 11.
1944-   "El Verdadero 'Pancho Villa'," *B-SCEH,* Vol. V,
1955   No. 2-6, 12; Vol. VI, No. 1-4, 6-7, 10-12; Vol. VII, No. 1-2, 4-7, 10-12; Vol. VIII, No. 1-5, 7-12; Vol IX, No. 1-3.

Terrazas Valdez, Alberto
  1941 "Fundación de la Missión de Nuestra Sr. de Guadalupe de Paso del Norte," *B-SCEH*, Vol. III, No. 4-6.
Tompkins, Frank
  1934 *Chasing Villa*. Military Service Publishing Company, Harrisburg.
Turismo (unsigned articles)
  1959 No. 111, July.
        "Doscientos Cincuenta Años de Educación
          en Chihuahua."
        "El Brillantisimo Historial de la Unión
          Regional Ganadera de Chihuahua."
        "Itinerario del Banco Commercial Mexicano, S.A.."
        "El Acta de la Fundación de Chihuahua."
        "Un Vasto Programa de Combate de Incendios."
        "La Empacadora de Chihuahua."
  1960 Unnumbered, January.
        "La Segunda Exposición Ganadera."
        "La Universidad de Chihuahua Entrega al
          Pueblo Sus Primeros Frutos."
        "Optimismo en la Celebración del 250
          Aniversaria de la Fundación de
          Chihuahua."
        "El Traje de la Tarahumara como Fuente
          Original del Traje Regional de
          Chihuahua."
        "Fué Brilliante la Participacíon de los
          Tarahumaras en los Festejos del 250
          Aniversario de la Fundación de
          Chihuahua."
        "La Crisis del Turismo Debe Corregirse."
  1960 No. 115, June.
        "La Industria Maderera de Chihuahua."
  1960 No. 116, August.
        "Obra Titánica, El Ferrocarril Chihuahua
          al Pacífico."
  1961 No. 117, January.
        "Inauguró la Tercera Exposición Chihuahuense
          de Ganadería."
        "Ecos de la Operación Seminario de Estudio
          Sobre Coníferas Latino-Americanas
          en el Edo. de Chihuahua."

"La Zona Arqueología de Casas Grandes."
"La Ganadería, Minería, y Agricultura
Chihuahuense."
"El Sr. Presidente López Mateos Realizó
Una Fecunda Jira por el Estado de
Chihuahua."
"Superficie, Población, y Clima del Estado
de Chihuahua."
1961   No. 118, July.
"El Ferrocarril Chihuahua al Pacífico,
La Obra Mas Grandiosa de México."
"Ojinaga: Puerto de Entrada Fronteriza."
"De Aldama a Ojinaga."
"El Sueño de Owen."
"La Alta Sierra Tarahumara que Atraviese
el Ferrocarril Descubre Milenarios
Yacimientos Metalificos."
"La Historia del Ferrocarril Chihuahua
al Pacífico Hasta 1940."
"El Ferrocarril Chihuahua al Pacífico
Puente de Hierro."
"Otro Puerto Libre."
"Bosques de Chihuahua, S. de R.I. da un
Ejemplo a las Empresas de Todo el Estado."
"El Turismo, Fuente de Actividad Commercial."
"Nuestras Bellezas Naturales."
Twitchell, Ralph Emerson
1912   *Leading Facts of New Mexico History*. Vol. 2. The Torch Press,
Cedar Rapids, Iowa.
Underhill, Ruth M.
1953   *Red Man's America*. University of Chicago Press, Chicago.
Valadés, José C.
1948   *El Porfirismo*. Editorial Patria, México. 2 vols.
Villagrá, Gaspar Perez de
1933   *History of New Mexico*. Trans. Gilberto Espinosa. The Quivira
Society, Los Angeles.
Webb, James Josiah
1931   *Adventures in the Santa Fe Trade, 1844-47*. Ed. Ralph P. Bie-
ber. The Arthur H. Clark Company, Glendale, California.
West, Robert C.
1949   "The Mining Community in Northern New Spain: The Parral
Mining Community," *Ibero-Americana*, Vol. 30. Berkeley.

Wheat, Joe Ben
1955 "Mogollon Culture Prior to A.D. 1000," *Memoir*, Society for American Archaeology, Vol. 10.

Whetten, Nathan L.
1948 *Rural Mexico*. University of Chicago Press, Chicago.

Willey, Gordon R., and Philip Phillips
1955 "Method and Theory in American Archaeology. II: Historical-Developmental Interpretation," *American Anthropologist*, Vol. 57, No. 5.

Wislisenius, A.
1848 *Memoir of a Tour to Northern Mexico, Connected with Col. Doniphan's Expedition in 1846-1847*. Washington.

Wolfe, Bertram D., and Diego Rivera
1937 *Portrait of Mexico*. Covici Friede, New York.

Woods, Betty
1962 "Pancho Villa State Park," *New Mexico Magazine*. March.

Zavala, Silvio
1943 "Los Esclavos Indios en el Norte de México. Siglo XVI," *El Norte de México y el Sur de Estados Unidos*. México.

Zingg, Robert M.
1940 "Report on the Archaeology of Southern Chihuahua." Center of Latin American Studies, University of Denver, *Publications*, No. 1. Denver.

Zuloaga, Pedro
1944 "¿Los Apaches, Eran Tartaros?" *B-SCEH*, Vol. V, No. 2.

INDEX